ATTENTION IN EARLY DEVELOPMENT

Themes and Variations

Holly Alliger Ruff
and
Mary Klevjord Rothbart

New York   Oxford
OXFORD UNIVERSITY PRESS
1996

Oxford University Press

Oxford   New York
Athens   Auckland   Bangkok   Bombay
Calcutta   Cape Town   Dar es Salaam   Delhi
Florence   Hong Kong   Istanbul   Karachi
Kuala Lumpur   Madras   Madrid   Melbourne
Mexico City   Nairobi   Paris   Singapore
Taipei   Tokyo   Toronto

and associated companies in
Berlin   Ibadan

Library of Congress Cataloging-in-Publication Data
Ruff, Holly Alliger.
Attention in early development : themes and variations / Holly
Alliger Ruff and Mary Klevjord Rothbart.
p. cm.
Includes bibliographical references and index.
ISBN 0-19-507143-3
1. Attention in children.   2. Child development.   I. Rothbart,
Mary Klevjord.   II. Title.
[DNLM: 1. Attention—in infancy & childhood.   2. Child
Development.   WS 105.5.C7 R923a   1996]
BF723.A755R84   1996
155.4'13733—dc20
DNLM/DLC   95–33048
for Library of Congress

9 8 7 6 5 4 3 2 1

Printed in the United States of America
on acid-free paper

Attention in Early Development

This book is dedicated with love and gratitude to our parents,

Ruth and Glen Alliger
Ruth and Olaf Klevjord

husbands,

John Ruff and Myron Rothbart

and children

Daniel and Michael Rothbart

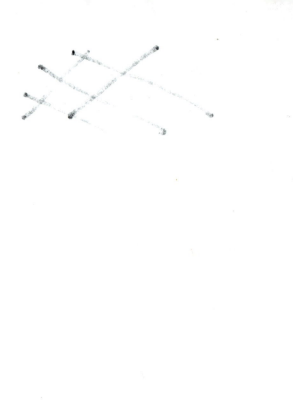

Preface

Infants and young children are faced with a complex environment and massive amounts of stimulation. To function well, they need to be selective, attending to only a small portion of the information available. At the same time, they must be responsive to important events as they occur. They must also learn to persist in tasks long enough to complete them despite obstacles and distractions, yet be able to disengage attention from fruitless or destructive activities. Flexibility in the deployment and management of attention requires activation of attention and behavior on the one hand and the inhibition of competing or inappropriate responses on the other. Infants do not come into the world fully equipped with the skills required for such flexibility. This book describes some of the means by which children gain these skills in the first five years of life. It is also an account of how individual children vary in what they bring to these developmental tasks and in the paths they take toward the regulation of their own attention.

The book has taken us three years to write. It would be hard to exaggerate how much the two of us have learned in that time. We brought very different perspectives to the subject of attention, and it has been a rich and rewarding experience for us to discover, debate, and resolve differences of opinion as we worked on the project. In trying to integrate the work and ideas of others into a coherent account, we realize how much we do not yet understand about the development of attention. Our thoughts are still very much in progress, and some sections of the book will reflect the tentative state of our knowledge. We have relied heavily on our own work because we understand it best. On the other hand, we have tried to include as much as we could of the current literature on attention in infants and children. If we have omitted a colleague's research or have missed the implication of some published findings, we apologize.

The book is organized around two overlapping structures. One is the division of attention into three conceptual domains: selectivity, state, and executive or higher level control. The second is developmental: we address the development of two attention systems during the early years. Changes in these two systems coincide with important developmental transitions at 2 to 3 months, 9 to 12 months, 18 to 24 months, and perhaps 4 years of age. As we discuss different domains of attention within this developmental framework, we concentrate on behavior, but include neurophysiological and neuropsychological data as they seem appropriate and helpful to our account.

The book is intended for advanced undergraduate and graduate students in psychology and education, as well as other students for whom knowledge of young children is important. We hope that our integration of research findings will also be of use to researchers and clinicians who work with young children. Finally, we offer a conceptual framework that we hope will stimulate further thinking about attention and early development.

Acknowledgments

We have many people to thank both individually and jointly.

Several of my colleagues deserve special mention as this project draws to a close. First, I thank Mary Capozzoli and Katharine Lawson for years of steady and cheerful comraderie in the research lab. Without them, I could not have accomplished as much as I have. I am also grateful to Michael Cohen, chairman of the Pediatrics Department at Albert Einstein, for his encouragement, support, and loyalty during my career here. Dan Anderson and John Richards have been friends in the struggle to understand attention and I thank them for many stimulating discussions. I feel particular gratitude for Sonia Graniela's help on the book, especially the bibliography. Even more important, her skillful handling of day to day affairs has helped to keep me calm. Finally, I acknowledge support from NICHD, NIMH, and NSF for grant funds to conduct the research described here.
New York, 1995   H.A.R.

I wish to give special thanks to Michael Posner, my close colleague in studying the early development of attention and a great supporter of this book. I also wish to thank Mick Rothbart, my husband, who is always available for discussion, care, and support. Colleen Vande Voorde is an outstanding secretary, the typist for my contributions to this book, and a close and much appreciated friend. I would also like to thank Leslie Tucker, Lisa Thomas-Thrapp, and Kendra Gilds, who have been laboratory coordinators for our infant attention and temperament work, and the many undergraduate students who have coded eye movements and facial expressions in the course of our studies. Graduate students Anne Clohessy, Catherine Harmon, Lisa Thomas-Thrapp, Gina Gerardi, and undergraduates Shaun Vecera and Lenna Ontai have also made important contributions to this research, which was supported by grants from NIMH and the Keck Foundation. Finally, thanks to the many mothers from the Eugene-Springfield area, who by their efforts and their desire to make a contribution to developmental science, have made the work possible.
Eugene, 1995   M.K.R.

Together, we would like to acknowledge several colleagues for their contributions to this book. We thank Michael Posner for his encouragement and his careful reading of early drafts of chapters. We also appreciate the prompt response by Patricia Miller and Gerald Turkewitz when Oxford requested their reviews of the next-to-final draft of the book. Their comments and suggestions were invaluable to the final revision and were instrumental in helping us to clarify and amplify certain sections and ideas. John Richards, Dan Anderson, Diane Kurtzberg, Barbara Rogoff, and Steven Tipper read parts of the book related to their own work and have helped to prevent some errors. Karen Adolph and Chris Schmidt read an early draft of the developmental section and made helpful comments. We are grateful to all of these individuals. We thank Carolyn Michelman and Lisa Stallings at Oxford University Press for their friendly and efficient handling of many details. Finally, we owe a special debt of gratitude to Joan Bossert, editor at Oxford University Press, for her faith in our ability to complete this project and for her wise counsel at all stages.

H.A.R.
M.K.R.

Contents

Attention in Early Development

1

Introduction

Words and phrases referring to attention are common in our language, attesting to the importance of attention in our everyday lives. We "pay attention," "concentrate," and become "preoccupied," "obsessed," or "distracted." We "notice" what others are doing; we ask them to "look closely" or to "watch" where they're going. We are sometimes aware of our own attention and often observe attention in others. When conversing with other people, we notice whether they are attending to us by their eye movements and facial expressions. By following the direction and intensity of others' attention, we learn something about their interests and concerns. Parents may attend selectively to some behaviors of their children, ignoring other behaviors that are seen as less interesting or less desirable. By observing the attention of parents and siblings, children can learn to distinguish between objects and events that are important to others and those that are not.

The importance of attention for adaptive behavior guides scientific work on attention and raises compelling questions. How do we keep from being inundated by the stimulation that surrounds us? What controls the intensity of attention and allows us to mobilize sufficient effort for demanding tasks? How can we react to new and important events when we are engrossed in an activity? What controls the shifting of attention so that we do not perseverate, but also are not pulled willy-nilly from one focus to another? What goes wrong when attention is maladaptive, when individuals are either overfocused or highly distractible?

In this book, we address these questions in the context of two major issues. The first concerns the development of attention over the first five years of life; the second concerns individuality among infants and young children in their deployment of attention. In this first chapter, we discuss briefly our framework for thinking about attention and offer an overview of the book's contents.

OUR APPROACH TO ATTENTION

Many of the principles we discuss apply to attention in general, but the book highlights visual attention. Also, even though attention can be focused inward, our

3

emphasis in this volume is on attention to objects, events, tasks, and problems in the external world. In the context of these emphases, attention often involves directing the eyes toward a source of information and maintaining a visual focus long enough to acquire information or solve a problem. Attention is thereby essential to perception and learning about selected events. Attention is also related to motivation. Some events are intrinsically so interesting that they compel involvement. On the other hand, the more formal aspects of education and employment often require us to attend to tasks that do not in themselves strongly elicit interest. The motivation to attend must then come from other sources, such as a desire for mastery or conformity to internal or external standards.

Attention is part of our adaptive response to the social and physical environment. Although attention can be distinguished from other aspects of functioning, we are ultimately dealing with the behavior of an integrated organism. Much has been written about the inseparability of perception and action (J. Gibson, 1979; Reed, 1982), and some have suggested that attention cannot be fully separated from either (E. Gibson & Rader, 1979). Actions often require less attention as they become smoother, faster, and more efficient with practice (Posner & Snyder, 1975; Shiffrin & Schneider, 1977). Other activities may require concentration for as long as we perform them. Thus, a fundamental problem in the study of attention is how attention is modulated to meet the demands of specific situations.

A functional approach to attention does not preclude a concern about the mechanisms that underlie attention. As Mesulam (1981) writes: "The effective execution of attention requires a flexible interplay among intense concentration, inhibition of distractibility, and the ability to shift the center of awareness from one focus to another according to inner needs, past experience, and external reality" (pp. 321–322). This quotation not only emphasizes the importance of regulating attention for adequate functioning but also suggests three general processes that need to be understood. These are the selection of a target, the engagement of attention, and the controls necessary to maintain and shift attention as necessary for the current situation.

This three-part definition of attention—selectivity, state of engagement, and higher-level control—serves as a framework for discussing specific processes underlying attention. These processes in turn can be studied in many different ways. In behavior, we observe facial expression (Izard, 1977), duration of looking, reaction time, quantitative aspects of performance on a task, and how often subjects turn their head and eyes away from a central event. Physiological measures include heart rate (Richards, 1988), respiratory sinus arrhythmia (Porges, 1986; Richards & Casey, 1992), adrenocortical activity (Gunnar, 1990), and neurotransmitter activity (Porges, 1976; Tucker & Williamson, 1984), to cite a few examples. Experiments can also be designed to identify the pathways and structures in the central nervous system involved in particular processes (Posner & Raichle, 1994). Understanding attention at one level advances understanding at other levels, and information from all of these approaches are necessary for a complete account of attention.

Regardless of the level of analysis, responses emerge from the interaction between the individual and the immediate context, and answers to fundamental questions about attention must incorporate the context in which attention is observed.

Six-month-old infants, for example, are particularly attentive to objects that come within reach and can be grasped and manipulated. Nine-month-olds begin to move themselves around by crawling and attend more to distant objects. In both cases, attention is jointly determined by the developmental level of the child and the location of objects in the immediate environment. In a parallel neurological example, Mountcastle (1978a) describes visual cells in an area of the monkey cortex that show a higher amplitude response when an object is within reaching distance than when it is not. As Mesulam (1981) suggests, however, neural responses studied in the laboratory may well be related to the physical restraint of the monkeys; under conditions of freedom, more "synaptic space" might be devoted to objects that are only temporarily out of reach (p. 313). Thus, interactions between the organism's condition and the physical situation are an essential component of both biological and behavioral approaches to attention.

Another essential component of an adequate treatment of attention is the integration of attention with constructs from other domains of study. If attention and its control are part of adaptive behavior, then we must explore the relationships between attention on the one hand and emotion, motivation, and cognition on the other (Dixon & Hertzog, 1988). The selectivity and concentration of attention, for example, are ideally high when individuals are in a cognitively demanding situation, such as an examination. How successful individuals will be in mobilizing the necessary effort for an exam will depend in part on their motivation and whether it stems from a desire to qualify for a job or to master a topic intellectually. Individual differences in temperamental characteristics will also contribute to the ease with which individuals can sit still, how distressed they become by questions without obvious answers, and how easily they can shift away from the focus of their distress. The intellectual preparation of some will keep them from being distracted by unimportant aspects of a question; others may not have the knowledge necessary for optimal selection. Emotions experienced by the test taker may influence attention. For example, fear or anger may hamper the student's ability to shift easily from one salient point to another. Interest or excitement, in contrast, may enhance attention and facilitate flexibility. The integration of attention with other domains of functioning can be approached from both behavioral and neurological perspectives and from concerns about self-regulation.

In summary, attention is a complex and multidimensional construct. It depends on distributed neural systems; it is linked to multiple sources of information from the environment and to complex motor, emotional, and motivational systems. Thus, in this book, we take a functional view of attention, are concerned with context and multiple levels of explanation, and hope thereby to illuminate the early development of attention and the variation in attentiveness found among children.

DEVELOPMENT OF ATTENTION

Infants are selective in their attention from the first day of life. Fantz (1961) demonstrated that the newborn infant will look longer at some pictures or designs than at others. His work was followed by an enormous amount of research documenting that infants attend to different aspects of pictures, objects, and events as they develop (Cohen, DeLoache, & Strauss, 1979; Fantz & Fagan, 1975). By about 2 months of age, for example, attention becomes less determined by the intensity of stimulation, such as size or brightness, and more by other aspects of stimulation, such as pattern or form (Ruff & Turkewitz, 1975, 1979). Over the rest of the first year, attention is governed in important ways by the novelty of objects and events encountered by the infant. Repeated experience reduces novelty, but also leads the infant to notice new and different details and features. Selectivity changes as new skills and knowledge emerge in development. Properties of objects and events salient to the infant at 3 or 4 months give way to object properties such as graspability and texture, as the infant learns to reach and manipulate, and still others, such as spatial relationships, as the infant begins to move independently (Bertenthal & Campos, 1990).

Time-related aspects of attention also change with development. Porges (e.g., Porges & Smith, 1980) has proposed a two-component model of attention that includes both reactive and sustained aspects of responsiveness to events; others have referred to these components as attention-getting and attention-holding (Cohen, 1972, 1973). The orienting reflex, a response to the onset of novel or moderately intense stimulation, develops into its mature form in the first 2 to 3 months (Graham, Anthony, & Ziegler, 1983). This reflex is important because it involves both alertness and selection, with sensory receptors directed toward potentially important sources of information. Orienting may then be followed by sustained attention and learning if the event is sufficiently novel or important enough to warrant further exploration. Reactive and sustained aspects of attention continue to change over the first year, with focused attention mobilized more rapidly when novel objects are encountered (Ruff, 1986) and maintained longer for complex events than simple ones (Oakes & Tellinghuisen, 1994).

As important as it is to be able to initiate and sustain attention, it is equally important to be able to shift from one focus to another. While very young infants are selective, they sometimes have great difficulty disengaging from highly salient targets. Indeed, in the first few months, they may try unsuccessfully to turn away from a visual focus, continuing to look even as they become distressed. By 4 months, however, infants seem to have much more control over the shifting of attention, making their attention more flexible (Johnson, Posner, & Rothbart, 1991; Posner, Rothbart, Gerardi, & Thomas-Thrapp, in press). Thus, in the first year of life, infants orient to novel and otherwise salient events; they sustain attention to those events for the purpose of exploring and learning. They gradually gain more control over their attention and can shift more easily from one focus to another. A system of attention, which we refer to as the orienting/investigative system, becomes functional early and governs attention in the first year.

As the infant develops into a toddler, a new system of attention emerges. Now selectivity is less influenced by novelty and more by what others attend to. Sustained attention in naturalistic settings increases dramatically as children play with toys (Ruff & Lawson, 1990) or watch television (Anderson & Levin, 1976). Attention comes to be related more to planned, self-generated activity with objects than to exploration. Plans are powerful organizers of behavior (Werner, 1948), and when a child can plan an activity, such as building a house with blocks, attention is recruited and maintained in order to carry the activity to completion. As plans and activities increase in complexity (Case & Khanna, 1981; Sugarman, 1982), so does the duration of attention.

Children become more able to focus their attention in a wide variety of settings, including some that are not intrinsically interesting (Weissberg, Ruff, & Lawson, 1990), and they are now less likely to squirm or walk away from assigned tasks (Levy, 1980; Ruff, Weissberg, Lawson, & Capozzoli, 1995). Children also become more aware that factors such as noise and their own level of interest will affect their attention (P. Miller & Zalenski, 1982), and they become more systematic in the deployment of their attention in memory-related tasks (Baker-Ward, Ornstein, & Holden, 1984; P. Miller, 1990).

These developments can be seen as part of the larger construct of self-regulation (Kopp, 1982, 1991; Posner & Rothbart, 1981)—the ability to modulate behavior according to the cognitive, emotional, and social demands of specific situations. Self-regulation is also increasingly manifested in inhibitory control (Reed, Pien, & Rothbart, 1984; Vaughn, Kopp, & Krakow, 1984), in the more frequent use of strategies in problem-solving and memory tasks (P. Miller, 1990; Wellman, 1988), and in the emergence of self-monitoring. Because much of this later attention requires some control over lower-level processes, such as orienting, we refer to the second system of attention as a system of higher level controls. This system continues to develop throughout the preschool years.

Behavioral development of attention is accompanied by neurological development. As noted earlier, attention depends on many parts of the brain. First, the brainstem helps control the general level of arousal in the cortex. From early infancy, it contributes to control of behavioral state, including sleep/wake cycles and levels of alertness when the infant is awake. Alerting functions continue to mature in the first few months, involving changes in the autonomic nervous system and changes in the nature of attention during cognitive activity (Porges, 1992; Richards, 1988).

Second, a spatial orienting network in the parietal cortex (Posner & Peterson, 1990; Tucker & Williamson, 1984; Mesulam, 1981) and an object recognition pathway in the temporal cortex (Ungerleider & Mishkin, 1982) are related to attention to specific locations and objects in the environment. Recent research (Clohessy, Posner, Rothbart, & Vecera, 1991; Harman, Posner, Rothbart, & Thomas-Thrapp, 1994) suggests that these networks become fully functional in the first year of life; their maturation may be involved in the extensive visual and manipulative exploration of the environment so characteristic of infants. Thus, these networks are important to the functioning of the first attention system.

Third, a complex system involving areas of the frontal cortex (Posner & Peterson, 1990; Rothbart, Derryberry, & Posner, 1994) is important in the inhibition of prepotent responses (Diamond, 1991) and in the development of planned, goal-directed behavior (Stuss & Benson, 1984). These cortical areas become more functional toward the end of the first year (Diamond, 1991), continuing to mature for several years after (Welsh & Pennington, 1988), and are the underpinnings of the second attention system.

Both neurological maturation and developmental changes in behavior take place in a social context. The newborn infant's regulation of state, the older infant's preference for novelty, and the preschooler's more voluntary attention all result from an interplay of the child and older, more experienced inhabitants of the child's social world (Wertsch, 1985). This interplay is possible, in part, because the child can share attention with others, an ability that develops in the first two years of life.

During the first few months, infants in our culture frequently engage in mutual attention during face-to-face interactions with adult partners (Stern, 1974). When infants become proficient at disengaging and shifting attention and at reaching and grasping, their attention is directed more toward the inanimate objects around them. Later in the first year, they begin to attend to objects jointly with adults (Adamson & Bakeman, 1991; Hubley & Trevarthen, 1979) and to follow the direction of others' attention to objects or events in the immediate environment (Butterworth, 1991). By 18 months, children demonstrate skills in coordinating attention to toys and to their partners in play.

Attention influences other aspects of development in important ways; at the same time, development in other domains contributes to the further development of attention. Joint attention between child and parent, for example, is important in early language development (Baldwin, 1991; Tomasello & Farrar, 1986); language, in turn, allows adults to relay information, values, and directions to the developing child. The child's ability to imitate (Meltzoff, 1990; Uzgiris, Benson, Kruper, & Vasek, 1989) also depends on attention to the actions of others and provides another mechanism for acquiring new behaviors. Social interaction facilitates the development of the child's internal controls on attention by conveying social expectations and standards (Kopp, 1991) and by providing examples of attitudes and strategies that can be internalized.

In summary, we propose that the development of attention in the first five years of life involves two general systems of attention. The orienting/investigative system becomes functional in the first year, and attention is strongly, though not exclusively, governed by novelty. This system diminishes in importance when the second system emerges, but never disappears. The system of higher level controls emerges toward the end of the first year and gradually becomes more dominant in the control of attention. Development involves continued refinements of this system and a consolidation of the underlying processes. Both systems function in a social context, but the later system is dependent on social input for its development.

INDIVIDUALITY AND DEVELOPMENT

In our discussion of the development of attention, we have briefly described important changes that occur with age. Equally important and fascinating, however, is the variability in attentiveness observed in normal children at all stages of development. Some children modulate their attention so that it can be concentrated and focused or wide-ranging and flexible according to current needs and goals. Others may be distractible and have difficulty staying with a particular task for long; James (1890/1950) described these individuals as those "whose work, to the end of life, gets done in the interstices of their mind-wandering" (p. 417). Still others persist in their attention to tasks to the point of perseveration and have difficulty shifting focus.

Variability in attention may reflect differences in speed of learning or in the amount of information acquired about given events. Variability may also reflect individual differences in temperament. Attention seems to be intimately linked to emotional tone (Rothbart, Ziaie, & O'Boyle, 1992); if a child is very prone to distress, that child may be generally less attentive than a child who is less susceptible to distress. Attention is also related to individual differences in inhibitory control (Kochanska, 1993; Rothbart, 1989b). Under conditions of low stimulation, adults characterized as extraverted—impulsive, sensation seeking, and responsive to rewards—tend to sustain attention less than introverts (Eysenck, 1976; Tucker & Williamson, 1984). After infancy, such a pattern may be seen in children as well (Douglas, 1983; Rothbart, 1989c).

Individual differences in attention are also related to processes of self-regulation. In the preschool years, as children are asked to become more attentive and less impulsive, individual differences in reactivity will contribute to the extent to which they can exercise control. Even weak inhibitory controls may be sufficient for children who are not very reactive to stimulation. Such children may, in fact, have to learn to stimulate or activate themselves in order to become appropriately engaged in a task. Other children who are highly reactive may need superior inhibitory skills to control their attention and behavior in stimulating and distracting situations.

Individual variation in attentiveness is likely to be related to physiological and neurological variation. Individual differences in autonomic reactivity (Porges, 1992) and the degree of inhibition exercised by the frontal cortex (Stuss & Benson, 1984) are two examples of functional variation. These may be tied to variability in neurotransmitter activity, affecting both peripheral and central nervous systems (Porges, 1976). Because attention is based on distributed but interrelated neural networks (Mesulam, 1981; Posner & Peterson, 1990), the possibilities for variation in neural structure are great. Thus, individuals vary in the neuroanatomy and neurophysiology they bring to different situations.

The assumption underlying any discussion of individual differences is that they are stable across extended periods. Differences in reactivity and tendency to sustain attention appear to be moderately stable in infants (Rothbart, 1981; Ruff, 1988), children (Ruff, Lawson, Parrinello, & Weissberg, 1990), and adults (Derryberry & Rothbart, 1988). Consistency across situations, however, tends to be modest, proba- bly because of the interaction between attentiveness and the immediate physical, cognitive, and social constraints of particular situations. For example, children who generally are not easily aroused may be very attentive in highly stimulating condi- tions; their attention may also increase under conditions of low stimulation if there are rewards to be reaped. The study of individuality necessarily requires an under- standing of situational variables; these variables are, in fact, an important part of the definition of individual characteristics.

Variation in children's attentiveness is also intertwined with developmental is- sues. Differences in temperamental characteristics are present early (Rothbart, 1981), and they contribute to the development of attention. Thus, positive affect and the tendency to approach objects in infancy, the tendency to sustain attention, and the infant's experiences in social contexts may interact to jointly determine the propensity to focus attention in later childhood. Infants who are fussy and tend to withdraw from novel objects and situations will have different life experiences and are likely to pick up different sorts of information about the world as they develop. On the other hand, a generally attentive infant may become an inattentive pre-schooler because the environment fails to provide adequate structure for developing self-regulatory skills. In the extreme, the child's social experiences may actively discourage the development of these skills. The different developmental trajectories of the two attention systems potentially serve as the basis for marked individual differences in the rate and profile of attentional development.

No treatment of individual differences would be complete without a discussion of attention deficits. In the psychiatric nomenclature (American Psychiatric Association, Diagnostic and Statistical Manual-IV, 1994), "Attention Deficit/Hyperactivity Disorder" is listed as a single deficit involving inattention, impulsivity, and hyper-activity. However, an important distinction has been made between subtypes of attention deficits with and without hyperactivity (Schaughency & Hynd, 1989). Some variants of attention deficit may even include *hypoactivity*—that is, difficulty focusing on a particular event or task because of a failure to be aroused by it. Deficits of attention may also be observed in perseveration or overfocusing, a failure to shift away from an event or task once engaged with it (Kinsbourne, 1991). Problems in sustained and shared attention play a role in other disorders, such as autism (Mundy & Sigman, 1989). Although disorders of attention are seen most clearly in school-age children, recent research suggests that their precursors can be observed in the early years (Campbell, 1985; Ruff, Lawson et al., 1990).

One of our goals in this book is to consider the subject of individual differences without minimizing the complexity and range of these differences. To accomplish this goal, we discuss underlying processes, how these processes are engaged by different situations, and how they are altered with development. At the same time, normal development of controls on attention cannot be fully understood without understanding the sources of individual variability in different phases of development.

ORGANIZATION OF THE BOOK

This chapter has included a brief review of the goals, framework, and content of our book. Structurally, the book has two major components. The first section (chapters 3 through 9) concerns common themes in the development of attention and thus deals with the average course of events. Topics in this section include the development of scanning, selectivity, state-related components, focused attention, and resistance to distractibility. In addition, we discuss the role of social forces in the development of attention and the relationship between attention and learning. The second section (chapters 10 through 12) deals with individual variations. These include individual differences in attention and related temperamental characteristics as well as vari-ability in patterns of development. We also consider early deficits in attention. The book concludes with a summary of major points and a discussion of the larger context for the book's content.

First, however, we need to deal more explicitly with definitions of attention. Because commonsense comprehension and use of the term "attention" is inadequate for scientific investigation, we explore, in chapter 2, more formal ways of defining attention and review operational definitions for its measurement.

2

Constructs and Measures

In 1930, Muriel Brown began the introduction of her article on attention with this comment:

A review of the literature discloses so many definitions of attention that one is [led] to wonder whether James could possibly have intended to include psychologists when he said "Everyone knows what attention is." (p. 256)

After many years, any single definition of attention is still problematic (Boring, 1970; Reason, 1984). At the same time, there has been significant progress in the study of attention (Posner, 1982), and the content of the book reflects this progress. Perhaps one of the most important advances we have made in recent years is to recognize that attention is not a unitary phenomenon but a complex set of functions that depend on a number of underlying processes (Posner & Boies, 1971; Pribram & McGuinness, 1975; Porges, 1976). Organized in a general way, these include: (1) selection of events; (2) general changes in state that underlie the engagement of attention; and (3) the intimate relationship between attentional control and the organization of behavior. In this chapter, we discuss the theoretical constructs relevant to these processes and address three questions concerning methods and measures. First, how do we determine what someone is attending to? Second, how do we know how strongly attention is engaged? Third, how do we investigate the issue of underlying control?

The methods we discuss include naturalistic observation, experiments, and the use of marker tasks. All employ a variety of measures that allow inferences to be drawn about attention. We discuss assumptions underlying particular measures, note advantages and disadvantages of each type of measure, and suggest some inherent limitations on interpretation.

Fortunately, researchers have available to them a rich array of both measures and methods. More confident inferences can be made when multiple measures at different levels converge in some theoretically meaningful manner. In addition, because each method has strengths and weaknesses, different methods can complement each other in elucidating the same aspect of attention. Our discussion of constructs, measures, and methods employed in the study of attention lays the foundation for our later treatment of development and individual differences in attention.

ATTENTION AS SELECTIVITY

Without a specific focus, the term "attention" would be meaningless; we always attend *to* something. Selectivity and the processes that underlie it are essential to the ability to manage the large amount of stimulation and information that is potentially available at any one time. Individuals may select external or internal events as the object of their attention. Several modalities—hearing, seeing, feeling—may be used in attending to selected events, or one modality may be dominant, as when one listens intently to a conversation in another room.

Selection of Objects and Locations

In this book, we emphasize visual selection of events in the environment. A major index of this selectivity is the orienting of the eyes in a particular direction. Since a given object is necessarily in only one place at a time, there is considerable overlap between attention to objects and their locations. A number of measures indicate to the observer that the subject is attending to a particular object or location, and we discuss them here.

Looking
Looking is a key measure of visual attention directed toward external events. Looking can be systematically observed in many situations; these range from presenting patterns to very young infants, to providing toys for preschoolers' play, to assigning complex search tasks to older children and adults. The *visual preference technique* is used so extensively in infancy research that it deserves special comment. Procedurally, the experimenter presents an infant with two objects or patterns and records the direction and duration of each look and the total duration of looking at each pattern. If infants reliably look longer at one pattern than another, we infer that infants discriminate between the two stimulus objects. We cannot conclude from differential looking that infants "like" one event better than the other because we cannot ask them directly. Different looking times might stem from one event being more arousing than the other, having been associated with more pleasant experiences, or requiring more time to process. Conversely, if infants look equally long at both patterns, we cannot assume that they *cannot* discriminate between them, only that they *do* not.

Although much work with infants is based on observing their spontaneous selection among simultaneously available patterns or objects, it is possible to induce or change selection through experience. The term "habituation" refers to a temporary decrement in the subject's responsiveness with repetition of or continued exposure to an event; it also refers to a methodology (Bornstein, 1985a). After a period of exposure to a target object, the familiar object and a novel object are presented, either simultaneously or in succession. In either case, it is expected that subjects will look longer at the novel object. This selection of the novel object depends on the child's immediately preceding experience and is one way for an experimenter to manipulate the child's visual selection of objects. This basic method has many applications in the study of both development and individual differences.

In our subsequent discussions, we refer to two methodological variations in the study of habituation. The first is the *familiarization procedure,* where one object or an identical pair of objects is presented for some duration, either a fixed amount of time or the time required to accumulate a given amount of looking (e.g., Rose & Wallace, 1985). When the trial is over, the infant is shown the now familiar object paired with a novel one. In the other method, the *habituation procedure,* a single object is presented for a set number of trials or, more commonly, until the infant reaches a criterion, such as two trials in which the infant's duration of looking is 50% of the duration on the initial two trials. The latter is often referred to as the *subject-controlled procedure* (Horowitz, 1975), where each trial lasts as long as the infant looks. When the trials are over or a criterion has been reached, a novel object and the familiar object are presented on successive trials. The mean looking time to each of these objects is then compared. Longer looking at the novel object is the expected outcome in either the familiarization or the habituation procedure. The subject-controlled procedure was designed to take individual differences into account and to decrease the number of subjects lost because of fussing; it seems to be successful in that respect compared to an habituation procedure involving a fixed number of trials (Horowitz, 1975). On the other hand, infants may be responsive to the novel display in a familiarization/paired comparison procedure in less time than required to reach the 50% criterion for habituation (see Fagan, 1974), suggesting that the process required for recognition of an object does not overlap completely with the process of habituation.

How is looking, the dependent variable in these methods, actually measured? The general direction in which an individual is looking is quite transparent to the average observer, and many studies require an experimenter simply to record whether and for how long the subject looks right, left, up, or down. This is done most easily and reliably when an experimenter or video camera, hidden from view, is positioned directly in front of and facing the subject, establishing a central reference point. Figure 2.1 shows one such arrangement. In other studies (e.g., Fantz, 1961; Smith, 1984), the criterion for recording whether a subject is looking at a specific display is a reflection of that display on the cornea of the subject's eye. This is a more taxing activity for the experimenter and is not necessary for reliable recording of the direction of looking (e.g., Ruff & Birch, 1974). Using corneal reflection also requires good light whereas the simple recording of direction can take place under less optimal conditions.

When experimenters need to have more specific information about where the subject is looking, actual *points of fixation* may be measured. Any given look at an object or event may be composed of many eye movements and fixations. Technically sophisticated methods are required to record these movements and pauses of the eyes (Hainline & Abramov, 1992). In one system (Maurer, 1975), four infrared lights are positioned behind a pattern. The changes in the reflected image of these

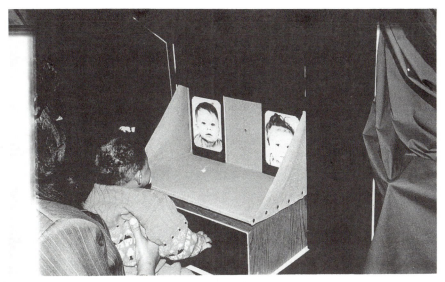

Figure 2.1. One experimental arrangement for recording infants' looking to pairs of pictures or patterns. (Top) The infant appears to be very interested in the two faces; (Bottom) an experimenter records the direction and duration of each look. (Photographs by Jefferey Jankowski, 1994.)

lights, which are not visible to the subject, are photographed by an infrared-sensitive camera at a rate of 2 to 4 per second; the distance between one or two lights and the center of the eye is then measured in each photograph. Because the location of the lights relative to the target is known, it is possible to determine the fixation point in each photograph; the exposure time of each photograph is intended to be long enough to produce a blur if the eye is moving rather than fixating at the time it is photographed. Other related systems may sample eye position as often as 60 times a second and can therefore detect smaller movements (Hainline & Abramov, 1992). These systems require restriction of head movement and ideally should be calibrated on each subject; for these reasons, few studies have been done with older infants and preschool children, who are more mobile than young infants and not as cooperative as older children and adults.

Visual following, often called *tracking* or *pursuit,* is a measure of looking obtained when subjects follow moving objects with their eyes. This behavior involves neural mechanisms different from those that govern looking at objects fixed in space (Aslin, 1981). Its use in studies of attention has been limited mainly to very young infants who are visually captured by moving objects more than stationary ones (McKenzie & Day, 1976; Volkmann & Dobson, 1976). In most studies of visual following, experimenters have used one pattern or object at a time, presenting it at the infant's midline, waiting for fixation, and then assessing how far the infant visually follows the pattern through an arc or along a straight path.

Looking is relatively easy to code and it often serves as a very reliable index of attention in naturalistic situations. We must remember, however, that to link looking to attention requires an inference. Somewhat different processes underlie movement of attention and eye movements, and one of the tasks of early development may be to coordinate looking and attention (Posner & Rothbart, 1981). The use of looking as a measure without additional information also makes it difficult to determine the level of engagement involved. Thus, we may mistake vacant staring for active visual attention to events. Research by Richards (1988), described in chapter 6, provides further support for this point.

Reaching and Other Motor Responses

Because direction of looking can sometimes be an ambiguous measure of whether attention is directed to a particular object or event, other measures of selection are also used. In "preference" tasks, for example, the experimenter can present infants over 5 months of age with two objects and observe which object is reached for and grasped. If subjects look at one object more than the other when they are out of reach, the probability is quite high that they will also reach for that object (e.g., Gottfried, Rose, & Bridger, 1977). Just as looking longer at one object rather than another shows that the object is more attractive, longer manipulation of an object in preference to another may do so as well. Reaching and manipulating, however, are not always governed by the same factors as looking. Steele and Pederson (1977) found that infants looked longer at objects of novel color, but did not manipulate one object longer than another unless the two objects varied in texture (see also Ruff, 1982).

In the tradition of behaviorism, "observing responses" are actions the subject uses to bring a stimulus event into view; these actions provide experimenters with a readily observable behavior that can be counted. For example, Schroeder and Holland (1968) investigated observing responses in a vigilance task where the subjects were asked to determine whether or not a specific signal had occurred. A press of a key illuminated a screen so that the subject could see whether a signal was present; if so, there was another response to make. Miller and her colleagues (P. Miller, 1990;

DeMarie-Dreblow & Miller, 1988; P. Miller & Harris, 1988) have used a similar technique very productively. In their design, the child is faced with a panel containing two rows of doors with pictures behind them. The child's task is to determine whether the two rows of pictures are the same or different. The pattern of door opening becomes a measure of selective attention as well as the extent to which the child employs strategic observation. Attention as measured by the observing response is, in principle, independent of performance on the task itself. Although reaching and other motor responses provide information about what is being selected for attention, an inference is still being made, as is the case with looking.

Selection of Attributes Within an Object

Selectivity can be based on factors other than location, such as properties of the objects or events attended to. Shulman and Wilson (1987), for example, found that adults, when asked to attend to the global aspects of a pattern, were more sensitive to probes (irrelevant stimulation) with large elements or low spatial frequency; in contrast, when asked to attend to the local features of the pattern, they were more sensitive to probes with small elements or high spatial frequency. These results demonstrate that subjects can develop a selective set that influences not only the main task but secondary tasks as well. Thus, attention can be directed to different aspects of a single event or object as well as to different events or objects in the visual field.

One way to assess such selectivity in infants is to manipulate the test trials in the habituation paradigm described above. As already noted, responsiveness that has decreased as a result of repeated presentations will recover when a novel object is presented. By varying the dimensions along which the novel and familiar objects differ, the experimenter can determine which aspects of the novel object are being responded to (e.g., Coldren & Colombo, 1994). For example, if infants are habituated to a red circle and their looking recovers to a red or green square but not to a green circle, we can infer that the infants are responding to shape and not color on the test trials; we may also conclude that the infants had been attending to shape but not color during the habituation trials.

ATTENTION AS STATE

The concept of state is as important to the definition of attention as is the concept of selectivity. Berlyne (1970) differentiates between selectivity and intensity, with the latter aspect referring to the degree of concentration and duration of attention once a focus has been selected. Porges (1976) suggests that we may distinguish between "an *attentional state* which facilitates or impedes stimulus intake from the *intellectual components* manifested in information processing—the intellectual components hypothetically being associated with cortical activity and the state components being associated with the central and peripheral autonomic nervous system" (p. 61, second emphasis is ours). The same general point has been made by Posner and Boies (1971) and Smothergill and Kraut (1989). Attention is a dynamic process that occurs over time, and changes in internal state mirror changes in the observed level of engagement. Thus, both behavioral and physiological measures are helpful in determining what general state a subject is in during an activity or task.

Behavioral Measures

A number of behavioral indicators have been used to assess how involved a subject is in an activity and how the intensity of involvement changes over time. We include here facial expression, degree of motor activity, and measures of performance.

Facial Expression

The coding of changes in facial expression over time has become central to the investigation of emotional responses to different events (Ekman & Friesen, 1975; Izard, 1977); it also has a place in the study of attention. In Izard's system (1979), interest/excitement is listed as one of the emotions and is intended to be synonymous with attention. Although not all investigators regard interest to be an emotion (Wozniak, 1986), a set of facial expressions has been identified as reflecting attention and effort (see figure 7.1 for examples). Izard, Dougherty, and Hembree (1989) describe the interest expression as "the brows are drawn together but neither raised nor lowered. In older children vertical furrows may appear above and between the brows. There is no movement in the eye or cheek region. The mouth is open and relaxed" (p. 12). Another expression, which Izard refers to as "hypothesized interest," is one in which no movements can be coded in any region of the face, but looking is clearly directed at a single target. The first variant of interest appears to be more intense than the second and is the reason for joining the term "excitement" to "interest."

Facial expression has not been coded extensively in studies of attention, but the few exceptions suggest that it can serve as a valuable adjunct to other measures. In particular, coding of facial expression during play or task performance may help to distinguish among qualitatively different levels of attention. Coding that requires attention to the details of facial musculature is, however, time-consuming and effortful. Izard et al. (1989) have recently introduced a less arduous system involving global judgments, which may facilitate the use of facial expression in future studies.

Motor Activity

Because motor activity in awake, alert subjects is consistently lower during cognitively demanding tasks than in other situations (Obrist, Webb, & Sutterer, 1969), level of motor activity provides another valuable measure in investigations of attention. The change in motor activity may be observed in reduced movement of muscles irrelevant to the task—for example, eye blinks or general body activity (Jennings, 1986). Obrist and his colleagues (Obrist, Webb, Sutterer, & Howard, 1970) presented adult subjects with a simple reaction-time task; they found that activity from muscles in and around the chin was directly related to reaction time, with subjects responding to the signal fastest when their muscle activity was lowest. The same kind of relationship has been observed in school-age children participating in a variety of tasks (Obrist, Howard, Sutterer, Hennis, & Murrell, 1973; van Hover, 1974).

Motor movements relevant to a particular activity or task should be distinguished from those that are irrelevant, because attention is associated only with a quieting of irrelevant movements. Direct observation and counting of movements is one method of recording degree of irrelevant activity; for example, the number of times a child gets up or off the chair during a task has been reliably counted in a number of studies (Campbell, Szumowski, Ewing, Gluck, & Breaux, 1982; Ruff, Lawson et al., 1990; Schleifer et al., 1975). There is less strain on observers, however, if movement is recorded either by mechanical means or by videotape to be scored later. One of the most common techniques is to have the subject sitting on a cushion containing several sensors that detect changes in pressure. These sensors are wired to a computer or other recording device so that a cumulative count is made automatically. Using a similar technique, Obrist et al. (1973) found that children from 4 to 10 years of age all decreased general activity when they were waiting to respond to a signal, with the magnitude of effects generally the same across age. In addition to automating the count, mechanical recording may be more sensitive than human observers to small movements that indicate squirming and fidgeting.

Another technique is to place electrodes directly over specific muscles to obtain an electromyograph, the record of electrical potentials generated by muscle movement. The chin and the corner of the eyes are common locations. These electrodes are connected to a recording device that calculates both frequency of movement and amplitude of muscle potential over the session. Using this method, van Hover (1974) showed that muscle movement in the chin decreased when the subject's task was to focus on an external task such as finding figures embedded in a complex pattern. Obrist and colleagues (1973) found that levels of eye blinking and muscle activity at the chin declined when subjects were waiting to respond to a signal.

It is not always necessary to depend on highly quantitative measures. In assessing movement, observers can make ratings or judgments about the degree of a child's activity on a simple rating scale. Such scales provide easily obtained measures that may capture somewhat different information than specific quantitative measures.

Performance on Tasks

When subjects are presented with a task, their performance can be assessed in terms of success, failure, speed of learning, reaction time, and number of errors. Many studies of attention involve *reaction time procedures*. A simple reaction-time task requires the subject to wait for a signal, usually auditory or visual, and then respond as quickly as possible. The cognitive demands of these tasks may be minimal or quite complex. Reaction-time studies have been helpful in identifying processes involved in thought and action as they occur over time (Posner, 1978). They have also been useful in studying attention and behavioral organization in children, with some successful adaptations for quite young children. For example, Weissberg et al. (1990) asked children as young as 2.5 years to push a button whenever they saw a rabbit appear on the screen in front of them. The rabbit appeared 20 times with unpredictable intervals in between.

In *vigilance tasks,* the signals are infrequent and the session is long, an attempt to push the limits of the subject's ability to concentrate over long periods (Mackie, 1977). In a more complex version, the *continuous performance task* (Rosvold, Mirsky, Sarason, Bransome, & Beck, 1956), subjects are asked to monitor a stream of visual or auditory signals, usually letters, in order to detect a particular letter or letter combination (targets). Subjects are instructed to respond only to targets and not to similar distractors. Performance on these tasks has a long history as an index of attention (Boring, 1970; Woodworth & Schlosberg, 1965); both alertness and sustained attention are inferred from fast responses and few errors of omission (i.e., missed signals). In studies of vigilance (Mackie, 1977), experimenters assume that variation within subjects in reaction times and error frequency reflect fluctuations in attention.

Although variants of the reaction-time task are among the most frequently encountered tasks in the literature on attention, attention has been inferred from performance on other tasks as well. For example, Humphrey (1982) tested recognition and recall, and Higgins and Turnure (1984) used simple and conditional discrimination tasks. When researchers use performance measures as indexes of attention, they assume that attention is a necessary component of good performance; there are, however, reasons other than variation in attention for variation in performance. As Jennings (1986) suggests: ''Attention can be convincingly inferred from a performance measure *only* when performance change cannot be explained by a change in environmental stimulation or cognitive activity (e.g., change in learned associations)'' (p. 271, our emphasis). Thus, independent measures of effort or expenditure of energy—physiological measures—are critical.

Physiological Measures

A number of physiological processes in both central and peripheral nervous systems serve as the basis for psychophysiological measures of attention. We include here a review of those most relevant to our subsequent discussions—heart rate, cortical electrophysiology, and cerebral blood flow—and omit others, such as galvanic skin response (Berlyne, Borsa, Craw, Gelman, & Mandell, 1965; Berlyne & Lewis, 1963) and pupillary dilation (Beatty, 1982; Kahneman, 1973), because they have not been used extensively with infants and young children.

Heart Rate
The primary autonomic indicator of attention and orienting has been heart rate. To collect data, the experimenter places electrodes on the subject's chest and then records the electrocardiogram, or EKG. The signals coming from the electrodes are translated into beat-to-beat intervals, which are then used to calculate changes in heart rate. Decrements in heart rate are considered to reflect attention to external events. Predictable decreases in heart rate occur with the onset of novel stimulation (Graham et al., 1983) and during execution of tasks considered to be attention-demanding (Porges & Raskin, 1969).

Just how directly heart rate decrements indicate attention is a matter of interpretation (Jennings, 1986). Obrist and his colleagues (Obrist et al., 1970) have argued that heart rate slowing is a by-product of the reduction in motor activity and respiration that occurs during sustained attention to an event or task. During performance of the simple reaction-time task described earlier, Obrist et al. (1973) measured heart rate and respiration as well as motor activity; heart rate was directly related to the level of general activity. Jennings (1986) suggests that both motor quieting and heart rate deceleration are manifestations of a central change in state. In either view, heart rate and attention are related. The relationship makes heart rate a valuable psychophysiological indicator and adjunct to behavioral measures; it may be particularly valuable in differentiating phases of attention (Richards, 1988), a possibility discussed in chapter 6.

Deceleration of heart rate seems to reflect attention to external events (Lacey & Lacey, 1970; Coles, 1984). Attention directed inward when solving mental or verbal problems, however, is more likely to be associated with heart rate acceleration. An index of sustained attention that seems to bridge these two conditions is a decrease in heart rate variability. Van Hover (1974), for example, presented school-age children with tasks requiring externally directed attention, such as visually discriminating between pictures, and tasks requiring internally directed attention, such as trying to recall a list of names. Heart rate declined for the external task and increased for the internal one, but heart rate variability decreased for both. Porges suggests (1992) that "during sustained attention[,] parasympathetic tone to the periphery is reduced[,] resulting in a slowing of digestion and other trophotropic [growth] processes" (p. 212), including the normal variability of the healthy heart.

Several measures of heart rate variability have been used. A measure that assesses parasympathetic control of heart rate variability is respiratory sinus arrhythmia (RSA), the rhythmic fluctuation in heart rate occurring at the frequency of respiration (Porges, 1986). These fluctuations involve an increase in heart rate with inspiration and a decrease with expiration. In situations that demand attention, RSA is suppressed, leading to lower levels of variability; the degree of suppression is often related to baseline levels of RSA (Porges, 1992). RSA is mediated by the vagus nerve. The vagus is the 10th cranial nerve originating in the brain stem with motor components connected to various organs, including the heart. Its activity contributes generally to homeostasis. It helps to regulate heart rate, in particular, via its connection to the sino-atrial node of the heart (Porges, 1991). For this reason, Porges (1992; Porges, Doussard-Roosevelt, & Maiti 1994) has argued that variability in RSA reflects individual differences in tonic vagal tone—that is, the degree of influence the vagus exerts over heart rate. Vagal tone is in turn seen as a direct outcome of central nervous system activity involved in the inhibition of the organism's behavior when attending to external stimuli. In a recent review, Berntson, Cacioppo, and Quigley (1993) have argued that RSA cannot be seen as directly equivalent to tonic vagal control of the heart because it is determined by multiple peripheral and central processes. They conclude, however, that RSA is an important noninvasive measure that "shows a high degree of sensitivity to psychological and behavioral variables" (p. 193).

The assumptions underlying the use of RSA as an index of attention are that (1) RSA is "a sensitive measure of brainstem regulation of the heart via the vagus" (Porges, 1992, p. 208); (2) the vagal system is important in the regulation of metabolism; and (3) sustained attention is metabolically demanding. Richards and Casey (1992) have expanded this analysis to suggest that RSA reflects "the broad network of CNS structures involved in attention" (p. 54). The correlation of internal changes, such as a slowing of respiration or heart rate, with behavior in demanding situations does not necessarily mean that these changes facilitate or cause changes in performance and behavior (Jennings, 1986). That is, the internal changes could be by-products of some other process and not be a necessary component of performance. However, temporary reduction or inhibition of normal physiological activity reduces metabolic demand and may therefore make energy available for mental work (Jennings, 1986; Porges, 1992); in this way, such changes could be integral to performance.

Cortical Electrical Responses

Electrophysiological measures of cortical activity also have a central place in the study of attention. The electroencephalograph (EEG) is a continuous recording of cortical electrical activity (see figure 2.2) obtained from electrodes placed on the scalp. Typically, 19 electrodes are placed on the scalp in a standard pattern. The resulting signals are amplified and can be translated by computer into a quantifiable analysis of waves of different amplitudes and frequencies. For example, some waves may be large and slow, others small and very rapid (Duffy, 1994). In the study of attention, the EEG can be monitored during a subject's participation in a vigilance task. Haider (1970) reports, for example, that the EEG slows down just before missed signals; thus the lapse in attention may be reflected in the EEG as well as in performance. Because the electrodes cover the scalp, the distribution of activity (topography) can also be determined (Duffy, 1994).

The derived event-related potential (ERP) is time-locked to specific stimulus events (see figure 2.3). The resulting electrical activity is analyzed into waves that vary in latency from the onset of the event, amplitude, form (sharp or spread out), and direction (negative or positive polarity). As with the EEG, the electrical activity is recorded from several different regions of the scalp, often interpreted in terms of underlying brain regions. The interpretation of ERPs is complex because the recording electrode is at some distance from the source of the neural activity and the tissue activated by the event (Steinschneider, Kurtzberg, & Vaughan, 1992). The assessment of the temporal parameters of neural activity, however, is very good.

An example of a study using ERPs to study attention comes from Hillyard, Munte, and Neville (1985). These investigators presented adults with brief events flashed either to the right or left visual field. Most events were bars 3° high, but a small proportion were only 2.5°. Attention was directed to one visual field or the other by an arrow; the subjects were instructed to press a button for every infrequent signal (short bar) occurring in that field. ERPs were collected from electrodes overlying the occipital and parietal areas. The investigators compared ERPs associated with events in the attended and unattended visual fields. They identified, among others, a negative wave or component of relatively high amplitude occurring at 190 milliseconds. This component was significantly larger at both occipital and parietal sites when the infrequent event occurred in the attended field than when it occurred in the unattended field; it was present even after several repetitions of the event. The

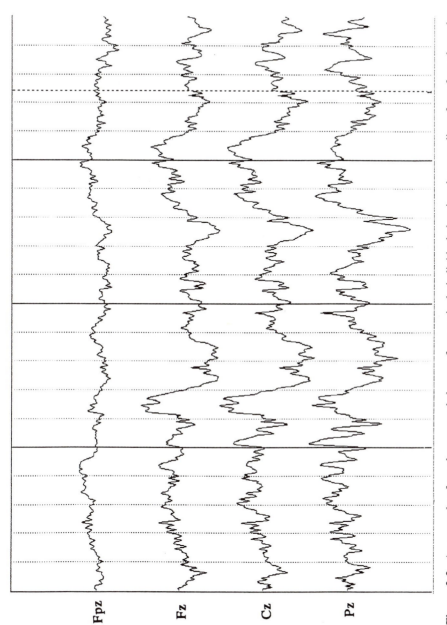

Figure 2.2. An example of an electroencephalogram from a single individual showing the recordings from four electrodes placed along the midline: on the forehead (Fpz), just above the hairline (Fz), at the top of the head (Cz), and slightly posterior (Pz). The solid vertical lines represent 1-second intervals; the dashed line indicates the occurrence of an event. (Tracings from Hilary Gomes, 1994.)

Fpz

Fz

Cz

Pz

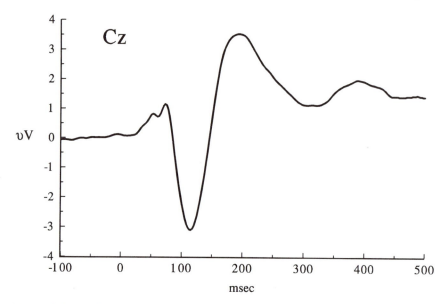

Figure 2.3. An illustration of an event-related potential. The latency to the first wave or component is determined by the onset of the event at 0 msec as seen in the scale at the bottom. The tracing represents the average of many trials from 10 subjects. (Tracing from Hilary Gomes, 1994.)

authors consider the component to reflect sustained visual attention to spatial locations.

Differential changes in the amplitude of ERPs from different brain regions may reflect increased sensitivity in specific neural pathways relevant to the task and decreased sensitivity or responsiveness in pathways not relevant to the task. Näätänen and Michie (1979) have shown, for example, that when a task is visual, amplitude of cortical evoked responses to visual stimuli is enhanced; at the same time, the amplitude of evoked responses to auditory stimuli is suppressed. Thus, some cells temporarily change the intensity of their response to particular stimulus events depending on the subject's current psychological set.

Desimone and his colleagues have pursued questions of intensity or state by making electrophysiological recordings directly from cells in the monkey brain (Spitzer, Desimone, & Moran, 1988). They found that when a monkey is given a discrimination task, the pertinent cells respond with higher amplitudes to stimulus events that are part of a difficult discrimination (\|) than to the *same* events that are part of an easier discrimination (__|). They argue that this pattern of response stems from the monkey's working harder when faced with the more difficult task.

In summary, electrophysiological techniques help to elucidate the functioning of the brain. Because information from the electroencephalogram and event-related potentials can be obtained from awake, alert subjects engaged in a variety of cognitive tasks, these techniques are invaluable in the search for brain-behavior relationships.

Cerebral Blood Flow

Another way to study brain function is to relate performance on particular tasks to patterns of metabolic activity in the brain. We briefly review the use of positron emission tomography (PET) because of its direct access to metabolism in the brain. One of various fluids containing positron-emitting radioisotopes is injected into the body and a scanner is used to image thin slices of brain tissue by detecting the distribution of the positron emitters. With certain fluids, the images reflect the blood flow to different regions of the brain. The denser the distribution of positron emission, the greater the blood flow and the more active the metabolism. In this way, researchers can map the distribution of activity in the brain during specific tasks (Taylor, 1990). For example, Corbetta, Miezin, Dobmeyer, Shulman, and Petersen (1990) showed subjects pairs of stimulus patterns and asked different subgroups to judge whether the pairs differed in color, shape, or velocity. Three different areas outside the primary visual area were activated on the trials; the location of activation depended on which stimulus characteristic the subjects were asked to attend to.

Because the PET scan technique is time-consuming and expensive, it is not likely to be used with large numbers of subjects; because it is invasive, it cannot be used with children, except when clinically indicated. Its temporal resolution or precision relative to external stimulation is more limited than the recording of event-related potentials. Its advantage, however, is that it offers more direct information about specific brain regions involved in specific activities. It also represents a way to validate and elaborate the speculation that attention is, in part, the process of allocating energy to different tasks. Knowledge obtained from both radiological and electrophysiological techniques, combined with the results of other kinds of research in the neurosciences, will help to specify the neurotransmitter pathways participating in neurally distributed attention networks (Posner & Peterson, 1990; Tucker & Williamson, 1984).

Recording cortical activity is most productive when used to investigate specific questions about the operations involved in the cortical control of attention. It is important to note that we are no closer to explaining a phenomenon when we show that a neuron responds to a given event than when we observe a behavioral response. The interpretation of both can be made only within the context of a theory or an understanding of the functional relationship of brain and behavior under specific conditions (see Posner & Raichle, 1994).

Marker Tasks

Experimental work with normal adults using neurophysiological techniques and tests of adults or nonhuman primates with brain lesions have made it possible to specify specific areas of the brain that are active during tasks requiring attention (Posner & Petersen, 1990; Wilson, Ó Scalaidhe, & Goldman-Rakic, 1993). This research represents an important advance in our understanding of brain-behavior relationships and provides a way of studying the development of brain-behavior connections in infants and young children. Marker tasks involve behavior that has been related to specific neural activity; when appropriate analogs to the tasks for adults or animals can be devised for use with children, then children's performance on the tasks can be used to study the development of both structural and functional aspects of particular neural networks.

One such marker task deals with the selection of locations referred to as "inhibition of return." Experimenters (e.g., Posner & Cohen, 1984) have shown that when an adult has examined an event at a particular location, there is a brief period of about 4 seconds during which a reorientation to that location is inhibited. The superior colliculus in the midbrain appears to be actively involved in this phenomenon because the behavior described is not seen in patients with damage to this area.

An infant test of this phenomenon will be described in detail later (Clohessey et al., 1991; Hood, 1993). The procedure involves pairs of trials. Before the first trial, a fixation is elicited by a flashing light at the center of a display; then a pattern 30° to the left or right comes on. When the infant's eyes move to it, the peripheral pattern is turned off, and refixation at the center is induced by the flashing light. On the next trial, two identical peripheral patterns are turned on, one to the right and one to the left (see figure 2.4). If the structures underlying inhibition of return are functioning, infants should, on average, turn in the opposite direction from the direction turned in the first trial.

Another example comes from the research of Diamond and Goldman-Rakic (1989). Dorsolateral prefrontal brain structures seem to be involved in performance on tasks where subjects must delay before responding differentially to two identical targets on the basis of spatial location (Passingham, 1993). By using the same tasks with young monkeys and infants in the second half of the first year, Diamond and Goldman-Rakic have demonstrated that graded steps approaching success develop in the same order, though at a faster rate in the monkeys. Then by studying monkeys with lesions in various parts of the brain, they have gathered data suggesting that development of successful delayed object search is specifically dependent on the maturation of the dorsolateral prefrontal cortex.

The use of marker tasks depends on advances in both psychology and the neurosciences, and we can expect an increasing number of such tasks to be used in the future. Even so, there is some need for caution. It is difficult to devise tasks for infants and adults that are identical in underlying demands, and it is possible for the same behavior in subjects of different ages to be governed by quite different processes (Nadel & Zola-Morgan, 1984).

ATTENTION AS EXECUTIVE CONTROL

Selectivity and state are overlapping constructs; when a focus of attention has been selected, changes in state occur both globally and in local neural pathways. In addition, attention occurs in time and can be either maintained or shifted to meet the ever-changing demands of daily life. Thus, both selectivity and state must be regulated. The concept of central executive functions is usually introduced to account for how we allocate attention, modulate concentration and effort, and plan for complex sequential activity; these functions are attributed to the frontal cortex (e.g., Stuss & Benson, 1984).

Given the multitude of activities possible at any given time, control and organi-

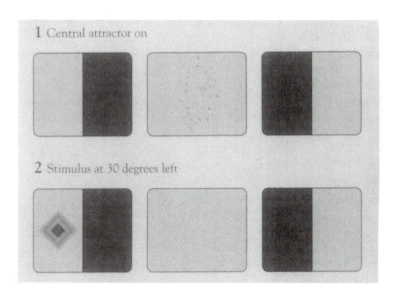

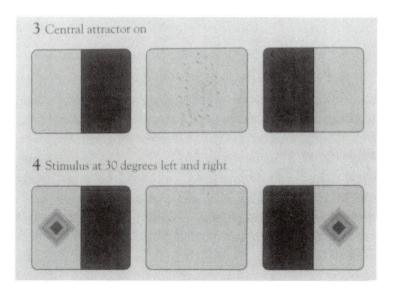

Figure 2.4. A schematic illustration of the displays used in testing inhibition of return in infants. From *Images of Mind* by M. I. Posner and M. E. Raichle. Copyright (c) 1994 by Scientific American Library. Used with permission of the authors and W. H. Freeman and Company.

zation of behavior are essential. Organization can occur outside of awareness because some events literally command our attention and other less salient events are behaviorally ignored, or possibly never detected. Organization also occurs at the conscious level, as when we list what needs to be done today and what can wait until another day. Executive or higher level control may be described as the process of determining which goals have the highest priority, given conflict among goals, and of controlling the nature, sequence, and timing of actions to meet those goals. Once priorities are determined, they may then lead to increases of energy to some activities and decreases to others (Jennings, 1986).

The allocation of energy and resources to meet current demands requires one or more processes that facilitate action in the face of local inhibitory mechanisms and inhibit action in the face of local facilitatory processes (Posner, 1982). Thus, for behavior to be organized, a higher level process must *select* among "the broad range of [activated] associations" (p. 174) or *counteract*, as necessary, "the basically inhibitory sensory processes" (p. 177). This is one way of defining modulation and control of attention. Posner and his colleagues (Posner & Petersen, 1990; Posner & Rothbart, 1991; Rothbart, Posner, & Boylan, 1990) suggest that the anterior cingulate gyrus could be the locus of this control in the central nervous system. Because the cingulate gyrus is part of the limbic system, its participation in the control of attention suggests strong ties between emotion and attention.

The concept of executive function tends to imply a homunculus, "a mind within the mind that carries out a full set of mental operations in miniature" (Tucker & Derryberry, 1992, p. 238). Thus, we are cautious in our use of the term "executive." The term implies hierarchical functioning in the brain, a model that is no longer prominent (e.g., Mountcastle, 1978b), for several reasons. First, as we have already noted, attention appears to be controlled by processes distributed throughout the brain and involves specific operations within specific pathways (Posner & Peterson, 1990; Mesulam, 1983). Second, even higher level activities, such as planning, emerge from the dynamics of specific situations. Many goals arise from immediate necessity and will change as the situation or the individual changes. Third, executive functions cannot be considered to reside in the frontal cortex; although frontal connections may be essential to conscious attention and planned, sequential activity, priorities are likely to be strongly influenced by input from subcortical pathways related to emotion. Thus, emotional factors play a determining role in what is important for adaptation, whereas control processes are important for translating emotion-determined priorities into organized action (Tucker & Derryberry, 1992). Throughout the rest of the book, we use the term "higher level" to refer to both facilitation and inhibition occurring when an individual has goals that are not compatible with immediate responses to environmental contingencies. With this term, we are not suggesting any specific processes, but the integration of many processes in the control of attention and behavior.

How do we measure higher level control? Because many situations and tasks may not require such control, it is important to observe subjects in the conditions that do require it. Norman and Shallice (1986, pp. 2–3) suggest that tasks involving higher level attentional control can be categorized as follows:

1. They involve planning or decision making.
2. They involve components of troubleshooting.
3. They are ill-learned or contain novel sequences of actions.
4. They are judged to be dangerous or technically difficult.
*5. They require the overcoming of a strong habitual response or resisting tempta-
    tion.*

Many of the measures already described can be useful in the context of experimental
manipulations that follow these general guidelines; results then allow the appropriate
inferences to be made. Here, we discuss three related concepts and the operation-
alization of them.

Voluntary Attention

The separation of attention into voluntary and involuntary modes represents a long-
standing distinction (James, 1890/1950; Ribot, 1911). James suggested that voluntary attention always involves secondary or derived motivations. That is, involuntary attention is immediate and motivated by the intrinsic appeal of the topic or
object; in contrast, voluntary attention is directed toward something intrinsically
uninteresting because it serves a remote, but important, goal. James thus considered
involuntary attention to be passive and effortless. Kahneman (1973, p. 4), however,
writes: "Voluntary attention is an exertion of effort in activities which are selected
by current plans and intentions. Involuntary attention is an exertion of effort in
activities which are selected by more enduring dispositions." Enduring dispositions
are responses to factors such as novelty and to motivationally important features of
events. We adopt Kahneman's view that both involuntary and voluntary attention
can be either focused and effortful or dispersed and casual.

If a person begins to look at something and maintains a steady gaze, we do not
know from this behavior alone whether the attention is voluntary or involuntary; the
underlying processes may be indistinguishable whether the visual target has "captured" the subject or the subject has deliberately chosen to attend to it. Because the
topic of voluntary attention is conceptually related to voluntary movement (James,
1890/1950), we often use a subject's actions to distinguish one form of attention
from another. If attention can be directed, maintained, and shifted on the basis of
instructions, we assume that subjects are exercising deliberate control over their
attention. Likewise, if attention is terminated when the task is finished, we assume
that attention was being maintained by some plan or goal. The methods used must
make it possible to observe subjects correcting errors, stopping when the goal is
reached, or halting an unproductive activity during the course of trying to accomplish a goal. Using these criteria, voluntary attention may be observed directly
during goal-directed activities where subjects indicate their goals and intentions by
word or action. In experiments with older children and adults, subjects can be
instructed verbally to solve a problem; to the extent that the subjects accept the
problem and work on it, the initiation, maintenance, and shifts of voluntary attention
can be measured.

Limited Capacity

The concept of limited capacity has wide currency in the field of cognitive psychology. The assumptions are that there is a relatively fixed quantity of attention or resources and that limitations may occur at both the local and the global level. According to Kahneman (1973), the metaphor for limits at the local level is a bottleneck that prevents the individual from perceptually exploring and understanding two events at the same time or from making two simultaneous and incompatible motor responses to an event. When two activities share the same local pathways, performing one activity will seriously interfere with the performance of the other.

The metaphor for the more general capacity model is one of a fixed amount of energy that can be distributed to various cognitive activities, the number of simultaneous activities limited by the amount of cumulative effort required (Kahneman, 1973). The total capacity available at any one time is fixed, but it fluctuates over time according to arousal level and the demands of the current activity. It may also change with development. Kahneman argues that it is impossible to work hard on an easy task. Even if the stakes are high, there is plenty of capacity left over for other tasks. During a difficult task, in contrast, we may expend a high degree of effort and have little spare capacity. The energy metaphor is consistent with the fact that cognitive activities make metabolic demands on an individual as do physical activities; thus, when the requirements are high for one task, the energy required for other activities, even vegetative functions, must be reduced (Porges, 1992).

Kahneman suggests that the empirical data do not fit either model perfectly and that both metaphors may be applicable. Structural limitations may, in fact, exist side by side with a limited, but nonspecific, capacity for attention and effort. Posner (1982) writes: "There is no incompatibility between the idea of structural limits to capacity within particular neural pools . . . and the idea of a more general structure that might coordinate information arising from more limited systems. . . . Indeed, it is a frequent trick of the nervous system to employ the same . . . organization at different levels of generality" (p. 171). It seems reasonable, therefore, to posit a global capacity for attention that can be deployed across different activities as the situation requires and also multiple, specific resource pools from which the individual can draw (Navon & Gopher, 1979; Wickens, 1984).

To test some of the tenets of the limited capacity model, investigators present subjects with two simultaneous tasks, one primary and one secondary, a procedure often referred to as a *dual task paradigm*. The experimenter assumes that the primary task will require more effort and that the subject will devote more attention to it than to the secondary task. A possible situation, for example, might require subjects to listen to lists of words and verbally recall them and, at the same time, to press a button whenever brief flashes of light or tones are detected (see P. Miller, Seier, Probert, & Aloise, 1991 for an example with children). The level of performance on the secondary detection task can be used to gauge how much attention is required for the primary recall task. If subjects can do both tasks well, the primary task is assumed to be less demanding than if they do poorly on the secondary task. By the same token, deterioration in recall memory may be interpreted as an indication that the recall task draws extensively on a central pool of resources or energy and that the secondary task is competing for those resources. By systematically varying the primary and secondary tasks, the investigator probes the limits of the theoretical model.

The same paradigm may be used to test moment-to-moment fluctuations in attention and effort expended for the primary task. When the subject is concentrating hard, signals in the secondary task may never be detected; when there is a pause in concentration, the signals are detected and responded to. These fluctuations are related to the concept of distractibility. Navon (1984), however, cautions against too glib an interpretation of dual task methods and suggests the possibility that the existing empirical data could be handled just as well without the concept of limited capacity. For example, concepts such as inhibition may explain interference or resistance to distraction just as well (e.g., Tipper, 1992). Further experimental manipulations would allow investigators to decide whether the data are best accounted for by a limited capacity (effort) model or a model involving inhibition of competing responses.

Automatic versus Controlled Processes

Because attention and behavioral organization are linked, limits on attention are related to the extent to which an activity has been practiced; some activities that have been repeatedly performed become extremely efficient and less demanding than they were at first. One interpretation of what happens with practice is that the activity becomes automatic (Shiffrin & Schneider, 1977; Posner, 1982). The term "automatic" implies that the activity does not require attention and, once initiated, runs to completion without further conscious thought. The activity itself will consume energy, but no expenditure of energy is necessary for central control mechanisms. Indeed, research with PET scans suggests that areas of the brain involved in a novel activity may not be the same areas activated by the performance of that activity after practice (Posner & Raichle, 1994).

Logan (1988) offers a somewhat different perspective on the concept of automaticity. He suggests that attention leads to obligatory perception and learning of the event attended to. The more often this occurs, the more quickly and efficiently the memory of that event can be retrieved in circumstances where it is needed. At all times, however, attention and intention can play an important role in initiating the automatic process and in completing it. Reason (1984) gives many examples of "slips of action" that occur even with well-practiced activities because the individual is preoccupied or distracted by something else. Spelke, Hirst, and Neisser (1976) offer yet another interpretation. Rather than practice causing behavior to become automatic, practice in doing two things at once promotes skills in managing both tasks at the same time.

Regardless of the theoretical perspective taken, it is undeniable that practice leads to a reduction in the demands made on people and increases their ability to perform two activities at one time. The processes involved are not obvious and must be discovered through experimental manipulation of the subject's experience. Practice on a task can be built into the experiment and the effects of practice within sessions observed. For students of child development, there are many opportunities to observe young children as they practice new skills. Short-term longitudinal studies allow the observer to trace the natural history of the skill as it becomes increasingly efficient. Experimental manipulations at different points in this history can then illuminate the effects of practice on the child's attention to other events in the environment.

In summary, executive control is a complex construct that implies some higher level management of lower level mechanisms. Mechanisms, such as orienting and habituation, can be facilitated or inhibited as necessary in pursuit of an individual's goals. Various methods are used to determine how much higher level control is being exerted, but most include the observation of subjects in settings with multiple tasks or sources of stimulation. The issue of automatic versus controlled processes and the related issue of limited capacity are both important in explaining children's growing efficiency in deploying attention in complex environments.

SUMMARY

We now return to questions posed at the beginning of this chapter: How do we determine what someone has selected for attention? What states of the individual are associated with attention? How do we investigate the issue of underlying control? We noted that a common approach to studying selection in children is to observe the direction and duration of looking. Variants on total looking time include the number, duration, and order of eye fixations at specific locations and the movement of gaze during visual tracking or pursuit. We cautioned the reader about assuming that the direction of the eyes is necessarily the direction of attention, distinguishing between overt orienting of head and eyes and the unobservable processes of attention. However, because the two often overlap in direction and move in synchrony, procedures using the direction and duration of looking have illuminated the central processes of attention.

Other behavioral indicators help to assess underlying states associated with attention at different levels of intensity. These include facial expression and motor activity. Physiological measures also contribute to our understanding of attentional state; these include heart rate, respiratory sinus arrhythmia, electromyographic responses, and cortical electrical responses, such as event-related potentials. New imaging techniques, such as PET scans, allow for more precise identification of brain areas activated during attention; these techniques have been particularly useful in determining brain activity associated with higher level control. Finally, marker tasks can be used in longitudinal studies to infer the development of particular regions and networks in the brain.

The executive or higher order functions are those that help to control attention and action and are thus essential to organizing complex behavior. The notion of higher level control needs to be integrated with information about the connections between cortical operations and emotional priorities. Related discussions in the literature revolve around contrasts between voluntary and involuntary attention and between automatic and controlled behavior; the concept of limited capacity to pay attention is also frequently invoked. Underlying processes need to be inferred from behavior in situations that are novel or otherwise demand careful monitoring of details.

Perhaps not everyone knows ''what attention is,'' but there is broad agreement that multiple processes are involved in attention. Therefore, investigations of several constructs at different levels are necessary for theoretical reasons; in addition, the use of multiple measures allows us to surmount the limitations of any given method. In the subsequent chapters, we provide many examples of such multidimensional approaches to the study of attention.

3

Looking and Visual Attention: Overview and Developmental Framework

This chapter focuses on the early development of children's looking, a potential index of visual attention at all ages. One of our goals is to provide a broad outline of issues to be discussed in more detail in the following chapters. A second goal is to cast these issues in a framework of early development. Within this framework we emphasize developmental transitions taking place around 2 months, 9 to 12 months, 18 to 24 months, and 3 to 5 years. These transitions are important in understanding the development of the two major attention systems introduced briefly in chapter 1. The first system is an earlier maturing system that underlies orienting and investigation of locations and objects, and the second is a later maturing system that underlies goal-oriented attention and the control of complex activity.

LOOKING IN THE NEWBORN

During the first 2 months of life, patterns of looking differ in important ways from those seen later in development. The newborn has only short periods of alertness, being awake 11 to 19% of the day in the first two weeks (Dittrichova & Lapackova, 1964; Wolff, 1987). When newborns are awake and alert, however, their looking is neither random nor confused; rather, it is organized and selective. In groundbreaking research, Fantz (1963, 1964) showed that newborn infants look longer at patterned stimulation than at plain fields of color and longer at some patterns than at others. Figure 3.1 shows two pairs of patterns used in Fantz's early work. The values under the preferred pattern from each pair show the percentage of infants' looking time directed at that pattern. His results indicate that newborns tend to look more at patterns and objects that have large features and high contrast. There is also evidence that newborns have preferences for looking at patterns composed of curved as opposed to straight lines (Fantz & Miranda, 1975).

Newborns are also able to track moving objects with their eyes, although this

70%   79%

Figure 3.1. Representative "preferences" of newborn infants. The values under one member of each pair represent the percentage of looking time directed at the preferred pattern. From "Pattern preferences and perceptual-cognitive development in early infancy" by R. L. Fantz and S. Nevis, *Merrill-Palmer Quarterly, 13*, p. 86. Copyright 1967 by Wayne State University Press. Adapted with permission.

tracking is not smooth and tends to lag behind movement of the object (Aslin, 1981). With moving targets, but not stationary ones, newborns selectively look at prototypical human faces compared to faces with scrambled features (Goren, Sarty, & Wu, 1975; Johnson & Morton, 1991). Infants in the first 2 months of life also tend to visually scan the external contours of stationary objects more than they do their internal features and to restrict their scanning to small sections of the contour (Salapatek, 1975). Figure 3.2 shows the young infant's pattern of scanning a face; successive fixations at 1 month are clearly concentrated at the edges (Maurer & Maurer, 1988).

At times, very young infants may have trouble looking away from a highly salient object once their attention has been engaged. Extended looking at high-contrast patterns is not uncommon. In the initial presentation of patterns to newborns in a study by Friedman (1972), mean looking time was 55 out of 60 seconds. Stechler and Latz (1966) allowed unlimited exposure to drawings of faces and bull's-eyes and observed one infant to look for 35 minutes at 10 days of life and another infant to look for 54 seconds with only brief interruptions. These periods of looking ended with considerable distress. The same kind of fussiness associated with lengthy looks was observed by Tennes, Emde, Kisley, and Metcalf (1972). These observations suggest difficulty with the process of disengaging attention.

THE TRANSITION AT 2 TO 3 MONTHS

All of these aspects of looking begin to change around 2 to 3 months of age, a time that has been identified as a major developmental transition (Emde, Gaensbauer, & Harmon, 1976). After 2 months, infants spend significantly longer periods of time

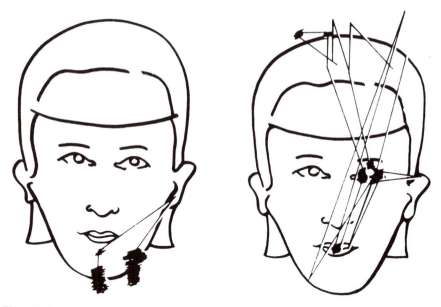

Figure 3.2. Visual scanning of human faces at 1 and 2 months of age. From *The World of the Newborn* (p. 123) by D. Maurer and C. Maurer, 1988. New York: Basic Books. Copyright 1988 by the authors. Reprinted with permission.

awake and looking around (Wolff, 1987). They are much more likely to select particular patterns, such as faces or bull's-eyes, regardless of whether they are larger or smaller, brighter or dimmer, than alternatives (Ruff & Turkewitz, 1975, 1979). Salapatek (1975) found a similar shift with quite different patterns—matrices of squares and lines (figure 3.3). During the first 2 months, infants looked longer at the squares than at the lines, presumably because the squares were bigger and brighter, and they did so regardless of whether the squares represented the majority or the minority of elements in the pattern. After 2 months, however, infants began to concentrate their looking on the smaller area that was discrepant from the rest of the pattern, regardless of whether that area was composed of squares or lines.

After 2 to 3 months, infants also begin to visually follow objects more readily (Ruff, Lawson, Kurtzberg, McCarton, & Vaughan, 1982). Their scanning of static objects is more likely to include the internal as well as the external contours and generally to be more widely distributed (Salapatek, 1975; Bronson, 1991). Figure 3.2 illustrates the more distributed scanning pattern seen at 2 months. After 3 months, "obligatory" looking seems to diminish and infants begin to disengage their looking more readily (Johnson et al., 1991).

The time infants spend looking at interesting objects during alert periods increases from birth to 3 months. The duration of looking at each age observed in a study by Keller, Schölmerich, Miranda, and Gauda (1987) is represented by the dashed line in figure 3.4. The displays used in this study included faces, checkerboards, and other high-contrast patterns. In this and following figures, age changes in total duration of infant looking are shown as a percentage of available time spent

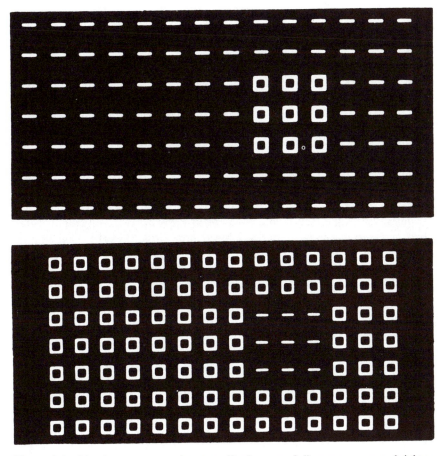

Figure 3.3. Stimulus patterns used to test effectiveness of discrepancy versus brightness. From *Infant perception: From sensation to cognition* (p. 223), L.B. Cohen and P. Salapatek, 1975, New York: Academic Press. Copyright 1975 by Academic Press. Reprinted with permission.

in looking, giving us a comparable measure across studies where different numbers of trials and trials of different lengths were used.

Social Implications of the 2- to 3-Month Shift

Face-to-face play between infant and parent is a good context in which to observe early changes in visual attention, changes that have an influence on social development. In the first 2 months, infants will look at their caretakers' faces some of the time, but at other times will fail to establish eye contact, often looking to the hairline or the edge of the face. Infants after 2 months are more likely to make eye contact (Keller & Gauda, 1987) and thus to select and invite the social partner to interact. The infant's state of alertness during interactions with the parent also changes over this period. Kaye and Fogel (1980) found that 24% of the time 2-month-old infants spent looking at their mothers in face-to-face interaction could be described as dull, with the infants' eyes glassy or partly closed; by 3 months, the proportion of dull looking had dropped to about 8% of total looking time.

The duration of social looking increases over the first few months, as it does for static patterns. The solid line in figure 3.4 illustrates the course of looking in a study by Lamb and his colleagues (Lamb, Morrison, & Malkin, 1987). In this study, infants were observed every four weeks from 1 to 6 months of age. Periods of social interaction with the mother and a strange woman were coded for a number of variables, including the duration of looking. As can be seen in the figure 3.4, the amount of the infants' looking at adults during interaction increased steadily from 1 to 4 months.

Robson and Moss (1970) asked mothers of young infants about when they felt their infants recognized them as special individuals, when they saw their infants as individuals, and when their own feelings of love for the child developed. Many mothers reported that these feeling developed around 6 to 9 weeks along with the child's eye contact, smiles, and vocal responses. Fraiberg (1977) describes the

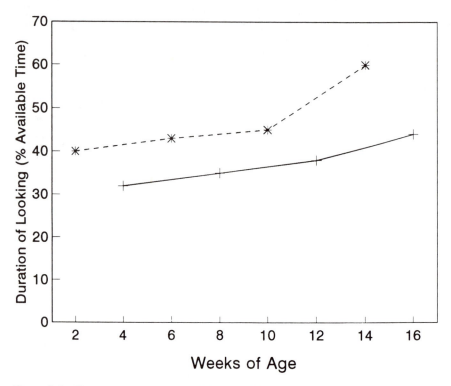

Figure 3.4. Changes in the duration of looking at objects and events in the first 16 weeks of life. Data were summarized from Keller et al. (1987; shown as asterisks) and from Lamb et al. (1987; shown as crosses). From *Curiosity, imagination and play* (p. 133), D. Gorlitz and J. F. Wohlwill (Eds.), Hillsdale, NJ: Erlbaum. Copyright 1987 by Erlbaum. From "The development of infant social expectations in face-to-face interaction" by M. E. Lamb, D. C. Morrison, and C. M. Malkin, *Merril-Palmer Quarterly, 33*, p. 250. Copyright 1987 by Wayne State University Press. Adapted with permission.

powerful social role of looking in this way: "During the first six months, the baby has the rudiments of love language available to him. There is the language of the embrace, the *language of the eyes,* the language of the smile, [and] vocal communications of pleasure and distress" (Fraiberg, 1977, p. 29, our emphasis). In this period, the long "obligatory" looking of the infant into the eyes of the parent might be seen by the parent as a sign of attachment (see figure 3.5). The transition marks the beginning of a period of developing attachment and mutual regulation of attention in face-to-face interaction (Schaffer, 1984).

Processes Underlying the Transition at 2 to 3 Months

Why does a dramatic shift in visual attention occur at 2 to 3 months? In part, some changes occur because 3-month-old infants can see better than newborns as a result of maturation of the visual system, including the retina. Lewis, Maurer, and Brent (1989) suggest further that, at this time, maturation of the cells and connections in the visual pathways to the cortex change the basis for discriminating and selecting among objects. In the newborn infant, looking may be guided predominantly by subcortical mechanisms (Bronson, 1974; Johnson, 1990; Lewis et al., 1989). Posner and Rothbart (1981) suggest that visual orienting and attention are governed by different processes and that, in the newborn, visual orienting or selectivity is not yet coordinated with attention. The shift to greater cortical control around 2 to 3 months makes it possible for processes of attention to assume greater control of eye movements. Thus, infants' patterns of looking begin to be determined more by attention and accumulated experience. More details of this transition will be discussed in chapters 4 and 5 on selectivity and in chapter 6 on state.

Figure 3.5. A mother and 12-day-old infant. (Photograph by Ruth Alliger.)

LOOKING AND THE DEVELOPMENT OF THE
FIRST ATTENTION SYSTEM

In the period from 3 to 9 months of age, there are steady changes in patterns of looking and their consequences. Throughout this period, infants begin to deploy their attention more flexibly and are influenced more readily by experience. Not only are they able to disengage visual attention more quickly, they also begin to develop expectations based on the repetition of simple events (Haith, Hazen, & Goodman, 1988; Johnson et al., 1991). The effects of experience are reflected in the increasing speed with which infants come to recognize repeated events through looking (Colombo, 1993). Colombo (1995) notes that there is a linear decrease in the amount of looking devoted to visual displays during familiarization and habituation procedures, possibly because infants learn about such displays more and more quickly (see figure 3.6). Within this age range, infants can also learn to visually recognize more complex events than younger infants (Cohen et al., 1979).

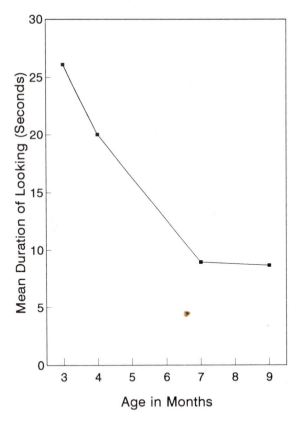

Figure 3.6. The mean duration of looking based on both longitudinal and cross-sectional samples over 3 to 9 months. From ''On the neural mechanisms underlying developmental and individual differences in visual fixation in infancy: Two hypotheses,'' by J. Colombo, 1995, *Developmental Review, 15.* Copyright 1995 by Academic Press. Adapted with permission.

Around 5 months, infants begin to reach, grasp, and manipulate objects that engage their visual attention, and by 9 months, infants are highly proficient at manipulative, as well as visual, exploration of novel objects. Schaffer (1984) suggests that, as the infant's attention shifts from primary involvement with the parent to the "world of objects" (p. 17), the incorporation of objects into social interactions promotes shared attention to objects, important for both social and cognitive development.

From 3 to 9 months, selective visual attention is strongly influenced by the novelty of events and objects and by the orienting/investigative system. A number of factors support the functioning of this first system of attention. The visual system matures rapidly during this time, and by 6 to 7 months, many functions, such as visual acuity and binocularity, have reached adult levels (Aslin, 1987). Visual orienting to novel events in particular locations in the external environment is supported by a network in the parietal cortex (Posner & Raichle, 1994). Results based on marker tasks derived from research with adults (Clohessy et al., 1991; Hood, 1993) suggest that the posterior orienting network becomes fully functional around 6 months of age, though it operates earlier to a lesser degree under some conditions (see chapter 5). The network involves a number of processes, including disengagement, shifting, and inhibition of return (Johnson, 1990; Johnson et al., 1991; Posner & Presti, 1987). Various accounts of the neural underpinnings of the orienting network (Derryberry & Tucker, 1990; Mesulam, 1983; Posner & Peterson, 1990; Posner & Raichle, 1994; Tucker & Williamson, 1984) agree that the network involves the posterior parietal cortex in conjunction with several subcortical systems; connections to the locus coeruleus in the brainstem, the major source of norepinephrine, seem to be particularly strong (Posner & Peterson, 1990; Tucker & Williamson, 1984).

The orienting network is strongly related to the movement of attention to specific locations in the environment; another network seems to underlie the recognition of specific objects (Ungerleider & Mishkin, 1982). This network involves the pathways from the primary visual cortex to the inferior temporal cortex, an association area that receives input about object properties such as form and color. The object recognition network is important for determining "what" something is, while the orienting network is important for determining "where" it is. Although not as much research has been conducted on the development of this latter pathway, an interesting study by Harman et al. (1994) is relevant. They found that infants at both 3 and 6 months had strong visual preferences for novel objects at novel locations. When novel locations were put in competition with novel objects, however, only the 6-month-olds preferred the novel objects. These findings, consistent with those by Colombo, Mitchell, Coldren, and Atwater (1990), raise the possibility that the "what" and "where" networks develop at somewhat different rates, with the parietal orienting network maturing before the temporal object recognition network. On the basis of event-related potentials recorded in the first year, Courchesne (1990) and Nelson and deRegnier (1992) hypothesize that an attention response to visual stimulation, indexed by a negative wave with greatest amplitude at central and frontal sites, is in place by 4 to 6 months. Courchesne (1990) notes that this negative component increases in amplitude with age, but according to Nelson and deRegnier

(1992), it changes very little in form or topography from 4 to 10 months. In contrast, a slow positive wave with the same distribution undergoes continued development over this period and is interpreted by Nelson and deRegnier as related to object recognition.

In brief, the first attention system underlies orienting to and exploration of objects in the environment, and it is composed of at least the two networks just described. For adaptive action, there needs to be communication between these networks (Milner, Carey, & Harvey, 1994). Indeed, Merigan and Maunsell (1993) argue that the two networks may be less separate than often supposed. Even if separate, the two networks play complementary roles: the "where" system directs attention to potentially important locations through stimulation in the periphery of the visual field; the "what" system then supports the gathering of detailed information through central vision. The information gathered, in turn, affects the direction of future looks. Although complex communication between these networks may continue to develop into the second year of life (Sinha, 1994), some additive influences seem to be present as early as 3 months (Wentworth & Haith, 1992; Harman et al., 1994). The coordination of these two networks supports the functioning of the orienting/investigative system. This system, in turn, underlies the strong preference for novelty and the extensive exploratory activity of infants in this age range (E. Gibson, 1988).

THE TRANSITION AT 9 TO 12 MONTHS

So many changes occur between 6 and 15 months, many of them emerging around 9 months, that 9 months is considered a major transition point in development (Bertenthal & Campos, 1990; Emde et al., 1976; Fox, Kagan, & Weiskopf, 1979). These changes include those in infants' looking, which we examine first before reviewing marked changes in other domains.

Developmental Changes in Looking

Six- to 12-month-olds' looking has been measured in two major contexts—presentation of static displays for viewing and presentation of toys for play. The first of these involves measuring the duration of looking at repetitions of stationary displays. Like figure 3.6, figure 3.7 shows a steady decrease in looking at such displays from 3 months to about 13 months. Stimulus events represented in the figure are flashing lights, slides of colored curved line segments (Lewis, Goldberg, & Campbell, 1969), and three-dimensional faces (Kagan et al., 1971). Each point indicates the percentage of available time spent looking, averaged over several trials of the same display. Thus, the decrease with age in the duration of looking is due, in part, to faster learning and habituation.

The other context in which length of looking has been measured is during infants' manipulative play with toys and other objects. When infants are presented with single objects, there appears to be little general change in looking (Ruff, Saltarelli, Capozzoli, & Dubiner, 1992), though older infants may look less at

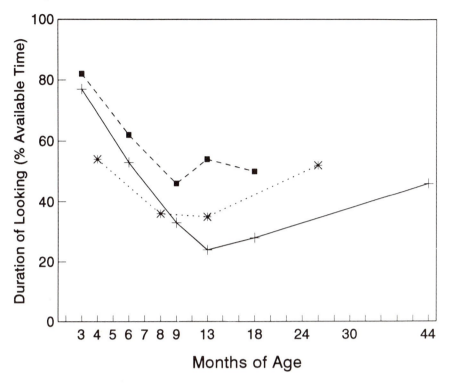

Figure 3.7. Decline in duration of looking from 3 to 13 months of age; note the suggestion of an increase in looking around 13 months. Data are summarized from Lewis et al. (1969; shown as solid squares and crosses) and from Kagan et al. (1971; shown as asterisks). From "A developmental study of information processing within the first three years of life," by M. Lewis, S. Goldberg, and M. Campbell, 1969, *Monographs of the Society for Research in Child Development, 34*, pp. 9, 16, 19, and 20. Copyright 1969 by the Society for Research in Child Development. From *Change and Continuity in Infants* (pp. 209–210) by J. Kagan, 1971, New York: Wiley. Copyright 1971 by John Wiley and Sons, Inc. Adapted with permission.

simple objects than younger infants (Oakes & Tellinghuisen, 1994). There are, however, some complex objects that elicit longer looking in older than in younger infants, perhaps because the older infants are more able to detect, explore, and manipulate subtle details of these objects.

When several objects are given to infants simultaneously, however, the dominant trend is for an increase in looking over this time period. Figure 3.8 presents overlapping curves from two studies. In one study (Ruff & Saltarelli, 1993), 7- and 9-month-old infants were put on the floor with a bucket of toys and allowed to play by themselves for 5 minutes while their mothers filled out a questionnaire nearby. Looking at the toys, which in this context is almost always accompanied by some manipulation, was significantly higher for the 9-month-olds than for the 7-month-olds. In another study, Bakeman and Adamson (1984) observed 6- to 18-month-old infants in their homes. In one condition, these infants were given toys to play with on the floor for 10 minutes while their mothers sat nearby. Engagement with the toys, which by their definition was roughly equivalent to looking, generally increased over that age range (Adamson & Bakeman, 1992).

The opposing trends seen in figures 3.7 and 3.8 suggest the possibility that as some influences on attention decline, others increase. The dip in looking between 9 and 13 months is another indication of possible changes in the factors governing visual attention. These changes are presumably due, in part, to the development Ruff of new skills for exploring and exploiting objects in the environment.

Two other changes in looking within this period have important social implications. One is that infants start looking more toward their mothers' faces when their mothers are at some distance from them. This phenomenon is often considered to be social referencing, a search for information from another person (Sorce, Emde, Campos, & Klinnert, 1985). It occurs at the same time that infants develop a transient fear of strangers (Bronson, 1972) and some behavioral inhibition to novelty or challenge (Rothbart, 1988b). More mature infants, as indexed by crawling, look more toward their mothers when physically separated and in novel or threatening circumstances than do younger infants or same-age noncrawlers (Bertenthal &

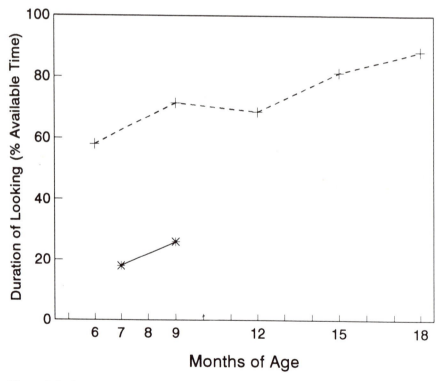

Figure 3.8. Duration of looking at toys during free play; data are taken from Ruff and Saltarelli (1993; shown as asterisks) and Adamson and Bakeman (shown as crosses). From "Exploratory play with objects: Basic cognitive processes and individual differences" by H. A. Ruff and L. M. Saltarelli, *New Directions for Child Development, 59,* p. 12. Copyright 1993 by Jossey-Bass. Adapted with permission. From unpublished raw data. Adapted with permission of L. B. Adamson and R. Bakeman.

Campos, 1990). Thus, infants begin to use their parents as a visual point of reference when they encounter ambiguous situations. Other investigators interpret these data as a reflection of attachment and a search for comfort (Baldwin & Moses, 1994). Regardless of the interpretation, infants change their patterns of social looking.

A second socially relevant change is that infants begin to share attention to toys or objects with adults who play with them; they do so by monitoring, through looking, both toy and partner. During periods of interaction, 12-month-olds show more coordinated attention to adult and toy than 6- or 9-month-olds (Bakeman & Adamson, 1984). Between 9 and 11 months, infants also become more likely to comply with the mother's instructions during play, to imitate her actions, and to attract the mother to a toy of their own choosing (Hubley & Trevarthen, 1979). As Schaffer (1984) notes: "the child's behavior now becomes much more flexible and coordinated. A more symmetrical relationship with the caretaker, based on reciprocity and characterized by intentionality, can thus be established around this age" (p. 17).

Changes in Other Domains

These changes in the duration and distribution of looking occur in the context of general developments in memory (Fox et al., 1979) and the control of action (Diamond & Gilbert, 1989). At 9 months, but not before, infants begin to imitate the action of others after a delay (Meltzoff, 1990). During this period of development, infants seem increasingly able to anticipate future outcomes on the basis of past experiences. Remembered details related to a goal, such as its location, influence their actions as long as that there is some physical reminder. Infants are able to find hidden objects after longer and longer delays (Diamond, 1985). Furthermore, as Piaget (1952) noted, infants are increasingly able to approach goals in a new way if the first approach fails. Willats and his colleagues (e.g., Willats & Rosie, 1989) have found that 9-month-olds begin to solve simple means-ends problems that require them to remove a barrier in order to grasp an object; by 12 months, infants are able to solve means-ends problems consisting of several steps. These developments require infants to attend to goals despite delays and obstacles.

Accomplishments during this period are evidence of emerging intentionality of action as goals are kept briefly in mind and infants employ a variety of means to attain them. These accomplishments may be a challenge for parents because infants' desires and preferences are now more clearly demonstrated, and with crawling and other self-regulative behavior, infants can move more easily toward what they want. Whereas the parent previously had a good deal of control over the attentional focus of the infant, the infant is now developing a "mind of its own."

Processes Underlying the Transition around 9 Months

Emerging motor skills, such as crawling, play an important role in this array of behavioral changes because infants, with their altered perspective, attend to new aspects of both the physical and social environment (Bertenthal & Campos, 1990).

Fox et al. (1979) suggest that these developments, along with stranger anxiety, are also due to increases in memory capacity. In a longitudinal study of 8 infants, they found parallel changes around 9 months in the tendency to compare novel and familiar objects, to succeed at standard object search tasks and tasks in which objects were surreptitiously removed or substituted, and to imitate actions with short delays. They write: "two related memorial competencies [emerge] during this era. . . . One is the ability to retrieve representations of past experience when minimal cues are present in the immediate perceptual field. The second is the capacity to engage in . . . comparison of retrieved knowledge with the transformations of current experience. . . ." (p. 95).

Kagan (1970) argues that the dip in looking and the subsequent increase, as seen in figure 3.7, are due to these new advances in memory and cognition. When young infants are looking at objects discrepant from their experience (see figure 3.9), they look only long enough to recognize that an object is part of an already experienced category of events. Older infants, on the other hand, begin to generate hypotheses about what they see, especially when current displays conflict with previous experience. Because older infants are more aware of the discrepancies, they attend longer than younger infants in an attempt to resolve or understand the discrepancy; thus, duration of looking increases.

The 9- to 12-month transition also includes the emergence of some inhibition of actions that are strongly or immediately elicited by the situation. Diamond (1985), for example, observed important changes from 6 to 12 months in infants' performance on the "A not B" task. This task involves shifting the location of a hidden object from A to B after the infant has already retrieved the object from A. Success requires the infant to adapt its response rather than repeat a previously reinforced action. Diamond argues that the younger infants are not simply failing to remember the correct location; they are failing to inhibit the primed response. In another reaching task developed by Diamond and Gilbert (1989), visual information about the appropriate route to a toy is put in conflict with the cues that normally guide reaching. An object is placed through an opening at the *front* of a box, but the toy is visible through the Plexiglas *top* of the box. Contact with the toy is possible only if the infant inhibits the tendency to reach directly for the visible toy. By 11 to 12 months, but not before, infants can retrieve toys through the opening irrespective of whether the opening is at the front, side, or back.

Evidence from research on monkeys with brain lesions (Diamond & Goldman-Rakic, 1989), EEG research (Bell & Fox, 1994), and PET studies on human infants (Chugani, 1994) suggests that parts of the frontal lobe are beginning to become functional during this period. In particular, Diamond and Goldman-Rakic (1989) have identified the development of dorsolateral prefrontal brain structures as important to success on the "A not B" and retrieval tasks. Their research comparing monkeys with lesions and human children on the same tasks suggests that the behavioral developments of this period are specific to changes in the prefrontal cortex; lesions in the hippocampus (Diamond, Zola-Morgan, & Squire, 1989) and parietal regions (Diamond & Goldman-Rakic, 1989) do not affect performance on these marker tasks.

These developments in attention and control over action represent rudimentary

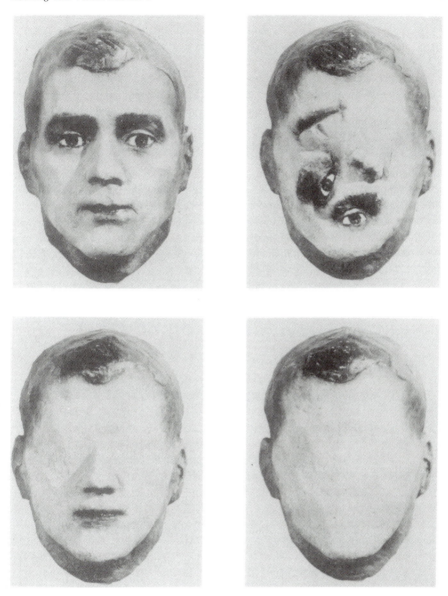

Figure 3.9. Three-dimensional masks of normal and distorted faces shown to infants from 4 to 27 months of age. From *Change and continuity in infancy* (p. 41) by J. Kagan, 1971. New York, Wiley. Copyright 1971 by John Wiley and Sons, Inc. Reprinted with permission.

elements of executive control. There are still many limitations on infants' actions, their comprehension of the world around them, and their ability to act and control attention on the basis of represented, as opposed to physically present, information. Thus, we see these changes around 9 to 12 months as the very beginnings of the second, higher level system of attention.

CONSOLIDATION OF THE SECOND ATTENTION SYSTEM AND THE TRANSITION AT 18 MONTHS

Dramatic changes in many areas of functioning occur around 18 to 24 months of age. There is, however, no inflection in the curve of looking to parallel that which we see around 9 to 12 months. What is happening to the duration of looking?

Developments in Patterns of Looking

Looking at complex visual displays, such as television shows, increases during the second year and continues to do so. Figure 3.10 presents the proportion of time in two studies that children spent looking at TV. The first was a laboratory study by Anderson and Levin (1976) of children from 12 to 48 months of age who were presented with a *Sesame Street* program. Similar age trends have been found in a more naturalistic survey of television viewing within the home (Anderson, Lorch, Field, Collins, & Nathan, 1986). The other curve comes from a study (Ruff et al.,

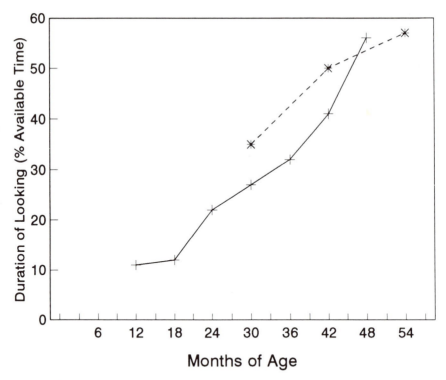

Figure 3.10. The duration of television watching by age. Data are taken from Ruff (1989; shown as asterisks) and Anderson and Levin (shown as crosses). From "Young children's attention to "Sesame Street," by D. R. Anderson and S. R. Levin, 1976, *Child Development, 47,* p. 808. Copyright 1976 by the Society for Research in Child Development. Adapted with permission.

1995) in which 2.5- to 4.5-year-old children were shown a specially created video-tape of puppet skits.

Looking during play with an array of toys continues to increase after 12 months. Figure 3.11 complements that of figure 3.7, which showed increases in looking during play. Krakow, Kopp, and Vaughn (1982) observed children from 12 to 30 months of age during six minutes of free play with an array of toys and found steady and significant increases over that period in their total time oriented to the toys. Ruff and Lawson (1990) observed children from 30 to 54 months of age during 10 minutes of free play and found a significant increase in looking from 30 to 42 months. Thus, looking at toys during children's play increases throughout the early preschool years.

The age trends depicted in these graphs are representative. It would always be possible to find a situation or set of toys that would lead to more attention in a 2-year-old than in a 4-year-old (Moyer & Gilmer, 1955), or a static display that would lead to a continued decline in looking throughout the preschool years. In general, however, the convergence of data from a number of different procedures strongly suggests a direct relationship between age and how long visual attention is sustained.

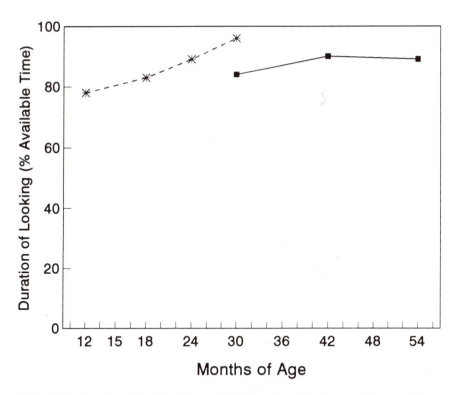

Figure 3.11. Duration of looking at toys during free play. Note the very high overall levels of looking. Data are taken from Ruff and Lawson (1990; shown as squares) and Krakow et al. (shown as asterisks). From *Sustained attention during the second year: Age trends, individual differences and implications for development,* by J. B. Krakow, C. B. Kopp, and B. E. Vaughn, 1982. Unpublished manuscript. Adapted with permission.

Cognitive developments occurring throughout the second and third years are related to these changes in looking. Improvements in comprehension of events leads to longer looking during television viewing in older than in younger children (Anderson & Lorch, 1983). In the free-play setting, older children appear to be better able than infants to manage the potentially distracting effects of having several toys at once to play with, leading to more organized and longer periods of sustained attention (Ruff & Lawson, 1990). By the end of the first year, the child's activity also takes on a new level of complexity as the child begins to combine objects—for example, putting one object on top of or inside another. Combinatorial skills thereafter become more and more complex (Brownell, 1988). In chapter 6, we discuss in more detail the implication of these developments for attention.

In addition to the increase in looking that emerges in the second year, other changes in visual attention are occurring. By 18 to 24 months, most children are skilled at following the glances and points of others (Butterworth, 1991), and their language comprehension is sufficient to understand when others use words to direct their attention (Anisfeld, 1984). They apparently use all these sources as information and as a motivation to shift the direction of their looking. At the same time, children gradually become more active in controlling the selectivity of others by pointing and vocalizing themselves and by checking to see whether other people are following their lead (Blake, McConnell, Horton, & Benson, 1992).

The 18-month Transition

Increases in comprehension and complexity of activity could be seen as a gradual accumulation of skills that influence visual attention. The steady increase in attention after a year of age supports this possibility. However, the shift around 18 to 24 months is also a qualitative one in many ways. These qualitative changes may underlie the emergence of new attentional skills not observable in looking alone (Posner, Rothbart, Thomas-Thrapp, & Gerardi, in press). In this section, we discuss some of the additional developmental changes and show how they are tied to the development of higher level functions.

Many behavioral changes reflect the major developmental shift occurring at this time. Perhaps the most salient of these is the "naming spurt," a sharp increase in labeling objects (Anisfeld, 1984). Although the beginning of spoken language stands out, Piaget (1952) links the development of language to the underlying emergence of symbolic functioning. Symbolic activity is seen at 18 months in pretend play and the ability to find hidden objects that have been displaced in ways not visible to the child. For Piaget, the significance of these changes is that the child now has some capacity to represent absent objects and events. Meltzoff (1990) argues that, although younger infants are able to "represent actual states of affairs from the past, there . . . is a profound deficit, before about 18 months of age, in representing what 'might be' or deducing what 'must have been'" (Meltzoff, 1990, p. 2). This is part of a shift from knowledge based on perception and action to more generalized and abstract knowledge.

Other important developments around 18 months include infants' self-referential ability. They begin, for example, to identify themselves in mirror images (Lewis &

Brooks-Gunn, 1979). Moreover, infants now have a sense of self, an important accompaniment to a new level of self-regulation. They can see themselves as agents who act on and alter the environment (Jennings, 1991). They begin to take pleasure in producing particular outcomes for themselves, such as putting a puzzle together (Jennings, 1991; Stipek, Recchia, & McClintic, 1992). They have a greater awareness of the extent to which their own behavior meets external standards (Stipek et al., 1992). The beginning of symbolic representation allows social interaction to be increasingly verbal (Schaffer, 1984) and greatly enhances the transmission of information about socially acceptable patterns of attention and action. At the same time, children become better able to anticipate future consequences and to plan ahead.

Processes Underlying the 18-Month Transition

It would be hard to overemphasize the importance of the development of language and planning for the development of executive or higher level functions. First, the ability to anticipate outcomes means that anticipations can influence action. The further ahead children can foresee consequences, the more they can plan how to handle them. To do this, they must keep plans firmly in mind and control their actions to be consistent with these plans. Although language may initially only accompany action (Anisfeld, 1984), it gradually comes to direct it (Luria, 1973). We previously discussed the emergence of rudimentary inhibitory skills; with this transition we now see greater inhibitory control over current and future action by symbolic and specifically linguistic means. These aspects of control over attention and behavior are dealt with in chapter 8.

The changes seen during the last half of the first year reflect the emergence of some primitive executive functions at both behavioral and neurological levels, and they seem to be supported by the development of the lateral prefrontal cortex (Diamond, 1991). The developments of the second year involve additional and improved functions, including the ability to act on the basis of represented, rather than present, information, such as verbal instruction from self or others. These changes may be related to the maturation of other parts of the frontal cortex.

Results of marker tasks suggest that the frontal cortex is undergoing further development in the 18- to 24-month period. For example, children's performance on tasks of delayed nonmatching to sample improves dramatically between 18 and 21 months (Diamond, Towle, & Boyer, 1994; Overman, 1990). In these tasks, a single object is presented; by picking the object up, subjects obtain a reward that lies under it. Then subjects are shown two objects and are rewarded only if they choose the object *not* presented before. In tasks that involve different objects on every trial, children must learn that only novel objects are rewarded and must inhibit a natural tendency to respond to the previously reinforced object. Delayed nonmatching to sample is much more difficult than a single reaching task, where novelty preference is seen, even after a delay, at a much younger age. Overman (1990) suggests that the inferior prefrontal cortex is important to this task. This section of the prefrontal cortex is connected to the object recognition pathway in the temporal cortex (Wilson et al., 1993).

Higher level control implies that lower level processes are being facilitated or inhibited in some way. If neural maturation in the second year includes new functional connections between frontal areas and the spatial orienting system in the parietal cortex on the one hand, and the object recognition system in the temporal cortex on the other, the possibility of higher level control is enhanced. Thus, by 2 years of age, the budding higher level controls observed at the end of the first year have developed into functional regulatory mechanisms affecting many aspects of development. The frontal cortex is, however, a complicated system with components that mature at different rates. Continuing maturation of the frontal cortex (Welsh & Pennington, 1988), along with new experiences and the emergence of new forms of motivation, leads to further changes in the second attention system during the preschool years.

THE PRESCHOOL YEARS AND INCREASING CONTROL OF ATTENTION

We have seen that attention during play with toys and during television viewing increases over age. So does persistence with toys that present specific problems to be solved, as documented by the literature on mastery motivation (Jennings, 1991). We assume that, in these situations, attention is governed by factors intrinsic to the setting and to the child. During the preschool years, however, more external demands are placed on the child, and more occasions occur when the child must be attentive to intrinsically uninteresting events. In these settings, unlike free play or television watching, the stimulus properties of the task are not very salient nor is there much room for child-generated invention and complexity. The child's motivation must come from other sources.

Behavioral Evidence

There have been only a few studies of preschoolers participating in dull, structured tasks. One example comes from Levy (1980). She asked children from 3 to 7 years to watch a computer screen and press a button whenever an "x" appeared in a stream of letters. Only 27% of the children 3 to 3.5 years were able to comply with all of the trials; 100% of children 4.5 years and older were able to do so. The difficulty preschool children have in such situations reveals much about their immaturities, not only in controlling their looking but also in coordinating and regulating behavior on demand.

In another study, children from 2.5 to 4.5 years of age were observed in several situations (Ruff et al., 1995). They were asked to watch a televised puppet show, to play with toys, and to perform a simple visual reaction-time task. The three situations made very different demands on the children. The puppet show required no physical activity and provided no objects to interact with. In contrast, the free-play situation allowed the child to choose from a range of activities, including pretend, construction, and manipulation. The reaction-time task, in which children were asked to press a button as soon as a rabbit appeared on the screen in front of them (Weissberg et al., 1990), provided a highly constrained situation with little cognitive demand, but requiring sustained alertness and readiness to respond. Several measures of attention and inattention were taken in each situation.

Table 3.1 shows what happens to the overall duration of looking and the duration of focused attention during the puppet show and free play. Focused attention is the portion of looking that reflects concentration on the target of attention, a topic to be discussed in more detail in chapter 7. Focused visual attention in both situations more than doubles over the age range studied, with the largest difference being between 2.5 and 3.5 years. The discrepancy in the strength of the age trend between overall looking and focused looking suggests the importance of making a distinction between them. In the reaction-time task, looking away from the screen decreased significantly with age, as did reaction time and the number of missed signals; the largest differences were between 3.5 and 4.5 years. In all situations, children also became less physically active, as reflected by the amount of time the children spent out of their seats and away from the work table. These changes demonstrate the extent to which preschool children gradually become less restless and more attentive in a variety of situations, some of which may not spontaneously engage their attention. For situations like the reaction-time task, motivations such as a desire to please the adult or to achieve a certain self-imposed standard become important.

Processes Underlying Development from 2 to 5 Years

Development in the period from 2 to 5 years of age could be seen as a consolidation of skills and the gradual accumulation of knowledge. Improved ability to plan ahead and to engage in complex activity must be the basis for at least some of the increases we observe in the amount of sustained, focused looking during play. The increased ability to sit still and to participate in adult-generated tasks requires a change in motivation and enhanced self-control. All of these abilities reflect improvements in

Table 3.1. Age-related Changes in Attention in Three Situations

	2.5 yrs	3.5 yrs	4.5 yrs
Puppet Show[a]			
Looking[b]	442.0	522.0	553.0
Focused attention	64.2	141.0	173.0
Time away from task	71.9	5.8	1.0
Free Play			
Looking	503.0	537.6	533.5
Focused attention	78.0	154.6	174.2
Time away from task	51.4	10.1	9.1
Reaction-Time Task			
Looking away from screen	45.9	52.5	24.5
Mean reaction time	3.6	3.2	1.9
Omissions	4.0	2.4	.3
Time away from task	14.3	.8	0.0

[a] All values are durations in seconds except number of errors of omission, which is a frequency count.
[b] The puppet show was approximately 600 seconds long; the free play was 600 seconds; the 20 trials of the reaction-time task took 200 seconds or less.

higher level functions, supported and mediated by continued maturation of the frontal cortex (Case, 1992; Welsh & Pennington, 1988).

As Llamas and Diamond (1991) note, the development of the frontal cortex is not only important for inhibition of motor activity but also for the organization of complex and sequential activity. Llamas and Diamond, studying children from 3 to 8 years of age, used several tasks requiring the child to inhibit a prepotent response in order to follow instructions (e.g., tapping twice when the experimenter taps once, and tapping once when the experimenter taps twice), to execute actions in a specific sequence, or to remember actions previously executed. The investigators observed marked improvements in performance on all tasks between 3 and 4 years of age and again between 4 and 5 years. As we will see in chapters 7 and 8, there is other evidence for increases in inhibitory control around 4 years of age (Reed et al., 1984).

In the trends over age presented in table 3.1, the largest changes in focused attention to the puppet skits and the toys occurred earlier than the largest changes in reaction time and errors. In contrast to the doubling of focused attention between 2.5 and 3.5 years, the reaction-time measures of looking away, response time, and errors of omission all improved from 40 to 85% between 3.5 and 4.5 years. The significant increases in performance on this task may signal a further change in attentional and behavioral control. The vigilance network (Posner & Raichle, 1994), involving right frontal pathways, may advance functionally within this age range or come under verbal control. Vigilance tasks require a "suspended state" in which the subject remains alert and prepares to respond to an infrequent or upcoming event (Posner & Rothbart, 1991). Heart rate slows down; brain activity generally diminishes; even metabolic activity in some frontal locations is reduced. Blood flow to the right frontal cortex, however, increases (Posner & Peterson, 1990). The right frontal cortex appears to control the orienting network, tuning it and increasing the signal to noise ratio. Although no data currently suggest specifically that connections with the vigilance network or the network itself become functional around 4 years of age, Thatcher (1994) argues that there is a growth spurt in the right hemisphere at that age.

While the notion of specific development in the vigilance network is speculative, several sources of evidence mark the period around 4 years as an important point in neurological development. A visual event-related potential recorded over the parietal area and linked to attention, P3b (P300), is not found reliably until between 3 and 3.7 years (Courchesne, 1990). Chugani (1994) cites data showing that metabolic activity in all areas of the developing brain reaches a maximum between 3 and 4 years of age. At that time, a plateau is reached, before the gradual decline to adult levels begins. Synaptic connections in some frontal areas reach a peak between 3 and 5 years, before being pruned to lower adult levels several years later (Huttenlocher, 1979). Measuring the coherence or correlation of activity in the EEG recorded at different sites, Thatcher (1994) argues for cycles of functional reorganization in the cortex with a subcycle from 4 to 5 years. The further development of the brain, particularly the frontal cortex, might account, in part, for some of the behavioral changes observed in the reaction-time task and for increases in inhibitory control. Therefore, we provisionally add a 4-year transition to the better-documented transitions already discussed.

SUMMARY

In this chapter, we have identified four major developmental transitions in early attention as reflected, in part, by infants' and young children's patterns of looking at the external world. In the first transition at 2 to 3 months, infants' scanning shifts from fixation of external contours of objects and patterns toward fixation of internal features. Infants also begin to emerge from a period of "obligatory attention" and to demonstrate more sensitivity to the novelty or discrepancy of objects. The first transitional period begins a time of close social interaction between the parent and infant, involving mutual gaze and often positive affect. It also coincides with the emergence of the orienting/investigative system of attention.

After an increase in looking at stationary visual displays during the first 3 months, looking times generally decrease from 3 months to the end of the first year. Around 5 months, infants are able to reach for and grasp objects. At this age, visual and manipulative investigation of the properties of objects is added to earlier visual orienting. When we observe looking times during infants' active interaction with objects, a different developmental pattern of looking emerges, with increases in looking from 5 to 12 months. In social interactions after 5 months, other people, including older children, frequently incorporate objects into their play with infants, and objects become the focus of shared attention.

A second major developmental shift occurs around 9 months of age. Now, infants appear to be able to remember past events with only a few cues available to support the memory. We see the beginnings of goal-oriented activity and the ability to inhibit some actions prompted by the environment. Changes during the 9- to 12-month period have been associated with development of dorsolateral prefrontal cortex. Children's increased development of intentionality at this time alters their contribution to adult-child interactions and sometimes challenges parents who wish to maintain control. This transition heralds the emergence of the second attention system of higher level control.

At 18 to 24 months, another major transition occurs, bringing further development of the second attention system. By late in the second year, the child can act on representations of events and can use language and other symbolic processes. Language now becomes a further means for parents to influence children and for children to communicate their needs and desires to others. At the same time, the child's developing sense of self as an active agent in the world leads to additional issues of control. Children are now increasingly able to direct their own attention to future or potential events and, thus, to plan ahead and modulate their behavior in accordance with those plans. These skills are important foundations for the process of socialization.

Finally, we have suggested that the second attention system continues to be consolidated throughout the preschool years with an enhancement around 4 years in the ability to inhibit actions on instruction from self or others. There is a leap in the child's ability to voluntarily direct attention to those aspects of the environment that are relevant to the task at hand and to inhibit responses to perceptually salient, but irrelevant, aspects. Thus, the child is better able to participate in structured, rule-

governed tasks, which may require waiting for instructions, attending to intrinsically uninteresting events, and closely regulating action.

In this chapter, we have provided only an outline of the story of how attention develops during infancy and the preschool years. The several chapters that follow tell this same story from different perspectives and in more detail. Chapters 4 and 5 are concerned with the development of selectivity—what happens to shifting selectivity during visual scanning and search and to changes over age in what is selected for attention. In chapter 6, we begin a discussion of the development of attention as a state, emphasizing arousal and the physiological changes that accompany the engagement of attention. Chapter 7 introduces an integration of state and selection through the concepts of focused attention and resistance to distraction. Chapter 8 concerns the role of social influences in the developmental shift from more external control of attention to more independent, voluntary control as the infant develops into a school-age child. Both chapters 7 and 8 are concerned with the development of higher level control from different perspectives. In chapter 9, we review the evidence linking selectivity, state, and higher level control to several types of learning. Within all of these specific topics, the major developmental transitions and the accompanying emergence of the two attention systems will be apparent.

4
Scanning, Searching, and Shifting Attention

Attention is a dynamic process that occurs over time, and selectivity can be considered within different time frames. The selection of objects and events may occur at a general level—for example, a child's watching the mother's activity rather than a television show; it also occurs in smaller time units as the child scans the features of the mother's face or shifts attention from her face to her hands. Chapter 5 will deal with general patterns of selectivity and how these change with age. This chapter is devoted to the relation between development and shifts of attention to new locations or parts of objects within relatively brief periods. These shifts include scanning—the sequence of fixations occurring when the eyes examine an object or scene—and short-term shifts in selectivity as the environment is explored or searched for something in particular. Patterns of eye movements and successive fixations, whether confined to a small portion of the visual field or extended broadly, inform us about the processes underlying looking and attention. In the final section of the chapter, we discuss the relationship between eye movements and attention; although we have previously alluded to inferential limits on using looking as a reflection of attention, we believe the topic deserves elaboration.

SHIFTING ATTENTION

The actual shifting of visual attention from one point to another in external space is determined by several processes. This first section of the chapter is divided into three subsections: (1) scanning of objects and pictures—here we emphasize the shifts of gaze from one point to another within a single look; (2) shifting attention from one event to another—here we emphasize exploring or sampling the environment through successive looks at different objects; and (3) visual search, or successive looks that involve anticipation and planning.

All of these subsections emphasize results stemming from the measurement of eye movements, using techniques described briefly in chapter 2. Eye movements can be observed over a wide age range, and there is considerable overlap between the motor activity of moving the eyes and shifts in visual attention. Haith et al. (1988) write:

There is no . . . motor system that is better practiced than the oculomotor system, nor is there any other motor system that so closely approximates the mature state in early infancy. By conservative estimate, by 3.5 months of age, a baby has experienced about 800 hours of alert wakefulness . . . and during those hours has made 3–6 million eye movements. That is a lot of practice. Further, by this age the infant has encountered untold numbers of occasions of predictable object motion. Thus, there is reason to believe that analogues to perception-action skills that emerge later will appear earliest in the sensory, perceptual-motor, and cognitive processes that comprise the visual system. (p. 476)

Scanning

Eye movements end in pauses or fixations, during which the fovea, the most sensitive portion of the retina, is directed toward details of the object. Scanning includes both eye movements and fixations and, in this context, is defined as the pattern of fixations to different parts of the object being viewed. Visual scanning during free exploration of objects undergoes considerable change with development. As expected, the period between 2 and 3 months marks an important transition in the nature of scanning.

Haith (1980) studied the eye movements of newborns in both lighted and darkened settings. In the lighted settings, the infants were exposed to large geometric figures and each successive fixation of the figure was noted. The additional investigation of eye movements in the dark tells us about spontaneous movements and helps to interpret patterns seen when the infant looks at a figure in the light. On the basis of his findings, Haith postulated a set of "rules" that govern looking at the beginning of postnatal life.

Rule 1: If awake and alert and light not too bright, open eyes.
Rule 2: If in darkness, maintain a controlled, detailed search.
Rule 3: If in light with no form, search for edges by relatively broad . . . sweeps of the field.
Rule 4: If an edge is found, terminate the broad scan and stay in the general vicinity of that edge. . . .
Rule 5: While in the proximity of edges, reduce the dispersion of fixations perpendicular to the edges as local and resolvable contour density increases. (p. 96)

A number of other studies are consistent with these rules in that infants under 2 months tend to select the external contours of objects or patterns and to ignore the internal details (Salapatek, 1975; Milewski, 1976). Presented with a large rectangle within which smaller elements are enclosed, the very young infant tends to move its eyes to the borders of the large rectangle and to scan back and forth across it. As we noted in chapter 3, the same patterns of scanning are seen when 4-week-olds look at the human face (Maurer & Salapatek, 1976); that is, they visually fixate the perimeter of the face more than the internal portions. By 2 months, infants distribute their fixations, *and presumably their attention,* more broadly. The change from 1 to 2 months can be seen in figure 4.1 (columns 4 and 5). As Bronson (1991) notes, "the scanning of very young infants can be described as markedly constrained by 'contour salience' effects" (p. 53), effects that diminish after 2 months of age.

As with all generalizations, however, we must be cautious. Hainline (1981) shows that infants at 1, 2, and 3 months of age all adapt their scanning to the size of the pattern being displayed, with more widely distributed fixations for large patterns than for small ones. In addition, individual infants at all ages sometimes scan narrowly and sometimes broadly, though the reason for such within-subject variability is not known (see figure 4.2). Hainline argues that the differences between her results and those of Salapatek may be due to differences in procedure and measurement. Hainline's infants were in an upright position; Salapatek's were lying down. Hainline also sampled eye position 60 times a second; Salapatek sampled 4 times a second.

The general developmental increase in the extent of scanning, though not absolute, may be related to the changing role that peripheral stimulation plays in directing eye movements. For humans of all ages, individual fixations within a look are terminated by saccadic eye movements to another portion of the stimulus pattern, and the direction of these saccades is strongly determined by the nature of nonfoveal, or peripheral, stimulation (Harris, Hainline, Abramov, Lemerise, & Camenzuli, 1988). For both infants and adults, the duration of fixations decreases—that is, saccades occur more quickly—when the competing stimulus pattern is larger than when it is smaller, presumably because large patterns offer more peripheral stimulation.

Two important factors involving peripheral vision may help to account for patterns of scanning in the first 2 months and for the changes seen around 2 months of age. First, as a number of investigators (Bronson, 1974; Johnson, 1990; Maurer & Lewis, 1991) argue, the early selection of contours for repeated fixations in the newborn, compared to the older infant, is based on the dominance of subcortical mechanisms over cortical mechanisms in the first month of life; these mechanisms are driven by peripheral rather than central vision. That is, the infant's eyes are drawn to the external contour of a pattern or object because it represents a larger, and therefore more effective, peripheral stimulus than the internal elements. If the internal elements of a pattern move, they are more likely to be fixated even by the youngest infants (Bushnell, 1979; Girton, 1979), probably because moving elements are more effective at stimulating the peripheral retina than static ones.

The second factor is the size of the visual field, as defined by responsiveness to different portions of the periphery; only in the second half of the first year are infants as sensitive to peripheral stimulation as adults (Maurer & Lewis, 1991; Mayer & Fulton, 1993). Given that peripheral stimulation leads to foveation, the tendency for eye movements of very young infants to repeatedly cross limited sections of large, high-contrast contours could stem from a combination of (1) relatively low sensitivity to events in the far periphery, and (2) a domination of events in the near periphery over foveal stimulation.

1-Month-Olds

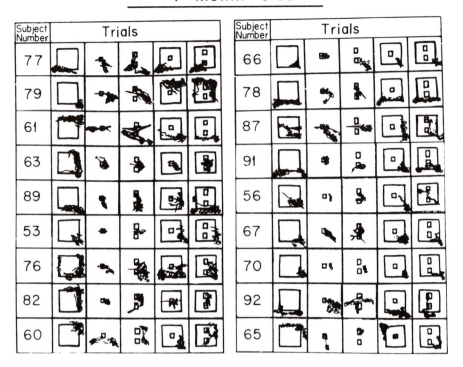

2-Month-Olds

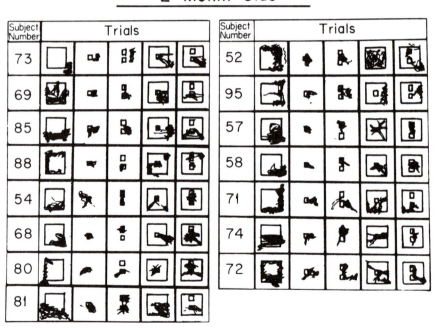

Figure 4.1. Changes in scanning from 1 to 2 months; note columns 4 and 5. From *Infant perception: From sensation to cognition* (p. 202), by L. B. Cohen and P. Salapatek, 1975, New York: Academic Press. Copyright 1975 by Academic Press. Reprinted with permission.

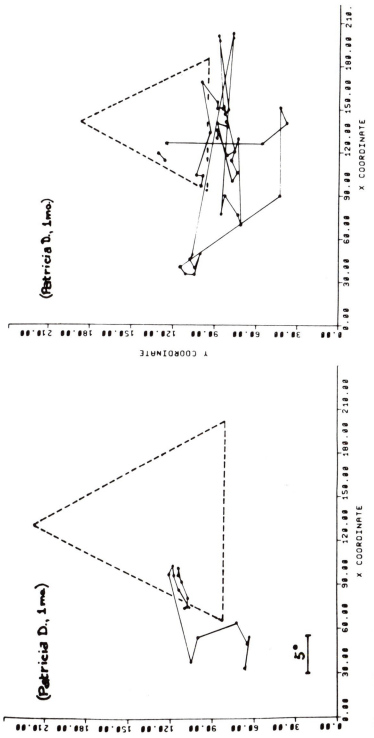

Figure 4.2. Variation in scanning within an individual infant (Hainline, 1981). From *Eye movements: Cognition and visual perception* (p. 16), D. F. Fisher, R. A. Monty, and S. W. Senders (Eds.), 1981, Hillsdale, NJ: Erlbaum. Copyright 1981 by Erlbaum. Reprinted with permission.

With development, two important processes lead to broader scanning and more attention to internal details. Pathways that inhibit collicular-governed eye movements become functional at about 1 month; consequently, 1-month-olds may actually turn away from a central stimulus *less* readily than the newborn (Johnson, 1990). Around 2 months, emerging cortical pathways begin to moderate the earlier developing inhibitory processes. In general, these newly functional pathways introduce the possibility of greater cortical control over eye movements. Second, by 3 months, the visual field of infants has expanded, so that they are responsive to information about shape, for example, in the near periphery (Maurer & Lewis, 1981) and are generally more responsive to events in the far periphery (de Schonen, McKenzie, Maury, & Bresson, 1978; Harris & McFarlane, 1974; Maurer & Lewis, 1991).

Johnson et al. (1991) studied this emerging process in 2-, 3-, and 4-month-old infants by drawing the infant's fixation to a central light display. After the central display was fixated, a display 34° to the right or left was turned on. The center display was left on, however, and the question was how long it would take the infant to turn from the central to the peripheral display. The 4-month-olds were significantly more likely to turn to look at the peripheral display (90%) within an 8-second period than either the 2- or 3-month-olds (35 and 45%). Considering only those trials in which the infants moved their eyes to the peripheral event, the older infants also moved them significantly faster. Both of these results suggest increased efficiency and flexibility.

The control of eye movements improves throughout infancy and the preschool years. Cortical potentials associated with eye movements have been measured during free scanning of pictures (Kurtzberg & Vaughan, 1979) and are related to the event-related potentials discussed in chapter 2; that is, electrical activity in the brain is time-locked to eye movements. These cortical potentials change in wave form between birth and 7 months; at that point, they are close to the mature wave form, but continue to decrease in latency for several years thereafter. Even at 4 and 5 years of age, children may show eye movements that are larger and more variable than those of adults (Kowler & Martins, 1982). Considering that preschool children's scanning of stationary patterns is less controlled than that of adults, Kowler and Martins (1982) suggest that scanning may represent a highly overlearned motor habit for adults—a habit that children have not yet had time to acquire. Strong generalizations, however, are precluded by the nature of the stimulus events in the study by Kowler and Martins; the children were presented with only a point of light and head position was rigidly maintained—not a situation where we would expect children to show their best performance.

Both eye movements and patterns of fixation are expected to come under increasing cognitive control as the second attention system develops. Accordingly, the "low-level automatic component of visual scanning in which saccades are triggered probabilistically in time by non-foveal stimulus features" may be overridden or inhibited by more cognitive factors (Harris, 1989, p. 401) and higher level functions. These cognitive influences include anticipation of complex sequences, goals, and strategies, all developing over a period of years rather than months. These influences should, in principle, make visual scanning more systematic, regardless of the parameters of the eye movements themselves. An adult who looks at a picture does so with eye movements and fixations that are systematic and reflect attention to informative details within the picture (Mackworth & Morandi, 1967). This is illustrated in a famous example from Yarbus (1967), who found that adults alter their scanning of details to fit the demands of the situation. Figure 4.3 shows variations in an adult's scanning of a picture when asked to answer different questions about the picture. These variations reveal the workings of a highly flexible system.

Relatively little information is available on the cognitive aspects of children's scanning patterns during free exploration of objects and pictures. In a task involving recognition of an object in a blurred photograph, Mackworth and Bruner (1970) found that 6-year-old children, compared to adults, concentrated a smaller proportion of their fixations on informative aspects of the picture. Children were also less consistent from one trial to the next and were more likely to focus on high-contrast contours. Zinchenko, Chzhi-tsin, and Taraknov (1964) found that 3-year-olds scanned simple geometric figures much less widely than 6-year-olds during a period of familiarization and free exploration (figure 4.4A). In contrast, when looking at pictures of a scene with animals and people, the 3- and 6-year-olds showed very similar patterns of scanning (figure 4.4B). These effects of context and stimulus event are not surprising, but they suggest that children may be less systematic and more variable in their scanning when performing adult-defined tasks of little interest to them (Aslin & Ciuffreda, 1983) than with complex and interesting events. A detailed developmental study analogous to the Yarbus experiment would contribute valuable results to this field of inquiry.

Shifting Attention Between Events

Scanning refers not only to patterns of fixation within a look at a given object but also to patterns of successive looks to different objects. A particular form of visual exploration studied at different ages is looking back and forth between two simultaneously presented patterns or objects. Peripheral stimulation surely plays a role here as well, and looking from one object to another may initially be the result of competition between the object or pattern currently being foveated and stimulation in the periphery. There is likely to be a transition, coincident with the developmental transition from 2 to 3 months, from simple competition to active sampling of two objects. Piaget (1952) describes his son in the second month:

During the second month we have seen Laurent look in turn at various objects or different parts of the same object, [for] example [,] three motionless people next to his bassinet or the hair and face of the same person. But in this case he looks at each image irregularly. On the other hand, during the third month, the emergence of the following behavior pattern may be observed: the glance compares, so to speak, two distinct objects while alternately examining them. For example, at 0;2(11) Laurent is looking at a rattle suspended from the hood of his bassinet when I hang a handkerchief parallel to the rattle. He then looks alternately at the handkerchief and at the rattle and smiles. (p. 69)

More experimental studies provide quantitative data on this point. Bronson (1991) found that the 2-week-olds in his study looked back and forth between two

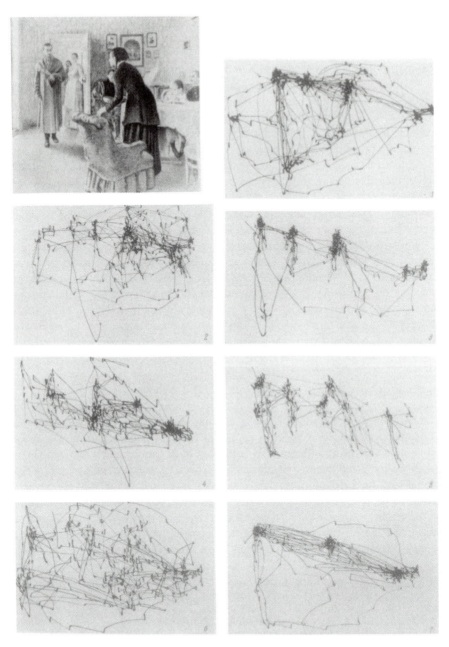

Figure 4.3. Variations in scanning of a single picture by an adult according to the questions asked about the picture. For example, scanning pattern 1 was during uninstructed inspection; 3 was after being instructed to estimate ages of the people; 6 was after being instructed to remember the position of both people and objects; and 7 was after being asked to judge how long the visitor had been away from the family pictured here. From *Eye movements and vision* (p. 174), by A. L. Yarbus, 1967, New York: Plenum. Copyright 1967 by Plenum. Reprinted with permission.

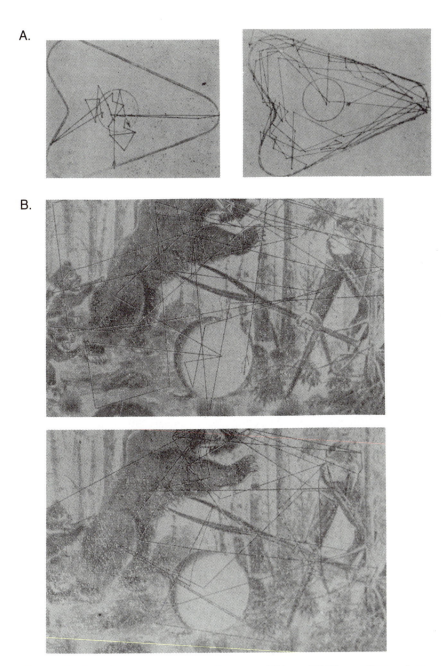

Figure 4.4. Visual scanning of pictures by young children. (A) The top figures show scanning of a 3-year-old and a 6-year-old looking at an abstract pattern; (B) The bottom two figures show the scanning of a 3-year-old and a 6-year-old looking at a picture with interesting content. From "The formation and development of perceptual activity" by V. P. Zinchenko, V. Chzhi-tsin, and V. V. Tarakanov, *Soviet Psychology and Psychiatry, 2*, pp. 7–8. Copyright 1964 by International Arts and Sciences Press.

patterns on less than 50% of the trials, while 12-week-olds readily shifted from one to the other. Ruff (1975) found a fourfold increase in looking back and forth between two patterns in the age range from 2 to 5 months, even when differences in total looking times were taken into account. Colombo, Mitchell, and Horowitz (1988) report a doubling of the rate of shifting from 4 to 7 months of age. Together, these last two studies of infants' responses to black and white patterns suggest that infants shift their visual attention once every 7 seconds at 2 months, once every 3 seconds around 4 months, and once every 1.7 seconds from 5 to 7 months. Slater, Morison, and Rose (1984), however, found that newborns shifted their looking from one member of a pair to the other once every 4 seconds in one study and once every 3 seconds in another. The combination of all these results suggests faster shifting in the newborn than in the 2-month-old. As described above, cortical maturation between 1 and 2 months may temporarily inhibit shifting by making disengagement difficult (Johnson, 1990).

If alternate glancing from one object to another is indeed the beginning of visual comparison, we should find that there is more shifting back and forth as two objects become harder to discriminate. Studies where pairs of patterns with varying degrees of physical similarity were used with 2- to 6-month-olds confirm this expectation (Harris, 1973; Ruff, 1975). There should also be changes in the degree of shifting with continued exposure and increasing familiarity with the stimulus events. In two separate studies (Ruff, 1975), shifting first increased and then decreased with repeated presentations. This pattern suggests that infants need a period of familiarity, and perhaps some degree of habituation, before shifting peaks. The decline with exposure may occur because the infants have learned something about the patterns and no longer need to compare them as much.

If infants' shifting from one object or pattern to another after 2 months is part of the orienting/investigative system, shifts should have a functional role. Although shifting gaze from one object to another suggests that infants are actively exploring the environment, further evidence is required for a confident inference about the role of attention in shifting. If, for example, information is acquired as a result of looking at both alternatives, we can infer a more active process of attention (Reznick & Kagan, 1981; Ruff, 1978). In one study (Ruff, 1978), 9-month-old infants were presented with pairs of objects for familiarization. The objects were all of the same shape, but varied in size, color, and orientation. After familiarization, the infants were presented with the old shape in a new size, color, and orientation paired with a new shape that was a rearrangement of parts from the old object (see figure 4.5). During familiarization, however, one group was presented with two different variants of the target shape within each trial (within-trial variation), such as the large orange form upside down paired with a small red form standing vertically (see figure 4.5). The other group was presented with the identical objects on each trial, but different variants on successive trials (between-trial variation), such as two large orange forms upside down on one trial and two upright small red forms on the next.

Because shape was the "relevant" variable, and color, size, and orientation were "irrelevant," it was expected that the infants who saw within-trial variation would learn to select the invariant shape more quickly than the group presented with between-trial variation. The results confirmed this expectation in that the first group attended more to the novel shape on the test trial than did the second group. The two groups did not differ in terms of the amount of time they looked at and manipulated the objects during familiarization nor in the response decrement over trials; *the within-variation group, however, tended to look back and forth between the two objects in a pair more often.* These data suggest that the information picked up when attention is shifted from one object to another is an important aspect of learning.

Although quite young infants alternate looks between two objects, one would expect, as noted before, that such behavior would come under more cognitive control as the child develops. Again, there are relatively few data in the preschool range. An exception is a study by White and Plum (1964), who presented children 3.5 to 5 years of age with a discrimination task in which two patterns were simultaneously displayed. They found that the children were more likely to look from one to the other just before they reached the number of successful trials set as the criterion for learning. This may mean that learning occurred when shifting peaked or, alternatively, that children finally realized the importance of active comparison and search in successful performance.

Visual Search and Expectation

Wright and Vliestra (1975) argue that an important developmental change in attention comes when children become capable of search as well as exploration. They describe exploratory activity as spontaneous and relatively unsystematic attention to novel objects and situations, determined largely by the physical salience of the objects in the environment. Search, in contrast, "is instrumental to the acquisition of information that will be used subsequently to organize and direct a goal-oriented behavior sequence" (p. 198).

Increasing experience with events in the world allows infants to deploy their attention based on expectations rather than immediate stimulation only (Neisser, 1979). Rudimentary anticipation is evident quite early. In a series of studies, Haith and his colleagues (Haith et al., 1988; Haith & McCarty, 1990; Canfield & Haith, 1991; Wentworth & Haith, 1992) have shown that infants at 2 or 3 months of age begin to make anticipatory eye movements toward events after repeated experience with simple spatio-temporal sequences of events. Figure 4.6 shows three such sequences. Infants in the 1/1, or simple alternation, condition are more likely to make eye movements to the other side in advance of the stimulus presentation after one presentation at the home side than infants in an irregular condition (Haith et al., 1988); infants in the 2/1 condition are more likely to shift fixation in anticipation of the target after two home presentations than after one presentation; and infants in the 3/1 condition are more likely to anticipate after three presentations in the home position than after one or two (Canfield & Haith, 1991). These data suggest that infants are shifting attention to the location of predictable events *before* the events actually occurred.

Infants of 3 to 4 months of age show this anticipatory attention more than younger infants (Canfield & Haith, 1991; Johnson et al., 1991), and infants at 4 months can predictably anticipate peripheral events on the basis of a central cue (Johnson et al., 1991). Clohessy (1994) found that infants of 4 and 10 months

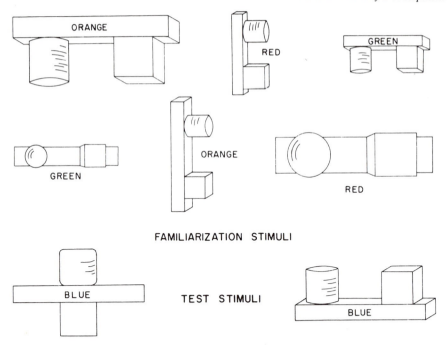

Figure 4.5. The objects used to examine the effects of within trial variation and between trial variation on infants' recognition of differences based on configuration alone (test objects). From "Infant recognition of the invariant form of objects" by H. A. Ruff, *Child Development, 49,* p. 298. Copyright 1978 by the Society for Research in Child Development. Reprinted with permission.

anticipate events occurring in simple sequences over three locations. Even so, in infants from 2 to 10 months of age (Canfield & Haith, 1991; DiLalla et al., 1990), most shifts in attention seem to be reactive—that is, occurring in response to the presentation itself. Haith and his colleagues have shown, however, that experience leads to some facilitation in that the infants respond more quickly after they have been exposed to a sequence. Anticipation and facilitation are both assumed to occur because the subject begins to form expectations about the sequence of events; the more regular the events, the more easily these expectations are formed (see also Smith, 1984). Thus, anticipatory attention appears to emerge very early in development and, in the absence of strong motivation, may not change much with age (see Ruff, Capozzoli, Dubiner, & Parrinello, 1990).

The ability to form simple expectations is thus a part of the orienting/investigative system in the first year. The same ability in more complex forms is essential to planning in the second, higher level system. As with other actions, eye movements can be controlled, to some extent, by a planned strategy. For example, Vurpillot (1976) showed 4- to 9-year-old children a pair of houses, one beside the other, and asked the children to say whether the two houses were the same or different. The structure of the houses, each of which had six windows, was identical, but the window dressings in each *homologous* pair of windows could be the same or different; there were four conditions: 0, 1, 3, or 5 differences. Vurpillot recorded the eye movements children made before answering the question. The eye movement patterns revealed a dramatic change over age in the approach to exploring the houses.

One would expect that fewer movements would be necessary to respond accurately in the case of 3 or 5 differences, while 1 or no difference would, on average, require a more exhaustive visual search. Using the 0-difference condition as a base, Vurpillot found that children from 4 to 5 years tended to concentrate their fixations on the upper left and center windows, while the older children dispersed their fixations more widely. Second, the most efficient strategy is to compare homologous windows—for example, the upper left window in one house with the upper left window in the other. Figure 4.7 shows, for the 0-difference condition, an idealized pattern of eye movements and fixations that is strategic and 100% efficient. The same strategy would apply to the other conditions of 1, 3, and 5 differences between

A. 1/1 (Alternating)   **B. 2/1**   **C. 3/1**

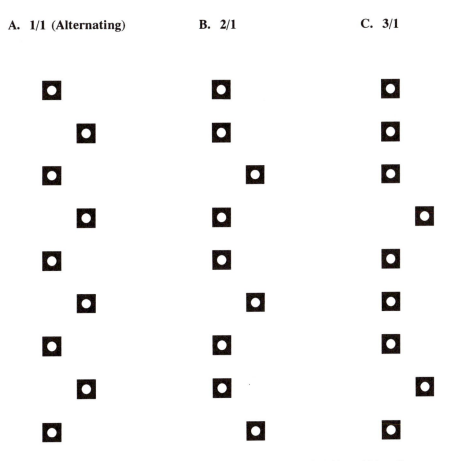

Figure 4.6: Three sequences used in the anticipation studies of Haith and his colleagues. From ''Young infants' visual expectations for symmetric and asymmetric stimulus sequences'' by R. L. Canfield and M. M. Haith, *Developmental Psychology, 27*, p. 203. Copyright 1991 by American Psychological Association. Adapted with permission.

houses, but the average number of movements required would decrease over the three conditions. When Vurpillot counted the number of times the children actually made such eye movements, the children of 5 years and younger did not differentiate among the conditions, while children older than 6 years made significantly more visual comparisons in the 0- and 1-difference conditions than in the 3- and 5-difference conditions. Figure 4.8 shows the actual patterns of eye movements observed in a child of 3 years, 11 months and a child of 8 years, 9 months, along with the children's answers.

Structured tasks may not engage the motivation of a preschool child to the extent they do a school-age child, thereby making the preschooler's performance less strategic and accurate. Young children may also have somewhat different definitions of "same" and "different" (P. Miller & Harris, 1988). P. Miller and her colleagues (e.g., DeMarie-Dreblow & Miller, 1988; P. Miller & Harris, 1988) have sought to eliminate these confounding factors. In one study, a story described twins putting away their toys; the problem for the child was to determine whether the toys had been put away the "twin way—the same way"—or not. Pictures of the toys were under two rows of closed doors, with one row belonging to each twin. The child was asked to show the experimenter the best way to find out whether the children had put

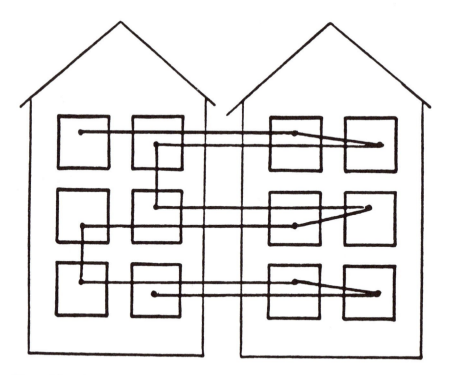

Figure 4.7. A hypothetical and idealized scanning pattern in a case where the windows in the two houses are identical. From *The visual world of the child* (p. 240) by E. Vurpillot, 1976, New York: International Universities Press. Copyright 1976 by International Universities Press. Reprinted with permission.

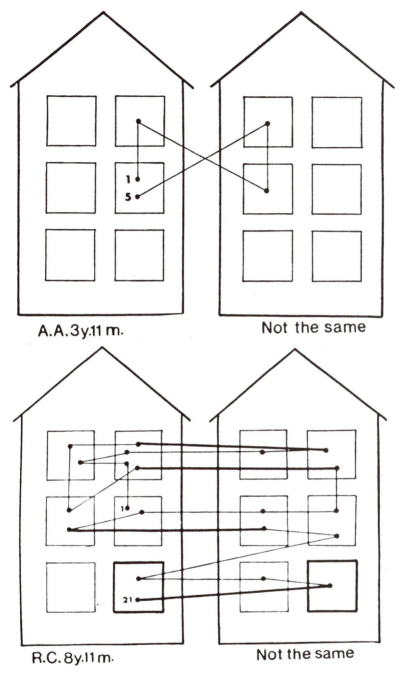

Figure 4.8. Two scanning patterns by children at different ages. In the top pattern, a child of 3 years, 11 months is faced with two identical houses, yet the scanning is incomplete and the child's incorrect answer is that the two houses are not the same. In the bottom pattern, a child of 8 years, 9 months is faced with two houses that differ in only one pair of windows (in bold). The scanning is quite thorough and the correct answer given was that the two houses were not the same. From *The visual world of the child* (p. 238–239) by E. Vurpillot, 1976, New York: International Universities Press. Copyright 1976 by International Universities Press. Reprinted with permission.

the toys away the "twin way." Instead of recording eye movements, these investigators observed the child's visual attention through the sequence of opening doors to look at the toys behind them. Again, the most efficient strategy involves inspecting homologous locations in the two rows—in this case, a vertical strategy of opening one door in the top row and then looking behind the door directly below. A control group of same-age children was presented with the same apparatus and much of the same procedure, but they were told to "open the doors just for fun" (P. Miller & Harris, 1988, p. 629); the behavior of this group is important to determine the degree of order in spontaneous door opening. The task is simpler than the one used by Vurpillot and the door opening was expected to be more motivating to the young child.

The subjects were 3- and 4-year-olds. A consistent pattern of opening vertical pairs of doors was considered most strategic, as well as most efficient, in dealing with the demands of the task. The 4-year-olds were much more likely than the 3-year-olds to use the vertical pairs approach (68% versus 38% of door openings); the older children showed more improvement over trials and were significantly more strategic than the control group. These results show how much more organized and systematic the older children were in their approach to the problem. Even so, to the extent that children at either age were able to produce the strategy consistently or partially, they were significantly more correct in their "same-different" judgments than children who did not produce the strategy at all.

Both the eye movement study by Vurpillot (1976) and the work by Miller and colleagues reveal developmental changes and suggest that children in their fourth and fifth years are able to participate in formal search tasks and to be at least partially systematic in their approach. Younger children do not behave randomly, but their search patterns are not as controlled or systematic as they will be in the later preschool years.

NONOBSERVABLE SHIFTS OF ATTENTION

To underscore what we have mentioned before, the direction of looking and the location of specific fixations or looks do not have to coincide with the object of attention. Because information can be detected by peripheral vision and because this information is important in guiding where an individual looks next, visual attention cannot be equated with foveation. Posner and Cohen (1984) argue that attention is often shifted covertly to a new location before an individual makes an eye movement to that point in space. The exact mechanisms by which the covert shift of attention occurs is still a matter of discussion (LaBerge, 1990; Posner & Dehaene, 1994). However, nonobservable shifts are usually followed so rapidly by an eye movement and by foveation of the new location that looking and visual attention are, in many cases, functionally related. Exceptions to this usual synchrony between attention and eye movements may occur during states of emotional vigilance, when an observer may be very alert to what happens in a particular direction without actually looking that way. Also, in social situations, we may wish to keep our eyes oriented in one direction even though we may be attending to peripheral events.

In this chapter, we have focused heavily on the role of spatial location in organizing selective attention. There is, however, another sense in which attention cannot be defined by a look at a specific location in space. Complex objects reside in particular locations, and complex events occur in defined spaces. Thus, although we can say that someone is looking at an object, or even fixating the upper right-hand corner of it, at a given moment, we cannot be certain what it is about the object that has engaged attention. Is it the object's shape? Its color? Its movement? Its function? Its texture? Repeated eye movements and fixations to a given location do not mean that attention is directed to the same aspects of the object each time. The details or aspects of objects focused on do, indeed, change with both repeated exposure and development.

Perceptual learning as discussed by J. Gibson and E. Gibson (1955) is, for example, a gradual process of differentiation that occurs spontaneously when attention is repeatedly drawn to the same object or event. With exposure, adults discriminate more readily among examples in a class of objects or patterns they are perceiving and attend to more details. Ross-Kossac and Turkewitz (1986) report that brief experiences with unfamiliar faces will lead to selection based on global aspects of the faces; further experience results in a shift of attention to distinctive features of the faces. In only a few studies has this process been investigated in infants. Colombo, Freeseman, Coldren, and Frick (1995) presented 4-month-old infants with global configurations (an hourglass or diamond) made up of letters (N or Z) in a familiarization/paired comparison task. One configuration was shown to each infant for a set amount of time and then two patterns were presented; one member of the pair contained a change in the overall configuration, and the other, a change in the component letters. Familiarization time varied from 10 to 30 seconds across subjects. For those infants who looked differentially at the two patterns, the preference was for a change in global configuration at 10 and 20 seconds and a preference for a change in detail at 30 seconds. Thus, even young infants show a shift from global to local aspects of stimulus events as a function of exposure to those events.

Jeffrey (1968) suggested a modification of the perceptual learning model with his serial habituation hypothesis. He proposed that children first select the perceptually most salient aspect of an object; when that aspect becomes familiar, they shift to the next most salient cue, and so on. D. Miller and colleagues (D. Miller, 1972; D. Miller, Ryan, Sinnott, & Wilson, 1976) investigated this hypothesis with 4-month-olds. They first established the infants' baseline responses to a circle, an X, and two dots. Subjects were then familiarized with a single stimulus pattern of the circle surrounding the X and the two dots to the right and left of the X. After eight 20-second trials with this combination, the infants were again tested on the elements separately. As predicted by Jeffrey's (1968) "serial habituation" hypothesis, the element attended to most in the pretest showed the greatest decrement in the posttest. Although this change may be a function of regression to the mean, it seems unlikely given the systematic decline in looking shown in habituation procedures. Habituation is thus another process that underlies shifts in attention within the same event or object. In neither perceptual learning nor serial habituation does simple direction of looking tell us what the basis of selective attention is.

Habituation may be particularly important to shifts of attention within the orienting/investigative system. Once children develop language and more attentional control, attention can be shifted from one dimension of objects to another according to instructions about what is relevant. In a reaction-time task, if children are asked to push a lever every time a red form appears in a moving array of colored forms of different sizes and shapes, their attention is likely to be on the color of the forms and not on the shape. But if the experimenter instructs them to respond when they see squares, their attention will probably shift to shape and away from color.

Thus, nonobservable shifts of attention occur for given individuals as a result of experience, learning, and instruction.

SUMMARY

In this chapter, we described early developments in infants' and children's eye movements and shifts of attention. When visual displays are presented to the newborn infant, eye movements occur until an edge or contour is found, with a tendency to maintain fixation in the vicinity of the contour. By 2 to 3 months, infants are scanning the visual field more broadly and scanning internal details of pictures and objects. Increasing cortical control over subcortical mechanisms during this period may account in part for these early changes. Scanning continues to increase in precision over the early years, but even preschool children scan in a less controlled manner than adults.

Scanning can be defined more generally as shifting attention from one object or event to another in the environment. In general, infants in the first year shift more rapidly from one object to another as they develop. The visual shifting of newborns may occur mainly because two objects compete peripherally for attention. The later, more rapid shifts may reflect a comparison of alternatives involving more cortical control. With further development, children's scanning is increasingly controlled by past experiences, expectations for the future, and task demands. Infants as young as 3 months show evidence of anticipating future locations of events, but as planning develops, scanning can become highly systematic as a result of efficient strategies for gathering information. In the next chapter, we describe other examples of this pattern of development.

Finally, we again distinguished overt orienting as observed in eye movements from orienting of attention, which must be inferred. We discussed shifts of attention, not related to eye movements, that can occur within single fixations or looks and reflect changes in the focus of attention from one object characteristic to another. We consider this in more detail in chapter 9, which deals with the relationship of learning and attention.

5

Development of Selectivity

The study of selective attention is an investigation not only of what is selected but also of the underlying processes that cause attention to be directed to particular events (Ruff & Birch, 1974). In this chapter, we describe the changing basis for visual selection across the periods of infancy and early childhood. The chapter is organized into several sections. In the first section, we discuss mechanisms that may account for the infant's initial "preferences" at the beginning of life and how the processes underlying selection develop in the first few months. We then address the increasing role of experience and the changing role of motivation in selection. Finally, we consider cognitive and social contributions to changes in selectivity in late infancy and beyond.

CHANGING VISUAL PREFERENCES IN THE FIRST FEW MONTHS

As noted in chapter 3 (figure 3.1), even newborns have visual "preferences" for some objects and patterns (Fantz, 1961). Although the existence of early preferences should not be taken to imply the emotional or cognitive activity that may govern the selectivity of more mature humans, any systematic basis for responding provides newborns with an organized experience of the world. We can learn much about the course of early development by observing changes in the types of objects and events selected and by considering the processes that govern selectivity at different ages.

Figure 5.1 illustrates a robust finding originally reported by Fantz and Nevis (1967). Before 6 weeks of age, infants look at a pattern of horizontal stripes as long as, or even longer than, a segmented bull's-eye. At 6 weeks, there is a major shift in preference, with the infants looking much longer at the bull's-eye than at the horizontal stripes. Why do very young infants prefer the stripes? What accounts for the change in preference at 6 weeks? When infants clearly select the bull's-eye, what is the basis for this selection? Do infants generally prefer curves? If so, is it because curves are more stimulating than straight lines? Because of infants' positive experience with other rounded objects, such as faces, eyes, and breasts? Because the

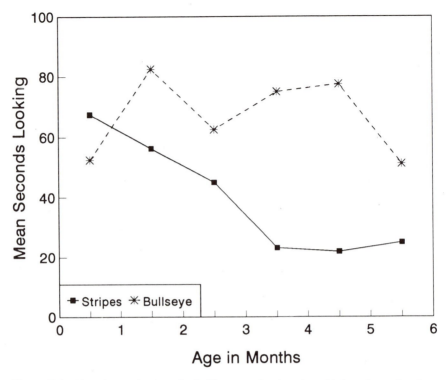

Figure 5.1. Changing preferences for bull's-eye and stripes from birth to 6 months of age. From "Pattern preferences and perceptual-cognitive development in early infancy" by R. L. Fantz and S. Nevis, 1967, *Merrill-Palmer Quarterly, 13,* p. 83. Copyright 1967 by Wayne State University Press. Adapted with permission.

bull's-eye is more discrepant from their previous experience than the horizontal lines?

Other research on this particular pair of patterns adds two important pieces of information about this shift in preference. First, even at 6 and 9 weeks of age, when infants normally prefer the bull's-eye to an equivalent-size pattern of stripes, the preference for the bull's-eye can easily be overwhelmed by making the stripes larger or brighter than the bull's-eye (Ruff & Turkewitz, 1975, 1979). For example, when bull's-eyes of different sizes are paired with an intermediate-size pattern of stripes, 6- and 9-week-olds look longer at the bull's-eye than at the stripes *only* when the bull's-eye is larger; when it is smaller, they look more at the stripes. Second, after 13 weeks of age, the bull's-eye is looked at longer than the stripes regardless of the size of the stripes or of the bull's-eye.

A Shift from Quantitative to More Qualitative Bases for Selection

These findings are consistent with the view that direction of looking in the first 2 or 3 months is based on quantity or intensity of stimulation. Kagan (1970) writes: "The infant naturally attends to events that possess a high rate of change in their physical characteristics'' (p. 827); these characteristics include contour, movement, and a large number of discrete elements. On the basis of other studies, Karmel and Maisel (1975) argue that preferences for visual patterns before 3 months of age are determined by the amount of contour in the pattern; longest looking times are generated by *moderately* dense contour, as in a checkerboard with medium-size squares.

Defining level of stimulation in relation to the individual organism, Schneirla (1965) hypothesized that the young of many species approach effectively moderate levels of stimulation and withdraw from effectively high levels. In the human newborn, directing the eyes toward an event would be equivalent to approach, and directing them away, equivalent to withdrawal. Using Schneirla's general theory, Turkewitz, Gardner, and Lewkowicz (1984) have argued that, under ordinary circumstances, infants in the first 2 months will orient selectively to objects and events on the basis of the total amount of effective stimulation, regardless of its source. For example, newborns tend to look more at complex checkerboards than at simple ones, but they look relatively more at less complex checkerboards if sound is simultaneously presented (Lawson & Turkewitz, 1980). The intensity of stimulation from the sound and the checkerboards appears to be additive, leading the infant to visually select the size of checks that contributes to optimal levels of stimulation.

Selectivity that is generally based on amount and intensity of stimulation does not mean that infants in the first 2 months of life *never* orient to patterns according to configuration or quality of stimulation. One example is the preference for curved over straight patterns seen in newborns under some conditions (Fantz & Miranda, 1975). Another is that newborns tend to visually follow prototypical face patterns more than scrambled ones (Goren et al., 1975; Johnson & Morton, 1991). Furthermore, in some cases, after repeated exposure to a pattern, newborns will sometimes look less at that pattern and more at a novel pattern composed of the same elements (Slater et al., 1984).

In general, however, quantitative aspects of stimulation are much more likely to determine the direction of looking before 2 months than after. After 2 months, aspects of patterns and objects related to form and configuration gradually become more salient. We can then ask what accounts for emerging preferences for particular patterns or forms. An analysis of the robust preference for the bull's-eye, emerging around 13 weeks, provides an example (Ruff & Birch, 1974). Three-month-old infants were presented with 10 patterns in all possible pairings. To separate the components of the bull's-eye and the stripes, the patterns varied in the number of line orientations and were curvilinear or straight, concentric or nonconcentric (see figure 5.2). The data suggested that the selection of the bull's-eye is based on all three variables, but that its concentricity is the dominant factor.

Neural Underpinnings for the Shift in Selectivity at 2 to 3 Months

Several theoretical models have been developed to account for newborn looking preferences and early changes in selectivity. All of these models stress the influence of neural maturation, but they differ in the site of the critical maturational events. In one model, early preferences are seen to be a function of the immaturity of the young infant's visual system. Very young infants select what they can see; as visual acuity

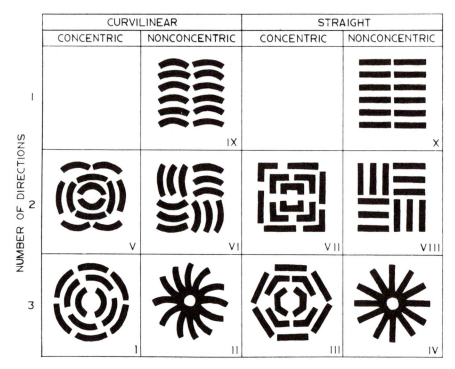

Figure 5.2. The ten patterns used to analyze the preference for the bull's-eye over the horizontal stripes. From "Infant visual fixation: The effect of concentricity, curvilinearity, and number of directions," by H. A. Ruff and H. G. Birch, 1974, *Journal of Experimental Child Psychology, 17,* p. 463. Copyright 1974 by Academic Press. Reprinted with permission.

and other aspects of the visual system mature, infants select more and different patterns. For example, Banks and Ginsburg (1985) discuss visual selectivity as resulting from the development of both retinal and more central mechanisms in the visual system. They propose that preferences in the first 2 or 3 months can be predicted from (1) the objective characteristics of objects or patterns, such as size of elements and degree of brightness contrast; and (2) the infant's visual acuity and sensitivity to contrast. Because, in this view, infants prefer those objects and patterns they can see most clearly, very young infants will look most at objects and patterns that contrast sharply with the background and have large elements. Banks and Ginsburg (1985) also suggest that, by foveating large, high-contrast contours, the infant will be exposed to patterned stimulation, a critical factor in the development of the cortical visual system. These early experiences may therefore lay the foundation for the more sophisticated selectivity of older infants, who are able to see many objects well.

While the Banks and Ginsburg model emphasizes maturation in both the peripheral and central components of the visual system, a second model emphasizes general maturation of the central nervous system. Graham, Anthony, and Ziegler (1983) argue that more intense, longer, and more frequent stimulation may be needed for visual orienting in the first 2 months of life because of the "slow conduction, uncertain synaptic transmission, and relative paucity of activatable neurons" (Graham et al., 1983, p. 372). This model suggests that degree of neural activation will determine what infants look at in the neonatal period. Later, with greater maturity, intense stimulation will no longer be as necessary to attract the infant's looking, and infants will be responsive to a wider array of objects and events. As with the first model, however, the maturity of neurons in the retina will affect the degree to which more central neurons can be activated.

A third set of models involves a differentiated account of the types of stimulation affecting different neural systems. Bronson (1974) proposed, for example, that eye movements in the first 2 months are controlled by pathways from the retina to the superior colliculus with little input from the primary visual cortex; thus, the stimulus factors that affect peripheral vision dominate those that influence central vision. These factors include size, brightness, and contrast—all quantitative aspects of stimulation. As cortical pathways mature, stimulus factors related to central vision and the perception and recognition of complex patterns can operate.

Johnson (1990) provides a related, more highly specified model. He notes that the visual system changes rapidly after birth, but does not suggest an absence of cortical functioning in the newborn. Rather, he notes that the deeper layers of the visual cortex are well developed at birth, but the more superficial layers are not. As these more superficial layers and their connections develop, a number of important changes occur. One change at about 1 month is the development of a pathway from the basal ganglia to the superior colliculus that provides inhibitory control over eye movements. This inhibition may diminish the effectiveness of those aspects of external events that tend to stimulate collicular activity directly. A second change is the development around 4 months of age of a pathway from the frontal eye fields to the superior colliculus and the parietal cortex. This new network allows selectivity to be controlled by more cognitive and experiential factors and is an important part of the orienting/investigative system.

In summary, intensity of stimulation is much less likely to determine the direction of infants' looking after 2 months. This general shift is related to improvements in visual acuity and contrast sensitivity that make it possible for the infant to see details and aspects of objects not available before. These improvements, in themselves, do not explain why there should be a diminished effectiveness of quantitative dimensions, but an increase in cortical control over subcortical mechanisms changes the basis of responsiveness dramatically (Bronson, 1974; Johnson, 1990). After 2 or 3 months, infants begin to exercise more control over their eye movements in much the same way as they will later control their hand and body movements. The increasing coordination between orienting and attention (Posner & Rothbart, 1981) is reflected in a shift toward selection based on experience and thus on variables such as familiarity and motivational significance.

SELECTION BASED ON PERCEPTUAL EXPERIENCE

Perceptual experience leads to greater differentiation of selected objects and events and to changing patterns of attention to features or elements within events

(E. Gibson, 1969). In the first year, infants' selective attention is strongly governed by the orienting/investigative system, and thus, by the novelty of events and objects.

Selection of Novel Objects and Events

Novel objects and events predictably recruit attention in all primate infants, as manifested in looking and active exploration. Selection for novelty is so pervasive in the first year of life in humans that it has been the foundation for much of the research on cognitive development during this period. Investigators use infants' preference for novelty not only to demonstrate that infants discriminate among objects (Fantz, 1961) but also to show that they categorize objects (Cohen et al., 1979; Younger, 1985) and are "surprised" by events that violate physical principles (Baillargeon, 1987; Spelke, Breinlinger, Macomber, & Jacobson, 1992).

Novelty is defined in terms of an individual's previous experience; there has to be some mechanism for registering this experience and orienting the individual to events discrepant from that experience. Sokolov (1963) suggests that an internal neural model is formed as a person becomes familiar with an event. Once the model is formed, other experiences will be compared to it. If the new experience is sufficiently discrepant from the previous ones, it will lead to an orienting response, a short-term phasic reaction characterized by both behavioral orienting and changes in the functioning of central and autonomic nervous systems (see chapter 6 for further discussion).

Preference for novelty depends on the child's having enough experience with an object or location to become familiar with it. Infants will sometimes select the familiar object rather than a completely novel one, and preferences for familiar sources of stimulation are often seen in very young infants. As we describe below, 3-month-olds are more likely than older infants to turn back to a location previously attended. Colombo and Bundy (1983) found that 2-month-olds were more responsive to a familiar tone sequence than to a novel one, while 4-month-olds were more responsive to the novel sequence. A number of studies have shown that infants between 6 and 8 weeks will look more at familiar patterns than at novel ones (Greenberg, Uzgiris, & Hunt, 1970; Weizmann, Cohen, & Pratt, 1971; Wetherford & Cohen, 1973).

Rose and her colleagues (Rose, Gottfried, Melloy-Carminer, & Bridger, 1982) hypothesized that very young infants need more time than older infants to learn enough about the initial stimulus event to recognize it quickly. They argue that, after a series of familiarization trials of fixed length, test trials may occur at a point when the original event is only partly familiar to the youngest subjects. They found that lengthening the familiarization period led 3-month-olds to look longer at novel patterns. Conversely, reducing familiarization times for older infants led them to prefer the familiar pattern. Wagner and Sakovitz (1986), reporting findings similar to those of Rose et al., suggest that infants sometimes prefer the partly familiar event over a novel one in much the same way an adult would resume an interrupted task in preference to doing something completely different (Zeigarnik, 1927, cited in Marx & Hillix, 1963).

With the development of the first attention system, infants from 3 to 9 months of age respond quickly and strongly to novel events, perhaps even being "hyperrespon-sive" (Graham et al., 1983, p. 413). Selection of novel objects may be adaptive for young organisms because they have so much to learn about the world. Though its relative importance in attention diminishes with age, novelty continues to be a factor in selective attention at all ages. Preschool children respond to the presence of a novel toy with a burst of exploratory activity, which then declines as the toy be-comes more familiar (Hughes, 1978, 1979). Parents sometimes take advantage of this phenomenon by removing familiar toys from the child's collection and later reintroducing them as relatively new toys. Preschool children will also respond to novel pictures with looking and phasic cardiac decelerations, both of which decrease in magnitude when a picture is shown repeatedly (Lewis & Goldberg, 1969).

The importance of novelty diminishes, in part, because children's increasing sophistication about the world leads them to encounter fewer really novel events as they develop. Because of their greater knowledge, however, older children may respond to some events as novel or discrepant from their past experience despite a lack of novelty in the physical characteristics of the event. A 2-year-old might be more surprised than an infant, for example, by a change in a routine activity because the older child has noticed and learned about the routine, whereas the infant has not. In general, however, with the development of the higher level system of attention, we see a decline in the salience of novelty as goals and planning become more powerful influences.

Selection of Novel Locations

Although our discussion has centered on the novelty and familiarity of objects and events, infants as well as older humans are also responsive to the novelty of locations at which events occur. Selective attention to locations in the environment is impor-tant because information provided by the events at an attended location will be acquired more efficiently than information from events at other locations (Posner & Presti, 1987). Mechanisms other than the orienting response, however, may be responsible for differential selection of novel places in the environment.

One example of preference for novel locations is the phenomenon of inhibition of return (IOR). As discussed in chapter 2, this is a decreased likelihood, lasting several seconds, of visually revisiting a previously attended location (Posner & Presti, 1987). Clohessy et al. (1991) studied the development of this phenomenon in 3-, 4-, 6-, 12-, 18-month-olds, and adults, using similar procedures at all ages. The subject's attention was drawn to a central fixation pattern (see figure 2.5 in chapter 2); the pattern was then turned off and a flashing visual display at 30° to one side was turned on (a unilateral trial). When the subject fixated the peripheral display, or when 5 seconds had elapsed, the display was turned off and the central pattern reappeared. After the subject again fixated the central target, flashing displays ap-peared at 30° on both sides of center (a bilateral trial). The primary measure was the percentage of bilateral trials on which the subject looked toward the new rather than toward the previously presented location. Responses of the 3-month-olds showed a bias toward the previous location (only 36% turned to the new location); responses of the 4-month-olds were at chance levels; and responses of all other age groups were significantly biased toward the new location (58 to 65%). For the older subjects, the period of inhibition was approximately 3.5 seconds.

Later studies, however, demonstrate IOR in both newborns and 3-month-olds. Three-month-old infants reliably show IOR at 10° but not at 30° (Harman et al., 1994), while newborns *can* show IOR to targets at 30° (Valenza, Simion, & Umiltá, 1994). The discrepancy may be related to the potency of the stimulus events in the two studies; Valenza et al. (1994) used lights in the periphery, while Harman et al. (1994) used patterns on a computer screen. The effectiveness of the event in eliciting a single and accurate eye movement is important because IOR does not occur if a single eye movement is not prepared for. Indeed, based on research with adults, Rafal, Calabresi, Brennan, and Sciolto (1989) have suggested that preparation of an eye movement, not an actual eye movement, is both necessary and sufficient for IOR. In the study by Valenza et al., only 61 trials out of a potential 351 were available for analysis because of poor and labile state, a lack of eye movements, or eye movements in the wrong direction. IOR was seen, however, on 71% of those 61 trials. On 90% of those trials, the peripheral target was fixated with one eye movement. A less effective stimulus might lead the infants' eyes to move step-wise to the target, a sign that the visual system has not prepared a single movement (Harman et al., 1994). The development seen after 3 months in the study by Clohessy et al. (1991) would reflect increasing alertness, compared to the newborns, increased peripheral sensitivity, and greater control over eye movements. All of these factors would facilitate the preparation and execution of efficient eye movements in many more situations and over a wider field. As these factors develop, therefore, IOR would become a more important influence on attention to locations than would be the case for the newborn, even though the underlying mechanism may be available at birth.

Attention in the orienting/investigative system is generally directed to the location of specific events or objects and is thus influenced by the characteristics of the event, including its familiarity. Harman et al. (1994) investigated the influence of both novelty of location and novelty of object on the patterns of looking in subjects 3 and 6 months of age. Infants of both ages showed strong novelty preferences (73% of trials) when they were presented with a familiar object at a familiar location versus a new object at a different location. When a novel object at the familiar location was opposed to a familiar object at a novel location, 3-month-olds showed no preference, but 6-month-olds showed a definite preference for the novel object (63% of trials), suggesting that object novelty, independent of location, may increase in importance over this period. In another study, Posner, Rothbart, Thomas-Thrapp, and Gerardi (in press) found that preferences for novel locations and preferences for novel objects were uncorrelated in a sample of forty 6-month-olds. Thus, both types of novelty preference come to influence selectivity in the short term and may help individuals to sample the environment widely when in unstressed conditions.

Spontaneous alternation, another preference for novelty based on spatial location, develops later than IOR. Spontaneous alternation is defined as the organism's unreinforced tendency to physically move to a location different from the location of its immediately prior response. Research on spontaneous alternation was originally conducted with rats and mice in T-mazes (Dember, 1989); older, but not younger, animals show a strong preference for visiting the arm of the maze not explored on the previous trial. In a study by Vecera, Rothbart, and Posner (1991), infants at 6 and 18 months were presented with a toy at a given location and allowed to play with it for a few seconds. The toy was removed and then presented again in its previous location with an identical toy in another location. The index measure was which toy the child reached for. The 6-month-olds were as likely to choose the toy in the familiar location as the toy in the new location, while the 18-month-olds alternated at a rate significantly above the chance level of 50%.

Because 6-month-olds do show IOR, these results suggest that a different mechanism underlies the manual selection of novel locations as tested here. Based on animal research, Vecera et al. speculate that the mechanism underlying spontaneous alternation is related to development of an anterior system that includes the anterior cingulate gyrus and the frontal supplementary motor cortex. Thus, IOR is linked to the functioning of circuits present at birth and to components of the earlier maturing orienting/investigative system; spontaneous alternation may be linked to components of the second, higher level system. The two forms of preference for novel locations may mature at different rates, but would eventually be integrated because there are anatomical connections between components of the first and second attention systems.

SELECTION BASED ON MOTIVATIONAL RELEVANCE

Our discussion has tended to emphasize the cognitive underpinnings of selective attention to novelty. These cognitive interpretations should not blind us to the importance of emotion in the individual's response. A novel or familiar pattern might be selected because it elicits positive feelings rather than because it matches or mismatches a cognitive representation of the pattern (Kunst-Wilson & Zajonc, 1980; Nachman, Stern, & Best, 1986). The development of behavioral wariness is interesting in this regard. Schaffer (1974) has observed that, although 6-month-olds will readily, even compulsively, grasp a novel object presented to them, infants older than 8 months seem more inhibited in their approach, sometimes showing avoidance and distress. Older infants who are rated by their mothers as somewhat more fearful tend to have longer latencies to approach novel objects (Rothbart, 1988b). Thus, whether novel or familiar objects or events are selected will depend on the child's emotional interpretation of them, and these interpretations change with development.

Motivation is another key factor. Although habituation directs the individual's attention away from familiar repeated events toward novel ones, this is the case mainly for events that are not emotionally charged or that cease to be motivationally relevant. Familiar objects continue to be selected in appropriate circumstances because they have been associated with satisfaction of basic needs or with social reinforcement. Other familiar objects are important to the attainment of goals. Thus, reinforcement and relevance to immediate goals attract attention to familiar objects. Waters and Wright (1979) argue that the probability of a selective response at any age depends on the balance between familiarity on the one hand and the consequences of that response for the integrity of the organism on the other. In this section, we address some of the changing consequences of events with development in the first few years and the resulting changes in what is selected for attention.

Social and Emotional Consequences of People

As we have noted, infants become highly social beings in the early months of life and they are very attentive to the faces of adult partners, often to the exclusion of other events in the environment. In the first few months, infants begin to preferentially smile to the faces of parents (Ambrose, 1961), perhaps because parents are so closely linked to regulation of arousal and other bodily functions (Hofer, 1981). Barrera and Maurer (1981) found that 3-month-olds also often look longer at pictures of their mothers than at pictures of strange women. Under other circumstances, however, infants will look longer at the faces of strangers than at those of their parents (Barrera & Maurer, 1981; Carpenter, Tecce, Stechler, & Friedman, 1970; Lamb et al., 1987).

Whether the child selects a parent's familiar, consequential face or a stranger's face almost certainly depends on the context of the child's choice. When the child is in physical or emotional need, selective attention to parents, with whom the child has achieved feelings of physical satisfaction and a pattern of mutual accommodation, makes adaptive sense. When the child's needs are satisfied, on the other hand, looking at and interacting more with a stranger has the advantage of exposing the infant to a wider range of social experiences and helps in the gradual process of differentiating and recognizing individual faces—an important social skill.

With the development of attachment, strange people may, for a time, cause distress rather than interest—a phenomenon associated with the 9-month transition. In a study of the changing response to the appearance and approach of a stranger (Campos, Emde, Gaensbauer, & Henderson, 1975), 5- and 9-month-olds were exposed to a stranger coming into the room when their mothers were either present or absent. The stranger approached to within 4 meters of the infant, then approached to within 1 meter, and finally came within 0.3 meters of the infant before departing. Of interest here are the facial expressions and heart rate responses to the different phases of this experience with the stranger. Figure 5.3 shows that the 5-month-olds generally looked "fascinated" and the 9-month-olds, sober or even frightened. Figure 5.4 shows that the heart rate response to each of these phases was decelerative for the 5-month-olds, typical of orienting, and accelerative for the 9-month-olds, a sign of defensiveness that is incompatible with orienting (Graham & Clifton, 1966). The response of the 9-month-olds was more extreme when the mother was absent than when she was present. The younger children responded much the same whether the mother was present or absent.

The reaction of the older infants was based not only on perceptual characteristics of the event but also on their emotional ties to the mother. Because of this connection of the orienting/investigative system to emotional systems, individuals develop different, but characteristic, tendencies to select and approach novelty. Campos et al. noted that, at either age, some infants were fascinated and others increasingly

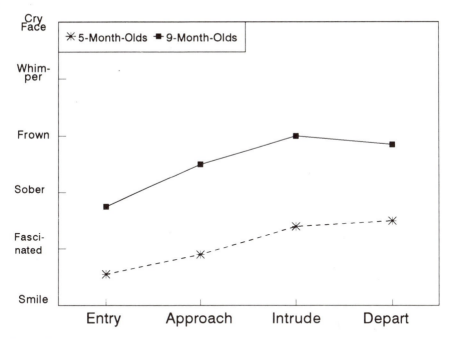

Figure 5.3. Facial expressions of 5- and 9-month-old infants in response to the approach of a strange adult. From "Cardiac and behavioral inter-relationships in the reactions of infants to strangers," by J. J. Campos, R. N. Emde, T. Gaensbauer, and C. Henderson, 1975, *Developmental Psychology, 11,* p. 594. Copyright 1975 by the American Psychological Association. Adapted with permission.

distressed and that the patterns of heart rate change differentiated them. Such individual differences will be considered in chapter 10.

Selection Based on What is Relevant to New Motor Skills

A decline in the intense attraction to faces seems to occur around 5 months of age and infants begin to attend more to distant events (Kaye & Fogel, 1980). Fogel (1977) describes a mother who tries to engage her infant in their usual intimate interaction only to find the infant straining to look elsewhere. Infants may begin to be uncomfortable in the relatively passive position in which they are usually placed (Field, Vega-Lahr, Goldstein, & Scafidi, 1987). By about 4 months, infants have also developed greater facility for disengaging attention from highly salient objects such as the mother's face (Johnson et al., 1991).

Although these factors are important, the increasing desire to look around at the external world surely stems, in part, from the infant's increasing means for perceiving, acting on, and controlling the objects in that world. The infant's ability to reach out and grasp objects leads to a fascination with small objects (Bushnell, 1985). As infants play with objects, they may be particularly attentive to the features of objects that can be manipulated, such as form and texture. Twelve-month-olds, after playing

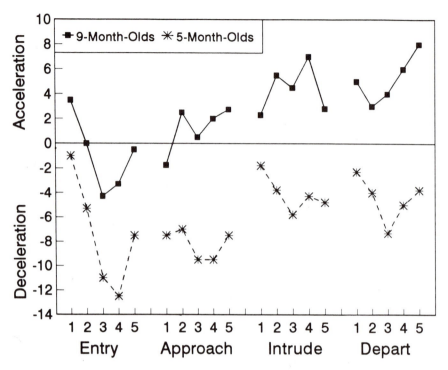

FIGURE 5.4. Heart rate responses (BPM) of the same 5- and 9-month-old infants in response to the approach of a strange adult. From "Cardiac and behavioral inter-relationships in
the reactions of infants to strangers," by J. J. Campos, R. N. Emde, T. Gaensbauer, and
C. Henderson, 1975, *Developmental Psychology, 11*, p. 595. Copyright 1975 by the American Psychological Association. Adapted with permission.

with a series of objects identical in shape but varying in color, preferred an object of
a novel shape to the familiar shape (Ruff, 1982). The results suggest that the infants
had learned something about the shape of the objects while looking at and manipulating them. In contrast, 12-month-olds who had played with a series of objects of the
same color but varying in shape showed no preference for a novel over the familiar
color. This failure to differentiate between colors may mean that little attention was
directed to the color of the objects during the familiarization period.

Casey (1979) reports similar findings. She trained 12-month-olds to make a
discriminative instrumental response for reinforcement—opening one door rather
than another for a smiling face as a reward. The infants learned to make the correct
response when the discriminative stimulus was the *shape* of the knob on the door but
not when it was only the *color* of the knob. The results from both of these studies
suggest that, in many situations, 12-month-old infants pay attention to object characteristics accessible to manipulation rather than those accessible only to vision—that
is, characteristics that have haptic consequences for the manipulating infant (see
Bushnell, Shaw, & Strauss, 1985, for an example with 6-month-olds).

From the point of view of selection, there was an interesting twist in the study by Casey (1979). She used a pretraining session in which only the "correct" knob (based on either color or form) was present, and responses always led to the smiling face when the door was opened. Thus, before the actual training trials, the infant made 10 reinforced responses to the doorknob that would be correct in subsequent training. Infants who were then trained to make a choice between two differently shaped doorknobs responded initially to the *novel* shape, while infants trained to make a choice between identically shaped knobs of two different colors responded more to the *familiar* color. Thus, the initial choice of infants in the shape discrimination group was not the choice that led to reinforcement. Even so, they were significantly more likely to reach the criterion for learning, which required responding to the familiar shape, than the infants in the color discrimination group. Both the initial response to novelty and the faster learning argue for the salience of form over color in this context. The pattern of results, however, also illustrates the difference between the momentary selection of novelty and more permanent learned shifts in selectivity.

The emergence of crawling and other modes of self-produced locomotion is related to further shifts in selective attention. Bertenthal, Campos, and Barrett (1984) speculate that the onset of crawling leads to changes in attention to spatial relationships, because spatial arrangements of objects in the environment become more critical. In some studies, for example, 9-month-olds, but not 6-month-olds, respond to a novel spatial arrangement when faced with novel and familiar objects composed of the same elments (Ruff, 1978). Variations along irrelevant dimensions during familiarization rule out discrimination on the basis of local contour. Bertenthal et al. (1984) used this paradigm and compared crawlers and noncrawlers of the same age (7.5 months). They found that infants who had already started to crawl were more likely to make a discrimination that could be based only on the configuration of identical elements. That is, their noncrawling 7.5-month-olds were more like the 6-month-olds in the Ruff (1978) study and their crawling 7.5-month-olds were more like the 9-month-olds (see figure 5.5). In a similar vein, Horobin and Acredolo (1986) found that continued attention to one of two hiding places was essential for 8- to 10-month-old infants' correct choices in an object search task. Infants who looked steadily at the correct location between the hiding and their responses were more mature, as indexed by length of time crawling, than infants who were visually inattentive.

Another source of information that is often more important to infants who are moving independently than to nonmovers is the mother's behavior and facial expression. As we noted in chapter 3, social referencing occurs when walkers ,and crawlers, separated from their mothers, look to their mothers and attend to the mother's expression and behavior in addition to the immediate context. Walden and Ogan (1988) studied infants from 6 to 22 months to document developmental changes in social referencing. When infants from 6 to 9 months looked toward the parent while playing at a distance, they were as likely to look at the parent's body as the parent's face. In contrast, children from 14 to 22 months not only looked more frequently at the parent but looked almost exclusively toward the face. These older

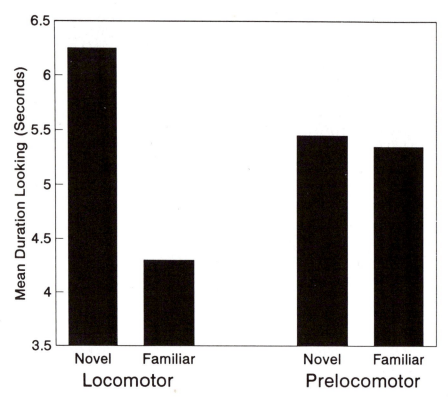

Figure 5.5. The response of crawlers and noncrawlers to novel and familiar objects that differ only in the spatial arrangement of elements. From "Self-produced locomotion: An organizer of emotional, cognitive, and social development in infancy" by B. I. Bertenthal, J. J. Campos, and K. C. Barrett, in *Continuities and discontinuities in development* (p. 200), 1984, New York: Plenum Press. Copyright by Plenum Press. Adapted with permission.

infants also looked more frequently at the parents' faces when the expression was negative than when it was positive. This differentiation suggests an enhanced interest in and attention to facial expressions.

The information infants receive by referring to adults begins to influence their behavior around 12 to 14 months. For example, Sorce et al. (1985) observed infants at 1 year on a visual cliff where there was a small visible drop-off, but tactual solidity. If the mothers, who were standing on the other side of the cliff, smiled or looked interested, children were much more likely to cross the "cliff" (74% crossed) than when the mothers frowned or looked fearful (only 6% crossed). Similarly, Hornik, Risenhoover, and Gunnar (1987) found that, when mothers' faces and voices registered disgust, 12-month-olds stayed farther away from toys and played with them less than when mothers expressed positive affect or remained neutral. These results indicate that by 12 months, infants are not only sensitive to variations in maternal expression of emotion but are also influenced by these emotions. The possibility exists, therefore, that as infants' motor development takes them into more distant and potentially hazardous activities, they begin to selectively attend to social cues that were previously less salient to them.

SELECTING WHAT OTHERS SELECT

Although important information may be conveyed to the child through social cues and through social reinforcement of the child's activity, attention is also guided, in a simpler fashion, by what others attend to. When we see someone, even a stranger, focused intently on something behind and above us, we often turn to look, curious to know what is so interesting. To be influenced in this way, we must be able to accurately perceive the direction and location of the looking of others (J. Gibson & Pick, 1963).

This skill emerges with the beginnings of the second, higher level system of attention and develops over the first 2 years of life. A number of investigators have been systematically charting its development. In a study of infants at 6, 12, and 18 months, Butterworth and Jarrett (1991) seated infants in the center of a room facing their mothers. On any one trial, there were four identical objects (plain yellow squares), two on the right of the infant, two on the left. Mothers were asked to play with their infants, maintaining eye contact, and, on a signal from the experimenter, to turn and look at one of the targets for 6 seconds. The 12- and 18-month-olds were more likely to respond to the change in the direction of their mothers' looking than the 6-month-olds, and when they responded, they looked at the correct target more than the incorrect one. Taking into account the number of times the infants looked in the wrong direction or never turned to look, Morissette, Ricard, and Gouin-Decarie (1992) found that, by 12 months, infants turned to the correct side significantly more often than they turned to the incorrect side or failed to turn at all. In contrast to the results of Butterworth and Jarrett, however, only 18-month-old infants looked directly at the correct target (the specific target toward which the mother was looking) significantly more often than they looked at the wrong target on the correct side.

These data suggest that infants of 6 months do not follow the direction of someone else's gaze, at least when they are required to select one of two identical targets. Butterworth and Jarrett (1991) found that infants at 6 months do quite well, however, when only one target is present at a time. The infants' scans were also more likely to terminate on the target as long as the target was within 90° of their midline. Under normal circumstances, of course, adults are most likely to shift attention away from the infant when novel or salient events occur—an important or interesting person enters the room or the telephone rings. Often these events will be salient to infants as well, facilitating their attention to the target of the adult's attention. As Butterworth and Jarrett (1991) note: "The mother's signal is informative because it specifies the *possibility* of an object, *somewhere* in visual space. Whether mother and infant actually engage in joint attention depends upon . . . the object singling itself out" (p. 70).

Even at 18 months, there are some limitations in joint attention. For example, 18-month-olds do not always turn to look at targets behind them even when the mother is looking at those targets (Butterworth & Jarrett, 1991). They are more accurate in locating a target behind them *if* there is no target within their current visual field; under these circumstances, they will be successful even if the mother makes only an eye movement. Accuracy is higher, however, when the mother makes both head and eye movements. A study by Butterworth and Cochran (1980) suggests that, unlike 18-month-olds, 12-month-olds still do not turn around to look behind them even when the visual field in front is devoid of targets. Although the authors interpret their results as selectivity based on an emerging appreciation of geometric space, the experimental paradigm forced the mother to rotate her head much farther to look at targets behind her (in front of the infant) than to look at targets in front of her (behind the infant); only older infants may be able to use the more subtle cues involved in the latter type of trials.

When people want to make certain that someone else visually attends to the same event they are attending to, they often point. Following the direction of another's point is a related skill that develops in the first 18 months. Butterworth (1991) asked mothers to either look at or look at *and* point to one of two mannequins. When the mother looked and pointed at the same time, most infants between 6 and 17 months looked at the correct target when it required only a 10° turn from midline. For other targets, only infants older than 10 months were correct more often than not. Murphy and Messer (1978) also found that infants' ability to follow the mothers' pointing was dependent on the location of the object. Nine-month-olds were successful only for some locations, while 14-month-olds were successful for all locations. In addition, the older infants looked at the object of the point faster than the younger infants. Descriptively, Murphy and Messer note that almost all of the mothers' points were accompanied by vocalization.

Speech is another factor in directing attention. Once children understand that words refer to objects or events, language becomes a means of indicating situations in the environment that deserve attention. Someone may simply tell the child to "look at this!" The child may understand what is being requested but may also be aroused by the sharp sound. More informative are words referring to specific objects. Ten- to 14-month-old infants pay more attention to objects that are labeled than to those that are not (Baldwin & Markman, 1989). By 18 months, infants will change the direction of their gaze to look where the mother is looking when she uses an object label (Baldwin, 1991). Ward (1990) proposes that young children recognize when adults use labels that are novel and that such labeling biases them toward selecting novel objects in the environment, especially if no other information is available about the object being labeled. As children gain experience, novel labels also tend to direct their attention to those attributes of objects that have been previously useful in categorizing objects. The shape of objects, including small parts, seems to be a particularly important attribute. Landau, Smith, and Jones (1988) presented 3-year-olds with an object accompanied by a novel label, such as "dax." Afterward, when asked to get another "dax," children tended to choose other objects that matched the original one in shape but not when they matched it only in texture, color, or size.

With the emergence of the second attention system, children become more adept at selectively attending to what others attend to. They also take more initiative in directing the visual attention of others. Children's own communicative pointing emerges in the latter half of the first year. By 14 months, their pointing is not only well established but often accompanied by a look at the person whose attention is being sought (Blake et al., 1992); this look suggests that children are checking to see whether the other person is attending to the target of interest. Early pointing is very likely to be accompanied by vocalization, another attention-getting device within the young child's capability (Leung & Rheingold, 1981).

In general, then, the infant's social interactions become based increasingly on a mutual monitoring of attention, first with adults and later with peers (Bakeman & Adamson, 1984). Anderson, Lorch, Smith, Bradford, and Levin (1981) report that 3- and 5-year-old children, when watching television together, influence each other's looking at and involvement in the program. As with attention in other settings, attention to television is episodic; children will attend to the television program at times but at other times play with toys or engage in social exchange. It might be argued that the observed synchrony between pairs of children is due to the common influence of features of the program, but the investigators found a significant degree of synchrony beyond what would be expected on the basis of the program alone. This could occur because both children monitor each other's looking, because the watching child comments on or laughs at the current segment, or because one child actively tries to recruit the other's attention by pointing or verbally requesting attention.

SUMMARY

In this chapter, we considered processes underlying selective attention. We first described changes in selectivity during the first 2 to 3 months of life and some theoretical models to account for them. Although what is selected for attention depends on the developing capacity of the receptors, a number of inhibitory mechanisms, such as habituation and inhibition of return, also ensure that, after 2 to 3 months, attention is more strongly influenced by experience.

Novelty, which is a function of experience, is especially important for selection during the period from 3 to 9 months of age, the period when the orienting/investigative system of attention is dominant. We distinguished attention to location from attention to objects, noting that the two processes appear to follow different time courses and to involve different underlying mechanisms. At 3 months, when novelty of location conflicts with novelty of object, the effects of location are relatively stronger than they will be later in development.

In addition to inhibitory processes, selectivity of attention depends on what is important for survival and is therefore linked to the child's emotions and motivation. Even highly familiar objects and places may be attended to if they have significant consequences for the child. Selection depends on momentary intentions and goals and on the context. Some changes in selectivity are related to motor development. Around 5 months, infants more readily disengage their gaze from the parent and scan the environment, looking toward objects that might be seized and manipulated. Selectivity also changes as a result of emotional development. Positive affect appears to be related to early selection of the parent, with fear of strangers and its attentional concomitants becoming evident by about 9 months.

With the development of the second, higher level system of attention, the young child becomes increasingly sensitive to others' line of regard, establishing a basis for joint attention and for social influences on what the child selects as important. Attention can also be guided by communicative gestures and language. At the same time, children become more skillful in directing the attention of others.

6

Development of Attention as a State

In chapters 4 and 5 we emphasized selective attention and the bases for directing attention to some events rather than others. The effectiveness of any particular event in attracting and holding a child's attention, however, depends not only on the physical characteristics of the event and the child's age and experience but also on the child's current state. Hofer (1981) defines state as:

*Internal changes [that] alter the tendency of an organism to behave, predisposing it to some kinds of behavior and causing others to be difficult or impossible to elicit. These time-related changes in the internal condition of the animal are generally called **states** if they persist for any appreciable length of time.* (p. 54)

Accordingly, in this chapter, we emphasize development of attention as an internal state that influences behavior.

Consider the infant in figure 6.1 (Maurer & Maurer, 1988); she is participating in a set of habituation trials where the same visual display is repeated. Her attention is initially captured by the display; she looks serious and engaged (frames 1 and 2). Her interest wanes, however, and she begins to look bored (frames 3 and 4). She then disengages her attention (frame 5) and finally finds something else to occupy her (frame 6). When a novel display appears (frame 7), she notices it and her attention is re-engaged in the task. These photographs nicely illustrate attention as changes in state over time.

In the first section of this chapter, we describe the processes underlying the engagement and disengagement of attention. Once attention is engaged, there are many factors that influence how long the state of engagement will last. These factors are the subject of the second section of the chapter. In the third section, we consider the role attention plays in regulating other states, such as emotional distress.

ENGAGEMENT AND DISENGAGEMENT OF ATTENTION

The engagement and disengagement of attention are dynamic processes that require time and are accompanied by physiological changes in both the autonomic and the

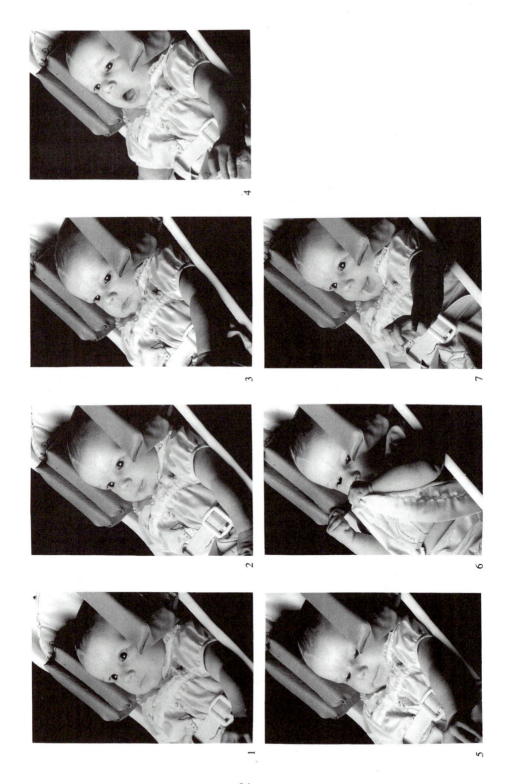

central nervous systems. Figure 6.2, taken from Richards and Casey (1991), summarizes these phases of attention as manifested in heart rate. An episode of attention begins with an orienting reaction to an event and the heart rate decelerates abruptly; visual attention is maintained for a period of time and the heart rate deceleration is sustained; the episode then begins to terminate as the heart rate accelerates back to baseline. Although heart rate is only one component of the attentional state, the specific model proposed here serves as a general guide to our discussion. In this section, we describe three phases of attention—the initiation, engagement, and termination of attention. Further, we discuss the phasic, or temporary, as well as the tonic alterations in physiology and behavior that define these phases and consider evidence for developmental change within each.

Initiation

Groves and Thompson (1970) suggest that every stimulus event both elicits a response and affects the state of the organism; they describe the latter effect as changing the "general level of arousal, activation, [and] tendency to respond" (p. 440). Attention will not be initiated without some optimal level of cortical and autonomic activation. One of the major ways attention is initiated is through the orienting response (OR) that occurs when an event "captures" our attention. The OR is a multicomponent, phasic process that occurs when an organism encounters a novel or otherwise salient event (Sokolov, 1963). With the OR, the organism is alerted; it prepares to learn more about the event and to respond appropriately. Jennings (1986) describes the orienting response as holding resources ready for whatever demands the event may impose. The behavioral and physiological components of the OR represent both general and specific alterations in the functioning of the individual. Physiological changes in central and autonomic nervous systems reflect general arousal (Sokolov, 1963), while the behavior of aligning the sensory receptors to the attended event helps to channel attention and may be accompanied by the alerting of specific neural pathways (Posner, 1978).

The OR is a relatively automatic or involuntary response to moderately intense changes in stimulation (Sokolov, 1963) that signal the possibility of interesting events to be explored. More intense and sudden changes are likely to evoke the defensive response or even a startle (Graham & Clifton, 1966). The OR is often seen in the context of novel events. Cohen and his colleagues (Cohen, 1972, 1973; DeLoache, Rissman, & Cohen, 1978) found, however, that stimulus complexity also makes a contribution; in their studies, 4-month-old infants turned more quickly to complex checkerboards than to simple ones. Thus, the OR is strongly dependent on the physical characteristics of events, such as intensity, novelty, and complexity.

Heart rate decrement, as seen in the second panel of figure 6.2, is the most studied physiological component of the OR. The typical heart rate response to the onset of novel stimulation may consist of two components; one is a very brief deceleration followed by acceleration, and the other, a longer term deceleration (Berg & Berg, 1987). The latter is considered to be the cardiac component of orienting and it is readily observed only after 2 months of age (Berg & Berg, 1987; Graham & Clifton, 1966). After 2 months, and until about 9 months, there is an age-

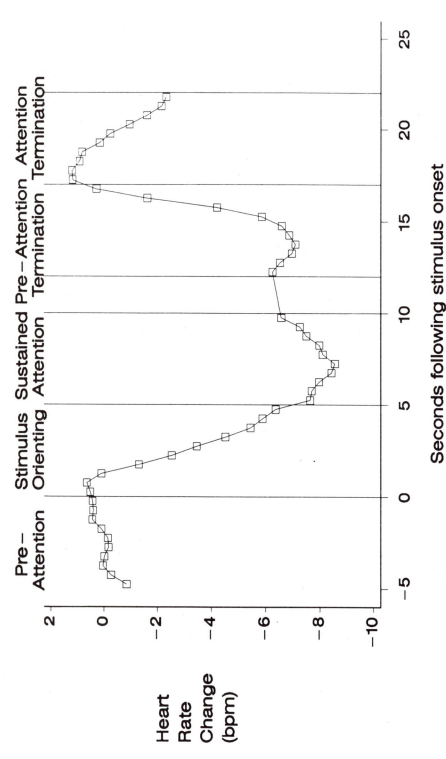

Figure 6.2. Model of the temporal phases of attention. From ''Heart rate variability during attention phases in young infants,'' by J. E. Richards and B. J. Casey, 1991, *Psychophysiology*, 28, p. 46. Copyright 1991 by the Society for Psychophysiological Research, Inc. Reprinted with the permission of author and Cambridge University Press.

associated increase in the amplitude of heart rate deceleration during the OR, at least for some stimulus events. Subsequently, the amplitude decreases until it approximates the adult response—a predictable, but small deceleration in response to novel stimulation (Graham et al., 1983). This period coincides with a time of strong behavioral attraction to novel events, as described in the chapter 5, and with the operation of the orienting/investigative system.

Habituation, resulting from repetition of an event, reflects a progressive reduction in the arousing capacity of the event itself (Smothergill & Kraut, 1989). This change can be seen in the gradually smaller heart rate changes elicited by an event as it is repeated. To illustrate this, figure 6.3 presents data adapted from Kagan et al. (1971); the mean heart rate deceleration becomes smaller with repetition of three-dimensional faces at 4, 8, and 13 months of age. The data also suggest development in the response to repetition. Although 12-month-olds show an initial deceleration that is somewhat smaller than that of the 4-month-olds (Graham et al., 1983; see chapter 5), they show the largest and most systematic decline with repetition.

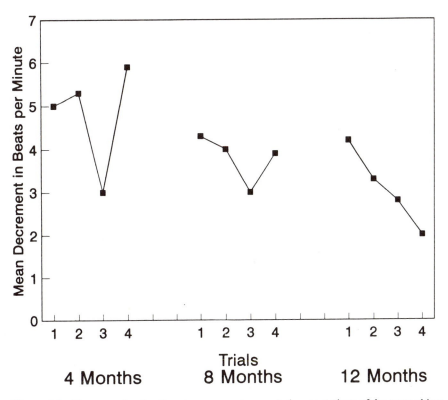

Figure 6.3. Heart rate decelerations in response to repeated presentations of the same object at 4, 8, and 13 months of age. From *Change and continuity in infancy* (p. 116) by J. Kagan, 1971, New York: Wiley. Copyright 1971 by John Wiley and Sons, Inc. Adapted with permission.

Decreases in the magnitude of the OR after 9 months may facilitate the initiation of attention guided by cognitive factors. If the OR continued to be strongly elicited by environmental events, intentional activity would frequently be interrupted and selectivity could not be maintained for long. Thus, as the second attention system develops, episodes of attention may also be initiated more slowly by intentions or plans. A decision to play a game or to work on a task sets in motion preparation relevant to the chosen activity. Once engaged, the processes underlying attention may be the same as those governing more externally controlled attention. It seems likely, however, that alertness will develop more slowly compared to the abrupt change in alertness seen in the OR; compared to the 3- to 5-second course of the OR, voluntary initiation may require many seconds or even minutes.

For example, Anderson (personal communication, October 6, 1992) observed a boy in a setting where toys and a television program were simultaneously available. The child spent the first part of the session playing with the toys, only occasionally glancing at the television. After one of these glances, however, he announced that he was "going to watch *Sesame Street*." He then put the toys away, lay down on his stomach, propped his chin in his hands, and looked at the television screen. This represents a deliberate choice that is superficially, at least, very different from the OR. The question is how different they are in terms of underlying mechanisms. The boy's announcement and his extended preparations indicate that his eventual looking at the television was voluntary, even though the look just prior to his announcement may have reflected an OR to a change in the program.

Engagement

A distinction has frequently been made between the reactive and the sustained aspects of attention (e.g., Porges & Smith, 1980), with the reactive component being equivalent to the OR. Cohen (1972, 1973) distinguishes between attention-holding and attention-getting properties of events. The initiation of attention in general, and the operation of the OR in particular, depend on the detection of some information about the world. This limited information is apparently used to make a preliminary evaluation of the importance and interest value of the event that elicited the initial response; thus, the processes involved are sometimes referred to as "pre-attentive" (Neisser, 1967). Important and interesting events are subject to more prolonged scrutiny and consideration; when this happens, some of the alterations seen briefly during the OR are prolonged either as an accompaniment to, or in support of, sustained attention. These sustained physical alterations include characteristic changes in facial expression, motor movement, and heart rate, some of which were described in chapter 2. Here we describe these changes in more detail, discuss developments in each, and suggest how they may indicate the level of attention.

Facial Expression. A number of studies include the facial expression of "interest" as one measure of attention. As we noted in chapter 2, Izard (1977) distinguishes between "hypothesized interest," which involves no movement of the facial muscles, and "interest/excitement," which involves raised or knit brows and a slightly open mouth. Other activity around the mouth could be included, such as the lower lip rolled under (Sullivan & Lewis, 1988) or the tongue protruding. Interest/ excitement appears to correspond to a higher level of engagement than does hypothesized interest. The frequency and duration of interest expressions should vary with both age and context, an expectation confirmed in a study by Langsdorf, Izard, Rayias, and Hembree (1983). They presented 2- to 8-month-old infants with three events—a live face, a mannequin, and a complex object. The duration of interest was lower than the duration of looking, but paralleled it; both increased over age and varied with the nature of the event. Infants at all ages showed more interest in the live person than in the mannequin and more interest in the mannequin than in the object.

Fähndrich and Schneider (1987) coded facial expression in their investigation of play in preschool children; the children's initial investigation of a novel toy involved facial expressions different from those in later, more playful, activity with the same toy. The investigators found more interest/excitement than joy during exploration of the toy, and more joy than interest during play with the toy. The only specific aspect of interest, however, that occurred more often in exploration than in play was knit brows.

Because the definition of focused attention used in several studies (Oakes & Tellinghuisen, 1994; Ruff, 1986; Ruff & Lawson, 1990) incorporates facial expression, a word of caution is in order. The context in which focused attention is measured most frequently is free play with toys. Whether a child is inspecting a novel object or playing in a more complex fashion with blocks or dolls, the activity tends to orient the child's head and eyes *down* to the objects. According to a study of 5- and 7-month-olds by Michel, Camras, and Sullivan (1992), contracted or knitted brows are more likely to occur when the head and eyes are down than when the head and eyes are raised. In contrast, the brows are more likely to be raised when the head and eyes are up. When infants and children look up to attend to something, such as a television program, the facial expression characteristic of focused attention may not be the same as that observed during free play. It is best, therefore, to think of facial expression as part of a coordinated complex of activity rather than as an isolated reflection of attention (see Weinberg & Tronick, 1994).

Motor Activity. Concentration of attention is linked to a reduction in many forms of motor activity. In awake, alert infants, the presentation of a stimulus event often leads to a suppression of general activity, sucking, and respiration (Graham et al., 1983), and reductions in activity level may increase with age, at least to 9 months (C. Turnure, 1971). By 3 to 4 months, however, bodily activity seems to be tightly coupled to variations in visual attention (Robertson & Bacher, 1992), as seen in figure 6.4. Visual attention may drive the motor system, causing increases and decreases in activity as attention is disengaged and re-engaged. The activity that follows an episode of attention may reflect a release from inhibition. We cannot rule out the possibility, however, that motor quieting, for whatever reason, physically facilitates the infant's ability to focus attention. Periods of activity could theoretically be independent of attention, with visual attention possible only during quiet periods.

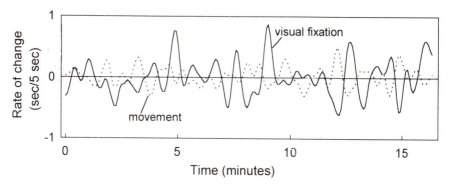

Figure 6.4. Cycles of bodily activity and visual attention in 3- to 4-month-old infants. From "Coupling of spontaneous movement and visual attention in infants," by S. S. Robertson and L. F. Bacher, 1992. Presented at the International Conference on Infant Studies, Miami. Reprinted with permission.

A link between attentional and motor systems is observed in older children as well. Activity and movement-related inattention continue to decline during the preschool years. As described in chapter 3, the amount of active inattention manifested by physically moving away from tasks decreases dramatically between 2.5 and 3.5 years. Levy (1980) had children sitting on a special chair that registered movement and reports that the frequency of small movements decreased significantly from 3 to 7 years. These developments parallel the general decrease in motor movement seen even in free play during this period (Routh, Schroeder, & O'Tuama, 1974). Although the precise relationship between the mechanisms governing attention and movement is not clear, movement can be seen as competing with sustained visual attention to an event or task.

Decrements in Heart Rate and Heart Rate Variability. Other investigators have studied the general distinction between higher and lower levels of engagement by examining relationships between looking and heart rate. Lewis, Kagan, Campbell, and Kalafat (1966) first noted that heart rate was lower during longer episodes of looking than during shorter episodes; they speculated that the use of both measures might make it possible to add "an 'intensity' dimension [to] the construct of attention" (p. 70). In line with this, Anthony and Graham (1983) found deeper decelerations for interesting displays than for dull ones. Richards (1988) suggests that, after the initial deceleration in heart rate to a visually presented pattern, the heart rate may remain low relative to baseline for some time (see panel 3 of figure 6.2). Richards's contention is that active, focused looking is associated with sustained heart rate decrements at levels below baseline; less intense attention is associated with accelerations back to baseline levels.

For many years, reductions in heart rate variability have also been associated with sustained attention (e.g, van Hover, 1974). In a series of articles, Porges (1972, 1986, 1991) has argued that the decrease in heart rate variability is due to a reduction in respiratory sinus arrhythmia (RSA), that portion of heart rate variability linked to fluctuations in respiratory rate and controlled by the central nervous system. As noted in chapter 2, Porges (1986) has quantified RSA in a measure that reflects vagal tone or the degree of influence of the vagus nerve on heart rate, an interpretation that has been validated in animal work (Porges, 1991). High vagal tone in resting states is related to well-defined reactivity to environmental events and to a sustained reduction in RSA during attention-demanding activity; the reduction is presumably a function of increased work and effort.

In the first year, there are dramatic developments in the neural control of heart rate. Heart rate variability and vagal tone increase monotonically with age in both rats and humans (Izard et al., 1991; Porges, 1992). Similarly, Richards and Casey (1992) report a threefold increase in baseline RSA from 8 to 26 weeks of age. Following Porges's (1991) argument, the general increase in variability, and RSA in particular, is an index of maturing neural integrity. Richards and Casey (1992) suggest that RSA is controlled by distributed attention networks that include limbic, frontal, and parietal pathways as well as the brainstem (cf. Posner & Peterson, 1990). Early development thus involves an increase in the "functional integrity of this entire system," which "may represent the capacity of the [individual] to respond with widespread neural, physiological, and behavioral responses during attention" (p. 54).

Integration of Response Systems. Sustained concentration is signaled by a number of behavioral and physiological changes. Interestingly, facial expression, motor activity, and heart rate changes seem to be interrelated. Langsdorf et al. (1983) found, for example, parallels between interest expression and heart rate; there was more interest and more deceleration as a function of age and increasing complexity (see also Brock, Rothbart, & Derryberry, 1986). There has been an extensive discussion (e.g., Obrist et al., 1970) of the close relationship between motor movement and heart rate, with attention accompanied by simultaneous reductions in both. In addition, Porges (1991) notes that vagal tone and facial expression are closely related both functionally and anatomically; "facial expressions are mediated by the central nervous system via cranial nerves that originate in brain-stem structures close to the cells giving rise to the vagus" (p. 117). We have presented little direct evidence for cortical changes related to state because, to our knowledge, almost no work with infants and young children has been designed to link sustained attention to prolonged alterations in central nervous system activity. As outlined in chapter 2, however, cortical changes are part of sustained attention as well. These interconnections suggest that developments in the engagement of attention are dependent, in part, on the developing integration of the various subsystems.

Disengagement and Termination of Attention

Once attention has been engaged, an active process of disengagement seems to be necessary before attention can be shifted to another object or location (Posner & Presti, 1987). Richards and Casey (1991; Richards, 1988) have identified a specific "attention termination" phase in their work with infants (panel 4 of figure 6.2). Simultaneous recording of both looking and heart rate reveals periods when looking continues but the heart rate begins to accelerate back to baseline levels. During this phase of attention termination, infants are more distractible than during the previous prolonged heart rate deceleration.

When the heart rate has completed its return, there seems to be a refractory period during which orienting to a novel event in the previous location or a nearby one is inhibited for a brief period, a process that may be related to inhibition of return. To demonstrate this, Casey and Richards (1991) conducted an experiment involving two stimulus events. When they presented the first event, *Sesame Street*, the heart rate in infants from 14 to 26 months slowed by approximately 7 beats per minute. In the absence of distraction, all infants continued to look at the screen while their heart rates returned to prestimulus levels. The experimenters then presented, on the same screen, a second stimulus event at 0, 3, 6, or 9 seconds after the heart rate's return. No deceleration—that is, no OR—occurred to the new event at 0 or 3 seconds. At 6 and 9 seconds, however, the deceleration approximated that seen with the first stimulus event; in addition, heart rate was significantly lower than on control trials where *Sesame Street* continued for another 10 seconds. The infants who looked at the new event but showed no heart rate deceleration may have been unable to actively attend and acquire information. Other studies would be needed to pursue this possibility, but the data are consistent with the idea that disengagement is an operation that takes time.

What happens to the process of disengagement with age? As we noted in chapter 3, infants in the first 2 or 3 months of life sometimes have considerable trouble turning away from salient objects and events. We noted that, after 4 months, infants look away from a central display more often and faster (Johnson et al., 1991). Casey and Richards (1988) also found that latencies to turn from a central event toward a peripheral one decreased with age—7.7, 4.4, and 2.8 seconds for 14-, 20-, and 26-week-olds infants, respectively. In a very different context, Lamb et al. (1987) found that the frequency of looking away in face-to-face interactions increased from 1 to 5 months before leveling off. A parallel increase in frequency of looks and total duration of looking shows that the older infants were looking many times for shorter durations. All of these data suggest that 4- to 5-month-old infants begin to engage and disengage attention much more easily than before. There may be several reasons for this: maturation of the neural mechanisms of disengagement (Johnson et al., 1991; Posner & Presti, 1987); expansion of the visual field (Maurer & Lewis, 1991); and faster habituation to the central display. All of these developments support the orienting/investigative system.

An important implication of the work on attention termination by Casey and Richards is that disengagement of looking is often gradual and that, without a particular alternative, infants may continue to look at something even though their attention is no longer strongly focused. At later ages, children may also disengage gradually from more complex activities involving attention. In a comparison of 1- to 4.5-year-old children, Ruff and Lawson (1990) found that episodes of focused attention during play with toys were often followed by continued orientation to the same toy; this was the case for 32%, 54%, 52%, and 47% of episodes at 1, 2.5, 3.5, and 4.5 years of age, respectively. Some episodes of focused attention were terminated by orienting to another toy (35%, 22%, 24%, and 24%) and others by looking away from the toys altogether (33%, 25%, 24%, and 29%). The 1-year-olds showed a somewhat different distribution from the older children, but the similarity in percentages across the three older ages suggests a lack of major changes in the termination of focused attention after 1 year of age.

With the development of the second attention system, children find it possible to disengage attention on the basis of instructions or a decision to do so. Following instructions or deciding to stop an activity requires inhibitory skills that infants and toddlers do not yet have. For example, a phenomenon related to disengagement of attention is interruption of an ongoing motor activity. Bullock and Lutkenhaus (1988) investigated children's ability and willingness to stop an activity when a goal had been reached, finding that spontaneous stopping increased from only 18% around 20 months to 75% around 32 months. These developments suggest that disengagement of attention from a pleasurable activity is not easily mastered and may develop later than the disengagement of looking.

FACTORS THAT SUSTAIN ENGAGEMENT

To some extent, the phases of attention are a function of both specific and non-specific arousal; cognitive factors also contribute to them. We begin this section with a brief discussion of arousal and then suggest several more cognitive factors that interact with arousal to determine how long attention is sustained.

Arousal

Arousal, like attention, is a complex construct and there is no single definition (Vanderwolf & Robinson, 1981). Kahneman (1973) identifies at least two states of high arousal related to attention. One is a "pattern of motor inhibition" reflected in the slowing of heart rate as well as reduced activity. The other is the "standard pattern of generalized sympathetic dominance, which invariably occurs . . . [during] problem-solving" (p. 33) and involves an increase in heart rate. This latter pattern may be seen more readily after 1 year of age when the second, higher level system is operating. Although our focus is on the former state, both may be accompanied by decreases in heart rate variability (van Hover, 1974), a factor which would distinguish the latter type of arousal from emotional arousal. With both types of arousal described here, the individual is "more active and alert" (Kahneman, 1973, p. 33) than when at rest.

Because the heart rate component of the OR is one of the initial manifestations of an increase in arousal, we may ask whether stronger ORs, as manifested in larger decelerations, lead to longer visual attention. In infants, this appears to be the case, at least in some circumstances. Finlay and Ivinskis (1982) found that infants who were oriented to a central event had deeper decelerations when they turned to a fast-moving peripheral event than when they turned to a slow-moving peripheral event; it also took longer for the heart rate to return to baseline in the trial with the fast-moving event. Although looking after turning to the peripheral target was at a ceiling in both trials, the duration of heart rate deceleration (see Richards, 1988) suggests that active, focused attention was longer in the trials with the faster moving stimulus.

In general, Richards (1985, 1988, 1989) has found that the magnitude and duration of the heart rate deceleration increase from 14 to 26 weeks.

Repetition leads to both a diminution of the OR and to less sustained attention. Figure 6.5 is taken from a study by Lewis and Goldberg (1969), in which 3.5-year-old children were shown repeated trials of colored slides. Decreasing arousal as manifested in the heart rate decrement parallels changes in visual attention as measured by duration of looking.

There are other indications that arousal helps to maintain attention over time.

A. Mean Looking Time

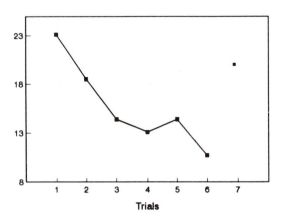

B. Mean Heart Rate Change (BPM)

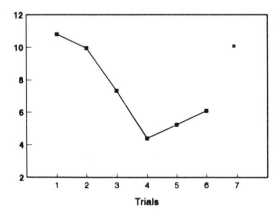

Figure 6.5. Parallel changes in heart rate and looking in 3.5-year-old children exposed to repeated patterns. The isolated dot represents the response to a novel event. From ''The acquisition and violation of expectancy: An experimental paradigm,'' by M. Lewis and S. Goldberg, 1969, *Journal of Experimental Child Psychology, 7*, p. 75. Copyright 1969 by Academic Press. Adapted with permission.

Several investigators, for example, have found that introducing a sound or changing it will cause infants to look more at a visual pattern (Colombo & Bundy, 1981, 1983; Horowitz, 1975). Lawson and Ruff (1984) found that a variety of both periodic and continuous sounds, including speech, facilitated visual tracking of moving objects. Visual following increased whether the sound remained spatially congruent with the moving object or was widely displaced from it, suggesting that sound had a general effect on arousal rather than a specific effect on localization. Similar effects are seen in older subjects (Berlyne, Borsa, Craw, Gelman, & Mandell 1965; Posner, 1978; Smothergill & Kraut, 1989).

Arousal interacts with learning to determine phases of attention. For example, we see the operation of both arousal and learning during habituation. As stimulus repetition decreases alertness, it also enhances the speed of acquiring information from the event (Posner & Boies, 1971; Smothergill & Kraut, 1989). In infant studies of habituation, both decrements in arousal and increases in speed of recognition would lead to a decline in the duration of looking over time. Learning about an event decreases the novelty of the event; as the novelty decreases, so does the event's alerting capacity.

The developmental decline in looking observed between 3 and 12 months of age (see figures 3.6 and 3.7) may be due to improvements in speed and efficiency of learning (Colombo & Mitchell, 1990). That this process continues for many years is suggested by Lewis et al. (1969), who report that the number of children whose looking declined within the number of trials presented increased monotonically from 3 to 44 months. The rate of habituation, calculated as the difference between total looking on the first and last trials adjusted for looking on the first trial, also increased. These developmental changes in speed of learning could be related to increases in neural transmission rates.

Cognitive Factors

As children develop the second system of attention, many cognitive factors may override habituation and contribute to sustained attention. We discuss three of these factors—comprehension, complexity of action, and a process known as attentional inertia.

Comprehension
With the development of symbolic function at 18 to 24 months and the increased knowledge that comes with experience, children are better able to understand events, including those accompanied by speech. For example, Anderson and Lorch (1983) argue that the television viewer brings certain expectations to a television program, and attention will be determined by the extent to which the viewer has "questions" that the program can "answer." If the program is completely predictable, attention will be lower than if the viewer has an incomplete but partial representation of the story line, which can be completed by watching closely to see what happens. Attention may be even lower if the viewer can make no sense whatever of the dialogue or action, as would be the case for a 3-year-old faced with a political analysis. Within a program, children pay most attention to those segments of a

program in which the dialogue refers to something concrete and present; presumably those segments are easiest for a young child to understand (Anderson & Lorch, 1983).

To test the hypothesis that comprehension actually leads to attention, Anderson, Lorch, Field, and Sanders (1981) controlled the comprehensibility of a television program independent of its formal features by: (1) scrambling the scenes in the program so that actions were hard to follow; (2) dubbing in the sound from a Greek *Sesame Street* program; and (3) dubbing the original dialogue backwards. As expected, 2-, 3.5-, and 5-year-old children looked less during distorted segments than during normal portions of the program. Anderson and Lorch (1983) conclude that children who play in front of a television set monitor the sounds of the program and look up when the sound track signals something visually interesting. Older children who understand more look up more often, and their total time looking at the television increases.

Complexity of Action

In the free-play setting, older children can engage in more complex activity as they develop; this ability in itself may lead to longer periods of sustained attention (Ruff & Lawson, 1990). One form of increased complexity results from gradually improved skills in combining objects and actions. Brownell (1988) defines combinatorial skills as "the [general] ability to produce integrated sequences of discrete behaviors" (p. 675). She found age-related improvements in such skills across the domains of language, pretend play, manipulative play with objects, social play with an adult, and motor activity. Children of 27 months combined more acts into longer sequences than did children of 20 months.

Case and Khanna (1981) found similar developments marked by an increase in the number of relations coordinated within tasks. Using block building as an example, building in one direction, as in constructing a tower, is simpler than building both vertically and horizontally. From her studies of early classification of objects, Sugarman (1982) concludes that children in the third year have developed the ability to consider two categories of objects at one time; younger children are limited to one. Similar increases in the number and variety of activities occur in symbolic play as it develops in the second and third years (Nicolich, 1977). At an early level of symbolic play, children may feed a doll; at a higher level, children may feed the doll, themselves, and their parents in succession; at a third and later level, children may feed the doll, wash it, cover it, and sing it to sleep. The results of all these studies give concrete form to the notion that children's activity increases in complexity. During play, children will sustain attention longer with age, in part because they are able to generate and carry out longer, more complex sequences of activity.

Attentional Inertia

Increasing comprehension and complexity of action are two cognitive factors that affect engagement and maintenance of attention, but are not themselves mechanisms of attention. Other cognitive factors may be more specific to attention. Attentional inertia has been defined by Anderson and colleagues (Anderson, Choi, & Lorch, 1987; Burns & Anderson, 1993) as a systematic change in visual attention over time;

specifically, the intensity of attention increases as a look continues, making it more likely that visual attention to a given source of information will continue even with a change or lapse in content or information. Anderson argues that attentional inertia is based on the individual's positive experience with a particular medium; this experience helps to maintain a focus on a source of information. For example, a child who has been listening intently to an adult tell a story may continue to attend to the adult even through pauses of a few seconds. The longer the child has been listening, the more likely that attention will be maintained, ensuring that the child is receptive to information when the adult resumes the story. Thus attentional inertia is a process that may override waning arousal if previous experience with the source has been sufficiently rewarding or adaptive.

This facilitative process may emerge after the first year. Mendelson (1983) reanalyzed data from his earlier studies of 4- and 7-month-olds. He concluded that, although the probabilities of continued looking followed the pattern described by Anderson, the pattern could be explained by artifacts that would not imply any process occurring within a look itself; thus, attentional inertia may not be operating at 4 and 7 months. Anderson and his colleagues (Anderson et al., 1987; Burns & Anderson, 1993) argue, however, that artifacts cannot account for attentional inertia observed in preschool children or adults where increasing length of looks is associated with decreased distraction and increased learning. Television programs represent more complex stimulation occurring over longer periods of time than the events used in the Mendelson studies; this difference may account for the discrepancy in findings and interpretation. Even so, we cannot rule out the possibility that attentional inertia may emerge or become stronger with age.

Attentional inertia is conceptually related to attention in situations where someone is waiting for an event to occur. In vigilance studies, for example, subjects will remain oriented to a screen although nothing is currently happening because they are expecting a visual event and are prepared to respond to it. Infants show this kind of attention when the expected events are potent enough (Ruff, Capozzoli et al., 1990), and such attention increases over the period from 2.5 to 4.5 years (Ruff, 1989). At all ages, however, there is a strong effect of content; children will remain oriented to a television screen longer when the expected events are colorful, lively, and complex than when the events are less salient. Thus, any changes with development may be due, at least in part, to changes in the extent to which events arouse and motivate children at different ages. The motivating properties of events in turn are related to the child's cognitive capacities.

MUTUAL INFLUENCES OF ATTENTION AND OTHER STATES

Even infants have some control over their arousal levels through selective attention. Infants' bodily comfort and internal activity will influence how much stimulation they can handle. A sated, well-rested infant is not subject to much internal stimulation and may be more inclined to attend to higher levels of visual stimulation than when hungry and tired. Gardner and Karmel (1983) found that internal and external sources of stimulation combined to determine whether newborns would prefer, in a paired comparison paradigm, to look at patterns of higher versus lower contour density or faster versus slower rates of flashing lights. They found that infants were more likely to look at more stimulating displays when they were fed and swaddled than when hungry and unswaddled. Thus, infants may orient to lower levels of visual stimulation at times when the overall amount of stimulation threatens to overwhelm them and orient to higher levels when arousal levels are low, thereby modulating their own states.

Looking toward and away from adults during social interactions occurs, in part, because of fluctuating arousal levels. Field (1981) and others have suggested that looking away is a result of an uncomfortably high arousal level, even when arousal is accompanied by indications of pleasure, such as smiling. Evidence for this is that heart rate tends to accelerate just before a look away and then decelerates (Field, 1981). Fogel's (1977) finding that his infant subject was most likely to re-initiate visual attention to the mother when she was quiet would be consistent with this interpretation of the look away. The potential for overarousal during face-to-face interaction, especially for very young infants, may be one reason why infants in the first 2 months do not readily establish eye contact (Keller & Gauda, 1987). Blass (1992) reports, however, that infants in the first 2 months will quiet and open their eyes when calmed by sugar. In such a state, the very young infant is capable of establishing eye contact if a face is available. After 2 months, sugar alone is not sufficient for the maintenance of the calm, alert state. When temporarily calmed by sugar, however, infants may actively search the environment, and eye contact at these times contributes to sustained calming (Blass, 1992).

The state of attention is incompatible with other states, such as emotional distress, making attention a potential influence in emotional control. The orienting response, for example, can influence the infant's level of emotional arousal by distracting the infant from distressing internal and external events. Infants after 2 months should be more easily soothed because the OR is more easily elicited. Posner and Rothbart (1981) report: "In our laboratory observations, we have noted than an orienting reaction may soothe the infant who has become distressed. As the infant's accelerating heart rate takes on a decelerating pattern in response to a new stimulus presentation, we see the infant's facial expression and body tension relaxing. Caretakers probably take advantage of this effect by presenting a distressed child with a distracting stimulus (e.g., an object or the caretaker's own voice or face)" (p. 38). Thus, it is not surprising that crying and other manifestations of distress markedly diminish over the first 6 months (Wolff, 1987; Rothbart, 1986) as the orienting response becomes well developed and there is more control over reactivity.

Under controlled laboratory conditions, Harman, Rothbart, and Posner (1995) observed that infants can be soothed by introducing distractors, such as small toys or attractive computer displays. They alternated 10-second periods of visual or visual/ auditory stimulation with periods of no stimulation for 3- to 4-month-olds who had become distressed. Infants were significantly less distressed during the presentation of distractors, although they tended to return to baseline distress levels during no stimulation. In a study with 3- and 6-month-olds, infants returned to the distressed state following distractions of 10, 30, and 60 seconds in length. Removing stimulation from nondistressed infants did not increase their distress levels, indicating that frustration at removal of the distractor is not likely to account for the finding. These studies suggest that an internal mechanism maintains the distress during distraction. Although the effect of short-term visual distractors may be temporary for young infants, development may bring with it the ability to use attention to promote more sustained changes in emotional state. Indeed, at older ages, ability to control attention has been found to be associated with lower levels of negative emotionality (Derryberry & Rothbart, 1988; Eisenberg et al., 1993; Rothbart & Ahadi, 1994). This is a topic we return to in chapter 10.

SUMMARY

Attention involves not only the selection of targets for cursory inspection or sustained engagement but also systemwide alterations that signal changes in state and level of engagement. Visual attention, along with these accompanying alterations, occurs in temporal phases. These phases generally include initiation, engagement, and disengagement. They can be distinguished by differences in behavior, such as distractibility, and by differences in physiological indicators, such as heart rate. Each phase shows developmental progress. In particular, children become engaged for longer periods in activities as they get older.

A number of processes work together to determine how long children will attend to different types of events and situations. Some of these processes are related to the properties of objects and events—how arousing they are initially and how familiar they become. Other processes are more cognitive in nature and appear to facilitate attention. After 1 year of age, decremental processes, such as habituation, are still operating, but they seem to be counteracted in situations where the potential for cognitive activity exists. At the same time, increasing cognitive capacities over the first few years lead to more complex activities that may simply demand more time to complete. The complexity of these activities helps to maintain a reasonably high level of engagement for longer periods as children develop. It is assumed that cognitively motivated episodes of sustained attention involve underlying physical changes (cf. Hughes & Hutt, 1979) and are related, in part, to arousal levels.

The incompatibility of the state of attention with states of high emotional arousal means that attention can sometimes be used to regulate emotional state. Children gradually learn that they can control their own levels of emotional arousal by directing and keeping attention away from events that are too exciting or distracting (see chapter 8).

7

Focused Visual Attention and Resistance to Distraction

Although it is not uncommon to separate the selective from the intensive or energetic aspects of attention (Berlyne, 1970; Hockey, Coles, & Gaillard, 1986), behavior is affected by both dimensions simultaneously. In reality, the two may be inseparable. In this chapter, selection and intensity are integrated through the concept of focused attention. First, we discuss the definition and conceptualization of focused attention. Second, we outline a framework for thinking about the development of focused attention. Third, we explore the implications of this framework for our understanding of infants' and children's ability to resist distraction and manage their attention in stimulating environments. Fourth, we raise the intriguing possibility that distracting conditions may sometimes serve to focus the attention of young children.

GENERAL CONCEPTUAL ISSUES

Focused attention is a term used by many investigators with varying operational definitions (Eriksen & St. James, 1986; Jonides, 1983; Posner, Cohen, Choate, Hockey, & Maylor, 1984). Theoretically, it refers to a state in which attention is directed more or less exclusively to one target or task and not divided or shared between targets or tasks. Our assumptions here are that, during focused visual attention: (1) selectivity becomes narrower and restricted to fewer elements; and (2) the degree of effort or energy directed at the target task is increased. These two assumptions underlie a hypothetical continuum that runs from casual, broadly deployed attention to highly concentrated attention.

How does attention become highly selective? How does the individual redistribute effort and resources toward one target and away from others? The answer seems to be the same for both of these questions. A motivating force needs to energize the system. In addition to this general facilitating process, however, inhibition seems to be essential (Houghton & Tipper, 1994). Because there are always multiple objects and events to respond to, highly focused attention to one object or event requires some blocking of responsiveness to others; otherwise, events that are not immediately relevant may interfere with effective action. Once this inhibition is operating, some redistribution of energy or resources toward the target activity may be inevitable.

Inhibitory processes can and do occur at many levels in the nervous system, and much discussion in the literature has centered around their influence on early versus late selection. In this framework, *early* refers to selectivity of input or perceptual information, *late* to selectivity of output or responses. Early visual selection, for example, occurs when the threshold for visual stimulation is reduced relative to other stimulation such as sounds. As noted before, when subjects are instructed to attend to visual events, responsiveness of the primary visual cortex is enhanced; at the same time, responsiveness in the auditory cortex is reduced (Näätänen and Michie, 1979). Spitzer, Desimone, and Moran (1988) have shown further that within the visual modality, cortical cells respond differently to the same objective stimulus depending on whether it is part of an easy or a difficult task. Such phenomena suggest higher level control over the responsiveness of cells early in the sequence of neural events leading to the behavioral response.

Late selection occurs when behavioral responses to a distracting event are inhibited after extensive analysis of the distractor, perhaps even after preliminary activation of response to the distractor. When response competition occurs, it can be inferred from several types of measures. One of these is longer choice reaction times and more errors when competing signals, as opposed to neutral signals, are in the periphery (Eriksen & St. James, 1986; Eriksen & Schultz, 1979). In a more direct test of response competition, Coles and Gratton (1986) asked subjects to hold a bulb in each hand and to squeeze the bulb in the right hand for one signal and the bulb in the left hand for another. Responses were defined as squeezes of more than 25% of maximum force; the force itself, however, could vary from 0 to 100%, reflecting different levels of response activation. This method allowed the investigators to measure muscle activity in both "correct" and "incorrect" hands, accuracy being defined by the target on a particular trial. The task was to respond to the letter at the fixation point (H or S); this letter was embedded either in an array of identical letters or in an array of competing letters (e.g., HHHHH or SSHSS where H is the target). The investigators monitored the initiation of hand movement with electromyographic recordings. Inhibition of a competing response was inferred when there was some muscle activity in the incorrect hand, but no overt squeeze. Houghton and Tipper (1994) argue that late selection allows the individual to attend more broadly to the environment than early selection; it also confers an advantage because, if a currently irrelevant dimension, such as shape, becomes relevant with a shift in activity, some necessary information has already been acquired. Late selection may be essential in tasks where the distractors are difficult to discriminate from target.

Cowan (1988) argues for an intermediate level of selection where partial information about distractors as well as targets is obtained. Preliminary information then becomes the basis for selecting the dimensions relevant to the task and the appropriate response. Tipper (1992) has suggested that inhibition is a general and flexible process that adapts to different task demands and different goals. Because selective attention is so closely tied to goals and tasks, inhibition is limited to those characteristics of distracting objects that fall along stimulus dimensions pertinent to the current task. For example, if the color red is relevant in a search task, then responses to other colors must be inhibited, but if the goal is to reach for a particular object on a table containing several objects, inhibition may be attached only to those objects that are in the path of the reach (Tipper, Lortie, & Baylis, 1992). Thus, in this view, selective attention is a central process, a component of higher level control; it allows inhibition to transfer between different stimulus modalities (Tipper & Driver, 1988) and different types of responses (Tipper, MacQueen, & Brehaut, 1988).

Although inhibitory processes may be the mechanisms by which attention becomes focused or concentrated, what causes them to operate? It would be hard to overemphasize the importance of motivation in determining the circumstances in which attention becomes more selective and behavior more activated. Motivation is closely tied to emotional reactions to events and the need for adaptive action. Brain systems important in evaluating the biological significance of events communicate directly with those responsible for attention and action (LeDoux, 1989; Derryberry & Tucker, 1990). Even highly cognitive activity is still connected to primary emotions and motivations, which stem from activity of subcortical regions from which higher brain structures have evolved (Derryberry & Tucker, 1990; Tucker, 1991). The general and flexible inhibitory process just discussed may operate best when motivation is moderate. It seems likely that the higher the stakes for the individual, the more strongly relevant behaviors are activated and the more widespread the inhibition (Fentress, 1989).

Thus, attention is part of adaptive behavior, not only permitting the selective gathering of information from the environment but also serving as a basis for organized action. Focusing attention narrows the effective range of stimulation and the range of activity. There are costs attached to focusing attention; these may include metabolic costs (Porges, 1992), reduced ability to monitor what is going on in the environment outside the task (Landers, 1980), and reduced speed of response to events outside the current field of attention (Posner et al., 1984). Assuming that the more narrowly attention is focused, the higher the costs, focused attention would be of benefit only in situations demanding detailed perception and highly organized nonroutine action; it could be detrimental in other situations requiring global perception of the environment, simultaneous attention to two tasks, or flexible responding.

FRAMEWORK FOR DEVELOPMENT

With these general comments in mind, we turn to issues in the development of focused attention. Much of the work on focused attention in infants and young children has been conducted in the context of play with toys, although looking at pictures or television has provided another, potentially contrasting, context for observations. Focused visual attention has been behaviorally differentiated from more casual or dispersed engagement with toys (e.g., Ruff, 1986, 1988; Ruff & Lawson, 1990; Ruff et al., 1992). In this work, focused attention has quite different temporal parameters and is affected differentially by experimental manipulations. Figure 7.1 shows examples of focused attention in children from 7 months to 3 years.

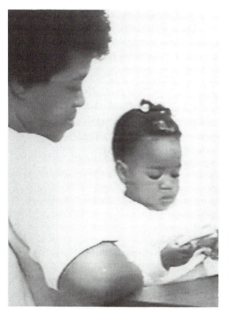

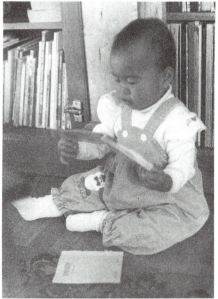

Figure 7.1. A 7-month-old, a 16-month-old, and a 3-year-old focusing attention on their respective activities. (Photographs by Holly Ruff, Merle Weiss, and Ruth Alliger.)

A striking aspect of focused attention during play in children is the extent to which concentration manifests itself in the same form despite marked changes over age in the nature of the activity. Whether we observe an infant absorbed in exploring an object, a toddler trying hard to put two Lego blocks together, or a 4-year-old concentrating on completing a puzzle, there is a characteristic downward cast of the eyes, a posture that seems to enclose the activity, a serious facial expression, and a quieting of motor activity extraneous to the task at hand. These behavioral manifestations suggest that children at all ages can be observed in a state of effortful attention quite different from that observed when they are relaxed and attention is more wide-ranging (see figure 7.2). As already noted, both activation and inhibition are likely to be involved in focused attention, but the nature of these opposing influences may change with development. In this sense, the similarity in appearance of focused attention at different ages does not mean an equivalence of underlying processes.

We suggest that the underlying processes change over the course of the first four or five years of life. Specifically, we propose that focused attention is supported by the orienting/investigative system in the first year of life and later, by the system of higher level control. Information in chapter 3 about underlying neural systems suggests that the two systems are anatomically and functionally separate and may mature at different rates; we expand on this information here as appropriate.

Orienting/Investigative System

The first system of attention underlies orienting to and exploration of objects in the environment and is composed of at least two networks involved in orienting to locations in space and object recognition, respectively (Ungerleider & Mishkin, 1982). Because it is important for our later discussion, we note that the orienting network may involve more than one type of orienting response. Foreman and Stevens (1987) describe one response as a short-loop, fast response and the second as a longer loop involving the frontal eye fields. The longer duration of the slower orienting response allows more environmental information to guide the motor response and may also involve an inhibition of the faster, reflexive response. Specifically, eye movements directed to targets in the environment may be controlled by the posterior network (Posner & Peterson, 1990) and the frontal eye fields (Johnson, 1990; Richards & Casey, 1992). When this network is engaged, reflexive eye movements to peripheral stimulation tend to be inhibited (Guitton, Buchtel, & Douglas, 1985).

The orienting/investigative system leads infants in the first year to be particularly responsive to novelty; however, novel objects that afford some direct action will elicit more responsiveness than novel objects out of reach. Thus, within the first attention system, selective and effortful attention is usually observed during exploratory manipulation of objects. Such periods of investigation can be considered a prolongation of the orienting response, sustained as long as the object retains some novelty and significance. When the alerting potential of the object wanes, the episode of attention is likely to be terminated, particularly if a novel event or object provides competition (Richards, 1988). Thus, the priority of novelty leads to an

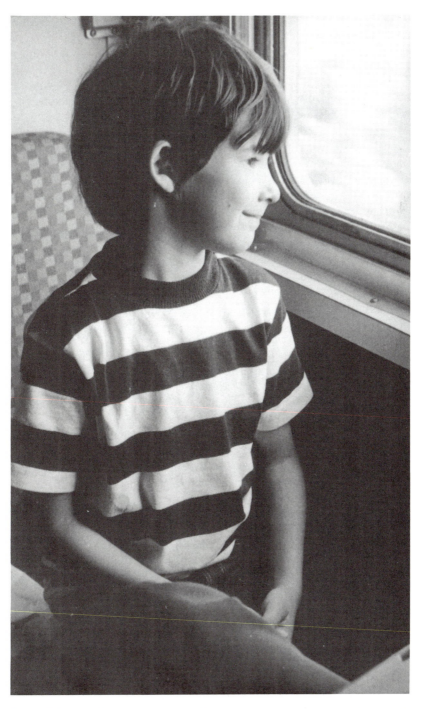

Figure 7.2. A child whose attention to the passing countryside seems relaxed and broadly deployed, ready to detect anything of interest. (Photograph by Myron Rothbart.)

"habituation bias" (Tucker & Williamson, 1984, p. 193), resulting in decrements of attention as exposure to objects and events is extended in time. Furthermore, habituation seems to be governed strongly by the physical attributes of objects and events, as opposed to semantic aspects (Cowan, 1988); these physical attributes include "biological importance, operant contingency, signal value, novelty, intensity, and unpredictability" (Waters & Wright, 1979, p. 111). Derryberry and Tucker (1990) suggest that the orienting system leads spatially to wide-ranging attention and temporally to "a short, present-centered attentional style" (p. 315).

Because attention systems are linked to both motivation and action, the nature of an individual's goals is a strong determinant of both attention and action. Jeannerod (1994) suggests that there are two levels of goals. At the lower level, associated with the orienting/investigative system, objects are goals. Although spatial location has a special status in the posterior orienting network, Jeannerod expands the function of this network to include actions on objects (cf. Mesulam, 1983). When objects are goals of particular actions, those attributes of objects important for the actions become salient. Important immediate goals for infants faced with interesting novel objects are grasping and manipulation. As infants respond quickly and attentively to novel objects, texture and shape appear to be more important than color and surface pattern in determining what actions an object affords (Ruff, 1982; see chapter 5).

System of Higher Level Control

The second attention system, supported by frontal structures and pathways, can be governed by language in the form of instructions from self or others and by information and expectations about future states (Posner & Rothbart, 1991). In this way, the system supports the formulation of plans, which then activate the appropriate behavior. This higher level system is connected to the orienting/investigative system, allowing lower level processes to be controlled more remotely by plans rather than by physical properties of the immediate environment (cf. Luria & Homskaya, 1970). Tucker and his colleagues (Tucker & Williamson, 1984; Derryberry & Tucker, 1990) suggest that this system, or something related, participates in focused, narrow attention with selection of a few elements among the many possible in the field. The system also supports preparation for action. According to the account by Tucker and his colleagues, the frontal attention system is important for integration of information over time and for anticipation and planning.

Likewise, Jeannerod's (1994) second level of goal specification as "long-term action planning" (p. 200) incorporates object-oriented actions into complex sequential activities occurring over longer periods of time. The goals involved are complex, and goal-related attention remains active until the goal is achieved. This second level of goals is clearly associated with the later-developing attention system.

Although there are a number of ways of conceptualizing the second attention system, a core feature is that it maintains sustained activity by facilitating and inhibiting the orienting/investigative system. On the one hand, orienting to irrelevant environmental events needs to be inhibited. On the other hand, habituation to the materials relevant to the task must be counteracted (Cowan, 1988). This second attention system supports "thinking about what you're doing" and is thus critical for completing components of a complex nonroutine activity in the proper sequence. Careful attention doesn't guarantee success, but even for routine activities, inattention leads to "slips of action" (Logan, 1988; Reason, 1984).

Development of Two Systems of Attention

In our review of developmental transitions in chapter 3, we cited evidence for the emergence and maturation of the orienting/investigative system within the first year of age. Within this system, periods of focused attention or examining tend to be relatively short and interspersed with other types of activity—mouthing, which may sometimes be investigative, and repetitive motor patterns, such as banging and waving. Because its development coincides with infants' strong responsivity to novel events (Graham et al., 1983), infants' focused attention is subject to habituation. At all ages between 5 and 12 months of age, focused attention is at its maximum when objects are novel and tends to disappear within 2 or 3 minutes of exposure to the same object (Ruff, 1986; Ruff et al., 1992).

The second system begins to emerge toward the end of the first year as the frontal cortex begins to contribute to the control of behavior, with further important changes occurring at 18 months and around 4 years. The maturation of this system provides a necessary substrate for the development of goal formulation and planning over the course of the next several years. To the extent that focused attention reflects the operation of this second system, it will be initiated and maintained by the child's planned actions toward a goal. The development of more highly articulated goals depends on both an increase in the complexity of cognitive and motor skills and an increase in self-regulatory skills, such as internalization of standards and self-monitoring (see chapter 8 for more detailed discussion). Thus, goals generally become more clearly defined throughout the preschool years. Perhaps in consequence, during the preschool years, episodes of focused attention become longer and appear with greater frequency and with shorter interruptions (Ruff & Lawson, 1990). Attention during play is no longer subject to habituation in the same way, probably because it is not tied so tightly to the physical properties of objects (see figure 7.3).

The time from 9 to 18 months of age represents a transition period as attention gradually comes under control of both systems rather than one. Changes in focused attention through the preschool years reflect the gradual ascendancy of the later-maturing system. The beginnings of the transition period may be marked by a decrease in the overall amount of time that children focus attention during independent play; children in this age range habituate more quickly to objects than do younger infants but are not yet capable of performing or planning for more complex activity. This possibility is somewhat speculative, however, and has not been studied systematically.

At the beginning of our developmental account, we noted a similarity in the appearance of focused attention from 6 months to 5 years. The similarity may stem from an equivalence of end-state in the attention of both infants and young children. Despite changes in the nature of the controlling mechanisms, focused attention in older children involves many of the same physiological and behavioral results—

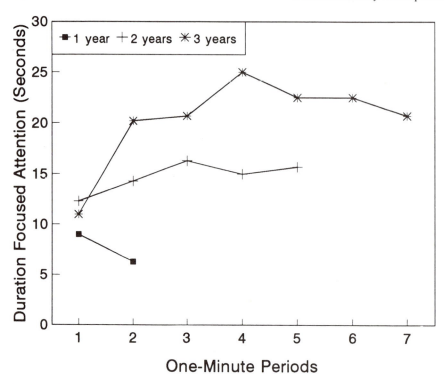

Figure 7.3. The duration of focused attention per minute of free play. From "Development of sustained, focused attention in young children during free play" by H. A. Ruff and K. R. Lawson, 1990, *Developmental Psychology, 26,* p. 89. Copyright 1990 by American Psychological Association. Adapted with permission.

lowered heart rate and inhibition of body motion—as the attention observed even in young infants (Richards, 1988; see chapter 6). Older children may assume the posture used in close inspection and manipulation of objects when engaged in activities that do not obviously benefit from such a posture. We observed one 5-year-old girl, for example, who started a fairly long pretend-play sequence by taking a doll, bringing it close to her eyes, and hunching over it while she talked through her pretend theme. The doll was apparently part of this scheme, but the girl's attention seemed to be concentrated on the story she was weaving and therefore was more internally than externally directed. Perhaps, the doll served as a way of narrowing her visual attention while she focused on her evolving theme.

IMPLICATIONS FOR DISTRACTIBILITY

Selective attention is critical to maintaining organized activity in the face of extraneous events or potential distractors. Whether a given event is a distractor depends on the individual's goals and skills as well as the demands of the situation. A systematic deployment of attention to two or more simultaneous events can occur under some circumstances. If two simultaneous activities remain organized and efficient, then one activity is not a distractor for the other. In our discussion here, we refer to situations in which it may be difficult to maintain an organized response to a target event because attention is attracted by extraneous events.

Given the presence of distractors, the more narrowly selective the attention and the more energized the target activity, the less likely distractors are to interfere with ongoing activity. This should be the case for the orienting/investigative system as well as the system of higher level controls. The orienting/investigative system is adaptive for exploration of the environment, and it thus facilitates orienting to the location of changes in the stream of stimulation. If attention is engaged via this system, distractors are effective to the extent that they compete or activate the same underlying processes. Thus, the organization of an infant's behavior is dependent on some objects and events in the environment being physically more salient than others. If an OR draws attention to an event in the first place and the OR is extended in time as the event is investigated, an OR to another event would most likely occur when the novelty of the original object wanes and the investigative impulse weakens. This appears to be what happens in studies of 3- to 9-month-old infants.

Richards (e.g., 1988), for example, has observed attention to televised events in 3- to 6-month-old infants; focused attention is indicated when extended slowing of heart rate accompanies looking. Richards has found that infants at all ages are less likely to turn and look at a peripheral event during the phase of focused or sustained attention than they are once their heart rates begin to accelerate back to baseline levels. If they do turn and look during the sustained attention phase, the latency to turn and look at the distractor is longer than during other phases. Presumably, when the heart rate begins to accelerate back to baseline, attention has already become less focused.

As we noted previously, graspability and manipulability give certain objects an edge for infants after 5 or 6 months of age because of infants' strong desire to act on objects within their reach. Oakes and Tellinghuisen (1994) and Saltarelli, Ruff, and Capozzoli (1990; Ruff & Saltarelli, 1993) have shown that infants can resist distractions when they are engaged in examining novel objects. On the assumption that examining is a behavioral manifestation of focused attention, infants would be expected to turn to a distractor less when their attention was focused on a toy during manipulative play than when they were only looking at the toy, without concentrated exploration. In a recent study (Ruff, Capozzoli, & Saltarelli, in press), 10-month-olds were presented with novel toys to play with and slides served as distractors; to look at a slide the infants had to turn approximately 90° to the right. The slides could be detected by peripheral vision, but the audible advance of the slide almost certainly contributed to distracting the infants from the toys. The interval between the slides was unpredictable, varying from 4 to 10 seconds. Focused and casual attention to the toys were coded independently of response to distractors.

As expected, the probability of a head turn was higher when the slides occurred during casual looking than when they occurred during focused looking (see figure 7.4A). When infants did turn their heads during focused attention, the time from the slide onset to the actual head turn was longer than during casual attention (see figure 7.4B). The study by Oakes and Tellinghuisen (1994) showed very similar results with somewhat different objects, distractors, and procedures, suggesting considerable generalizability of these phenomenon. In addition, the study reported here showed that, when the distractor interrupted focused, as opposed to casual, attention, the infants spent less time looking at the slides, and they were significantly more likely to return to focused attention within a second of turning away from the distractor (see figures 7.4C and 7.4D).

In these studies, a turn to look at the distractor suggests an interference with current attention to the toys and a disruption of play activity. At the same time, the relative lengthening of the latency to respond to the distractor during focused examining hints at an inhibitory process at work during focused attention.

Within the second attention system, the attention of toddlers and preschool children may be motivated by interest in more complex activity, but the same resistance to distraction should be observable during periods of high engagement. Using degree of distractibility to define level of engagement, Anderson et al. (1987) hypothesized that an uninterrupted look at television involves "progressive attentional engagement" (p. 800). Three- and 5-year-old children were shown a *Sesame Street* program; slides preceded by a sound were presented to the right on a variable

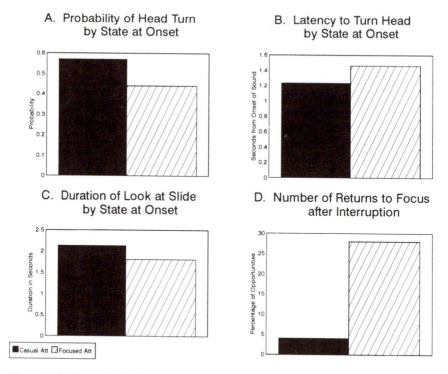

Figure 7.4. Four related effects of attentional state on responsiveness to distractors: (A) decreased probability to turning to look at distractor during focused attention; (B) increased latency to begin a head turn; (C) decreased look at the distractor; and (D) increased probability of returning immediately to focused attention on the target object. Based on Ruff, Capozzoli, and Saltarelli (in press).

schedule. Children at both ages were significantly more likely to be distracted by the slides during looks less than 15 seconds in duration (short) than looks of 15 seconds or more (long). Other work (Burns & Anderson, 1993) suggests that the short looks were not simply those truncated by a turn to the slide, because short looks are similar to early parts of long looks in the amount of information acquired; more information seems to be picked up during the latter part of long looks. In addition, when children were distracted during long looks, it took significantly longer to begin the head turn than during shorter looks. Choi and Anderson (1991) found essentially the same results in a study of 5-year-olds playing with toys. The results suggest that the degree of focus changes *within* looks at a television program and episodes of attention to toys. In turn, these changes may reflect an increase in the intensity or scope of inhibition.

Although these results demonstrate that children from 3 months on can resist distractors given the right conditions, they do not tell us much about developmental changes in distractibility. It is commonly stated that children become less distractible as they develop (Lane & Pearson, 1982), but that generalization does not begin to capture the complexity of the developmental picture we have presented here. We might predict that distractibility would be greater in infancy than in early childhood because the orienting/investigative system supports shorter episodes and habituation to the target, and thus, leaves the child more vulnerable to distraction. However, there has been so little developmental research on infants and preschool children in equivalent attentional states that we do not know whether infants, *given that their attention is focused,* are any more distractible than 5-year-olds. We can, however, reasonably predict that distractibility at all ages will be determined by the interplay of the child's motivation and internal state, the nature of the distractors, and the nature of the child's activity.

Conceptual Issues in the Study of Distractibility

Because there has been relatively little research on distractibility in infants and young children, we mention several principles that may be useful in the future study of the development of resistance to distraction. First, children should be observed in situations where their motivation is fairly high; otherwise, activation is low and there is little impetus for the necessary inhibition. Preschool children in experimental settings may not see the importance of the task posed for them, even if they understand the instructions. Thus, they may exert less effort than older children or adults who accept the experimenter's view of the situation. Tipper and McLaren (1990) also argue that children may show less selectivity and inhibition in unfamiliar conditions than they do in familiar ones. As we have already seen, during play with toys, even infants spontaneously provide evidence for selection and inhibition.

Second, different types of distractors may be effective for children at different developmental levels. Infants may be more vulnerable to distractors that are optimal for eliciting an orienting response. For this reason, infants can often be soothed by the presentation of novel objects and sounds (Harman et al., 1995). In contrast, older children may be more vulnerable to high-interest topics signaled by the semantic content of conversations or events around them—events that would leave infants unmoved. Thus, older children may be more readily soothed by distractors such as stories involving their names. In a later section, we elaborate on possible developmental changes in the nature of effective distractors.

Third, when children of different ages are being compared on performance in the same situation, they may differ in degree of distractibility because the situation offers varying degrees of challenge at different ages. Assuming the same level of motivation, younger children who find a task difficult may actually be less distractible than older children who find the task easy. That is, if responding to distractors does not interfere with the performance of older, more capable children, there is little reason to inhibit such responses. By the same token, in dual task situations, where children are asked to perform a primary and a secondary task at the same time, younger children who find the primary task more difficult may show more interference from the secondary task than do older children (Lane & Pearson, 1982).

With these caveats in mind, we explore possible mechanisms underlying focused attention and resistance to distraction in early development. We first discuss mechanisms that may be common at all ages and then consider mechanisms that may emerge only with the second attention system.

Common Mechanisms

We suggest that some inhibitory mechanisms are common to all developmental levels, at least after 6 months. Common mechanisms could include: (1) reduced responsiveness to peripheral stimulation, or peripheral narrowing; and (2) habituation.

Peripheral Narrowing

No matter which attention system is dominant, under most conditions of high motivation, an individual brings the desired or significant target into central vision. This action permits the acquisition of detailed information and the operation of centrally controlled mechanisms to prevent unwanted stimulation from interfering with the current activity. One possible mechanism is a specific inhibition of responsivity to peripheral stimulation, sometimes referred to as "peripheral narrowing" (Landers, 1980) or "tunnel vision" (Mackworth, 1965). In this context, focused attention is associated with central vision (Eriksen & Yeh, 1985; Eriksen & St. James, 1986), which can be narrowed to a visual angle of 1°.

If attention is limited to the location of a motivating event, then that location can be sampled with only the head and eye movements necessary to foveate the event. For young infants, this may mean focusing on a particular object in a particular place. For older children, head and eye movements during more complex activities may involve attending sequentially to more than one location, as a musician in an orchestra must read the music but also attend to the conductor and nearby musicians at the appropriate times. At all ages, casual or dispersed attention would be directed to an area as broad as eye and head movements would allow, with broad peripheral sensitivity within fixations and looks and few constraints by task demands.

What evidence is there for peripheral narrowing in infants and young children? A large literature on the development of central and peripheral vision in infants shows that sensitivity to peripheral stimulation generally increases in the first six months of life. Of interest here, however, are results of competition between peripheral and central targets for the child's attention. Harris and MacFarlane (1974) found that for both newborns and 2-month-olds, the effective visual field was smaller in the presence of a competing central event than in its absence; when the central event was present, infants at both ages moved their eyes only 15 to 16° toward bright contours in the near periphery; when the central event was removed as the peripheral event was presented, the infants were responsive to events as far as 26 to 36°. MacFarlane, Harris, and Barnes (1976) confirmed these results and showed that, in infants between 1 and 2 months, sucking may narrow the effective visual field as well. De Schonen et al. (1978) presented stationary central targets (red and yellow pompoms) and moving peripheral targets (also pompoms) to infants from 2 to 5 months. They found a continued expansion of the effective visual field through that age range; in the 2- and 3-month-old infants, however, there was also a greater contraction of the field when the central stimulus was near, and presumably more attractive, than when it was far, even though retinal size was equated.

If young infants, in particular, are "captured" by central events, then it may be difficult to test the full extent of their peripheral acuity (Mayer & Fulton, 1993). Maurer and Lewis (1991) argue that the presence of a salient central event reduces orienting to peripheral events without reducing peripheral acuity. Thus, visual attention involves central mechanisms that control focal and peripheral responsivity (Richards, 1991; Richards & Casey, 1992). Eye movements to peripheral events are controlled, in part, by a pathway involving the superior colliculus; this pathway is inhibited during focal attention, which is controlled by pathways involving the frontal eye fields. Johnson (1990; Johnson et al., 1991) suggests that these latter pathways develop around 4 months of age, making inhibition of reflexive eye movements more efficient (see also Richards, 1991).

Finlay and Ivinskis (1984) found that 4-month-old infants, presented simultaneously with central and peripheral targets, sometimes showed heart rate responses to peripheral stimulation even when they did not turn to the peripheral target. The heart rate responses during these trials were larger than during trials with only the central target, but smaller than during trials where the infants turned to the peripheral target. These results are open to other interpretations and need to be replicated. Further work along these lines would help to determine whether and when infants can detect targets but inhibit behavioral responses at the same time.

Preliminary results from Richards's laboratory (Richards, personal communication) are also intriguing. During the focused or sustained phase of attention, as defined by heart rate, 6-month-olds show distorted eye movements when they look toward the periphery; in contrast, during attention termination, they make normal eye movements to the periphery. These data in conjunction with those from Finlay and Ivinskis (1984) suggest an inhibitory process operating by 4 months at the level of motor responses. Further research using different types of central and peripheral targets would help to separate developmental changes due to increased speed of disengagement and changes due to increased efficiency of inhibition during central engagement.

Very little research on older children is relevant to this issue. Once the inhibitory interaction between eye movements directed by attention and more reflexive eye movements to the periphery matures in the first year, it should continue to operate as children develop. In addition, the mechanism of peripheral narrowing might operate no matter what the source of motivation or the nature of the particular activity, but it would be associated only with more intense motivation and higher levels of engagement.

Habituation

Habituation is another inhibitory process affecting responsiveness to distractors (Waters & Wright, 1979); it occurs simply with the repetition of events and may be effective even in situations where motivation is not particularly strong. Behaviorally, habituation refers to the decrease in responsiveness that occurs when an object becomes familiar or a signal is repeated. Habituation proceeds more rapidly to simple than to complex events. It occurs across all ages, but tends to progress more quickly with age (Lewis et al., 1969).

Habituation plays an important role in preventing irrelevant events from disrupting current activity. One way of demonstrating this is to compare subjects who have been exposed to the distractors before the primary task with those for whom the distractors are novel. Both adults (Waters & Wright, 1979) and school-age children (Lorch & Horn, 1986) perform better on cognitive tasks with pre-exposure, presumably because they have had an opportunity to habituate to the distractors.

Without some habituation, it seems to be difficult not to orient to irrelevant stimulation (Waters & Wright, 1979). Thus, habituation to distractors supports maintenance of attention to the target and helps keep attention from being pulled rapidly from one event to another in a busy environment. Because the attention of infants in the first year is so bound by novelty and habituation, infants' span of focused attention is likely to be short because they habituate to all events, whether defined as targets or distractors. On the other hand, habituation to the target object allows attention to shift, but this effect may not be so important in older children who can focus and shift attention more deliberately.

Despite an expected increase in rate of habituation with development, habituation may have a more marked effect on resistance to distraction in younger than in older subjects. For example, studies by Lorch and Horn (1986) and by Tipper, Borque, Anderson, and Brehaut (1989) suggest that younger school-age children benefit proportionately more from pre-exposure to distractors than do older children and adults; a marked difference in procedures in the two studies underscores the potential generality of this trend with age. It would be of great interest to know whether such a trend would be observed during the first five years.

Habituation involves inhibition of previously elicited responsiveness, but the inhibition involved is involuntary because it does not require any effort and is thought to occur with repetition regardless of the individual's goals. In this sense, it is a passive process. With the development of the second attention system, however, the buildup of inhibition caused by repetition may be overridden by voluntarily attributing significance to the habituated event (Luria & Homskaya, 1970; Cowan,

1988). Thus, it becomes possible to focus on events that have little inherent power to attract and hold attention.

Summary

From a very early age, focused attention is linked to and dependent upon inhibitory processes as well as facilitative processes, such as arousal. Habituation, though important at all ages, may be relatively more important in infants and very young children because other, more active forms of inhibition are unavailable to them.

Developmental Changes in Mechanisms

In this section, we discuss a number of potentially important developmental changes in distractibility that reflect the operation of one attention system in the first year and two systems thereafter. One is that location as a means of discriminating between distractors and targets becomes less important with age. Another is that, with age, children are able to inhibit responses that are partially activated, and in consequence, are better able to manage competition among responses. A third is that the complex activity of the older child, especially in spontaneous play, may be less vulnerable to interruptions because of the child's goals and plans.

Environmental versus Embedded Distractors

Because the orienting/investigative system helps to direct and maintain attention to spatial locations of novel or significant objects, infants may find it relatively easy to resist distractions in locations other than the one they are focusing on, but more difficult to ignore distractors occurring in the same location. Much of the work on distractibility in children concerns distractors embedded in the task—that is, centrally located or in the near periphery. When the distractor is located some distance away, the discrimination between the distractors and the relevant features of the situation is easy. Under these conditions, restriction of attention to the central field and inhibition of eye movements to peripheral stimulation could also operate to prevent distraction. In contrast, the nearer the distractors are to the central field, the more difficult they are to discriminate from target items on the basis of location and the greater the probability that they will be responded to with attention-directed, nonreflexive eye movements.

Humphrey (1982) showed that the type of distractor interacted with both age and the complexity of the task. She used recognition and recall tasks, with recall considered to be more demanding, and three kinds of distractors—environmental (a mirror), simple embedded (irrelevant elements within the task could easily be discriminated from relevant ones), and complex embedded distractors (irrelevant and relevant elements were harder to discriminate). The mirror was external to the task and was spatially separated from it, while the embedded distractors occupied the same general space as the task-relevant features. The children served as their own controls by being tested under both nondistraction and distraction conditions. Humphrey found disruption of performance in 4-year-olds for both simple and complex tasks under all conditions of distraction. The performance of kindergartners was disrupted only by the embedded distractors, the performance of second graders only by embedded distractors on the complex task, and the performance of fourth graders not at all. These results suggest a systematic change in distractibility with age, with younger children managing more distant, highly discriminable distractors earlier than closer, less discriminable ones.

In most research on distraction in infants and preschool children, only external distractors have been used. There are, however, a few direct investigations of the effect of embedded distractors on infants and toddlers. Bahrick, Walker, and Neisser (1981) presented infant subjects with two filmed events superimposed on each other. Their previous work had demonstrated that adults could readily attend to one event and ignore the other. Four-month-olds also seemed to be able to detect and attend to one of the events and attend less to the superimposed one. The method used was ingenious and requires some explanation. Infants were presented with two superimposed films (e.g., two people playing a clapping game and another person moving a slinky between two hands) while the soundtrack from one film was played. The reasoning, based on previous work (Spelke, 1976), was that infants would attend selectively to the actions that matched the soundtrack. The films were periodically separated and projected side by side without sound; the question was whether infants would look longer at the "novel" action. This indeed was what happened. The infants apparently became familiar, during the presentation of superimposed films, with the event for which there was a matching soundtrack; they then preferred the event they had not been following before. The proportion of first looks directed to the novel film in the paired tests was 0.66—virtually identical to the proportion shown in a previous study presenting only one film and soundtrack during familiarization. Because the paradigm was successful with such young infants, the results do not imply much development in selectivity or resistance to distractors in the same location.

Another possible form of embedded distraction, however, is to present multiple rather than single objects for manipulation and play. When a child is playing with one toy in a confined space, other toys occupy approximately the same spatial location and are readily detectable by peripheral vision. In a study of 12-month-olds (Ruff & Lawson, 1990), total duration of focused attention was longer with a single object than with many objects present. The difference between the two conditions was seen in mean duration of focused attention episodes (6.2 seconds versus 3.3 seconds) but not in the number of episodes of focused attention (3.9 versus 3.6). The assumption that the infants were distracted from one toy by another is bolstered by the high degree of overall attention to the toys as a group. The infants spent more overall time oriented to the multiple objects than to the single objects (85% versus 69%). Thus, the presence of several toys specifically interfered with focused attention rather than with general orientation to the toys.

Duration of attention to particular toys and activities, even with many toys to choose from, increases throughout the preschool years, perhaps because children are less distracted by currently irrelevant toys. These results and our explanation suggest a decrease in distractibility over age, while those of Bahrick et al. (1981) do not. The discrepancy may be related to the very different demands of the two situations. In the Bahrick study, the different visual rhythms of the superimposed events, along with the auditory accompaniment to one of them, may have led to easy discriminability of the two events. Perhaps more important, there would have been no strong response competition, as there is for 12-month-olds exposed to several interesting toys within reach.

Management of Response Competition

Infants in the first year of life may have only limited types of inhibition available and thus limited means of preventing interference from distractors. When the second attention system is engaged to meet nonimmediate goals, additional inhibitory mechanisms may serve to narrow selectivity and increase effort. The flexible system of inhibition described earlier (Tipper, 1992) permits individuals to selectively attend to the aspects of the situation relevant for current goals and to selectively inhibit aspects of the situation that may interfere with achieving those goals. Thus, it is likely that this process operates well only after the first year or two. In addition, inhibition of activated motor responses becomes increasingly possible throughout the preschool years (e.g., Reed et al., 1984; see chapter 8). When older children have selected an object for focused attention, actions toward objects in nearby but irrelevant locations may be inhibited even though information about properties of objects in those locations is acquired.

Vulnerability to Interruption

The essence of the second attention system is the ability to attend to distant goals and block interfering responses to keep attention and action directed toward reaching those goals. The extent to which activity is goal-directed during play is a relative matter, with younger children formulating plans much more loosely and opportunistically than older children. Younger children's goals emerge from their play; they often spend relatively long periods perusing the available toys before focusing attention on a particular activity. Even then, children's plans are often dependent on the constraints placed by the materials themselves. For example, although nesting barrels may be used creatively, the relationship among the barrels presents a strong demand to reassemble them in order. Whatever the source, goals help the child sustain attention and act appropriately, even if attention is not always highly focused. As a result, not all interruptions of focused attention necessarily disrupt children's activities. For preschool children, compared to infants, interruptions may be tolerable because children can keep their goals in mind and because the materials remind them where they were when they return.

Summary

Preventing interference and maintaining organization of behavior is important at all ages. We suggest that inhibitory mechanisms are essential, but that the specific mechanisms may change with both age and task.

CAN DISTRACTORS HELP PERFORMANCE?

Most of the work with distractors has been designed to look at interference from stimulation irrelevant to the current task. Yet there are circumstances when the intended distractors actually seem to facilitate performance. We first illustrate this with a remarkable example from the adult literature. In an early study, Morgan (1916) asked adults to perform a precursor of the continuous performance task under two conditions—relative quiet and noise. In the noisy condition, he bombarded subjects with sounds, such as hammers hitting metal beams and a fire gong sounding only 8 feet away! He found, first, that subjects had *faster* reaction times at the end of noise trials than during quiet trials, even though noise was initially disruptive. Second, he found his subjects pushing the response keys with greater force and talking to themselves more, both indications of greater physical and cognitive effort. A later study by Hockey (1970) suggests that noise may narrow the effective visual field.

Studies with preschool and school-age children show that distractors can be facilitative for them as well. Furthermore, the effects may increase with age. Investigating the effects of environmental distractors on performance in discrimination learning tasks, Turnure (1970) found that 3.5- to 5-year-old children exposed to the sound of typing or a record of children's songs made fewer errors than children without the distractors. Of the children who reached the criterion for learning, the distraction subjects reached criterion in an average of 13 trials, while the control group did so in an average of 24 trials. When the duration of time spent looking away from the task was corrected for the number of trials to criterion, the children in the distraction condition looked away less than the control group. A smaller group of children at 3 years, 3 months did not show this enhancement effect and glanced away from the task more than control children. The number was small, however, and it is hard to know whether their failure to resist distraction was an effect of age or of sampling.

In a more recent study, Higgins and Turnure (1984) varied both noise level and task difficulty and found that any level of noise disrupted the performance of preschoolers on both easy and difficult visual discrimination tasks. The performance of sixth graders, in contrast, was better on both tasks at both levels of noise compared to quiet. The number of times the child glanced away before reaching criterion was higher in noise for the preschoolers, but lower for the sixth graders, suggesting that the older children were inhibiting irrelevant responses more efficiently. In a study of children from 4 to 9 years of age, Humphrey (1982) found similar results using a large mirror next to the task as a distractor, suggesting that the effect is not limited to auditory distraction.

The evidence from these developmental studies, though not entirely consistent, suggests that distractors are more disruptive of performance in younger than in older children. As already noted, however, preschool children may be less likely than school-age children to be motivated by experimenter-defined tasks. Perhaps when they are attending spontaneously in play or other activities they would show the same narrow focus and expenditure of effort and would inhibit their responses to distractors.

Suggestive evidence for such a possibility comes from observations of both infants (Ruff, Capozzoli, and Saltarelli, in press) and preschoolers (Ruff, 1992) exposed periodically to auditory/visual distractors (slides with an audible sound when advanced) during their play with objects. Ten-month-old infants were given one object at a time for manipulative play; 3.5-year-olds were presented with a set of toys. At both ages, focused attention was distinguished from casual visual attention to the toys. Infants and children in the distraction condition were compared to groups presented with the same toys to play with but no experimental distractors. The subjects exposed to the distractor slides actually focused their attention *more* than the control subjects (see figures 7.5 and 7.6).

The difference between the distraction and the control conditions is particularly striking when overall amount of looking at the objects is compared. The control groups at both ages spent more total time oriented to the toys. Thus, when focused attention is considered as a proportion of looking time, the difference between the distraction and the control groups is even stronger. At 10 months, the proportion of focused attention is 40% of looking time for the distraction conditions and 28% for the control condition. The equivalent values for the 3.5-year-olds is 35% versus 28%, though the gap increases with time so that the difference is 52% versus 31% in the last 2 minutes of play.

One possible explanation is that the distractors, particularly the auditory component, raise the general arousal level of the child, increasing the probability that the children will show focused attention. Such a mechanism might underlie the report

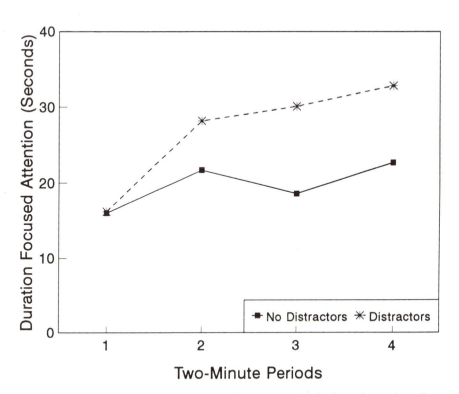

Figure 7.5. The duration of 10-month-olds' focused attention in distraction and nondistraction conditions. Based on Ruff, Capozzoli, and Saltarelli (in press).

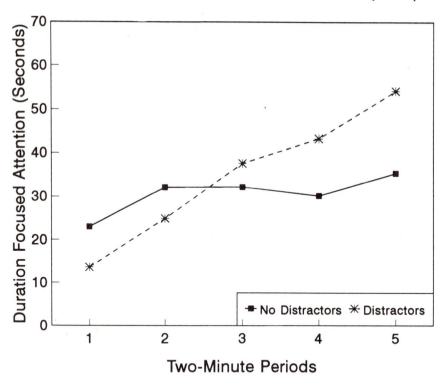

Figure 7.6. The duration of 3.5-year-olds' focused attention in distraction and nondistraction conditions. Taken from Ruff, 1992.

that some individuals have a hard time concentrating without some background noise, such as the radio. A radio provides highly variable input, but the distractors in these studies were more repetitious. Thus, the alerting function of the distractors would be expected to diminish with increasing exposure (Smothergill & Kraut, 1989). According to an arousal explanation, however, this reduction in alerting potential should lead to a decrease in focused attention, which is contrary to the results shown in figures 7.5 and 7.6.

Another plausible mechanism might involve habituation to the distractor, since turning to the distractor declined significantly over the session for both age groups. Habituation may reduce the arousal potential of these objects and therefore the degree of interference. It would not, however, explain why children in the distractor group actually showed more focused attention than the nondistraction group. However, if habituation moderated the salience of the distractors, they may have then activated ongoing behavior rather than disrupting it (Fentress, 1989).

If we assume that individuals generally seek to maintain some level of organization, narrowing the focus of attention and increasing the effort devoted to a particular object or task may actually constitute a defense against too much stimulation. Easterbrook (1959) proposed that arousal, whatever its source, decreases the range of information attended to. Increased arousal may thus improve performance if irrelevant aspects of the situation are ignored; if arousal is too high, however, performance would be expected to suffer because information important to the task is also ignored. Stress may lead to arousal and therefore to peripheral narrowing. Studies consistent with this hypothesis suggest that several different arousers and stressors, including noise (Hockey, 1970), heat (Bursill, 1958), and incentives (Davies & Jones, 1975), can contribute to a redistribution of effort and selectivity away from the peripheral visual field and toward the center.

SUMMARY

An important functional aspect of attention is the ability to become narrowly selective when necessary or appropriate and to redirect energy and resources to the selected activity. In this chapter, we defined this ability as focused attention and outlined a conceptual framework in which motivation and inhibitory processes were central. We argued that mechanisms for both early perceptual selectivity and later inhibition of competing responses are necessary for understanding focused attention. We cited examples of a flexible process of inhibition that can be considered a higher level function.

Next, we considered the development of focused attention, which can be observed in infants as well as older children with both behavioral and physiological measures. We suggested, however, that the processes underlying focused attention change with age as first one, and then two, attention systems become available. Some of the processes supporting focused attention seem to be available by 6 months of age, or even earlier. Focused attention in the first year, when the orienting/ investigative system is operating, is observed most often during exploratory activity. It is engaged rapidly when the infant encounters something novel, but it also habituates rapidly. The higher level processes critical for the more voluntary control of attention, however, begin to emerge at the end of the first year. These take a giant step forward at 18 months and continue to develop throughout the preschool years, leading to longer and more complex actions guided by plans and goal-oriented attention. Thus, focused attention is no longer as subject to habituation and can be sustained for long periods, if necessary for the completion of planned sequences of activity. Although there should be many commonalities in the underlying state in both infants and children, the route to achieving that state is likely to be quite different.

The development of two attention systems has important implications for the child's ability to resist distraction. Even infants can resist distractors that compete for their attention and responsiveness, but they are more likely to do so if the distractors are in the periphery of the visual field and if they have habituated to the distracting events. With the development of the second system, children become more flexible in inhibiting responses to distractors and can begin to manage response competition even when extraneous stimulation is present in the central visual field.

Finally, we reviewed evidence for a facilitating effect of distractors on focused attention under some conditions. Studies of both adults and children suggest that distractors, such as noise, may increase attention to a task and improve performance.

We also presented evidence for a similar effect during infants' and preschool children's play with toys. Although speculative, we suggested that noise and other stressors may increase visual focused attention by narrowing sensitivity and responsivity to events in the peripheral visual field. The current research findings hint that this effect becomes stronger with age, perhaps because the second attention system allows more deliberate deployment of focused attention. In our next chapter, we explore further the development of this later system and demonstrate its dependence on contributions from the social environment.

8

Increasing Independence in the Control of Attention

In the previous chapters, we have described the development of many dimensions of attention. We have emphasized underlying physiological and cognitive mechanisms related to changes in selectivity and capacity for concentration. Still to be considered are important experiential and social influences on the development of attention, particularly higher level control. In this chapter, we chart the shift in the balance from dependence on external control for regulation of attention to more independent control. Many elements of this shift occur during the preschool years and are closely tied to the child's experience with adults and to increasing awareness of self and of social standards.

A number of recent reviews have dealt with the general issue of self-regulation (Kopp, 1982, 1991; Patterson, 1982; Rothbart, 1989c). Kopp (1982, pp. 199–200) writes:

Self-regulation, a complex construct, has been variously defined as the ability to comply with a request, to initiate and cease activities according to situational demands, to modulate the intensity, frequency, and duration of verbal and motor acts in social and educational settings, to postpone acting upon a desired object or goal, and to generate socially approved behavior in the absence of external monitors. . . . self-regulation demands awareness of socially approved behaviors and thus represents a significant aspect of the socialization of children.

In this chapter, we stress the implications of developing self-regulation for control of attention. The chapter has two major sections. The first deals with the ways that parents and other adults help to regulate infants' state and attention during face-to-face interactions and during shared attention to objects. We also consider larger cultural influences on attention. The second section documents the developmental shift from more external to more internal control of attention. Important processes in this shift include increasing awareness of standards relating to attention, increasing awareness of factors affecting attention, changing motivations, and the growth of skills related to voluntary attention.

ADULT AS REGULATOR

Although children's ability to regulate their own states contributes to attentional control at all ages, young children would not acquire many of the skills necessary for self-regulation of attention without attachment to and interaction with the more experienced members of their communities. In what ways do adults contribute to children's growing ability to regulate themselves?

The Role of the Parent in State Control

Modulation of reactivity and arousal level is an important aspect of attentional control. When infants are too aroused by stimulation, they may withdraw from it by turning away, closing their eyes, or crying until an adult removes them from the source of distress, provides a pacifier, or otherwise adjusts the situation. Adults may anticipate circumstances where particular infants would have difficulty and avoid those situations whenever possible.

Adults may also stimulate a sleepy baby to keep its attention engaged with events in the outside world. Korner and Grobstein (1966; see also Frederickson & Brown, 1975; Gregg, Hafner, & Korner, 1976) observed that the alertness of infants younger than 2 to 3 months depends on their posture; infants are particularly alert when held upright against the adult's shoulder, perhaps because of vestibular stimulation. Talking and vocalizing to infants can also arouse them from sleepiness to quiet wakefulness. Although there may be no optimal amount of time for an infant to spend in an alert state, the infant who is alert for long periods of time will have different early experiences from the infant who is sleepy most of the time. Adamson and Bakeman (1991) argue that the later shared attention of child and others stems, in part, from early periods of shared alertness (see figure 8.1). They suggest that an alert infant who experiences pauses between sucking bouts during feeding—pauses in which the mother talks to the infant or moves it rhythmically—may also experience a rudimentary form of "turn-taking" that will later develop into an important aspect of social interaction and communication.

From 2 months on, infants are capable of shared attention with partners, first in extended periods of face-to-face play and later in joint play with objects. During face-to-face play, mothers are likely to spend most available time looking at their infants (Fogel, 1977; Stern, 1974). The observed cycles in these interactions thus stem from the infant's patterns of looking toward and away from the mother's face. The behavior of the adult partner, however, has an important influence on the proportion of time the infant spends either attending to or avoiding the adult face.

Field (1979, 1981; see also Symons & Moran, 1987) manipulated mothers' activity by instructing them to interact normally or to simply imitate their 3-month-old infants' facial expressions. Field also included two conditions with a Raggedy Ann doll, one in which the doll was suspended and still in front of the infant and another in which the doll's head nodded and "talked" via a recording. Infants' looking in the four conditions, from the lowest to highest amount, was ordered as follows: the spontaneous interaction between mother and infant; the mother imitating; the animated doll; and the quiet doll. In addition, the mean change in heart rate

Figure 8.1. The development of shared attention from early mutual looking to joint attention to objects with adults and peers. (Photographs by Mary and Myron Rothbart, Merle Weiss, and James Antczak.)

from baseline to the 3-minute periods for each event showed an acceleration during the spontaneous interaction (+3 beats per minute), small decelerations during the mother's imitation and presentation of the animated doll (-1 to -2 beats per minute), and a larger deceleration during presentation of the still doll (-5 beats per minute). Figure 8.2 presents these results graphically. Field (1981) interprets the results in terms of emotional arousal, with visual attention shorter and less likely in conditions

A. Percent Time Looking

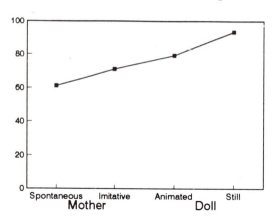

B. Heart Rate Change (BPM)

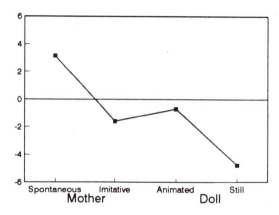

Figure 8.2. Mean durations of looking and changes in heart rate according to the type of interaction. The data here are for the full-terms from the original study. From ''Infant arousal and affect during early interactions,'' by T. Field, 1981, *Advances in infancy research, 1,* p. 68. Copyright 1981 by Ablex. Adapted with permission.

of high arousal. A mother's activity may therefore enhance or interfere with her infant's attention during social interaction.

In a more fine-grained analysis of a single mother-son pair observed several times between 6 and 13 weeks, Fogel (1977) noted that the mother's visual attention to her infant son was steady, while the infant's visual attention cycled through many episodes of attention and withdrawal. In this way, the mother was prepared to interact and share attention whenever the infant was (see also Stern, 1974). The mother addressed her infant with exaggerated mouth movements, nodding, and vocalizing. Onsets and offsets of these activities were just as likely to occur when the infant was looking away as when he was looking at his mother, possibly reflecting the mother's attempts to get the infant's attention back again. Although the infant was most likely to look back at his mother when she was still and quiet, the duration of her activities was longer when the infant was looking, suggesting that they were used to sustain the infant's attention.

Although our emphasis and that of many studies is on the influence of the mother's face and voice on arousal and attention, other modalities are also important, particularly in this early period. A mother's neutral or expressionless face when looking at the infant leads to less looking at the mother and often to distress (Gusella, Muir, & Tronick, 1988). Stack and Muir (1992) found, however, that mothers' touching of their 5-month-old infants maintained both the infants' visual attention and their smiling, despite the neutral face. These results indicate the importance of multimodal information from the mother in visual attention during early social play.

Shared Attention to Objects

Later in the first year, when shared attention between mothers and infants often occurs in the context of play with objects (Adamson & Bakeman, 1991), the adult can play several roles—stimulating, directing or teaching, and inhibiting the child's action. As in earlier face-to-face interaction, adults may stimulate the child's interest in a particular toy or activity or calm the overaroused child so that its attention can be focused more effectively. Thus, whether the mother seeks to lower arousal level or to raise it will be related to the context and to the age and temperament of the child.

The effect of stimulation was assessed in a study by Parrinello and Ruff (1988). Level of adult stimulation was manipulated by varying loudness and frequency of vocalization, frequency and speed of demonstrating action on the toy, and distance from the infant. A moderate level of stimulation raised the level of focused attention as well as the expression of positive affect in 10-month-olds during play with objects. The effect was particularly strong for children who had shown relatively little focused attention when they played independently. The moderate level of stimulation seemed to increase the *number* of episodes of attention but had less effect on the *duration* of attention. This pattern of results suggests that an adult can be effective in redirecting or refocusing infants' attention when it flags by raising arousal level. The equal effectiveness of a noisy toy further supports such a possibility.

In addition to alerting the infant at appropriate moments, adults' activity may convey information to the infant and thereby enrich the infant's experience. Demonstrating how to manipulate an object and produce an effect is a technique used frequently by parents in a teaching role (Bornstein, 1985b; Lawson, Parrinello, & Ruff, 1992). The ability of infants and young children to learn by observation and to imitate actions makes this technique useful in expanding the child's repertoire of behaviors and in influencing attention to objects. Infants manipulate objects more in specific ways, such as fingering, when adults are demonstrating such actions for them than when they play alone with objects (Lockman & McHale, 1989).

The nature of intervention by parents is important, however, because many parental activities with toys can limit the child's opportunity to act on those same toys. Lawson et al. (1992) found maternal demonstrations to be related to increases in infants' looking at the toys; thus, demonstrating could reasonably be said to increase attention. Demonstrations, however, were also related to *decreases* in infants' active exploration of the objects. In contrast, the mother's pausing and holding the object after a single demonstration was related positively to the amount of active exploration or focused attention and not to the duration of looking, underscoring the importance of leaving room for the infants' own activity. Thus, parents and other adults may encourage different types and levels of attention. A number of activities are effective in getting the infant to watch the adult, but other kinds of activities, or the lack of them, may be important for encouraging more active and focused attention.

Adults may also influence the attention and activity of children by providing constraints. Lawson et al. (1992) found, for example, that the more mothers physically restricted the movement of their 12-month-old infants sitting on their laps, the greater the level of the infants' attention to the toys. This effect may have a straightforward explanation; when a child is physically prevented from engaging in responses or activities incompatible with close attention to the objects, focused attention is more likely to occur. The mere presence of a parent or other adult in the same room may also lead to more mature activity in a child without any interaction with or intervention from the adult (Labrell & Simeoni, 1992). The presence of adults may be arousing, may remind young children of activities in earlier interactions, or may encourage children to inhibit competing activity more efficiently than when they are on their own. Although this possibility has not been systematically investigated in a developmental framework, Draeger, Prior, and Sanson (1986) found the performance of school-age hyperactive children on a continuous performance task to be improved by the experimenter's presence. When the adult was absent, the hyperactive children, compared to normal children, were more active and less accurate. Draeger et al. argue that the adult's presence exerted some external control on the hyperactive children's activity and attention.

Over the course of the preschool years, young children are increasingly expected to regulate their own attention. A documentation of this shift from other-regulation to self-regulation for visual attention is presented by Wertsch, McNamee, McLane, and Budwig (1980), who observed six mother-child pairs at each of three ages: 2.5, 3.5, and 4.5 years. Mothers and children were asked to put together a puzzle of a truck according to a model. The model was presented along with an identical set of puzzle pieces to which a few extra pieces had been added. The central problem was to match the truck's cargo, consisting of squares of different colors, to the model; the extra pieces were distractors, squares of colors that were not in the model.

There were no significant age differences in the number of times the children looked at the model or the mean number of looks per placement of cargo pieces. Mothers were successful in getting their children to look at the model about 90% of the times they tried. The ratio of looks attributable to the mother's direction relative to total looks, however, changed dramatically with age—0.76 for 2.5 years, 0.29 for 3.5 years, and 0.13 for 4.5 years. Children's looks to the model were thus increasingly self-governed. Even taking this difference into account, mothers of the youngest children were significantly more likely to intervene with specific help between the child's look at the model and the actual placement of a cargo piece—0.96 for 2.5 years, 0.56 for 3.5 years, and 0.33 for 4.5 years. The investigators interpreted these age trends as showing that children take increasing responsibility for their attention and performance in joint tasks. The greater intervention after looks at the model in the youngest group also "suggests that children from different age groups did not have the same understanding of the strategic significance of this gaze behavior" (p. 1221). Both social and cognitive factors may therefore play a role in helping the child to move toward more independent control.

Cultural Influences

Social factors in development include more than the direct influences of the parent-child relationship; influences of the larger culture on attention are also mediated by family interactions. For example, Bornstein and his colleagues (Bornstein, Azuma, Tamis-LeMonda, & Ogino, 1990; Bornstein, Maitel, Tal, & Baras, 1995; Bornstein, Tamis-LeMonda, Pêcheux, & Rahn, 1991) have examined the mother's role in directing 5-month-olds' attention toward either social interactions or the environment. Mothers and infants were observed in their homes and mothers were asked to behave as usual. The coding relevant for attention included mothers' active stimulation of attention versus passively providing an opportunity for stimulation; an example of the latter might involve putting the infant in an infant seat where the infant could observe the objects and activity in the room. Active stimulation was further subdivided into didactic versus social activities, depending on whether the mother was trying to engage her child's attention in surrounding objects or in social interaction with her. If the infant was alert and paying attention, the infant's visual attention was coded as directed to objects or to the mother. Tactual exploration was also coded.

The investigators' use of the same methods in four cultures—United States, Japan, France, and Israel—makes cross-cultural comparisons possible. Mothers in all four societies directed attention to objects in the environment more than to themselves. Infants in all four groups attended more to the environment than to their mothers. However, Japanese and American mothers were more active in directing their infants' attention to objects than were French and Israeli mothers; French mothers were least likely to direct attention to the social interaction. Israeli mothers seemed to let their infants direct their own attention by passively providing opportunities more than did mothers in the other cultures. Japanese and French infants were relatively less attentive to objects than were American and Israeli infants, while Japanese infants exhibited the lowest level of attention to the mother.

These data suggest that mothers' and infants' activities are not completely parallel. Interestingly, within the Japanese and American cultures, the amount of mothers' didactic stimulation was strongly associated with the amount of infants' attention to objects (.63 and .79). This association was weaker for French dyads (.38) and nonexistent for Israeli dyads ($-.04$). Mothers' direction of attention to social interactions and infants' attention to their mothers was associated in all except the Israeli dyads ($-.10$). The low correlations in the Israeli data may stem from their greater reliance on unmediated or passive opportunities for infants to direct their own attention. In all cultures, however, the amount of tactual exploration was associated with the number of passively provided opportunities. These data suggest that families in four different modern societies, while similar in some respects, vary in what they encourage children to select for attention.

Studying the very different culture of the !Kung San in the African country of Botswana, Bakeman, Adamson, Konner, and Barr (1990) found that adults paid little attention to infants who were exploring objects. Although, once mobile, infants' exploration was not restricted in any way, the older members of the society were less likely to vocalize, smile, or encourage infants when the infants manipulated and investigated objects. In contrast, adults were more likely to be attentive, interactive, and encouraging when infants offered an object to another person. Thus, the attention of other members of society conveyed to the infant that offering and sharing objects was a more valued activity than exploring objects on their own.

Rogoff, Mistry, Göncü, and Mosier (1993) describe cultural differences in the way older children deploy attention in naturalistic settings. In some cultures— Mayan families in Guatemala (Rogoff et al., 1993) or Marquesan families in Hawaii (Martini & Kirkpatrick, 1992)—it is assumed that, because children attend to what others are doing, they will learn by observation and do not need to have their experiences structured in a didactic way. In societies where children are separated from adults working, adults may need to provide more explicit instruction and arrange special contexts for the practice of important skills (Rogoff et al., 1993). The nature of the work has an influence because some work-related skills require long periods of tuition and preparation and cannot be acquired by observation alone.

Thus, the extent of external control may vary with cultural context, but so may the need for narrowly versus widely deployed attention. Rogoff et al. suggest that children who depend on observation and eavesdropping may learn to attend carefully and simultaneously to more than one source of information; an example might be visually monitoring and listening to a conversation between adults while also exploring a novel toy. In societies where it is expected that adults must teach children, the attention of caregivers and children tends to be more narrowly focused. These investigators compared toddlers (12 to 24 months) in Mayan families to toddlers in middle-class families in the United States by (1) identifying episodes in which the toddler was focused on something but another event competed for attention, and then (2) rating the episode for the type of attention dominant in that episode: attending to both; alternating rapidly between them; or appearing unaware of the second event.

Mayan toddlers were more likely to attend simultaneously to two events than were toddlers in Utah (2.0 versus 0.3 episodes per observation out of a possible 5). In contrast, the Utah toddlers were more likely to be unaware of ongoing events when they were engaged in an activity (2.3 versus 1.2 episodes). Mayan and Utah mothers show much the same pattern as their toddlers. Figure 8.3 shows the relative proportion of simultaneous attention, rapidly alternating attention, and attention focused on only one of two concurrent events in both Mayan and American samples. Perhaps more significant events occur simultaneously in the Mayan households, giving children more to monitor; such a cultural characteristic would encourage more wide-ranging attention. Rogoff et al., however, emphasize that wide-ranging

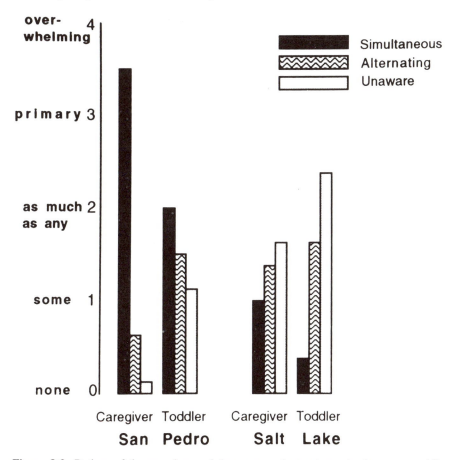

Figure 8.3. Ratings of the prevalence of three types of attention—simultaneous, rapidly alternating, and unaware (only a single focus)—in toddlers and mothers in San Pedro (Guatemala) and Salt Lake City, Utah (USA). From "Guided participation in cultural activity by toddlers and caregivers," by B. Rogoff, J. Mistry, A. Göncü, and C. Mosier, 1993, *Monographs of the Society for Research in Child Development, 58,* p. 143. Copyright 1993 by the Society for Research in Child Development. Reprinted with permission.

attention does not mean that the children are distracted; instead they are managing attention to more than one event, a skill that may come with practice (Spelke et al., 1976).

In summary, parents help to regulate the attention and action of infants and young children. They do so by observing the child's degree of arousal and by acting to decrease or increase it to optimal levels. They teach the infant by example and by verbally directing their children in play and in more task-oriented situations. They provide structure and constraint, increasing the likelihood that their children will attend to some things and not others. Although the process is a long one, the child gradually takes over more of these regulatory functions.

THE SHIFT FROM OTHER-REGULATION TO SELF-REGULATION

Wertsch et al. (1980) write: "In cases where other-regulation is involved, many of the child's overt behaviors may be identical with those carried out through self-regulation, but the adult will have taken over the strategic responsibility for directing these behaviors" (p. 1216). The equivalence of observable behavior, whether the control is exerted by external influences or by the child, is in keeping with the systems approach. That is, child and environment are considered an integrated system, and neither is privileged in accounting for the child's behavior (Fogel & Thelen, 1987; Sameroff, 1983). An intriguing question is just how the processes underlying attention differ when children, rather than others, are responsible for their control. When adults play a critical role in activating and sustaining children's attention, does adult action "trigger" the same neurological processes "triggered" by children themselves? Would the same pathways of the brain be metabolically active in both conditions? We assume that a major factor in the development of attention is bringing lower level processes, such as alerting and orienting, under higher level, internal control.

Although we remain subject to external factors throughout life, the development of the second attention system in the preschool years makes it possible for the child to exert more independent control on attention and action. Mechanisms of control become more independent in three ways. First, children's awareness of attention-related phenomena expands. Second, their awareness is translated into action by means of changing motivations. Third, children acquire volitional skills (Lütken-haus & Bullock, 1991), including the ability to inhibit action and to use private, self-regulatory speech.

Increased Awareness of Attention in Self and Others

As children develop, they come to perceive and know more about the events and people surrounding them. They also become aware of themselves as independent individuals. Gallup (1979) originally developed a measure of self-awareness that separated the performance of monkeys from that of the great apes. Gallup's findings were extended to the study of children by Lewis and Brooks-Gunn (1979). In these studies, 6-month-olds reacted to their mirror images as if the image were another infant; infants 18 to 24 months of age, however, reacted to the reflected image of a spot of rouge that had been surreptitiously applied to their noses. They touched their noses or otherwise indicated that they recognized the mirror image as reflecting themselves. With these developments, children also become more aware of how others react to them.

When children manipulate objects appropriately and produce desired outcomes, they generally take pleasure in the mastery of those objects and gain information about the efficacy of their own activity (Jennings, 1991). Other situations are more ambiguous; in these cases, when parents praise their child for particular actions, the child is not only reinforced for the activity but may gradually become aware that certain kinds of activity are valued by the parents and other kinds are not. This is the beginning of an awareness of family and social standards. The more emphasis parents and the larger society put on sustained attention to and persistence in particular activities and events, the more likely children are to see such characteristics as worthwhile. As children's awareness of a standard increases, so does their awareness of the extent to which their own behavior approximates or falls short of that standard.

Stipek et al. (1992) explored young children's awareness of standards and related reactions. In situations where the children worked with an experimenter on tasks, children 15 to 21 months of age looked up at the experimenter as often when the experimenter completed the task as when they did themselves. Older children, however, increasingly referenced the experimenter only when they themselves had accomplished something. In similar situations with their mothers, children older than 21 months actively called the mother's attention to what they had done.

In a second study, Stipek et al. studied reactions to success and failure in 2- to 5-year-old children. Children younger than 2 years were not included in the study because experiences of failure could not be induced; they simply redefined the task and made no attempt to do what the experimenter had requested. The procedures for older children in the failure condition were to (1) show them a puzzle or nesting cup in its completed form; (2) disassemble it and surreptitiously substitute a piece that was a little too large to fit; and (3) ask the child to put it back together. The procedures for the success condition were the same, except no pieces were substituted. At all ages, children reacted to failure by looking away from the experimenter, turning their bodies away, and adopting a closed rather than an open posture. Children in the failure condition were also more likely to frown and *withdraw attention* from the task than were children in the success condition. These results suggest the potentially important role of experience with success and mastery in the development of attention.

We assume that focused attention is a desirable state under many conditions and that many parents, at least in our culture, will promote it in their children when necessary. Children themselves, as they seek to maintain attention in various situations, also develop an increasing awareness of factors that facilitate and interfere with attention. P. Miller and Zalenski (1982) found that children between 3.5 and 4.5 years understand that both noise and a lack of interest will affect their ability to focus attention. Miniature rooms were used to pose problems; in each room there were four noisy and seven quiet objects. The children were first told about a boy listening to his mother tell him how to play new games or a boy trying to learn his numbers. Then they were asked to remove one item that would help the boy listen or learn. More children than expected by chance chose a noisy object to remove.

In the next problem, four noisy objects (e.g., a vacuum cleaner) were put in one room and four quiet objects in the other. The children were asked to choose the better room for listening to the mother or for doing numbers. A majority of the children (75%) chose the quiet room. In an analogous problem, two dolls were placed in one room—one with a smile and one with a frown. The children were told that one boy liked to listen to his mother tell about new games or to learn numbers but the other did not; they were then asked which boy would listen more or learn his numbers better. Significantly more children than expected by chance chose the smiling doll. Although children might be biased toward the smiling doll regardless of the question, a further test showed that children made the same choice simply on the basis of being told about the doll's preferences.

In a related study, O'Sullivan (1993) reported that 4.5-year-old children considered the degree of both effort and incentive to be influential in recall memory. Given a choice between pictures of a child with a serious expression and tightly knit brows and a child with a more neutral expression, most children thought the first child would remember more of an array of items after the items had been removed. They also thought a child would remember more if rewarded by a box of crayons than by a pencil. Other results suggested that the subjects thought the effect of incentives was mediated by effort—that is, children would work harder for a larger reward than for a smaller one.

All of these results suggest that preschool children understand some influences on attention, but they do not tell us whether children can or do use such understanding. Pillow (1988) tested children's practical understanding about the effects of competing stimulation on their ability to attend. Three- and 4-year-old subjects were asked to decide whether they would listen to two stories at once or separately. In the two-speakers condition, the children were then told that two puppets would each tell a story, and that they should try to learn as much as possible about both stories so they could tell the stories to a friend. They were given a choice of hearing both puppets speak at the same time or one after the other. The children were also asked whether it would be easy or hard to understand if the two puppets talked at the same time, and whether it would be nice or not nice if they did so. These two questions were designed to separate a genuine understanding of the difficulty of attending to two simultaneous messages from the knowledge that it is not polite for someone to talk at the same time as another person. In the tape-recorders condition, procedures were the same, but no puppets were involved. Playing two tape recorders at the same time would not be impolite, but would make comprehension difficult.

The 4-year-olds chose turn-taking more often than the 3-year-olds in the tape-recorders condition, suggesting that they had a greater practical understanding of the problems simultaneity causes for comprehension. The 3-year-old group chose turn-taking more in the two-speakers than in the tape-recorders condition, perhaps because they were aware of the impropriety of two people talking at the same time but not the problems it would create for comprehension. This interpretation is supported by their answers to direct questions from the experimenter. The results suggest that there are limits on the young child's practical understanding of the optimal conditions for attending to and remembering information. A second experiment showed that, although 3-year-olds do not readily anticipate problems with attending to simultaneously presented information, they do notice the difficulty when actually trying to cope with such situations.

Using a within-subjects analysis, O'Sullivan (1993) found that 4.5-year-old children who were offered a larger or preferred reward for recalling items from an array would visually examine the objects for longer periods of time and spend less time off task than children offered a smaller reward. These results corroborate those of Pillow and suggest that children may use their own experiences with different types of reward to develop an appreciation of attention's influence on performance in task-oriented situations.

The Role of Changing Motivations

Although control of attention is related to an increasing awareness of social standards and the effects of circumstances, the shift from external to internal control is also related to changes in motivation. Vygotsky (translation by Cole, John-Steiner, Scribner, & Souberman, 1978) writes: "if we ignore the child's needs, and the incentives which are effective in getting him to act, we will never be able to understand his advance from one developmental stage to the next, because every advance is connected with a marked change in motives, inclinations, and incentives" (p. 92). Although developmental advances are based on other factors as well, major changes in motivation occurring in the toddler and preschool years contribute to the development of attention. One of the differences between the infant and the preschooler lies in the types of motivation that can be attached to basic processes, such as orienting, terminating, and maintaining attention.

Developmental changes in motivation are dependent, in part, on the child's social experience. From these experiences emerge not only greater knowledge of social standards but also a desire to please adults and a concern for what might happen if one is not compliant. Thus, in situations where stimulus events are in themselves uninteresting, children may accept a task's demands and share in a process of evaluating their own performance. Concern with the attainment of standards of performance is developmentally related to a desire to master the environment and to be socially acceptable; children's control of attention and action becomes more autonomous as standards are accepted as their own.

An adult's praise may be reinforcing in many situations, but it is also informative (Kohlberg, 1971). By example and through verbal communication, parents not only motivate children but also provide instruction on how to meet expectations. Compliance with parental directives increases in the second year. Schaffer and Crook (1980) note that, during this period, children begin to comply more at several levels. Two-year-olds are more likely than 15-month-olds to look where adults ask them to, to handle the toys they are encouraged to, and to follow specific instructions regarding the toys. Parents' verbal commands to act are more successful if they make sure the child is attending to them at the time the command is delivered. Language comprehension is also an important factor. Kaler and Kopp (1990), after independently measuring comprehension and compliance with directives, found a significant increase in both comprehension and compliance from 12 to 18 months. The two were directly linked; children rarely complied when they did not understand the words in the command, and they rarely failed to comply when they did understand them.

In later development, when language is not so much an issue, compliance with adult wishes continues to increase. Vaughn et al. (1984), using a cleanup task with the mother, found that compliance increased significantly from 18 to 30 months of age. The amount of noncompliance, however, did not vary with age, but tended to change form, with older children arguing more. Mothers recognize these changes in their children by altering the way they offer direction; they rely more on explanation and reprimand and depend less on simply distracting the child from undesirable activity (Kuczynski, Kochanska, Radke-Yarrow, & Girnius-Brown, 1987).

Although the older child may be motivated by social factors, intrinsic motivation—the motivation that comes from an activity itself—continues to be a critical force in determining attention. The two forms of motivation do not necessarily reinforce one another. In the study by Stipek et al. (1992), children were not simply motivated by praise; the more often the mothers defined the task rather than the children themselves, the less positive affect the children displayed. Motivation for mastery and pleasure in accomplishing their own goals were apparently still important (Jennings, 1991; Kohlberg, 1971). Lepper and Greene (1978) observed the amount of time preschool children spent drawing in their nursery school classrooms. Those showing high interest in drawing were selected to participate individually in an experiment. Each child was randomly assigned to one of three conditions: some children were asked to draw in order to obtain a certificate; some were asked to draw and afterward received the same certificate unexpectedly; and some were simply given an opportunity to draw. When these children were again observed in the classroom, the children in the first condition showed a significant decrease in drawing, while the other two groups continued to draw at their previous levels. Lepper and Greene concluded that extrinsic rewards can interfere with intrinsic motivation by turning an intrinsically attractive activity into a means to an external goal. They ruled out alternative explanations, such as the reward's causing a general change in affect. Whatever the explanation, their results have important implications for attention in different contexts. The encouragement and praise of parents may be most helpful in situations where the materials are not intrinsically interesting to the child but the activity is valuable or necessary for other reasons. In situations where the activity is interesting and pleasurable in its own right, the parents' encouragement may actually diminish the child's enthusiasm.

Volitional Skills

At the same time as the child's awareness expands and motivations change, the development of voluntary control also contributes to increasing independence of attention. The development of voluntary attention was of central concern to Russian psychologists (e.g., Luria, 1973; Yendovitskaya, 1971). Luria wrote: "Features of the most elementary, involuntary attention of the type which is attracted by the most powerful or biologically significant stimuli can be observed very early on, during the first few months of the child's development" (1973, p. 258). In contrast, Luria adds, "the formation of voluntary attention has a long and dramatic history, and the child acquires an efficient and stable, socially-organized attention only shortly before he is due to start school" (p. 263). Many specific skills make such voluntary control possible.

Inhibitory Skills

Voluntary control of attention is closely tied to the control of behavior and action. Both involve inhibitory skills. As described in chapter 3, rudimentary inhibition that might be described as voluntary becomes evident by the end of the first year. Inhibition of approach can be observed in infants during the last quarter of the first year of life. Infants who readily reach for a novel object at 6 months may by 8 or 9 months show caution in approaching the object (Rothbart, 1988b; Schaffer, 1984). This early kind of inhibition reflects the development of fear, and even mild fear acts as a brake or control on behavior. A 12-month-old will also inhibit a direct reach to a toy behind a glass barrier and reach around and get the toy. A 6-month-old, in contrast, will reach repeatedly in a direct line only to be frustrated by the barrier. On the basis of research with both human infants and young monkeys, Diamond and Gilbert (1989) argue that development of the prefrontal cortex underlies the infant's emerging ability to inhibit such strongly elicited, but inappropriate, responses.

In the second and third years, children begin to gain control over impulses or actions that are strongly activated by the situation. Vaughn et al. (1984) studied this development in children between 18 to 30 months, using several tasks where children were asked not to approach an attractive object, such as a wrapped gift, until given permission by the experimenter, who then left the room. Large and highly significant increases in the duration of delay and resistance to temptation were observed from 18 to 30 months. Measures across the different delay tasks also became progressively more intercorrelated with age. The median correlations were − .13 at 18 months, .08 at 24 months, and .32 at 30 months. The investigators write: "The capacity to delay or inhibit responsiveness to attractive stimuli can be readily, though fleetingly, observed in 18-month-old children; nonetheless, for these young children, delay capacity is quite variable and not necessarily maintained across time or tasks. With increasing age the exercise of self-control increases with respect to both capacity and coherence" (p. 1001). The emergence of language and the continued development of the frontal cortex may underlie further advances in impulse control, and these advances are directly related to the increases in sustained attention also observed in the same period (Krakow et al., 1982).

After 3 years of age, inhibitory skills continue to improve. In a study by Reed et al. (1984), children from 40 to 49 months were presented with several tasks designed to assess some aspect of inhibitory control: (1) spontaneous alternation, the tendency to switch from one object location to an alternative one; (2) a pinball game; and (3) a version of Simon Says. The first is assumed to assess involuntary buildup of inhibition, while the second and third are assumed to assess voluntary inhibitory control. With age partialled out, the Simon Says, pinball, and alternation tasks were moderately and significantly related to one another (.41 to .54). Performance (or degree of inferred inhibition) on all three tasks showed improvement with age. The authors conclude that an underlying dimension of self-control is manifested in different contexts. The parallel changes in spontaneous alternation, an uninstructed form of inhibition, seem to rule out the possibility that the results were based solely on developmental increases in the motivation to comply.

As another illustration, Levy (1980) presented children from 3 to 7 years of age with the task of drawing a line from one point to another. On three trials, the children were uninstructed, then instructed to draw a line as slowly as possible, and finally, to draw the line as fast as possible. The older children were slower in the uninstructed trial than were the younger children, with the time increasing from 2.8 seconds at 3 years to 4.4 seconds at 7 years; the decrease in speed reflects the general change in overall motor activity already alluded to. All age groups were able to slow down when asked to, though the older children slowed down considerably more, 4.4

seconds to 33.5 seconds, than the youngest children, 2.8 seconds to 7.1 seconds. The older children were also more able to increase their speed when asked to, though the youngest children in the uninstructed condition may already have been close to a ceiling on speed. Being able to increase and decrease speed in accordance with instructions is strong evidence for an activity's being under voluntary control, as we noted in chapter 2. Performance on this task, not a measure of attention as such, was related to reaction time and errors on a continuous performance test, demonstrating that voluntary control is developing in several areas at once. These developments in inhibition may be related to further development of the second attention system and the possible transition at 4 years.

Unlike behavioral inhibition motivated by wariness or fear and emerging in the second half of the first year, the type of impulse control that emerges with the second attention system may be seen as more deliberate and effortful (Rothbart, 1989c). Using this distinction between fearfulness and effortful control as a foundation, Kochanska (1993) hypothesizes that both are important elements in children's development of conscience, an internalized manifestation of behavioral control. That is, the earlier form of inhibition still operates in the preschool years and is part of the gradual increase in inhibitory skills.

Planning

We earlier described a significant increase in focused attention during play in the preschool years. We suggested in chapter 6 that several factors, including arousal and cognitive development, contribute to this increase; another is the ability to plan. All types of play can unfold without a plan or a script, but older preschool children increasingly think about and plan ahead for their activities. With age, children are not only more likely to formulate goals for their play, their goals become more articulated. Plans or goals have a powerful organizing influence on behavior and on sustained attention (Werner, 1948). If a 4-year-old girl decides to build a castle with a set of blocks, she is likely to maintain that activity until she reaches her goal—a castle that meets her particular standards. When she reaches her goal, the relevant activity stops, and she shifts to another activity that may or may not include the castle. This is quite different from a 2-year-old boy who may not have a very clear idea about what he wants to build. He begins to put blocks together, concentrating on making them balance. If he looks up and catches sight of one of the dolls on the floor next to him, he may interrupt his construction and start playing with the doll. Because he doesn't have a plan, there is no definite end to the activity of construction and no particular reason not to shift. During play, attention may therefore be sustained to the extent that the child's play is goal-oriented.

Adapting Action to a Goal

Planning is important for all complex, nonroutine activity. Planning can influence activity, however, only if children can adapt their behavior to specific goals, employing alternate means when a first attempt is not successful or modifying action in mid-course. Such adaptation implies coordination of attention, activity, and intentionality. This coordination develops significantly from 9 to 18 months of life and involves the important transitions around 9 and 18 months (see chapter 3). Further developments in the third year add to the child's ability to maintain and succeed in goal-oriented activity.

As children are better able to anticipate an end result, they discover that specific activities or sequences of activities are necessary to reach the goal. They must then be able to carry the activities through to completion, an ability realized through the development of "volitional skills" (Bullock & Lütkenhaus, 1988), such as keeping the goal in mind, "waiting or searching for appropriate opportunities to act, resisting distractions, overcoming obstacles, correcting actions, and stopping [the action] when a goal is reached" (p. 664). At the same time, the child develops a concept of self as agent.

Bullock and Lütkenhaus (1988) observed children in four age groups: 15 to 18 months, 19 to 22 months, 23 to 28 months, and 29 to 35 months. Each child was presented with three tasks—building a tower from three blocks, cleaning a blackboard, and "dressing" a block figure with blocks. In the first and third tasks, there were extra blocks not needed for completion; for the second task, a bowl and sponge were distractors in that they supported interesting activities other than cleaning the blackboard. Each child's performance on each task was categorized as belonging to one of five categories: (1) no attention to standards; (2) a rudimentary and wrong standard, and no evidence of stopping when the goal was reached; (3) a wrong standard but stopping at goal completion; (4) a correct standard but no evidence of stopping; and (5) a correct standard and stopping at goal completion. As we noted previously, interrupting a pleasant activity is not always easy and the ability to do so may depend on more than the clarity of the child's goal.

Summary scores based on the five categories showed that the number of children oriented to outcome rather than to the activity itself increased over the four ages: from 41% at 15 to 18 months, to 59% at 19 to 22 months, to 87% at 23 to 28 months, to 98% at 29 to 35 months (averaged over tasks). Only the oldest children were actually correct on a majority of trials (1.7%, 4.7%, 32%, and 65%). Stopping when the task was completed also increased with age (18%, 21%, 57%, and 75%).

In addition to rating the five categories, Bullock and Lütkenhaus measured how much the children monitored their own performance. Using the first task as an example, they observed whether children took care in placing and aligning a single block, took care with the whole tower, or made corrections, such as taking an unnecessary block off the tower and replacing it with the correct one. Children became more careful and more likely to make corrections with age (20%, 38%, 73%, and 84%).

Finally, the children watched the experimenter complete some tasks, and the investigators noted whether or not the children showed "outcome reactions"—more positive affect to their own completion of a task than to the experimenter's completing it. The percentages of children showing an outcome reaction at the four ages were 32%, 62%, 75%, and 90%, respectively. Performance was reliably better on those trials with outcome reactions than on those without, suggesting that children were evaluating their own performance appropriately.

Bullock and Lütkenhaus (1988) suggest a developmental sequence. Before 18 months, children are oriented mainly to an activity rather than to outcomes, focusing attention more on the flow of activities than on their consequences. By 20 months, children become concerned about producing particular outcomes, although they are not yet adept at monitoring their progress toward goals nor do they reliably stop at completion. By 24 months, children regulate their behavior according to a goal, but are not nearly as likely as older children to correct their actions along the way. After 30 months, children are more likely to monitor and correct specific details of their actions as they progress toward a goal.

Private Speech.

As children shift toward monitoring and regulating their own actions, one important development is the emergence of regulatory, as opposed to communicative, speech. Language both facilitates action and helps to inhibit it when appropriate. Initially, adult speech is used to direct, activate, and inhibit actions of the infant and young child; this speech is eventually internalized and used by the child as a means of self-control (Vygotsky, 1978; Yendovitskaya, 1971). Such speech has been referred to as egocentric (Piaget, 1955; Vygotsky, 1962), or private. Private speech is defined as speech not directed to a listener; it includes word play, expressions of affect, and comments and questions that may or may not be relevant to the current task (Bivens & Berk, 1990).

To establish that task-relevant private speech has a functional role in development, several criteria must be met. First, we must show that adult speech does, in fact, influence behavior. Any experiment showing that children respond differently after instructions than before suggests some verbal control over behavior. For example, young children usually comply with instructions if they comprehend them (Kaler & Kopp, 1990); children 3 years and older will draw lines more slowly when instructed to do so than in uninstructed conditions (Levy, 1980). It is, in fact, difficult for children *not* to respond to commands to act, even when previously instructed not to do so (Reed et al., 1984; Strommen, 1973). Masters and Binger (1978) found a clear developmental trend in the ability to stop playing with an attractive toy on command from an adult. At 2.5 years, only 43% of the children did so compared to 71% at 3.5 years and 77% at 4.5 years. In the first two and a half years of life, then, adult speech becomes more effective in directing and controlling children's behavior.

Second, children's own speech must actually function to regulate their behavior. This criterion can be met by experimental manipulations of children's speech. For example, Tinsley and Waters (1982) presented 2-year-old children with a hammer-and-peg toy that had only one peg and asked them to hit the peg once. After six trials with no further instructions, the children were instructed to say either "one" (task-relevant) or "toy" (irrelevant) at the same time as hitting the peg with the hammer. With either word, children improved significantly from baseline and were more likely to hit the peg only once and to do so without delay. The results suggest that saying the word may have been related to the arousing properties of the sound, because the effect was not specific to the task at hand. A second study compared children between 2.5 and 3.5 years of age with children between 3.5 and 4.5 on a more difficult task. Both younger and older children performed better at hitting three pegs in a specified order when instructed to say the color of the peg as they hit it, but older children improved more than younger children. Though not definitive, the results are consistent with the view that speech comes to have a regulatory function.

Third, we must demonstrate that private speech is used in contexts where it is needed. Several investigators have shown that private speech increases when tasks are demanding (Berk & Garvin, 1984; Goodman, 1981). The second study by Tinsley and Waters (1982) showed that the child's verbalization helped more when the task was difficult than when it was easy. In the more naturalistic setting of working on puzzles, Goodman (1981) found preschool children's spontaneous verbalizations of plans to occur more often around failures to place puzzle pieces than would be expected by chance.

Thus, children appear to shift from a dependence on the immediate instructions of adults, to being able to use their own speech, whether induced or spontaneous, to regulate their own behavior. After the preschool years, such speech tends to become silent and is then observed only in chin and mouth movements during difficult tasks (Bivens & Berk, 1990; van Hover, 1974). Berk and her colleagues (Berk, 1986; Bivens & Berk, 1990) have shown that, at least in school-age children, silent task-relevant private speech is positively associated with focused attention and decreased motor movement. These associations further support the contention that private speech eventually helps to control attention and behavior.

Voluntary Control of Attention

In the preschool years, children come to accept the value of tasks that may not in themselves compel attention and learn to attend voluntarily. Yendovitskaya (1971) suggests that one route to voluntary attention is through language. Parents use words to direct the child's attention to the external world, and children gradually learn to use the same means for directing and organizing their own attention. Thus, to enhance their own attention, children may instruct themselves.

Children's awareness of factors affecting attention also helps them to see ways of reducing distraction. They may, for example, remove themselves from noisy situations or eliminate the noise. Children may also learn that attention cannot easily be focused or behavior organized for a given activity without a simultaneous inhibition of competing responses. Because gross motor activity generally decreases in the preschool years (Routh et al., 1974), even in situations not demanding inhibition or control, children may find it easier to inhibit irrelevant motor activity, thereby reducing one source of distraction. In addition, a deliberate reduction in motor activity alone may promote attention—a peripheral influence that could add to the central mechanisms already suggested.

Children become more able to attend to adult-defined tasks and perform them well, in part because they deliberately resist distractions over which they have no control. Patterson and Mischel (1975), for example, gave 4- to 5-year-old children instructions on how to remain oriented to a copying task in the face of invitations from a "clown" to play. The experimenters offered three possibilities to each child: (1) look at your work and say "No, I can't [play]: I'm working"; (2) say to yourself "I'm going to keep working so I can play with the fun toys . . . later"; and (3) pretend that "there's a brick wall between you" and the clown so that you wouldn't be able to see him even if you did look up (p. 371). Instructed children spent a significantly greater portion of the session engaged in the task than control children to whom no strategies were suggested. The data suggest that, by the end of the preschool years, children may be able to resist distraction by instructing themselves to keep working, at least for short periods of time.

In studies that involve waiting rather than working, the physical presence of rewards makes waiting much more difficult for children (Mischel & Ebbeson, 1970; Yates & Revelle, 1979). To explore the basis for this difficulty, Mischel, Ebbeson & Zeiss (1972) experimentally instructed children from 3.5 to 5.5 years in different strategies to use during the delay period. Children who played with a toy or thought of something fun during the delay period were able to wait much longer than children who were not instructed and as long as children for whom the rewards were not visible. Directing attention toward a toy or to a thought was equally effective, but Mischel and his colleagues reasoned that the type of thought might be critical. Children were therefore asked to think of something fun, think of something sad, or think about the rewards themselves. Waiting times during "thinking sad" and "thinking rewards" were as short as without instructions and did not differ from each other; children asked to think of something fun were able to delay much longer. Mischel (1983) reports that he and his colleagues also explored children's spontaneous strategies for managing delay periods with rewards present. The spontaneous techniques varied. Some children hid their eyes or turned their backs on the rewards to avoid looking at them. One child even fell asleep! Other children creatively distracted themselves: they talked, sang, and played games while they waited. Yates and Revelle (1979) found that children who waited the entire period in the presence of rewards were significantly more likely to talk to themselves about matters unrelated to the rewards than were children who did not wait. Conversely, children who did not wait were more likely to stare at the rewards.

These results show that, at least by 4 years, children can resist distractions in order to attend to a task. They can also create distractions for themselves and redirect their own attention in the service of managing something onerous. There are limits, however, on the extent to which children, or even adults, can exercise control. One intriguing example (Ruff, 1991) involved children of 2.5, 3.5, and 4.5 years of age presented with a series of 20 videotaped puppet skits; the skits were separated by intervals of 5, 10, 15, 20, or 25 seconds, and presented randomly in four blocks of five trials each. The puppet skits were intended to be moderately interesting but not absorbing; they were presented in black and white, the puppets were fairly plain, and the skits were simple. The relatively low physical salience of the skits, combined with the blank intervals between skits, provided a challenge to the children's developing capacity to cooperate and attend. Children were seated in front of the video monitor and told only that there was something for them to watch. All sessions were videotaped, and the durations of the children's looking and focused visual attention directed toward the screen were scored from the videotapes. Focused visual attention was coded when the child seemed to be actively engaged; observers reported that they based their judgments on the child's spontaneous utterances, decreased motor movement, interested facial expressions, and active scanning of the screen.

Figure 8.4A shows the mean changes in looking time within the sessions for the three age groups. Older children looked at the screen more than younger children, and looking generally decreased over the four trial blocks. However, an interaction between age and trial blocks emerged; the decline in looking over trial blocks was very strong for the 2.5-year-olds and nonexistent for the 4.5-year-olds. Contrast these results with those for focused visual attention in figure 8.4B. Here all age groups showed decreasing attention over trials. The fact that the older children were able to maintain their looking to the screen, *despite* declining engagement, is likely a consequence of their greater compliance and voluntary control. Although the experimenter's introduction was vague and made no specific demands, the older children may have been more ready than the younger children to interpret the situation as one requiring particular behavior. The decrement in focused attention, however, suggests how difficult it may be to deliberately control the intensity of attention and

A. Looking at Puppet Skits

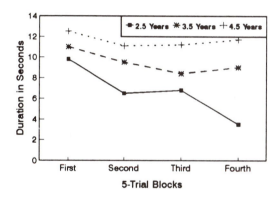

B. Focused Attention During Puppet Skits

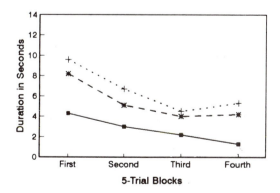

Figure 8.4. (A) Changes over time in looking at a videotape of puppet skits by 2.5- to 4.5-year-old children. (B) Focused attention over time to the same videotape in the same children. Adapted from Ruff (1991).

effort. In line with our discussion of focused attention in chapter 7, we suggest that children may develop deliberate—and therefore self-conscious—techniques for selecting and maintaining orientation to an event or task. The materials or problem itself, however, must eventually capture and hold attention if attention is going to be focused. Without that absorption in the task at hand, individuals remain vulnerable to distraction by external events, by mind-wandering, and even by thoughts about themselves engaged in the task.

SUMMARY

Development of attention involves increasingly independent higher level control of lower level processes such as arousal and orienting. The processes that underlie higher level control of attention are dependent in large part on the social context in which the child develops. Initially, parents and other older members of society play a role in the early development of attention by helping infants maintain calm, alert states conducive to attention. They help to arouse infants who are not alert and calm those who are distressed. In the later months of the first year, they may assist and share in the attentive exploration of objects. When children develop language, parents exert some verbal control over attention and action. Gradually, however, children assume more control over their own attention.

In the toddler and preschool years, developments in self-regulation and control are a function of children's increasing awareness of their own activity and its consequences. Children also become more aware of what adults expect of them. The development of self-regulatory skills is also a function of emerging motivations that depend on such awareness. These motivations include a desire to master more complex aspects of the environment, to succeed in tasks according to preconceived standards, and to please others.

Expectations and motivations together define what behavior children and their parents consider to be acceptable. In particular, children desire and are expected to participate in many more structured, adult-defined activities. Cognitive and language development along with neural maturation provide children with new and more efficient means of controlling their own attention and actions and of complying with the higher levels of functioning required by the social context. These means include inhibitory skills, private speech, and more deliberate deployment of attention. To some extent these new skills depend on the self-conscious strategies a child may adopt in order to accomplish a goal or comply with expectations.

There are, however, limits on the extent to which individuals of any age can control the intensity and narrowness of their attention. The power of events and ideas to elicit focused attention, for example, remains strong. Thus, although the attentional and behavioral changes occurring in the preschool years can be considered as a shift toward more voluntary or independent control, children's interest and attention to events and activities also change spontaneously as a function of their growing comprehension of the world and their increasing ability to be challenged and intrigued by complex situations and problems.

9

Attention in Learning and Performance

In this chapter, we explore an issue that cuts across the topics of selectivity, state, and higher level control: the reciprocal relationship between attention and learning. The acquisition of knowledge and skills during development depends on how well infants and children pay attention to the events around them, to their parents' behavior and instructions, and to the consequences of their own actions. At the same time, what children learn influences their attention by redirecting it and making selection and effort more efficient. This chapter has four sections. We first review briefly the role learning and performance play in defining attention. Second, we discuss the possibility that learning and performance are facilitated by attention, particularly focused attention. These two issues can be seen as different perspectives on the same relationship. Third, we consider the specific contribution attention makes to performance in three types of paradigms—discrimination learning, sequence learning, and observational learning. For each type of learning, we address the implications that stem from the development of the two attention systems. Finally, we examine a central issue in early development—the limitations imposed by the child's concentration on emerging skills.

LEARNING AND PERFORMANCE AS DEFINING ASPECTS
OF ATTENTION

A common notion is that attention should be defined, in part, by what and how much is learned. Should we, for example, refer to selective orienting in the newborn as attention? We have previously noted that looking is not an unambiguous measure of attention, and this would seem to be particularly true in the newborn where neural pathways that might be closely connected later are still very immature (Posner & Rothbart, 1981). Even so, if we can determine that the alert neonate, with its eyes open and directed toward an event, is actively acquiring information about that event, then we are more justified in referring to early looking as attention. Habituation studies are helpful in this regard because a decrease in looking that cannot be accounted for by fatigue provides some evidence of learning. Although such decrements are not readily observed in the first month, a number of examples (e.g., Friedman, 1972; Slater et al., 1984) demonstrate that habituation can occur in neonates, albeit at a slower rate than later.

Dannemiller and Banks (1983) have suggested that some habituation in newborns could be explained by neurophysiological adaptation. That is, a particular display excites a set of feature-detecting cells; with repetition, these cells become less responsive; a new display then stimulates a different set of fresh cells, which are readily excited. This explanation is consistent with the neural activation models discussed in chapter 5 and may be adequate for many of the observed instances of response decrement in the first two or three months of life. It implies that changes in looking are tied to processes in the primary sensory areas of the cortex and do not involve any control by or change in higher neural centers. In contrast, Slater and Morison (1985) argue that selective adaptation is not adequate to explain all the findings on newborn attention and that psychological processes, such as attention and learning, are necessary to account for some results. They argue that habituation based on selective adaptation should be faster in the newborn than in older infants because cortical neurons should become fatigued more easily in very young infants. Yet, the rate of habituation is slower in younger than older infants. Although the extent to which attention governs patterns of looking in the first month remains an unresolved question, the controversy illustrates the nature of the issue.

More formal tests of performance and learning are possible with older subjects. In chapter 7, we cited several studies in which distractors led to better learning and performance on a task; the conclusion was that attention to the task was increased in the presence of distractors and learning was thereby enhanced (Turnure, 1970; Higgins & Turnure, 1984). We also noted previously that vigilance tasks, which usually require a motor response to an unpredictable and infrequent signal, provide a means of observing fluctuations in attention through variations in speed of response and number of errors. The reasoning is that subjects' reactions will be faster and less prone to error during attention to the task than during lapses of attention. Thus, we see that reactions slow and errors increase at the end of a session compared to the beginning (Parasuraman, 1984; Weissberg et al., 1990). Likewise, 4-year-old children are faster and miss fewer signals than 3-year-olds; they also do not need to be reminded to pay attention, whereas 3-year-olds need frequent reminders (Weissberg et al., 1990). These results suggest that increases in attention with age contribute to age differences in performance on such structured tasks. Because neuronal transmission and motor speed also increase over this age range, some caution is needed in making inferences about attention from performance.

DOES ATTENTION ENHANCE LEARNING AND PERFORMANCE?

Inferences about the role of attention in performance and learning are stronger in studies that include measures of attention independent of the measures of performance. Some examples of such measures are physiological changes, extraneous motor movement, facial expression, or glances away from the task (J. Turnure,

1971; Higgins & Turnure, 1984). Krupski and Boyle (1978), studying second graders, found that slow responders in a simple visual reaction-time task glanced away from the task more than fast responders. A similar pattern has been observed in preschoolers (Ruff & Capozzoli, 1991); the duration of time spent looking away from the computer screen was correlated with reaction time to a visual signal ($r =$ .57). Another finding is particularly relevant for our current discussion. Higgins and Turnure (1984) found that children 4 years and older glanced away for longer periods after reaching the criterion for successful learning in visual discrimination tasks. Children were apparently more attentive while they were actively learning to select the relevant variables than after the task was mastered.

In other studies, attention is manipulated and performance measured. Rovee-Collier, Earley, and Stafford (1989) observed infants learning to kick for reinforcement from a mobile hanging over their cribs—the more they kicked, the more the elements of the mobile moved around. The investigators had earlier noted the tendency of 2-month-olds to focus on one block and not to scan the entire mobile, behavior consistent with the scanning patterns discussed in chapter 4. Reasoning that the amount of learning and memory was determined by the number of cues the infants noticed in the course of training, Rovee-Collier et al. compared memory after 24 hours in two conditions. In both conditions, the mobile consisted of five hanging cubes. In the first condition, each of five identical cubes had a different pattern on their five visible faces; in the second condition, each cube was different from the other four and had the same pattern on each of its faces. Thus, in the first condition, an infant who focused on only one of the blocks would be exposed to the same five cues as an infant in the second condition who scanned the entire mobile. The investigators tested 2-month-olds, expecting that the type of mobile would be important for learning and memory. The results confirmed their expectations. Memory scores were significantly better in the condition that provided five cues in each block than in the condition presenting five cues over the entire mobile. Thus, the investigators manipulated the circumstances to take infants' patterns of attention into account and found superior learning and memory. A reasonable inference is that visual attention is a factor in infants' learning the contingency between a specific mobile and their own behavior. However, the investigators did not assess the infants' looking at the mobile directly.

In another example, Hayes, Ewy, and Watson (1982) found the amount of visual attention 3-month-olds paid to a simple visual display during baseline to be positively related to learning a contingency between foot kicking and a visual reinforcer in the same location as the baseline display. The investigators then manipulated attention level by exposing infant subjects to the visual reinforcer for 5 minutes before the learning phase. A majority of infants showed a marked decline in looking at the display—that is, they habituated to it; these infants failed to learn the contingency in the subsequent training period. Those infants who remained attentive to the display throughout showed significant learning. Although the separation of subjects into groups was based on a post hoc analysis of attention, the results suggest that attention during the contingency phase was causally related to learning the contingency. As the authors note, "infants in what has generally been considered an optimal state for learning, i.e., awake, alert, and happy, nevertheless are not all

equally attentive and prepared to analyze the contingencies in their environment''
(Hayes et al., 1982, p. 43).

Behavioral Evidence for the Role of Focused Attention

Because it is possible to differentiate among levels of attention, a further question is
whether intense or focused attention enhances learning more than less focused
attention. Here we summarize evidence suggesting that it does. In one study (Ruff,
1986), infants from 6 to 12 months of age, when encountering novel objects, were
likely to show visually focused exploration of objects first, and only afterwards to
engage in other activities involving less focused attention, such as mouthing or
vigorous repetitive activity. These results suggest that attention is recruited and
focused when the object is new and at its most novel. In another study of 5- to 11-
month-old infants (Ruff et al., 1992), focused attention at all ages declined during
manipulative play as an object was exposed longer and presumably became more
familiar. Other looking and manipulating, not judged to be focused, showed no
systematic relationship to degree of exposure. When novel objects were presented,
recovery was observed only for focused attention (see figure 9.1). Although indirect,
these results suggest that focused attention is related to, and probably involved in,
learning to recognize objects through exploratory play.

Sullivan and Lewis (1988) recorded degree of attention in 12-month-olds' facial
expressions during a task where the children were to learn that pushing a lever would
activate a slide with music. They found that the duration of ''knit-brow interest''
was related to progress in learning; children who eventually learned to systematically produce the reward showed more ''knit-brow interest'' than children who
never learned. Compared to nonlearners, learners also sucked or rolled in their lower
lips, a possible sign of concentration. The results suggest that children who recognized the contingency between their actions and the onset of the slides were more
focused or concentrated than the other children. The learners may have become
more attentive only after they recognized the contingency, rather than the reverse,
but the differences in facial expression between the two groups were present from
the earliest trials. Thus, the best interpretation seems to be that focused attention
facilitated learning.

There has been no similar research in preschool children, but Burns and Anderson (1993) present data from adults suggesting dependence of learning on state.
They found that recognition of program content in a television show was better if the
subject's look at the program had progressed past 15 seconds than during earlier
segments of those same long looks or during short looks. Better recognition for
content presented in the later parts of long looks than earlier parts rules out the
possibility that short and long looks were different to begin with. Rather, attention
seems to intensify within the look. As described in chapter 7, preschool children
watching television are less distractible after 15 seconds of looking than they are
after shorter periods of looking. If results similar to those from Burns and Anderson
were found with preschool children, we would have evidence that recognition
memory is better when children are more focused, as indexed by degree of distractibility, at the time the material is presented.

EXAMINING

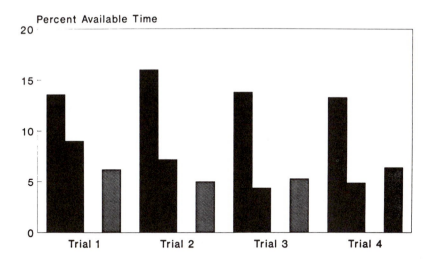

OTHER LOOKING/
MANIPULATING

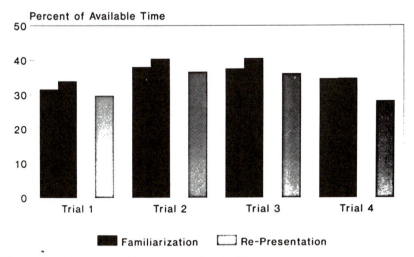

■ Familiarization ▢ Re-Presentation

Figure 9.1. The course of focused attention (in this case, examining) and casual attention during infants' manipulative play with objects. Each trial is separated into two halves and is followed by a re-presentation of the same object; the following trial involves a novel object. From "The differentiation of activity in infants' exploration of objects" by H. A. Ruff, L. M. Saltarelli, M. Capozzoli, and K. Dubiner, *Developmental Psychology, 28,* p. 856. Copyright 1992 by American Psychological Association. Reprinted with permission.

Taking a somewhat different approach, Renninger and Wozniak (1985) studied the influence of preschool children's interests on recognition and recall memory. Interest was individually determined for each child by observing the toys the child spent most time with in the preschool. Items of particular interest were interspersed among comparison items and incorporated into the tasks. In the recall task, the experimenter held a toy box and showed each child nine toys for 3 seconds apiece, with the toy representing the child's interest always in position 5. At the end, when all the toys were in the box and out of sight, the children were asked to say what objects were in the box. As can be seen in figure 9.2, the children exhibited the well-documented recency effect—that is, better recall of the last item presented—but they were equally good at recalling the toy at position 5. The objects of particular interest for each child may well have been the most familiar ones for those individual children; even so, the data suggest that objects subject to the most attention are learned and remembered well. In addition, Renninger and Leckrone (1991) suggest

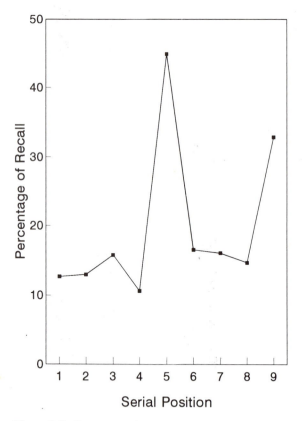

Figure 9.2. Percentage of correct answers on the recall task by serial position. The object chosen on the basis of the child's activity of greatest interest is in the fifth position. The values shown here are averages for the younger and older age groups in the original study. From "Effect of interest on attentional shift, recognition, and recall in young children," by K. A. Renninger and R. H. Wozniak, 1985, *Developmental Psychology, 21,* p. 630. Copyright 1985 by the American Psychological Association. Adapted with permission.

that activities or objects of particular interest to children "play a major role in determining . . . [how] the child learns about general principles of problem solving (e.g., planning, strategy, and revision)" (p. 212).

This array of findings suggests that children learn best when they are alert and focused. Using a paradigm with a warning signal and reaction times to a same/ different judgment, Morrison (1982) found that 5-year-old children were slower than adults to achieve maximum alertness and maintained alertness more poorly. He then used the observed alerting functions to make predictions about performance on an independent task. At the point of their maximum alertness, 5-year-olds were as quick to pick up information and respond as were adults. These data raise the possibility that age differences in learning and performance are related more to arousal and attention than to speed of detection and acquisition of information. Similar kinds of studies with preschool children would provide further information about the development of these processes.

Physiological Differentiation

Physiological manifestations of attention are also related to learning and performance. Porges (1972) has shown that heart rate variability is lower during attention-demanding tasks than in other situations. In the interval between the warning signal and the response signal in simple reaction-time tasks, heart rate variability in adults and children is reduced (Porges, 1972; Porges & Smith, 1980); the greater the reduction, the faster the reaction time. Porges and Raskin (1969) found similar results for a matching task. DeGangi, DiPietro, Greenspan, and Porges (1991) found that infants who showed greater reductions of respiratory sinus arrhythmia (RSA) when being given a standardized developmental test performed better than infants with smaller reductions of RSA.

Using heart rate deceleration as the measure of focused attention, Linnemeyer and Porges (1986) found that only 6-month-old infants whose heart rates decelerated during stimulus presentation showed behavioral evidence of recognition memory. Along similar lines, Richards (1994) conducted a systematic study in which the timing of exposure to the stimulus event was experimentally linked to the level of attentional engagement, as indexed by heart rate. He presented visual patterns to 14-, 20-, and 26-week-old infants at two different phases of attention: (1) during sustained, active attention, when there is a prolonged lowering of heart rate relative to the resting baseline; and (2) during attention termination, when heart rate begins to accelerate back to baseline. After 5 seconds of exposure during the sustained attention phase, infants preferred a novel pattern to the previously exposed one. There was no such preference in children who were exposed to the same pattern for the same length of time during attention termination or in control children who were never exposed to the pattern at all. These data suggest that the infant's state at the time of exposure influences how much information they will acquire about objects and events.

The infant's state during the recognition test also appears to be important. Richards and Casey (1992) found discrimination between novel and familiar events during sustained attention, but not during attention termination, even though both phases involved looking. During recognition test trials, the phase of sustained attention lasted an average of 11.8 seconds with infants looking 7.3 seconds at the novel pattern and 4.5 seconds at the familiar pattern. During the phase of attention termination, in contrast, the infants looked 3.1 and 2.7 seconds at the novel and familiar patterns, respectively. Thus, focused attention during exposure to an event facilitates learning to recognize the event, but demonstrating such learning may also depend on the sustained and focused state.

SPECIFIC TYPES OF LEARNING

In this chapter, we have tried to demonstrate a general link between attention and learning, a link that is evident in some form at all ages. There are many forms of learning, however, and by discussing some of these in detail, we may be able to specify more precisely the nature of the relationship between attention and learning. Here, we deal with discrimination learning, sequence learning, and observational learning.

Discrimination Learning

Discrimination learning occurs when a subject learns to discriminate between two targets and to choose the one that consistently leads to reinforcement. As Stevenson (1970) notes, the child involved in a discrimination learning task must be

capable of attending to the relevant stimuli, of inhibiting attention to irrelevant cues, of discriminating the differences among the stimuli, of remembering the stimulus chosen, of being appropriately influenced by the consequence of his response, of being motivated to persist in trying to be correct, and of not elaborating the problem so that it becomes more difficult than it actually is. (p. 868)

Faced with a choice between a large blue square and a small red sphere on every trial, learning is usually fast. The task can be made more difficult by changing the specific targets on every trial, but keeping the connection between reinforcement and a given feature—the color red, for example—constant across trials. In an influential theory, Zeaman and House (1963) suggested that discrimination learning depends on the subject's attending to the correct dimension. During training, the subject might attend to many different dimensions of the stimulus objects. In most cases, the dimensions attended to would not be consistently associated with reinforcement; consequently, attention would shift to another dimension, an example of the nonobservable shifts of attention discussed in chapter 4. Once the subject attends to the relevant dimension, however, learning proceeds rapidly.

An assumption of this theory is that subjects attend to dimensions, such as color or shape, as well as to specific features, such as red or round. To test this theoretical assumption, a new variant of the task involves shifting the contingencies, so that reinforcement is now associated with either a new feature within the same dimension or a feature within a new dimension. For example, green squares and red squares could be paired with red triangles and green triangles, with the subject reinforced for responding to the squares, regardless of color. Then reinforcement would be shifted either to triangles, a feature within the originally reinforced dimension, or to red, a feature outside the original dimension. As predicted, children find shifts within dimensions easier to master and they learn the new contingencies faster than they do when the shift is to a new dimension (Zeaman & House, 1963). The ability to selectively attend to dimensions does not appear to undergo much development because there is evidence for it in infants.

In a recent monograph, Coldren and Colombo (1994) provide both an excellent review of the developmental literature and a series of interesting studies with 9-month-olds. They trained infants to look at one of two patterns in a series of pairs varying in color, shape, and lateral position. The reinforcement was an audio recording of a woman's voice continuing to speak as long as the infant looked at the correct target. Each infant was presented with eight training trials; each trial lasted until the infant had accumulated 10 seconds of looking to one or both of the targets. The relevant dimension was either color or shape. When shape was relevant, the infant had to choose between a circle and a triangle; the irrelevant dimension, however, varied across trials, so that sometimes the infant would be reinforced for looking at a blue circle, and sometimes, a green circle. Following the training trials, the stimulus targets were changed and the infants were either reinforced for choosing one of two shapes (square or cross) or for choosing one of two colors (red or orange). The first condition represents an intradimensional shift and the second, an extradimensional shift. The theory proposed by Zeaman and House (1963) predicts that infants would find the intradimensional shift easier because they would not have to shift from the dimension of shape to the dimension of color. This appears to be what happened because, on the first block of trials, infants looked more at the correct target when the shift was within a dimension than when the shift was to a new dimension (see figure 9.3).

A second prediction from the Zeaman and House model is that learning should be rapid from the point that the subject attends to the correct dimension. However, the amount of time different subjects spend in the period before isolating the correct dimension would vary. To test this prediction, Coldren and Colombo trained a group of infants to a criterion; trials were stopped when, on two consecutive trials, infants looked 50% longer at the correct target than on initial trials or looked 65% of the time at the correct target. When the proportion of looking time was plotted backward from criterion, the infants' looking appeared to stay around 50% to each target until criterion was met (see figure 9.4). In the absence of postcriterion training trials, the sudden upsurge in looking at the correct target might be an artifact of the criterion, but the results are consistent with the attention model proposed by Zeaman and House and with their empirical findings.

Under ordinary conditions of learning, cues will vary in the extent to which they attract attention. Learning may be dependent on habituation to highly salient but irrelevant cues. Repetition of low-salience cues would ordinarily lead to fast habituation, but when these are attended to and associated with reinforcement, they will receive more attention in the future. Thus, reinforcement is facilitative and counteracts the inhibitory process of habituation. Jeffrey (1968) gives an example of

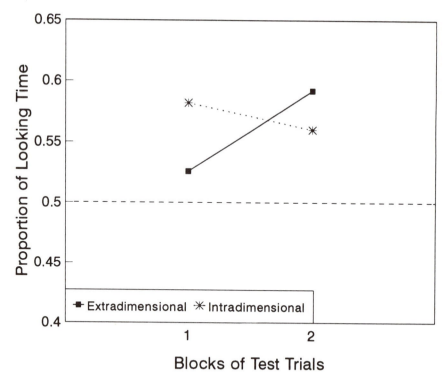

Figure 9.3. The test trials represent either an extradimensional shift where infants were reinforced for looking at targets on the basis of a different dimension from that reinforced during training, or an intradimensional shift where infants were reinforced for looking on the basis of a different feature within the same dimension as that reinforced during training. The figure shows the proportion of time spent looking at the reinforced target on the first four test trials and on the second four. Chance level of .50 is shown by the dashed line. From *The nature and processes of preverbal learning* by J. T. Coldren and J. Colombo, 1994, *Monographs of the Society for Research in Child Development, 59,* p. 42. Copyright 1994 by Society for Research in Child Development. Adapted with permission.

how salience of a cue can be changed by pairing it with a more attention-demanding event. The example is based on the difficulty children as old as 5 to 6 years have in discriminating between oblique lines (Rudel & Teuber, 1963), such as a leftward diagonal line and a rightward diagonal line (\/). The difficulty may be related to young children's confusion with mirror images (Pick & Pick, 1970). Jeffrey (1968) suggests that attention to directional cues could be increased by attaching these low-salience cues to more salient ones—that is, cues of greater intrinsic interest. In a study by Jeffrey

marbles rolling down an oblique line were used to elicit attention to the directional cue. Learning proceeded readily. . . . Furthermore, there was considerable transfer to a more difficult labeling task involving the oblique lines as discriminanda. These results lend some support to the assertion that once a subject's attention to a critical cue is elicited, the salience of that cue will be increased if reinforcement follows. (p. 329)

The presence of discrimination learning and transfer based on dimensions of stimulation at 9 months (Coldren & Colombo, 1994) suggests that there is relatively little change in the processes underlying discrimination learning, at least after 9 months. Further work with younger infants would be valuable in assessing whether there is a transition in the basis of discrimination learning at 9 months along with the other changes occurring at that time. A lack of development in the basic mechanisms, however, does not mean that older children are no better at these tasks than younger ones. As children mature and gain knowledge and experience, they are able to isolate relevant variables in problem-solving tasks more quickly. They become better able to ignore or inhibit responses to irrelevant variables. Perceptual learning and analysis of detail also allow them to make discriminations too subtle for the younger child. Finally, the functional use of language, as discussed in chapter 8, makes it more possible for their learning to be based on explicit rules. By 4 or 5 years, children's learning, at least in some contexts, may be less dependent on direct control by reinforcement contingencies and be "governed [more] by rules of the subjects' own devising" (Bentall, Lowe, & Beasty, 1985, p. 177).

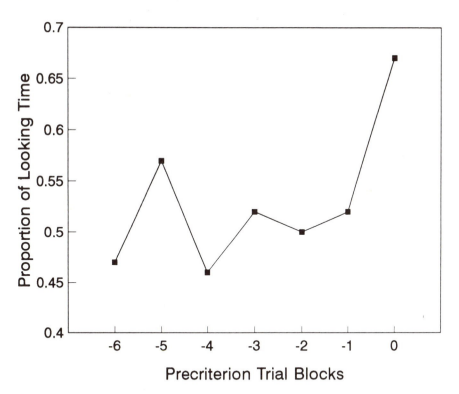

Figure 9.4. Backward learning curves suggesting that responses tend to remain at chance level until just before criterion. From *The nature and processes of preverbal learning* by J. T. Coldren and J. Colombo, 1994, *Monographs of the Society for Research in Child Development*, *59*, p. 49. Copyright 1994 by Society for Research in Child Development. Adapted with permission.

Sequence Learning

The literature on sequence learning in adults raises the possibility that only some types of sequences can be learned within the orienting/investigative system of attention, while learning other types of sequences may require the development of the second system of higher level controls. Several investigators working with adults have hypothesized that some learning of sequential patterns occurs without awareness, in the sense that subjects cannot explicitly state what they have learned. Nissen's research (e.g., Nissen & Bullemer, 1987) suggests that both implicit and explicit learning require attention because learning and performance in both cases deteriorates when a distracting secondary task must be carried out simultaneously. Curran and Keele (1993) argue, however, that a type of sequential learning may occur with almost no attention. Cohen, Ivry, and Keele (1990) found that adults' reaction times decrease to the repeated presentation of events in a series of locations, where each location predicts one and only one subsequent location (e.g., a sequence such as 1-2-3-1-2-3). Under these circumstances, adults show a kind of habitual learning of the locations without consciously knowing the sequence, and they can learn even while carrying out a simultaneous attention-demanding task of counting tones. When sequences do not show unique associations (e.g., 1-2-3-2-1-3), however, a simultaneous attention-demanding task interferes with learning, even though subjects seem to learn without awareness.

The subjects, of course, had to be looking at the task events and so were attending at some level, but the ability to carry on despite high levels of distraction suggests that almost no effort was involved. Sequential learning, according to Curran and Keele (1993), may proceed on the basis of two different processes occurring in parallel: The "nonattentional" type may be particular to the learning of sequential patterns of responses and to faster reaction times as a measure; the "attentional" type may be more general and account for a larger share of the learning that does occur. They found, for example, that subjects who were explicitly aware of the sequence responded significantly faster than subjects who were unaware or only partly so.

In the development of such learning, however, the important question is what kinds of sequence learning are possible in the first attention system and which require the second system. Clohessy (1994) tested 4- and 10-month-old infants in a setting where events occurred in three locations under these conditions: (1) randomly; (2) in a simple, predictable sequence (1-2-3-1-2-3); or (3) in a complex sequence where the location of the event depended on the context (1-2-1-3-1-2-1-3). Infants at both ages learned to anticipate events in the simple sequences, but infants at neither age learned to anticipate the complex sequences. In contrast, a more recent study from the same laboratory (Rothbart, Rundman, Gerardi, & Posner, 1995) suggests that 18-month-olds can learn the context-dependent associations in a complex sequence. The investigators speculate that these complex sequences require an executive attention network (Posner & Rothbart, 1991) that leads to explicit learning of sequences in adults. This network would be included in our more general system of higher level control that is operating at 18 months in some form, but is not operating at 4 to 10 months.

Although infants in the first year attended to sequential events, their learning was limited to highly predictable sequences with no ambiguity about the location of the next event (see also Smith, 1984; Smith, Jankowski, Brewster, & Loboschefski, 1990). A theory of possible relevance is provided by Jones and Boltz (1989). They theorize that observers attune themselves to the spatio-temporal structure of events by entraining their own rhythms to those of the event. The observer's attention, however, may be set to large units of time and structure or to small units of time and structure; these are termed "referent periods." Jones and Boltz argue that attention to smaller units is more effortful and may be characteristic of the early phases of learning. In addition, they suggest that "infants may be differentially selective to events that offer relatively small referent periods . . . whereas older people may increasingly entrain with longer periods as referents" (p. 470). Thus, infants may expend their energy on learning the details of a sequence as associations within pairs. By 18 months, children may begin to focus on the larger spatio-temporal structures and to pick up information about the larger context containing associations between pairs of events. Their expectations then become more long-range and complex.

Observational Learning

Children learn by doing, but they also learn a great deal by watching others' actions. The research on imitation attests to children's readiness to learn new actions by observation, an ability that becomes highly functional at the time of the 9-month transition (Piaget, 1962). Meltzoff (1988b) found that 9-month-olds, after a single exposure to an adult demonstrating a target action, later reproduced that action on the same object more than would be expected by chance, even though they had not been given an opportunity to perform the action immediately after the demonstration. The behavior of a control group ruled out the possibility that imitative actions occurred because the adult's activity was arousing and simply increased the probability of any action. The control group watched the adult manipulate the object but not perform the target action; later their execution of the target action was at chance levels.

In further work (Meltzoff, 1988a), 14-month-olds demonstrated imitation after a week's delay; this delayed imitation was not limited to actions already in the children's behavioral repertoires, but included novel actions with no probability of occurring spontaneously. These results suggest that infants' imitation is based on observation of particular actions and translation of observed action into the child's own activity. As Meltzoff (1990, p. 13) points out, "Imitation serves the function of providing 'no trial' learning in our species precisely because it allows the direct pick-up of novel behaviors from the observation of others." Imitation or observational learning of novel actions emerges with the beginnings of the second attention system; with the added influence of language and symbolic function on that system, observational learning can lead to new symbolic representations of appropriate behavior (Bandura, 1965).

Uzgiris et al. (1989) emphasize the social nature of imitation and the extent to which both partners in an interaction match one another's actions. They write that "an act of imitation captures the juncture of the individual and the world with which the individual interacts" (p. 108). Bandura (1965, 1986) also underscores the role of observational learning in social development. He incorporates attentional processes as an integral part of his model of observational learning in at least three ways (Bandura, 1986). First, some instances of modeling are more salient by virtue of the sounds and interesting sights provided by the modeled action. In addition, modeled actions may alter the child's subsequent attention by highlighting certain aspects of the environment. Second, with cognitive development, children become aware of and attend to more subtle aspects of the events they observe. The child may even imitate or match the attention of the person observed (Bandura & Walters, 1963). Finally, children are not equally attentive to all models. For example, they imitate adults and other children who are rewarded more readily than other models. Bandura (1965) notes that the child's anticipation of being similarly rewarded increases learning by "enhancing and focusing" (p. 8) attention to the model. Indeed, individual differences in observational learning may be largely ascribed to differences in direction and degree of attention during the modeled actions.

Adults frequently seek imitation from the child; they employ appropriate attention-getting techniques, make sure the child is watching, and then model the desired action (Bandura, 1986). Much imitation, however, occurs without adult intervention because adult behavior is fascinating to children; they watch and imitate even when the adult is paying no attention to them. As an example, a mother and her preschool child were shopping in a grocery store. When they came to the fruits and vegetables, the mother selected grapefruits by hefting them to see whether they were heavy and juicy. She then moved on; when she turned around to see where her son was, she saw him lifting grapefruits and moving them up and down just as she had. Although he probably had no idea why she had behaved in that particular way, he copied her action and may have learned something about grapefruits as a result.

An interesting study by Azmitia (1988) explored the collaboration between 5-year-old novices and experts on a construction task. Children were pretested by asking them to create a Lego structure according to a Lego model in front of them; their scores on this task determined whether they were novices or experts. During the pretest, those children later labeled as novices looked less frequently at the Lego model than the experts and spent less time engaged in the task. The novices were then paired either with other novices or with experts. The novices paired with experts began to look more at the model and spent more time observing their partners than did novices paired with other novices. Experts paired with other experts spent more time observing their partners than did experts paired with novices. These results suggest that children are more likely to observe another child if that child's actions are effective; they may also be aware of when another child is performing better than they are, although such social comparison may not be strictly necessary to explain the results observed here. Kohlberg (1971) suggests that young children are motivated to meet challenges that circumstances set for them; when they recognize their limitations, they are more likely to observe and imitate older or more expert partners because such activity provides them with information about how to do well. As Rogoff (1990) notes, "Observation may be a very important and commonplace way for a novice to be involved in skilled processes" (p. 205).

ATTENTION AND PRACTICE OF NEW SKILLS

The limited nature of human attention sometimes makes it impossible to attend to all information relevant to an activity (see chapter 2). When this happens, actions are inefficient and often ineffective. An important factor in overcoming limitations is practice. Some actions may become so highly practiced that they require little attention and can therefore be carried out at the same time as an activity demanding attention. This process, in principle, underlies some developmental changes in attention and learning.

Practice of Emerging Motor Skills

Emerging motor skills themselves require attention, so for a time the child's attention may not be free to be directed to other aspects of the immediate environment or task. For example, shortly after visually guided reaching emerges at about 4 months, infants practice it intensively and compulsively. In the period from 4 to 9 months, however, reaching becomes markedly more efficient (von Hofsten & Lindhagen, 1979) and ballistic in the sense that, once objects are located, infants can accurately grasp them without watching either their hands or the objects. Bushnell (1985) argues that the decline in *visually guided* reaching frees the child's attention for perceiving and learning about other aspects of the situations in which reaching occurs. To quote Bushnell,

between the ages of 4 and 8 months, the act of executing an accurate reach demands a great deal of the infant's attention. The target and the hand are concentrated on throughout the act, which may be said to fill a whole frame of consciousness. Hence, it would not be possible for memories, perceptions, or activities attended to prior to or after the reach to be meaningfully connected with the reach nor with one another. This restriction would naturally interfere with the encoding of many cause-effect, means-end, or other such sequences of events. For example, the reappearance of an object could not be related to the reach for the cloth with which it was covered nor to the memory of its prior disappearance. Similarly, the reach for an object on which a second object rests could not be related to the subsequent retrieval of the second object. When the bridging act of reaching no longer fully occupies the infant's attention, however, the before and after states or the actions and consequences in such instances can be encoded together. By this reasoning, the automatization of may be considered prerequisite to the attainment of these familiar cognitive milestones. (p. 151)

Koslowski and Bruner (1972) provide an example in the second year of life. They systematically observed children in three age groups—12 to 14 months, 14 to 16 months, and 16 to 24 months—trying to solve a problem. A toy was attached to a rotating lever and the children were given 15 to 20 minutes to retrieve the toy. The solution was to rotate the lever away from the body in order to bring within reach the toy resting on the lever. Several approaches to the task were used by the children according to their ages.

The first, most common among the 12-month-olds, was a direct reach for the object. Failing to reach it, some children walked around the table to grasp the object directly. Being foiled by the experimenters, they tried again or switched to a second approach—moving the lever back and forth, but always bringing it back to midline. These children seemed to appreciate the fact that the lever rotated, but not that rotation would bring the object close enough for a direct reach. In the third approach, 14- to 16-month-olds rotated the lever part way, or even all of the way, but made no attempt to reach for the object even when it came close to them. They may have been attending so carefully to the relationship of lever and toy that they were, as the authors put it, "operationally preoccupied" (p. 795). This third approach involved a strategy apparently requiring so much attention that the goal motivating the activity in the first place was forgotten. The last approach, used only by the 16- to 24-month-olds, was to rotate the lever until the toy was just within reach and then to grasp it. Although the specific situation may have been a novel one for them, the older children would have brought to the situation experience with other rotating objects. This experience would have made the operation more routine, allowing the strategy and the goal to be attended to at the same time.

Drawing is an example relevant to older children. Although the scribbles of a 2-year-old do not meet a very high standard of depiction, children of this age lack the necessary fine motor skills to do better. The quality of their drawings, however, may not arise simply from a failure of coordination. Their attention is initially devoted to *making* marks on the paper; only later when that skill becomes well practiced and efficient can they begin to pay close attention to the final product (Di Leo, 1970).

Attention to Emerging Cognitive Skills

It is easy to think of motor skills in terms of practice, but the same freeing of attention by increasing efficiency can also be seen in more cognitive realms. For example, Bloom and Beckwith (1989) argue that infants and young children have two systems for expressing themselves: One is affective, involving posture, vocalization, and facial expression; the other is linguistic. They found that, when children were at the stage of acquiring their first words, there was a diminution of positive affect for several seconds preceding the onset of a word and a peak in affect expression immediately after. At the later "vocabulary spurt," however, the dip in expressiveness before the spoken word was not as great and the subsequent peak in affect expression was higher. The authors consider the reduced expression of affect before the word to reflect the cognitive demands of speaking words at a time when the ability is just emerging. At the vocabulary spurt, children have had more practice; the cognitive demands are less and the dip in expressiveness is accordingly less pronounced.

Wiener-Margulies, Rey-Barboza, Cabrera, and Anisfeld (in press) tested the hypothesis that attention absorbed by activity during play would lead to lower levels of talking in children whose skill in combining words was emerging. They observed 11 children when the children had just begun to combine words; their average age was 22 months. The children played with two sets of toys at the first visit and with two other sets of toys approximately six months later. Videotapes of their play sessions were coded for three levels of engagement: focused attention to the toys, casual attention to the toys, and no attention to the toys. The presence or absence of speech was coded every 2 seconds. The major dependent measure was the proportion of 2-second episodes in which speech occurred over the total number of 2-second episodes in the different levels of engagement. Every child spoke much less during focused attention than during casual attention. The children might have talked during casual attention because they were engaged in some social interplay with the mother. However, the same pattern of results emerged even when cases of speech directed to the mother were eliminated. The differences among the levels of engagement were less at the second visit than at the first, as might be expected on the basis of six months of practice with talking.

Although toddlers have mastered many aspects of attending to both toy and adult during joint play, Rocissano and Yatchmink (1983) suggest that children just beginning to acquire language will have difficulty attending to toys and to adult speech at the same time. In their study, preterm children of mothers who followed the children's lead in what toys to attend to, talking about those toys, were compared to children of mothers who more often asked their children to shift their focus of attention. Children of mothers who followed their lead had more advanced language development.

To emphasize the continuing nature of this process, we cite an example offered by Sorsby and Martlew (1991), who found the demand on 4-year-olds' representational capacity to be greater during reading than during play with materials such as Play-doh. When looking at books with their children, parents are more likely than during play to ask children questions requiring some operation on objects and events not currently present, such as "What is the same about an apple and an orange?" Children's answers are also more likely to be fully adequate when the questions occur during book reading than during play. The authors suggest, in concert with our current theme, that because book reading does not require physical action, children's attention is freed for concentration on symbolic activity. That is, constraints imposed on representational skills by attention will be greater in situations requiring the coordination of several subskills or components. By limiting the number of components, book reading offers a better opportunity for practicing the emerging capacity for abstract thinking than do other play settings. With more practice, children become better able to coordinate abstract thinking and play with concrete materials.

Effort Involved in Emerging Use of Strategies

When children are faced with situations challenging their abilities to manage the demands made on them, specific strategies for dealing with demands are useful. Miller (1990) has reviewed her research on strategies of selective attention. As described in chapter 2, her task involves an apparatus with 12 doors, two rows of 6 each. On each door is a picture of either a cage or a house. Children are told to remember, for example, the location of specific animals under the doors with cages because they will later be asked to recall those locations. The most efficient strategy is to open only the doors with cages and ignore those with houses. Miller outlines a developmental sequence occurring during the period from 3 to 6 years: (1) initially, children do not produce the selective attention strategy; (2) next, they produce partial strategies—that is, they open relevant doors but less than 75% of them; (3) they then produce the selective strategy but with no improvement in recall;

(4) finally, children both produce the selective strategy and appear to profit from it.

Miller hypothesizes that, when strategies first emerge, there is a "utilization deficiency"—the strategy is used spontaneously but it does not seem to improve performance. She argues that this lack of improvement is due to limited capacity and the amount of attention and effort required to execute the strategy. Support for this argument comes from a study using a dual-task paradigm (P. Miller, Seier et al., 1991). Finger tapping was interfered with more when younger children used a systematic door-opening strategy than when older children did, suggesting that the strategy was more effortful for the younger children. Execution of a strategy is effortful for at least three reasons: Children have to search for relevant information, inhibit inefficient but salient response tendencies, and monitor the consequences of their own behavior. When particular strategies become more practiced, more attention can be paid to the task. A substitute for practice would be to have an adult help with the task. When adults opened the relevant doors while the children watched, age differences in performance were reduced (P. Miller, Woody-Ramsey, & Aloise, 1991). For children who do not spontaneously use a strategy, the experimenter is both supplying and executing the strategy, thereby enhancing the children's performance.

In summary, a preoccupation with means rather than ends suggests that exercise of an unpracticed skill, whether physical or cognitive, takes considerable effort. Until the skill becomes more practiced or automatic, the child may not be able to selectively attend to combining the various components required to solve a problem involving that skill. This aspect of skill development is repeated again and again; when children use new skills, attention and resources are co-opted and cannot be directed to other requirements of the task.

SUMMARY

In this chapter, we discussed the way in which measures of learning and performance are used to infer that a subject's attention is focused on a task. We also reviewed evidence suggesting that children learn about those objects and events they attend to and that learning and performance are enhanced when children focus their attention.

We then introduced three types of learning and considered the relationship between attention and learning inherent in the different types. First, the Zeaman and House model of attention in discrimination learning has received support from recent work on discrimination learning in infants. We concluded, along with others, that the basic mechanisms of orienting to a dimension of stimulation may not change, at least after the first six months of life. On the other hand, older children may be able to selectively attend to more subtle differences between objects and events and thus learn in a larger number of situations. In learning to anticipate events in a sequence, however, there do seem to be important changes in underlying processes. Learning of complex sequences is very difficult before about 18 months of age. Infants can easily learn to anticipate predictable events in a simple sequence because processes of the orienting/investigative system are adequate. The second attention system and other changes around 18 months make it easier to learn complex sequences in which the location of an event is not predictable from the immediately preceding event. Finally, much learning proceeds from children's spontaneous observation of the activity of others and requires little direct intervention by adults.

In the last section, we reviewed evidence of children's limited capacity to attend and the role practice plays in overcoming those limitations. Because the number of events occurring simultaneously is large and the capacity to attend is limited, there are costs when an activity requires close attention. At times of transition in early development, these costs are evident as children practice newly and barely acquired skills. Once the skills become routine, attention is freed for learning about new relations. In this way, learning influences the development of attention as much as attention affects learning. Both processes underlie children's expanding knowledge of the world.

10

Individual Differences in Attention

In the preceding chapters, we have outlined a number of developmental trends in attention. Embedded in these developmental trends are individual differences in attentiveness that can be observed in specific activities, such as duration of looking, or in general attributes of behavior, such as persistence or distractibility. The term "individual differences" refers to behavioral variation *among* individuals that transcends both time and context. It does not refer to the variability *within* individuals due to temporary fluctuations in alertness, motivation, physical condition, mood, and so on, even though these are important concurrent influences on behavior. Individual differences in attention are related to variability in both cognition and temperament and constitute an important influence on the development of self-regulation.

In this chapter, we discuss the evidence for stability and consistency in individual children along the attention-related dimensions of behavior discussed in previous chapters. We begin with a brief review of methods used to determine whether stable individual differences exist. The second section is a discussion of individuality in three aspects of attention: reactivity to environmental events; sustained visual orienting to displays and events; and focused attention during play and tasks. In the third section, we consider individual differences in three dimensions related to attention: activity level, impulse control, and emotionality.

STUDYING INDIVIDUAL DIFFERENCES

Researchers assess individual differences in behavior by recording or rating the behavior of children at different times or in different situations. The investigator's task is to consider the many sources of behavioral variation and to determine, by analytic methods, how much individual children's responses vary because of the tendencies they bring to the situation. There are two general designs for investigating individual differences. The first is to use correlational techniques to examine the degree of association between measures taken at least two times or in two contexts.

Averaging over multiple measures tends to cancel out temporary fluctuations. Thus, the more times or the more situations in which measurements are taken, the more reliable the estimate of stability and consistency within individuals (Epstein, 1980).

A second method is to separate a group of children into two or more subgroups based on behavior at one time and then observe them at other times or in different situations. The question is whether the subgroups continue to differ along the same or related dimensions of behavior. The grouping of children can be achieved in several ways. One is splitting a sample at the median of the relevant variable. Another is to consider only the extremes of a continuum (e.g., Kagan, Reznick, & Snidman, 1987). For example, children who fall at the upper and lower 25% (or 33% or 10%) of the distribution in looking time on one occasion could be compared on their attentiveness on a second occasion. The disadvantage of this method is that it fails to include the entire range of variation. Nevertheless, it can be sensitive to individual differences not captured by overall correlations.

Within either method, a variety of measures can be used. Some are based on direct observation and recording of children's behavior. These measures generally lead to the type of results discussed in previous chapters. Many of the measures to be reported, however, are based on responses to questionnaires by parents or teachers. Because of the extensive use of questionnaires, we discuss their rationale briefly.

On questionnaires, parents or teachers may rate more global items—"My child fidgets during quiet activities" (Fullard, McDevitt, & Carey, 1984). Or they may rate more specific items—"Enjoys riding a tricycle or bicycle fast and recklessly" (Rothbart, Ahadi, & Hershey, 1994; Rothbart, Ahadi, Hershey, & Fisher, 1994). In questionnaires with more global items, it is assumed that respondents will be drawing from a wide range of experience with the child. In questionnaires with more specific items, several items will be directed at a dimension of behavior, such as activity level, in particular situations; the experimenter then averages over those items to get a general picture of the child's behavior. As one of us (Rothbart, 1989d) has noted,

When we gather information across a broad set of items, aggregating an overall score across those items, our expectation is that the temperamental "signal" will become enhanced, while the "noise" from other influences of mood, need state, and personal history will tend to cancel each other out. (p. 61)

At times, researchers may find no "signal" and the underlying rationale for the items will have to be reconsidered or the items revised. On the other hand, there is always a possibility that a general attitude about the child will bias a respondent's answers to all items, producing a spuriously strong signal. Despite some disadvantages, a major strength of questionnaires is that parents are basing their ratings on the child's behavior in normal circumstances and across many more situations than are accessible to the researcher (Rothbart & Goldsmith, 1985; Rothbart & Mauro, 1990).

Correlational and subgroup analyses are complementary and can often be used on the same data set. Likewise, direct behavioral observation and questionnaire data can provide validation for each other as well as converging results on the topic of individual differences. This multidimensional approach is important to our interpretation of patterns of behavior over time and across situations.

INDIVIDUAL DIFFERENCES IN ASPECTS OF ATTENTION

Our intent in the following sections is to summarize and integrate the available evidence for the proposition that children vary in: (1) the readiness with which they react to external events; (2) the tendency to remain oriented to those events; and (3) the tendency to narrowly focus or concentrate on objects, events, and activities. For each of these aspects of attention, we summarize the evidence for stability over time, consistency across situations, and underlying mechanisms that may account for differences. In general, we report correlations that tend to be modest. In some cases, the low to moderate level of the intercorrelations could be due to unreliability of measurement, but they are often modest for substantive reasons to be clarified in each section.

Reactivity

Reactivity has been defined as "the characteristics of the individual's reaction to changes in the environment, as reflected in somatic, endocrine, and autonomic nervous systems" (Rothbart & Derryberry, 1981, p. 37). Reactivity is not a unidimensional construct; there are dissociations across response systems and differences in the time course of different reactions (Gunnar, 1990; Lacey & Lacey, 1962; Rothbart & Derryberry, 1981). We can therefore think of reactivity in terms of attention, emotion, autonomic response, and so on. We are most concerned here with aspects of reactivity related to attention, but in a later section, we indicate how different aspects of reactivity may be related.

Characteristics of reactivity include the timing and intensity of responses to environmental events. Individuals vary on how much stimulation or change in stimulation is required to elicit a reaction, how long a response takes to develop, and the vigor of the response. Reactivity is clearly related to the behavioral and autonomic features of the orienting response, discussed in chapter 6, to respiratory sinus arrhythmia as discussed in chapters 2 and 6, and also to the concept of alertness.

Behavioral Reactivity

We begin with research on individual differences in behavioral alerting in the newborn infant. Brazelton's Neonatal Behavioral Assessment Scale (NBAS: Brazelton, 1984) was developed to assess variability in the newborn's behavioral responses that might be related to patterns of coping with the physical and social environment (Brazelton, Nugent, & Lester, 1987). The NBAS is carried out in conjunction with assessment of newborn reflexes and contains 28 items. It is administered in a way that varies somewhat from infant to infant because the examiner attempts to elicit the best possible performance from each infant.

Factor analyses on NBAS scores from several samples point to an underlying set of dimensions that characterize variability in infants' NBAS performance (Kaye, 1978; Strauss & Rourke, 1978). One factor includes items assessing both alertness and orienting (visual tracking and turning to sound). From the first to the second week of life, infants seem to be somewhat stable in their scores on these items if scores from several assessments are combined (Kaye, 1978). Consistency of alertness across situations in the newborn has also been reported. Osofsky and Danzger (1974) found that alert newborn infants who oriented more in NBAS testing tended to be more alert during feeding and achieved more eye contact with their mothers. Bakeman and Brown (1980) reported that scores on orienting for preterm and fullterm newborns were positively related to measures of the children's social participation and social competence at 3 years of age. Birns, Barten, and Bridger (1969), however, found little stability between alertness in the newborn period and later laboratory assays of alertness at 3 and 4 months of age.

Investigators attempting to relate NBAS alerting and orienting scores to later infant performance in habituation studies have not found the earlier measures to predict the later measures (Frankel, Shapira, Arbel, Shapira, & Ayal, 1982; Moss, Colombo, Mitchell, & Horowitz, 1988). Moss et al. (1988), however, did find a relationship between a measure of newborn behavioral state organization and later length of infant looking toward a novel object. Infants whose state tended not to reach distress levels, yet who were nevertheless responsive to stimulation, later showed longer looks to presentation of a *novel* stationary pattern at 3 months of age. Barten and Ronch (1971) found a negative relationship between newborns' visual following of a schematic face and duration of their first looks to such faces at 3 and 4 months (Barten & Ronch, 1971). That is, newborns who showed longer visual pursuit were at the later ages likely to show shorter looks toward a schematic face, presumably a *familiar* configuration. As we will see in the next section, shorter durations of looking at familiar displays and longer looking at novel displays is considered a more mature distribution of attention than vice versa. The familiarity or novelty of displays, therefore, help determine whether there are positive or negative relations with earlier measures.

Just as orienting in the newborn period may reflect reactivity to external stimulation, some of the dimensions derived from temperament questionnaires may assess reactivity in older infants and preschool children. In parent-report measures of alerting, Hageküll and Bohlin (1981) found modest stability for a dimension of infant variability they called ''attentiveness'' across 4 to 13 months. This dimension, extracted through factor analysis, includes ratings on items assessing reactivity to physical differences in people and voices, reactivity to taste and to preparations for feeding, and differential reactions to adults and children.

A related dimension—approach to novelty—is well correlated across four different temperament scales and is modestly stable (Rothbart & Mauro, 1990). One extreme of this dimension—very rapid approach—might stem from moderately strong reactivity. Rapid approach to new objects would reflect high positive reactivity and attention. A distinction can be made, however, between positive and negative reactivity (Rothbart, 1989c). Some extremely reactive children might respond negatively to stimulating events and withdraw, making them relatively inattentive to those events. Behavioral approach and withdrawal both have implications for attention, but they may be different processes (Rothbart, 1989a; Schneirla, 1965) and should not be thought of as two ends of a continuum.

Physiological Reactivity

Early attentional reactivity can also be observed in heart rate responses to the presentation of stimulus events in the laboratory. Lipton, Steinschneider, and Richmond (1961) found individual differences in heart rate reactivity to a standard stimulus event by measuring the time to newborns' peak magnitude and recovery of heart rate responses. Bridger, Birns, and Blank (1965) also found that newborns consistently differed from one another in magnitude of heart rate during stimulus presentation and that peak heart rate was related to peak behavioral excitement; these results suggest variability among newborn infants in vigor of responsiveness. Other investigators have focused on heart rate variability; they have shown that higher levels of resting variability are related to larger heart rate decrements to stimulation (Porges, 1974; Porges, Stamps, & Walter, 1974). Lipton, Steinschneider, and Richmond (1966) found that, like behavioral alerting, heart rate reactivity was not stable from the newborn period to later ages; considerable stability, however, was found from 2.5 to 5 months. Graham, Strock, and Ziegler (1981) have suggested that some aspects of cardiac control mature around 2 months. The lack of early long-term stability in both behavioral alerting and heart rate reactivity may be related to the major transition occurring at about 2 months, as discussed in chapters 3, 4, and 6.

In her review of heart rate research, von Bargen (1983) reported that heart rate reactivity to stimulation is more readily observed and more reliable in older than in younger infants. Richards (1989) found stability of heart rate from 3 to 6 months. He also found some modest evidence for stability in the extent of heart rate deceleration to the onset of stimulation. In a study of older children between 6 and 18 years, Lacey and Lacey (1962) found relatively high stability (rs ranged from .50 to .76) over four years for overall heart rate reactivity in the laboratory, with reactivity to warnings and subsequent stressful events showing higher stability than baseline heart rate. Their measures included both heart rate and heart rate variability. Moderate stability in resting respiratory sinus arrhythmia (RSA) has been found across the period of 3 to 13 months of age (Izard et al., 1991) and between 5 to 14 months (Fox, 1989). Baseline RSA appears to be strongly related to heart rate responses to stimulation (Richards, 1989) and to parental rating of the infant's tendency to approach new objects (Richards & Cameron, 1989). In both behavior and heart rate, individual differences in aspects of reactivity are apparent early in life and seem to become more stable as children develop.

Sustained Visual Attention

To date, most research on individual differences in visual attention during infancy has focused on looking, as was the case for developmental studies in this age range (see chapter 3). Duration of looking can be defined as the total accumulated amount of looking across trials, the length of the longest look during an experimental session, the length of the first look to a display, or scale scores from a questionnaire. Duration of looking is an interesting measure of individual differences because it has emerged as a predictor of both concurrent measures of infants' cognitive capacity and later individual differences in children's performance on intelligence tests (Bornstein & Sigman, 1986; Colombo, 1993; McCall & Carriger, 1993).

Stability

Using parent-report measures assessing attention span and persistence, McDevitt and Carey (1981) reported a moderate degree of stability in parents' ratings from the period of 4 to 8 months to the period of 1 to 3 years, and Huttunen and Nyman (1982) found modest stability from 6 to 8 months of age up to 5 years. Duration of Orienting, a subscale from the Infant Behavior Questionnaire (Rothbart, 1981), shows modest stability between 3 months and 6 or 9 months and quite strong stability across assessments at 6, 9, and 12 months.

Duration of looking has also been studied extensively in the laboratory. Stability over time has been assessed within the familiarization/response to novelty paradigm and the habituation paradigm described in chapter 2. Using the familiarization method, Colombo, Mitchell, and Horowitz (1988) found measures of infants' looking to be moderately stable over one week at 4 and 7 months and over the three months between 4 and 7 months. Measures included the number of separate looks at the displays, the amount of exposure time required to accumulate a criterion amount of looking, and preferences for novelty on paired comparison tests. The percentage of time spent looking at the novel display in paired comparison trials, in turn, was positively related to the number of looks and the exposure time, suggesting that infants who looked frequently and briefly at the display during familiarization were more responsive to the novel display. Although all infants discriminated between the two test displays by looking longer at the novel than at the familiar display, infants with short looks had significantly *stronger* preferences for the novel display.

Examining the same issue at older ages, Rose and Feldman (1987) presented infants at 6, 7, and 8 months with six different sequences of familiarization trials followed by paired test trials. Averaging over the six sequences, they found correlations from .30 to .51 across the different ages for the percentage of time spent looking at the novel picture, and from .32 to .38 for the amount of exposure time required to accumulate a fixed amount of looking. Fenson, Sapper, and Minner (1974) found that 12-month-olds' duration of first look and total duration of looking at a series of slides were highly correlated to the same measures obtained three weeks later ($rs = .64$ and .74). The results of all these studies demonstrate a moderate degree of stability within the first year in key measures of looking and visual discrimination.

The infant habituation paradigm also reveals stability across time in infants' duration of looking at visual displays. Colombo, Mitchell, O'Brien, and Horowitz (1987) found that the peak look in an infant-controlled habituation paradigm was moderately correlated over the short term at 4, 7, and 9 months of age and across the age range from 3 to 9 months. Measures of the magnitude of habituation were also significantly related in sessions a week apart and across several months. However, when peak fixation was partialled out, the correlations for magnitude of habituation were no longer significant; this suggests that magnitude of habituation is dependent on peak fixation and thus does not provide unique information about the infants' patterns of looking. There was no evidence of stability in measures of recovery to a novel display presented after habituation.

In studies of stability of looking time over even longer periods, the correlations are quite low. For example, D. Miller et al., (1979) found low to moderate correlations of .30 from 3 to 27 months, .28 from 27 to 39 months, and .26 from 3 to 39 months. But, as Colombo notes, the low correlations may be due, in part, to a decrease in the extent to which the same paradigm will motivate older children. As suggested in chapter 3, there may also be a discontinuity in the processes governing looking.

Although many studies of individual differences in duration of looking have involved continuous measures, investigators have also identified subgroups of infants with patterns of looking that are somewhat stable. Bornstein and Benasich (1986) examined profiles of habituation within sessions and concluded that most 5-month-old infants could be characterized as showing one of three patterns. The most common was a steady decline in looking over trials; the second most frequent pattern was a fluctuating one; the least frequent was an increase in looking followed by a decline. Infants tended to show the same patterns over a 10-day period. The correlation between the two visits was .37, with 66% of the infants showing the same pattern on the second visit. Interestingly, Colombo (1993) argues that the fluctuating pattern is characteristic of older infants and thus may reveal greater maturity in 5-month-olds than the other patterns.

Colombo and his colleagues (e.g., Colombo, Mitchell, Coldren, & Freeseman, 1991) suggest that infants are consistent enough to allow analyses of subgroups referred to as "short lookers" and "long lookers." The identification is usually made on the basis of the length of the infant's peak look during 20 seconds of accumulated looking at a photograph presented before the habituation session. Infants are then separated into two groups at the median or at some criterion—for example, those with peak looks below and above 9 seconds. The duration of peak look, as we have noted, is moderately stable over one-week to six-month intervals (Colombo et al., 1987).

Consistency Across Situations

Duration of looking has shown some consistency at 3 months across both visual paired comparison tasks and social interaction with the mother. In a study by Coldren (1987), the highest correlations were between duration of peak looks on visual tasks and number of looks to the mother during interaction, with shorter peak looks related to more frequent, and presumably shorter, looks toward the mother. Pêcheaux and Lécuyer (1983) found a moderate, but positive, relationship between 4-month-old infants' duration of looking at two-dimensional displays and duration of looking at a three-dimensional toy. Jacobson and colleagues (Jacobson et al., 1992) found that mean duration of looks at static patterns at 6.5 and 12 months was related to mean duration of look on the visual test trial in a haptic to visual cross-modal task at 12 months. For girls, Fenson et al. (1974) found a positive and substantial relationship (.70) between duration of looking to slides and duration of visual-manual contact with a single toy. As we will see in the next section on focused attention, however, duration of looking at displays in familiarization and habituation procedures are often not correlated with concurrent measures of focused looking at toys during manipulative play.

Predictive Value of Looking Measures

Measures of looking are associated with both concurrent and later cognitive measures. Concurrently, shorter durations of looking during infancy are related to (1) greater responsiveness to novel displays and toys; (2) more advanced motor development; and (3) better concept formation and discrimination learning (Colombo, 1993). In these cases, more mature performance on the cognitive tasks is related to infants' looking for shorter periods of time. Duration of looking between 2 and 8 months of age is also predictive of performance on intelligence tests up to 8 years of age (Bornstein & Sigman, 1986; Colombo, 1993; Fagan, 1984; McCall & Carriger, 1993); shorter looking predicts higher scores. These predictions have been of particular interest to developmental researchers because attempts to predict later intelligence from tests of mental capacity in infancy have not always been successful. There is also a suggestion in the data that results from infants of 2 to 8 months are most predictive (McCall & Carriger, 1993); this period is associated with the strongest influence of novelty on selective attention (see chapter 5).

Tamis-LeMonda and Bornstein (1993) recently reported that infants who show shorter peak looks in an habituation paradigm at 5 months tend to have higher scores on a measure of exploratory competence at 13 months. The 13-month exploratory competence score is a measure derived from a combination of attention span (the average of infants' two longest looks at toys during free play) and level of symbolic play with toys. Exploratory competence at 13 months was also predicted from extent of 5-month "activity"—a home-based measure that included looking at the mother and looking at objects. A final analysis of the unique predictive value of 5-month measures for 13-month outcome revealed that high levels of later attention during exploration were predicted by shorter looks during habituation, more activity, and higher maternal IQ.

Underlying Processes

Here we consider several possible interpretations of individual variability in duration of looking during infancy. The variability might, for example, reflect individual differences in the degree to which the infant is actively learning about the visual world, with more complete learning accomplished by infants who look for longer periods. This interpretation, however, has been rejected on the basis of the predictive relationships described above. In addition, average duration of looking tends to decrease across age in infancy, so that developmentally "mature" performance is measured by shorter, not longer, looking (Colombo, 1993). Finally, although an infant may be looking at a display, measures of heart rate and distractibility suggest that the infant's attention is not necessarily engaged (Richards, 1988). Thus, long looks are not an adequate reflection of attention span.

Another currently held interpretation of individual differences in duration of looking is a differential encoding hypothesis; infants who look longer do so because they require a longer time to acquire sufficient information for visual recognition (Colombo, 1993; Colombo & Mitchell, 1990). Support for a negative association between average duration of looking and speed of acquiring information comes from the study by Jacobson et al. (1992). They performed a factor analysis on a number of measures taken from a sample of infants observed at 6.5 and 12 months of age. The factor analysis revealed a clear first factor, "speed," composed of two reaction-time measures from Haith's visual anticipation task (Haith et al., 1988; chapter 4) and duration of looking during both visual and cross-modal tasks; longer durations of looking were associated with slower reaction times.

Jacobson et al. (1992) suggest that infants who look for shorter times may "have a more developmentally advanced or integrated CNS (e.g., their neural transmission rate may increase as a function of postnatal myelination or synaptogenesis)" (p. 721). Jacobson et al. also found a negative correlation between baseline reaction time and novelty preference, similar to a finding by DiLalla et al. (1990) with a sample of twins observed at 7 and 9 months of age. These latter findings are consistent with the relationship, noted earlier, between short looks during familiarization on the one hand and strong responses to novelty on the other.

A process that may help to account for individual differences in infants' time to learn about static patterns is their rate of scanning the pattern. Bronson (1991) studied a small sample of subjects whose fixation patterns were coded in detail, allowing him to link infants' visual scanning patterns to their preference for novelty. Three-month-old infants who later showed relatively low preferences for a novel test figure tended, during their inspection of the standard pattern, to look at parts of the figure for extended periods and to show less extensive scanning across the figure. Bronson's (1991) analysis of the scanning style of 2-week old infants also showed a tendency toward long looks and narrow scanning. Thus, 3-month-olds who showed less novelty preference scanned the patterns in ways similar to younger infants, raising the possibility that differences in scanning reflect differences in rate of development. A maturation lag interpretation would agree well with the concurrent relationships found between duration of looking and other performance measures (Colombo, 1993).

Bronson hypothesizes, however, that infants who show more rapid and distributed scanning patterns may be disposed, on a more permanent basis, to engage in acquiring new visual information. From this perspective, movement of gaze is driven by the infant's motivation to learn about the visual world. Because preference for novel displays is related to shorter looks at familiar ones, this possibility seems reasonable; it also fits with Berg and Sternberg's (1985) argument that interest in novel situations is an important aspect of intelligence at all ages.

Another basis for early differences in looking may lie in the infant's ability to disengage attention from one position in space and move it to another (Hood & Atkinson, 1993; Johnson et al., 1991). Long looks at familiar events may reflect a weakness in the "infant's capacity to turn off attention" (Sigman, Cohen, Beckwith, & Parmelee, 1986, p. 790). Individual differences would then reflect differences in sustaining and then disengaging attention to particular events. In a related formulation, McCall and Mash (1995) argue that the critical difference among infants may involve inhibition. Because infants can distinguish between novel and familiar displays in paired comparison trials before showing habituation (Fagan, 1974), encoding may not be the most important aspect of habituation studies.

McCall and Mash suggest that acquisition of information actually occurs rapidly, with habituation of looking more dependent on the infant's ability to inhibit responding to low priority stimuli. They speculate about a potential association between short durations of looking in infancy and efficient inhibition in cognitive processes during the preschool years (see Bjorklund and Harnishfeger, 1990).

Colombo and his associates (Colombo et al., 1991; Freeseman, Colombo & Coldren, 1993) have explored the possibility that infants who look for shorter or longer times at static displays may be attending to different levels of information in those displays. They hypothesize that infants with shorter looks may be responding more to the global aspects of the display, and infants with longer looks, to details within the display. In a study (previously described in chapter 4), Colombo and his colleagues (1995) presented infants with overall shapes, such as an hourglass and a diamond, composed of little letters, *N*'s and *Z*'s. After familiarization, the investigators pitted global and local properties against each other in test trials by pairing a familiar global pattern composed of novel elements with a novel global pattern composed of familiar elements. As expected, short-looking infants preferred the novel global pattern after short familiarization times and the novel local details after longer familiarization times. Long-looking infants did not discriminate between the two displays until familiarization time was extended; even then, their initial discrimination was seen in a preference for novel details.

To further explore the hypothesis that long-looking infants tend to focus on local details of a display, Colombo and his associates (Ryther, Colombo, Frick, & Coleman, 1994) investigated long- and short-looking infants' responses to visual "pop-out" effects such as those seen in figure 3.3 of chapter 3. The detection of an odd element within a homogeneous field of different elements, for example, a *Q* among *O*s, is more likely with a global analysis that involves broad scanning of a display. In their study of 4-month-olds, short-looking infants responded differentially to displays with and without discrepant elements, while long-looking infants of the same age did not. These findings are interesting because Adler and Rovee-Collier (1994) have observed that 3-month-old infants' learning and memory over a week's time can be enhanced by using a pop-out effect to highlight the critical stimulus feature. Thus, short-looking infants, compared to long-looking infants, may be more sensitive to the information available only when the whole display is attended to; this sensitivity, in turn, may lead to more general learning about the visual environment.

Colombo (1995) has recently speculated about possible neurological underpinnings for the classification of infants into short and long lookers. He first notes that there are two different neural pathways involved in pattern recognition, one responding to low spatial frequencies (global aspects of the display) and the other responding to high spatial frequencies (details). The neurons in the first, low-frequency pathway (magnocellular) fire more rapidly than those in the second, high-frequency pathway (parvocellular); thus, information from the first visual pathway may reach higher cortical centers slightly before information from the second pathway. This, in itself, may account for the general tendency to detect global properties more quickly than details, the "global precedence" effect (Navon, 1977).

Colombo then cites evidence that the slower, high-frequency pathway may mature sooner than the faster, low-frequency pathway and thus may be a more dominant influence on the looking of young infants. Lewis et al. (1989) make a similar argument. Finally, he argues that infants with long looks, compared to those with short looks, may be more influenced by the slower pathway and respond more on the basis of details—that is, they may be immature. Although both "long lookers" and "short lookers" require longer periods of inspection to show novelty preferences for local details than they do for global patterns, Colombo suggests that the long-looking infants may be learning about the global aspects of the pattern through a slower process of integrating detailed information into the whole, rather than apprehending the whole based on the faster, low-spatial-frequency pathways. Colombo speculates that a long period of dependence on the slower, high-spatial-frequency pathway could lead to a permanent dominance of that pathway in visual perception and recognition.

The research of Colombo and his colleagues has provided important information not only about individual differences but also about underlying processes. Colombo's speculations are well considered and lead to interesting predictions that can be tested with further research. A word of caution may be in order, however. The original distinction between short and long lookers involved splitting groups of infants at the median of the distribution of looking times. Thus, roughly half the infants in any study will be long lookers and half will be short lookers; within each subgroup, there will be considerable variation. There is no reason to think, however, that any of the infants fall outside the normal range in their responses to the displays; therefore, we should view the observed differences as normal individual differences in attending to such displays and not as deficiencies in some infants. Some infants at the extreme of long looking might eventually experience difficulty in controlling their attention and in functioning adequately in demanding circumstances, but infants at the very extreme of short looking might do so as well.

Interest in the duration and pattern of looking has inspired much research and theoretical speculation. We expect research on this topic to be vigorously pursued in the future, leading to progress in accounting for the basic facilitatory and inhibitory processes involved in visual attention. One interesting direction for future research in this area will be to compare the effect of various manipulations on the duration of looking and the duration of focused or active looking. We now turn to individual differences in focused attention.

Focused Attention

The measurement of focused attention provides us with a more differentiated index of attention than do measures of looking or simple orienting to toys during play. As discussed in chapter 7, focused attention is defined as narrowed selectivity and increased cognitive energy expended in the selected activity. Focused attention, or concentration, during play may be readily observed from 5 months on. The amount of focused attention is strongly governed by situational demands, increasing during exposure to new information and during complex tasks (Oakes & Tellinghuisen, 1994; Ruff, 1986). At the same time, at every age, there is wide variability around the average duration. To what extent can this variability be attributed to stable differences among individual infants and children?

Stability

Although it is not common to gather such information, we present data on the relative variability in focused attention within individual children versus the variability across children. In a study of eighty-four 10-month-old children, Parrinello-Ruttner (1986) presented each child with four different objects for 60 seconds apiece. A recent reanalysis of her data shows that the ranges in focused attention between the child who showed the least focused attention to an object and the child who showed the most focused attention were 41.5, 56.3, 56, and 56.8 seconds for the four objects, respectively. When a range was calculated across objects for individual infants—that is, the difference between the object with the least focused attention to the object with the most focused attention—the average range was 24.5 seconds and varied from 3.8 to 46.5 seconds. These results demonstrate that individual infants showed less variability *across* the four objects than the group did *within* each object.

The mean duration of focused attention from one set of objects to another within the same session is quite strongly correlated, about .70 (Parrinello-Ruttner, 1986), and the stability coefficient over two weeks is estimated to be about .60 (Ruff & Dubiner, 1987; Ruff, 1988). The short-term stability coefficient over one to two weeks in the preschool years is .64 (Ruff, Weissberg et al., 1995). All of these results are evidence for individual differences in duration of focused attention.

The information about long-term stability is somewhat more complex. In one study (Ruff, Lawson et al., 1990), the duration of focused attention during children's play was not stable from 1 year to 2 years or from 2 to 3.5 years. However, a global rating of attention made at 2 years (1 = very inattentive, 2 = of average attentiveness, and 3 = very attentive) was significantly related ($r = .39$) to duration of focused attention at 3.5 years. The discrepancy in predictive value of duration of focused attention at 2 years versus the global rating of attention illustrates an important aspect of measurement. Quantitative measurement is objective and clearly definable. Qualitative, global ratings are not as well defined, but may incorporate more information than any single quantitative index, taking into account context and subtle cues from behavior. Particularly in the arena of individual differences, both types of measures are valuable in assessing the extent and quality of children's behavior.

Consistency Across Situations

Focused attention to toys in 7- and 9-month-old infants is moderately related ($r = .44$) across settings within the same session (Ruff & Saltarelli, 1993). Whether infants were sitting on their mother's laps playing with a single toy or on the floor playing by themselves with a bucket of toys, the infants who focused attention to toys in one condition tended to do so in the other. In this study, as well as others (Ruff, Capozzoli et al., 1990), focused attention while playing with toys is either not related to the duration of watching more distant events, such as a puppet show, or it is *negatively* related. These low to negative correlations suggest that focused attention accompanying a child's activity with toys involves somewhat different processes from looking at ongoing events that cannot be controlled.

The moderate correlations across play settings using the same measure suggest that individuals are somewhat consistent when the same construct is measured, but may not be consistent across settings if the relevant processes are different. In the study cited earlier (Ruff & Saltarelli, 1993), Duration of Orienting as assessed with the Infant Behavior Questionnaire (Rothbart, 1981) was positively related to duration of focused attention to toys but negatively related to the duration of looking at ongoing events—further evidence of a distinction between the measures of attention in those two situations. By the same token, looking at static displays early in infancy may not predict, or be based on the same processes as, later focused attention in more active play.

During the preschool years, focused attention measured in different contexts shows only modest consistency (Ruff, Weissberg et al., 1995). When the duration of a child's concentration during play is correlated with a measure of concentration while viewing an experimental videotape of puppet skits, the associations are positive but in the range of .20 to .40. Focused attention during play or during viewing of videotapes is not related at all to speed of response or number of missed signals in a concurrent visual reaction-time task. Although these latter measures also indicate how well attention is focused on the task, the reaction-time task places attentional and motor demands on the child that are very different from those involved in playing with toys or watching television. These differences stem from the reaction-time task's infrequent and relatively uninteresting signal and from the request for a highly specific response. The low to modest correlations across situations are not due to unreliable measures, because internal reliability for all measures is quite high (.71 to .94) and short-term stability is substantial.

Underlying Processes

Why do individuals differ in the tendency to focus attention, even in situations, such as free play, that do not demand it? To some extent, the observed variability reflects different styles of approaching play. A child who is generally reflective may see a tray of toys as an opportunity to generate interesting activities that challenge cognitive skills and are conducted with thoroughness; focused attention would be a necessary component. As an infant, that child may have explored novel objects with an eye to detail and a propensity to return to features already explored. A child who is active and needs a high level of stimulation may use the toys to generate stimulation, quickly discarding toys that are no longer novel and creating fast and noisy activities that involve little planning. As an infant, this child may have spent little time examining objects and more time banging and throwing them. The first child may linger over details of objects and pick up finer and more specific information than the second child. On the other hand, the second child may grasp more readily the global features of a situation.

Autonomic Accompaniments of Focused Attention

Focused attention is accompanied by tonic alterations within the autonomic and central nervous systems (see chapter 6). Psychophysiological measures thus help us to assess the intensity or degree of concentration during various activities. In our discussion of reactivity we briefly considered research employing heart rate measures, either directional changes in heart rate or respiratory sinus arrhythmia (RSA). These measures, which show a range of variability in normal children, also signal differences in attention during sustained tasks. Variations in resting RSA, a measure obtained while the child is sitting still before the experimental procedures begin, has perhaps been the most studied individual characteristic. Richards (1985, 1987) has reported less distractibility and larger heart rate decelerations to visual events in infants with higher baseline RSA. Huffman, Bryan, Pederson, and Porges (1988, cited in Porges et al., 1994) found more rapid habituation in 3-month-olds with higher RSA. Linnemeyer and Porges (1986) also found that 6-month-olds with higher baseline RSA looked longer at novel displays.

Changes in RSA in *reaction* to environmental events have also been related to duration of focused attention. DiPietro, Porges, and Uhly (1992) measured reactive RSA, or vagal tone, in 8-month-old infants. Infants were presented with a jack-in-the-box (music followed by a clown popping up), with RSA measurements made before, during, and after the presentation. Three toys were also given to the infants to play with for two minutes apiece; play was coded on a scale that included examination as its highest level. The investigators found a systematic relationship between RSA reactivity and duration of examining. Infants who showed an increase in vagal tone to the jack-in-the-box (augmenters) subsequently demonstrated longer periods of examining and a greater variety of actions with the toys than did infants who showed a decrease in vagal tone to the jack-in-the-box (suppressors). Figure 10.1 compares the augmenters and suppressors, displaying the general patterns of focused attention over the four 30-second intervals of play with objects. The pattern of focused attention for the augmenters was described as an initial exploration followed by "intensive examination of the unique properties of the object through manipulation, followed by a readiness to move on to the next toy . . ." (DiPietro et al., 1992, p. 837). The authors suggest that the infants with suppressed vagal tone never explored the object enough to become familiar with it, while augmenters maximized their intake of information when the object was novel.

Higher Level Control

With development, focused attention becomes increasingly involved in the pursuit of goals. Work on individual differences in the preschool years suggests that children differ in their ability to control action (Kochanska, Murray, Jacques, Koenig, & Vandegeest, in press; Vaughn et al., 1984; Reed et al., 1984) and emotion (Eisenberg et al., 1993). These controls seem to be related to the ability to control the direction and intensity of attention (Ahadi, Rothbart, & Ye, 1993; Rothbart, Ahadi, Hershey, & Fisher, 1994). In addition, some children develop inhibitory and attentional control earlier than others (Diamond, Werker, & Lalonde, 1994; Kochanska et al., in press). We develop our discussion of individual differences in effortful control in the next section in this chapter, pointing out the relationships between attentional controls and other aspects of inhibitory control.

RELATED DIMENSIONS OF INDIVIDUALITY

Having reviewed evidence for individual differences in specific measures of attention, we now turn to the issue of individual differences along other dimensions related to attention. Characteristics of attention are not isolated; they constitute part

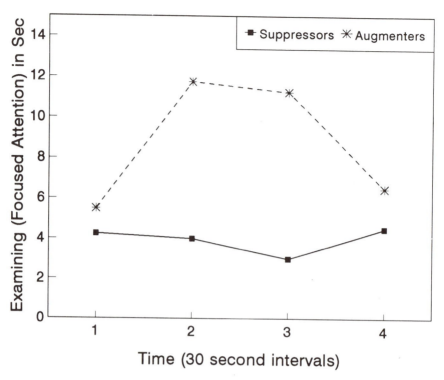

Figure 10.1. The response of two subgroups of children to toys. The subgroups were defined as augmenters or suppressors on the basis of their reactivity to a highly stimulating event. During a subsequent play period, the augmenters showed more focused attention to toys than the suppressors. From "Reactivity and developmental competence in preterm and full-term infants," by J. A. DiPietro, S. W. Porges, and B. Uhly, 1992, *Developmental Psychology, 28*, p. 837. Copyright 1994 by the American Psychological Association. Adapted with permission.

of a complex individual. To convey the important interrelatedness among attention and other characteristics, we explore activity level, impulse control, and positive and negative emotionality.

Motor Activity

In our earlier chapters, we argued that inhibition or quieting of nonrelevant motor activity is an important accompaniment of attentiveness—so much so that it is sometimes considered a defining feature of attention (see chapter 6). In this discussion of motor activity, we include large body movement as well as wiggling and fidgeting. As Buss (1989) states, activity level refers to the "sheer expenditure of physical energy" (p. 49), which is higher when the pace of activity is fast and the intensity and force of actions are greater. As we noted in chapter 2, activity level can be measured by mechanical means and by direct observation; it can also be derived from questionnaires for parents and teachers. Activity level is one of the most commonly studied individual differences in temperament and is included in almost all temperament and behavior questionnaires for infants and preschool children. Here, we are concerned not so much with activity level as such, but with the implications that activity level has for the child's ability to pay attention.

Stability

Earlier we noted that activity level, in absolute terms, tends to decrease from 1 to 5 years of age; even so, at every age tested, there is considerable variability across children. To what extent do children maintain a stable rank order in baseline activity levels over age? Birns et al. (1969) found activity level in newborn infants to be stable over short periods of time but unrelated to activity level after 4 weeks of age. This discontinuity may arise because of disparate underlying bases for activity level. Activity level in newborns may be related to negative emotionality, with activity increasing directly with level of distress, while after a month of age, activity level gradually becomes more related to positive emotionality (Rothbart, 1989c).

Activity level has been assessed in the first year with both the Infant Behavior Questionnaire and direct observation (Rothbart, 1981, 1986). Measures of activity level based on parents' reports were quite stable from 3 to 12 months with correlations for 3-, 6-, and 9-month intervals ranging from .48 to .78. In a later study, infants were observed in their homes at 3, 6, and 9 months of age; although correlations between measures of observed activity level were lower than for simultaneously collected questionnaire data, they were significant for 3- and 6-month intervals, .27 to .35. Although stability of activity level has been found within the first year of life, evidence suggests that there is discontinuity in activity ratings between the first and second years (Rothbart, 1989c). This discontinuity may be related to the development of the second attention system.

In the toddler years, Schaefer and Bayley (1963) measured activity level through ratings made by experimenters on the basis of direct observations; ratings of both vigor and speed were highly intercorrelated (about .85) at ages 10 to 12 months, 13 to 15 months, 18 to 24 months, and 27 to 36 months. Both vigor and speed were consistent for girls from 1 to 3 years, with the average correlations between .51 and .70. Boys were less consistent over the same age range (.39 to .59), but still showed modest to moderate stability. Buss, Block, and Block (1980) studied children wearing actometers, a mechanical device, and obtained measures of activity on three occasions at 3 years and four occasions at 4 years. The investigators then averaged over the multiple samples at each age to achieve more reliable estimates. They also obtained ratings of activity level at 3, 4, and 7 years of age from teachers who had several months of experience with the children. For both boys and girls, the average actometer measures at 3 and 4 years were moderately but significantly correlated. Teachers' judgments at the three different ages were intercorrelated to roughly the same degree (.45 for girls, .54 for boys). Consistency across the two types of measures obtained at the same age averaged .49 for girls and .57 for boys. These correlations suggest that, in the later preschool years, there is a stable trait related to the amount, pace, and vigor of motor activity.

Although we have mentioned only a few of the existing studies of activity level, the evidence suggests that, at least after 3 months, there is both short- and long-term stability of activity level. The use of questionnaires and the same respondent at different ages introduces the possibility of inflated correlations, but the conclusion is also based on data that stem from direct observation of children.

Consistency Across Situations

Mean levels of motor activity are influenced by the contexts in which they occur (Routh, Walton, & Padan-Belkin, 1978). Relatively little is known about the consistency within children across contexts and whether children tend to maintain their rank order even though mean levels may increase or decrease. Consistency across context is essentially built in to some parent-report instruments, such as the Infant Behavior Questionnaire (Rothbart, 1981), because items that relate to diverse, but specific, situations are preselected to be intercorrelated. Using mechanical recordings and direct observation, Halverson and Waldrop (1973) found boys' activity levels to be consistent from outdoor to indoor activities in a preschool setting. Havill and Halverson (Havill, personal communication, 1994) coded a variety of specific activities in preschool children, such as running and climbing, and also obtained readings from actometers worn by the children. When scores were aggregated over occasions, outdoor and indoor measures showed a moderate degree of correlation. Actometer readings were highly correlated to outdoor observational measures, but less so with indoor measures, perhaps because variability was reduced by the structure of the indoor activities.

Tempo

Tempo during play with toys is a factor studied in its own right and refers to the frequency with which children change activities or toys. One way to measure tempo is to count the number of times an infant or child changes toys or activities during a given period of play. Wenckstern, Weizmann, and Leenars (1984) found that the number of changes shown by 8-month-old infants was moderately consistent across sets of toys in the same session (.60) and moderately stable over a two-week period for both sets (.55 and .60). Kagan et al. (1971), in contrast, found little evidence of stability in tempo from 8 to 13 months or from 8 to 27 months.

Motor Activity and Attention

In considering the relationship between attention and activity, there are several general points to consider. First, if a child is currently moving around a great deal, that movement will have to be curbed before the child can look at an object or event for any length of time or with any concentration. Second, the curbing or inhibition of activity may be either spontaneous or deliberate. Some spontaneous inhibitory process must be involved when a child's interest is captured by an event. We have, for example, seen infants stop sucking when they catch sight of a novel object. Figure 10.2 presents another example: an 18-month-old girl's hand is suspended in mid-reach as she suddenly becomes absorbed in a skit from *Sesame Street*. In the later preschool years, however, children may deliberately control their activity level because they want to, or feel they should, pay attention to a task. Third, the inhibition or control required to quiet motor movement should be greater for a child who has a high baseline level of activity than for a child who tends to move slowly

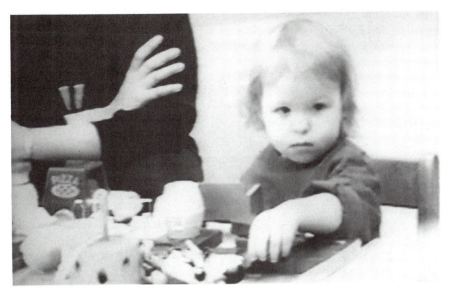

Figure 10.2. An 18-month-old who was playing with toys when her attention suddenly shifted to the TV as a *Sesame Street* song and routine started. She held this pose for almost 30 seconds and then continued her play. Photograph by Mary Capozzoli.

and infrequently. Children who are generally highly active may continue to move a little even though their attention is apparently riveted by an event, while children who tend to be inactive may become absolutely still. Thus, an estimation of baseline activity should be considered when assessing the role of movement in children's concentration.

Motor activity tends to be negatively related to measures of attention and behavioral control. Buss et al. (1980) examined the relationship of activity level, averaged over actometer readings at 3 and 4 years, and teachers' ratings of behavior at 3, 4, and 7 years. More active children were judged to be less reflective and planful at all three ages; they were less "attentive and able to concentrate" at 3 and 4 years; they tended to be less "strongly involved" in what they did at 3 years, but they were also judged to be more "curious and . . . eager for new experiences" at that age (p. 405). In a study of older children (Martin, 1989), ratings of activity level in elementary school classrooms were negatively related to frequency of "constructive self-directed activity" and positively related to "inappropriate behavior" (p. 454). In the school setting, however, children may differ not only in their baseline activity but also in the extent to which they can control their own level of activity. In line with this, Havill and Halverson (Havill, personal communication, 1994) found that teachers' ratings of activity level were positively related to the amount of running indoors, where it was inappropriate, but not to the amount of running outdoors, where the children were allowed more freedom.

We do not want to leave the impression that active children are inevitably inattentive. The important issue for attention is whether activity level is modulated in accord with the demands of the situation. Highly active children may have more difficulty slowing down, but with the development of higher level controls, they may be able to effectively inhibit body movement when necessary. Some children may fall at the opposite extreme and be so quiet that they could be described as passive and unreactive.

It is of value, then, to assess activity level in contexts where sustained focused attention based on higher level controls might be expected. A measure of activity during structured tasks is the frequency with which the child gets up off the chair and the frequency of leaving the table (Schleifer et al., 1975). In a longitudinal study (Ruff, Lawson et al., 1990), this form of active inattention was found to be modestly stable from 2 to 3.5 years. At each age, it was also negatively related to focused attention to toys during free play. Within a session, active inattention appears to be quite consistent across various situations in children from 2.5 to 4.5 years of age; significant correlations range from .34 to .55 (Ruff, Lawson et al., 1990; Ruff, Weissberg et al., 1995). Interestingly, in these studies, mother's ratings of activity level were not related to active inattention (Lawson & Ruff, 1995b; Ruff, Weissberg et al., 1995), suggesting that mothers may judge activity level on a quite different basis. Teacher ratings of behavior in the classroom might, on the other hand, be expected to correlate with this measure because teachers observe children in more structured situations.

One theory to account for individual differences in activity level is that activity provides stimulation and that individuals vary in the level of stimulation most satisfying to them (Zentall & Zentall, 1983). The implication is that highly active individuals prefer more stimulation. If so, it would be expected that children who seek higher levels of stimulation would habituate more quickly to objects and events and thus would pay less overall attention to them as they search for novelty. As a result, they may change activities so quickly that not enough attention is paid to a given event to learn many details about it. At the same time, a child who is very inactive may spend so much time with one activity that too little is learned about a broad range of events. Escalona (1968) suggests that less active infants may not encounter enough novelty and challenge on their own and may therefore be more dependent on others to provide the stimulation important to cognitive development. As described in the next chapter, such explanations underlie some accounts of attention deficits in children.

Higher Level Control of Impulses

We now turn to the child's self-regulation of behavioral impulses. The system of higher level controls emerging in the last quarter of the first year of life and showing continued development throughout the preschool years are related to children's ability to keep goals in mind and to effortfully direct activity toward goals not physically present. This capacity is closely related to the development of the ability to delay action in order to attain future rewards and to children's general development of self-control.

Stability and Consistency Across Contexts

Vaughn et al. (1984) studied children's self-control, including ability to delay in response to adults' directions to inhibit behavior. Subjects in this study were 18 to 30 months of age. Krakow et al. reported that several measures of children's ability to inhibit action were related to each other as well as showing strong effects of age (see chapter 8). Across the 12-month period that the children were studied, the authors also found moderate stability of these measures. Reed et al. (1984) investigated abilities to delay in 3- and 4-year-old children. Significant effects of age emerged on two self-control tasks—a pinball game and a "Simon Says" game—both of which demanded inhibition of strongly activated responses. The investigators also found a sizable correlation across inhibition tasks, suggesting individual differences in effortful self-regulation. A more recent study by Kochanska et al. (in press) found high internal consistency in a battery of tasks assessing inhibitory control.

As we described in chapter 8, Mischel and his colleagues (Mischel, 1983) have investigated processes underlying impulse control in the preschool years; they have shown that delay and control are facilitated by plans for resisting distractions and interfered with by the presence of concrete rewards. Some children are able to deliberately direct their attention elsewhere, thereby managing distractions and making it easier to wait for a delayed reward. Thus, children vary in their ability to inhibit activated responses and in their deliberate deployment of attention.

Relationship Between Behavioral Control and Attention

Krakow et al. (1982) found that the ability to delay was positively related to young children's length of sustained attention in play with toys. Quite remarkably, individual differences in length of delay at 4 years (Mischel, 1983) are also related to children's attention as adolescents (Shoda, Mischel, & Peake, 1990). The number of seconds children delayed as 4-year-olds when rewards were present predicted later parent-reported attentiveness when the children were juniors and seniors in high school. Children who were relatively unable to delay in the preschool years were reported later by their parents as more likely to go to pieces under stress. In contrast, children who had been able to impose delays on themselves, using attentional strategies when rewards were present during the waiting period, were described 10 years later as more attentive, persistent, planful, able to concentrate, and likely to use and respond to reason. Delay times were also positively related to later performance on scholastic aptitude tests. This pattern of characteristics identified by parent ratings is similar to the concept of *ego resiliency* (Block & Block, 1980). Ego resiliency is defined in terms of a person's ability to flexibly employ different levels of ego control—the "characteristic expression or containment of impulses, feelings, and desires" (Block & Block, 1980, p. 43)—in order to meet the demands of the moment.

Additional research suggests that impulse control may be related to other dimensions of temperament. Scale-level factor analyses of results from the Children's Behavior Questionnaire (Rothbart, Ahadi, Hershey, & Fisher, 1994; Rothbart, Ahadi, & Hershey, 1994) have consistently recovered three broad temperamental dimensions for children from 3 to 8 years of age; there are strong similarities in factors for 6- to 7-year-olds in both China and the United States (Ahadi et al., 1993). The first factor extracted represents Extraversion ("Surgency" in the original article) and includes subscales of impulsivity, activity, and experience of high-intensity pleasure, with a negative loading for shyness. The second factor, Negative Affectivity, includes subscales of discomfort, fear, anger/frustration, and sadness, with a negative loading for soothability. The third factor, labeled Effortful Control, includes subscales measuring children's capacity to focus and shift attention, ability to inhibit action when it is called for, and response to low-intensity stimulation and reward. The Effortful Control factor involves control of action combined with control of attention and is likely to be related to the development of the second attention system.

Separate groups of children at 3 years, 4 to 5 years, and 6 to 7 years show a similar general factor structure (Rothbart, Ahadi, Hershey, & Fisher, 1994). For the 3-year-olds, however, the factor structure is not as clear, with attention related to soothability. This relative lack of clarity may reflect the smaller number of children contributing data or their immaturity. Another interesting possible difference with age is that attention and soothability are more closely related for the 3-year-olds than for older children, and attention and inhibitory control less related.

Based on this temperament research and research on behavioral inhibition (Kagan, Reznick, & Gibbons, 1989; Rothbart, 1989a; Rothbart & Ahadi, 1994), two temperament-related control systems appear to be associated with children's impulse control. One of these is behavioral inhibition—that is, reluctance to act based on wariness, anxiety, or fear. The second is effortful control as discussed above, where restraint of impulsive behavior is controlled by self-regulatory mechanisms, including attention. Behavioral inhibition, the first control system, may be considered a type of passive control, related to Gray's (1982) Behavioral Inhibition System. The second control system is more related to higher level attention and may be considered active in that impulses are deliberately controlled (Rothbart, 1989c). It has been associated with social behavior in the early school years; higher levels of effortful control are related to lower levels of aggression and negativity and to higher levels of empathy and guilt (Rothbart, Ahadi, & Hershey, 1994).

Kochanska and her colleagues (e.g., Kochanska et al., in press) have been investigating the contribution of these two systems to the developing ability to restrain impulses and to delay in achieving a desired end. They observed children between 2 and 3.5 years of age in the laboratory and also obtained questionnaire reports from parents. The children's behavior toward forbidden toys was coded into three categories: (1) no restraint, (2) partial restraint, and (3) committed and self-regulated restraint. Mothers completed the Children's Behavior Questionnaire (Rothbart, Ahadi, & Hershey, 1994); aggregated scores for fearfulness and inhibitory control were derived from the questionnaire items. Inhibitory or effortful control increased significantly across the age range in both behavioral coding and maternal report. The temperament scores derived from the questionnaire showed that both fearfulness and inhibitory control predicted the category of restraint independently of the contribution of age. Of particular interest here is that the behavioral restraint observed in girls was more strongly related to fearfulness or behavioral inhibition, and the restraint observed in boys was more strongly related to inhibitory control, though both dimensions were operating in both boys and girls (Kochanska, personal communication, 1994).

Eisenberg et al. (1993) have found results that support this suggestive difference between boys and girls. In their study, both teachers and mothers rated preschool children's emotionality, coping, and attentional regulation. For boys, teachers' ratings of attentional control were positively related to the boys' social skills as assessed by adults and popularity as assessed by peers; more negative affect was associated with lower skills and popularity. For girls, mothers' reports of avoidant or fearful reactions were positively related to girls' teacher-rated social skills.

Attention is related in important ways to behavioral control in the preschool years. Reciprocally, the emergence of behavioral control has an important influence on children's ability to pay attention in situations that may be intrinsically dull but involve adult-imposed or self-imposed standards to be met. In those situations, some children may be more able than others to resist distractions and temptations because of stronger underlying regulatory mechanisms. Other children who may not be particularly reactive to distracting stimulation would not need such strong controls to maintain attention. The distinction between the tendency to be reactive and impulsive and the level of control required to inhibit action toward irrelevant or prohibited objects is worthy of further investigation, because these tendencies will interact with children's socialization to help determine the development of attention.

Attention and Emotionality

In the previous chapters on development, we had several occasions to underscore the relationship of attention to motivation and emotion. An important relationship in the realm of individual differences is between negative emotionality and sustained attention. Even in newborn infants we see some evidence for an association between longer episodes of attention and emotional state. Scores on the Neonatal Behavioral Assessment Scale, as we noted before, can be separated into different factors. Strauss and Rourke (1978) found that the visual orienting/alertness factor was related to a fourth factor that included state control. Infants with longer periods of orienting tended to be less labile in state and to approach the peak intensity of their responses less rapidly.

After the newborn period, there are relationships between disengagement of attention and lower levels of distress. At 4 months, the more readily infants disengaged visual attention to a central event when a peripheral event occurred, the less distressed and the more soothable they were according to mothers' reports (Johnson et al., 1991). At 13.5 months, infants' ability to shift attention away from highly arousing stimuli was modestly related to lower levels of negative affect (Rothbart et al., 1992). Infants in the laboratory who looked for shorter periods at small toys they were holding smiled and laughed more in the laboratory and were described by their mothers as higher on temperamental smiling and laughter and less fearful than infants who looked at these toys for longer periods (Rothbart, 1988a).

We have already discussed some of the relationships between effortful control and affective characteristics of children and adults. A relationship between effortful control and lower levels of negative affect can be seen in Mischel's studies (Mischel, 1983; Shoda et al., 1990) where earlier ability to delay was associated with later tendencies to remain calm in stressful situations. In the study by Eisenberg et al. (1993), ratings from both teachers and mothers for preschool boys, but not girls, revealed a negative relationship between attentional control and negative emotionality. These results are consistent with adults' and early adolescents' reports that show negative relationships between attentional control and their experience and expression of negative affect (Capaldi & Rothbart, 1992; Derryberry & Rothbart, 1988).

Respiratory sinus arrhythmia (RSA) has also been linked to emotional reactivity and affective aspects of temperament as well as to attention. DiPietro, Larson, and Porges (1987) found newborn infants with higher baseline levels of RSA to be more irritable. In a longitudinal study by Stifter and Fox (1990), higher RSA in the newborn period predicted mothers' ratings of the infants at 5 months as being more easily frustrated and slower to approach novel situations. In the same study, a concurrent positive relationship existed between 5-month RSA and negative reactivity elicited in the laboratory; mothers also reported that infants with higher RSA smiled and laughed less and were more active. Using a continuous measure of insecurity of attachment rather than the typical classifications, Izard et al. (1991) found that measures of RSA at 3 months and heart rate variability from 3 to 13 months were positively related to insecurity of attachment at 13 months. These data, most of which involve infants in the first 6 months of life, suggest that higher RSA is associated with more negative affect.

The nature of the relationship between RSA and emotionality, however, seems to be somewhat different after 5 or 6 months, with more associations between RSA and positive emotionality. Richards and Cameron (1987) found baseline RSA to be positively related to concurrent parent-reported measures of approach at 6 and 12 months of age. Similarly, Fox and Stifter (1989) found a concurrent relationship at 14 months between RSA and infants' short latency to approach a stranger. Stifter, Fox, and Porges (1989) found that 5-month-olds with higher RSA looked away more often to a stranger's approach than did infants with lower RSA, but they were also more expressive, showing higher levels of joy and interest. This pattern of relationships was not seen at 10 months, suggesting a change with age in the relationship of RSA and reactivity, perhaps related to the developmental transition at 9 months. Fox and Field (1989) found that 3- year-old children with higher RSA levels made a more rapid adjustment to preschool; higher levels of RSA were also related to positive affect and greater adaptability.

Porges et al. (1994) relate the developmental change in the pattern of relationships between RSA and behavior to the emergence of regulatory mechanisms. Infants with high baseline levels of RSA are initially highly reactive. These infants have the potential for intense attention and emotion, but early in the first year, when regulatory mechanisms are immature and unstable, their reactivity to environmental events often generates irritability. As self-regulation of state becomes more possible in the latter half of the first year, their reactivity leads to concentration when interest is the primary factor, and to more expressiveness when other emotions are ascendant (see also Rothbart & Derryberry, 1981). The accumulated results suggest that individual differences in attention and emotionality are mediated, in part, by autonomic activity.

Overall, the relationship between attention and emotion influences the adaptive capacity of the individual. Because affect is related to both attention and behavioral control, the relationship between attentional control and positive and negative affect is best understood in terms of mutual influences (Rothbart, Derryberry, & Posner,

1994). Affective-motivational systems such as fear, anger, and positive anticipation help to direct attention toward motivationally relevant information. On the other hand, attentional control can be used for calming infants, for self-distraction, for reframing the meaning of events, and for solving problems and coping with stress, all of which serve to minimize negative affect. As we come to understand these processes better, it is likely that our view of them will be both complex and heartening. The complexity can be seen in the developmental changes in the relationships among the domains, as discussed above. The heartening aspect is that an individual who is highly reactive emotionally need not be a victim to this reactivity; self-regulation through attention can help control negative affect just as it can help to control behavior.

SUMMARY

In this chapter, we moved from a discussion of themes in the development of attention to variations in attention-related characteristics at different points in development. We described measures and methods in the study of individual differences, followed by descriptions of substantive findings. Early individual differences have been found in several attention-related measures. First, individual children show early individuality in the speed and magnitude of their reactions to stimulation. In the newborn period, stable differences are observed in both behavioral and physiological indices of reactivity. These initial differences, however, seem to reflect mainly short-term stability with longer term stability emerging only after 2 months.

Second, individual infants vary in the amount of time they spend looking at visual displays. These differences are quite stable across time and situations in the first year and are related to later measures of cognitive ability. We considered possible underlying mechanisms for these attentional differences. One possibility is that duration of looking reflects the amount of time required to encode or learn about a display, with faster infants looking for shorter durations. Infants who look for shorter durations may, however, be attending to different features of the displays or using different processes. In some situations, shorter looks may stem from more efficient inhibitory processes than longer looks.

Most of the research on individuality in duration of looking has been conducted with young infants. With older infants and preschool children more research on sustained attention involves focused attention during play and structured tasks. Children show moderate stability over time in the duration of focused attention during play. Consistency across situations is more modest. Individual differences in autonomic measures, such as heart rate and respiratory sinus arrhythmia, are associated with focused attention.

We also related these individual differences in attention to the temperamental dimensions of activity level, impulse control, and positive and negative emotionality. Not only do children differ in their level of activity but these differences have implications for individuality in sustained attention and self-control. Children vary in their tendency to inhibit impulses for proscribed or irrelevant actions. Impulse control is related, in part, to the ability to shift or maintain attention as needed. More reactive children may require stronger controls over behavior to behave flexibly during changing circumstances and challenging situations. We described two developing self-regulatory or control systems on which children differ. The first of these, behavioral inhibition, is emotional in character and related to the development of fear. A later developing attentional control system corresponds to the higher level system of attention. We noted that children may differ in their rate of development of these controls and in the strength of control, once developed. Some children thus may develop self-regulatory skills at an earlier age than others.

Finally, we addressed the relationship between attention and emotionality. Young infants who react strongly to environmental events may initially be irritable, but later may be capable of sustained and intense concentration. Children who develop strong and flexible higher level controls on attention seem to have better emotional control, at least in part, because they can voluntarily focus and shift their attention to minimize emotional distress.

Individuality in attention is part of a complex interrelationship among cognitive and temperamental differences. These differences have important implications for all aspects of development, including socialization. At the extremes, they may also have implications for our understanding of attention deficits, a topic we turn to in the next chapter.

11

Early Manifestations of Attention Deficits

A discussion of individual differences in attention would not be complete without some consideration of children who develop problems with attention. Deficits of attention, variously referred to as hyperactivity, hyperkinesis, and attention deficit disorder, have been described and diagnosed in school-age children for many years. As we have emphasized, however, attention is multifaceted; thus, we should expect to see a variety of deficits, diverging in their underlying processes. In addition, we have seen that attentiveness is not an isolated characteristic but part of constellations of characteristics that help to define individuals. In this chapter, we explore a range of difficulties young children may experience in the control of attention. We first discuss attention deficits as conceptualized by investigators who work with school-age children. We then review research suggesting possible precursors of these disorders in infants and preschool children. Next, we expand our treatment to include other at-risk populations of children who have difficulties with attention. Finally, we describe some of the theoretical ideas put forward to account for the development of attention deficits.

ATTENTION DEFICITS IN SCHOOL-AGE CHILDREN

Statistics reveal that a large number of school-age children are either diagnosed or perceived as having trouble with overactivity and poor attention. Bosco and Robin (1980) summarized the prevalence of attentional deficits in the school system in Grand Rapids, Michigan. Parents and teachers independently reported that between 3.2 and 3.4% of children had been diagnosed by a physician as having attention deficit disorder; 75% of those had been treated with medication. In addition, parent ratings put another 5% of the children two or more standard deviations above the mean on the Conners Parent Questionnaire (Goyette, Conners, & Ulrich, 1978). With this instrument, parents rate their children on such items as "excitable, impulsive," "restless, always up and on the go," "fails to finish things," and "distractibility or attention span a problem."

Many children currently diagnosed with attention deficits with hyperactivity (Attention Deficit/Hyperactivity Disorder; *DSM-IV,* 1994) also have problems with aggression and oppositional behavior (Lahey, Schaughency, Hynd, Carlson, & Nieves, 1987); from 30 to 50% of children with Attention Deficit/Hyperactivity Disorder have dual diagnoses (Hinshaw, 1994). Some investigators (e.g., Raine & Jones, 1987) have argued, on the basis of questionnaire data, that the underpinnings of conduct disorder and hyperactivity are independent; others (e.g., Rutter, 1989) question the meaningfulness of a "pure" syndrome of attention deficit with hyperactivity. Thus, there are still unresolved diagnostic issues in the field.

Although aggressive children diagnosed with attention deficits with hyperactivity seem to draw special disapproval from other children (Milich & Landau, 1989), nonaggressive children with the same deficits also tend to be disliked (Whalen & Henker, 1985). According to Whalen and Henker (1985), children with Attention Deficit/Hyperactivity Disorder court trouble by "saying or doing things that seem immature, irritating, situationally inappropriate, highly salient, and perhaps also provocative" (p. 448). They also seem to have difficulty modulating their behavior to meet changing social demands (Jacob, O'Leary, & Rosenblad, 1978; Landau & Milich, 1988).

Problems with attention and impulsivity as well as antisocial behavior may continue into adulthood for many young people with attention deficits and hyperactivity (Hinshaw, 1994; Weiss & Hechtman, 1986). Because very few studies have included children with other psychiatric diagnoses for comparison, we do not know the extent to which problems observed in adolescence and adulthood are specific to a diagnosis of attention deficit (Thorley, 1984). Despite uncertainty about the specificity of the prognosis, children diagnosed with attention deficits and hyperactivity are at increased risk for later difficulties with attention, impulsivity, and antisocial behavior (Rutter, 1989; Thorley, 1984). On the positive side, however, not all children so diagnosed will be showing signs of the disorder in late adolescence; the absence of earlier aggressive behavior may be a favorable prognosticator (Thorley, 1984).

Clear definitions and scientific explanations of attention deficits have been slow to evolve, despite extensive research and discussion (Prior & Sanson, 1986; Rutter, 1989). Although a detailed treatment of this topic is outside the scope of this book, we begin by considering a few major issues guiding our consideration of possible precursors in the development of attention deficits.

Excess Motor Activity and Attention

The first issue is whether poorly controlled attention is necessarily associated with excess motor activity in young children. Conners and Wells (1986) argue that if children are constantly moving around, they will not be able to finish what they start; poor attention and lack of persistence will then be closely related to excessive activity. This view would be consistent with the close link between activity level and engagement of attention reported in our earlier chapters. At the same time, excessive activity in situations calling for restraint, rather than activity level per se, is most relevant to a discussion of attention deficits (Conners & Wells, 1986).

Although there may be a relationship between overactivity and attention in some impulsive children, Schaughency and Hynd (1989) have reviewed the results of a number of factor analytic studies and conclude that the two are independent dimensions of behavior. Their conclusion is supported by the existence of a subgroup of children whose attention is poorly controlled but whose activity level is better described as "sluggish." In two separate factor analyses of teacher ratings, Lahey et al. (1988) described two orthogonal dimensions as Inattention-Disorganization and Motor Hyperactivity-Impulsivity. The results were consistent with previous failures to find an independent dimension reflecting *only* impulsivity. Some diagnosed children are high on both of these dimensions; others are high chiefly on the first dimension. Both subgroups of children tend to show lower academic achievement than do control children; however, some studies suggest that children characterized by attention deficits without hyperactivity are especially prone to learning disabilities (Goodyear & Hynd, 1992).

Because, for the most part, we are not focusing on psychiatric disorders as such and because the nomenclature has changed periodically in recent years, we wish to use the term "attention deficit" in a general way. In our subsequent discussion, we refer to two major subtypes of attention deficit—attention deficit with hyperactivity and attention deficit without it or with *hypo*activity. The latest Diagnostic and Statistical Manual (*DSM-IV,* 1994) makes the same distinction with somewhat different labels. For convenience, we will sometimes use the term "hyperactivity" when referring to the first subtype.

Relating Disorders to Different Processes

A second issue is the relationship of attention deficits to the multiple facets of attention discussed in this book. Are children diagnosed with attention deficits less aroused and less reactive to stimulation than normal children? Are they less selective and less able to ignore distracting and irrelevant events? Are they less able to exert effort and sustain attention over time? Are they less able to control and organize behavior? Considerable research has provided tentative answers to such questions.

Following an extensive review of previous research, Douglas (1983) argued that hyperactive children are consistently underreactive, although they may become overreactive in certain situations, particularly those that involve concrete rewards for performance. Conners and Wells (1986) report that hyperactive children who are not anxious have lower resting arousal levels according to autonomic measures, and in response to some task demands, have "extremely sluggish or late-responding autonomic function" (p. 73). In keeping with this, Douglas (1983; Douglas & Peters, 1979) argues that hyperactive children do not appear to be more distractible than normal children. Moreover, they show normal levels of discrimination and average ability to handle simultaneous events. Sergeant and Scholten (1983) agree with this assessment.

A number of investigators in the field (notably Douglas and Conners) argue that the major problem characteristic of children with attention deficits and hyperactivity is difficulty mobilizing and sustaining the effort necessary to persist at intrinsically dull tasks, such as continuous performance tests. Conners and Wells (1986) cite an unpublished study by Sergeant in which hyperactive children "were persuaded to perform a vigilance task over several hours. Their performance decrements over time were no different from matched controls, and their ability to attend selectively was unimpaired. What did distinguish them was the amount of effort required to keep them engaged in the task'' (p. 82). In this case, the effort was supplied by the experimenter! These results are reminiscent of those reported by Draeger et al. (1986), in which young hyperactive children performed as well as normal children as long as an adult was sitting near them, but more poorly when left on their own.

Finally, a number of investigators consider a core feature of attention deficits with hyperactivity to be impulsivity or the inability to restrain responses inappropriate to the current situation (Lahey et al., 1987). Such poor control would link the deficit to the general category of disinhibitory disorders (Gorenstein & Newman, 1980). It would also be related to Gray's (1982) theory of temperament; Gray postulates a dimension of behavioral activation opposed by a dimension of behavioral inhibition. A general weakness in inhibitory skills may also be the basis for the frequent co-occurrence of hyperactivity and aggressive behavior (Lahey et al., 1987).

In summary, a major form of attention deficit represents a constellation of characteristics implicating several dimensions of behavior. According to Douglas (1983), these include: (1) difficulties in investing, organizing, and maintaining attention and effort; (2) difficulties in inhibiting impulsive responding; (3) difficulties in modulating arousal level according to the demands of the situation; and (4) a strong inclination to seek immediate reinforcement. However, another variant of attention deficit, as already noted, may involve cognitive disorganization, low sensory reactivity, and sluggish tempo (Lahey et al., 1987; Schaughency & Hynd, 1989), a different constellation of characteristics. We would not expect poor attention in all conditions; children with either constellation of symptoms should have most difficulty in situations that are not intrinsically motivating.

POSSIBLE PRECURSORS OF ATTENTION DEFICITS WITH HYPERACTIVITY

Given the poor prognosis for school-age children diagnosed with attention deficits, a search for early precursors becomes important. Compared to the research on school-age children, there is relatively little work on preschool children. The existing research, nevertheless, strongly suggests that manifestations of such deficits are present in the first five years of life.

Early Signs of Hyperactivity

Waldrop, Bell, McLaughlin, and Halverson (1978) reported that the number of minor physical anomalies, such as malformed ears and missing creases on the palm, observed in newborn boys was related to their behavior in the preschool years. The predicted behavior included attention span and degree of involvement in free play, attention span during storytelling, and extent of aggression and impulsivity in relation to other children. The more anomalies, the less attentive and the more aggressive the boys were. These results demonstrate that measures of attention in the preschool years can be useful indices of differences among children and suggest a possible biological marker.

Prior, Leonard, and Wood (1983) compared a group of 4- to 5-year-old children who had been diagnosed as hyperactive with a matched control group of children who had never been considered problematic by parents or teachers. Measures from parent and teacher ratings of temperament and behavior were combined with behavioral measures based on observation; these were subjected to factor analysis. Two major factors were isolated: (1) a dimension reflecting the child's manageability, including attention and adaptability; and (2) a dimension of hyperactivity and negative interactions at home. The two groups differed significantly on both these dimensions even controlling for IQ, which was lower in the diagnosed group.

Alessandri (1992) compared a group of twenty 4- to 5-year-old children diagnosed with attention deficit and hyperactivity to a well-matched group of 20 normal children. Both groups of children participated in a preschool program that allowed data on attention and behavior to be collected in free play as well as more structured settings. During the free-play periods, the children with attention deficits spent less time playing; they engaged in more functional play, characteristic of younger children, and less construction and dramatic play. While the two groups spent equivalent amounts of time in solitary play, the children with attention deficits spent less time playing beside or with other children. The children with deficits were less likely to converse with other children, and their exchanges with teachers were more negative. They also were less compliant during periods set aside for putting toys away and straightening up after play.

All children were observed in two structured settings, one where they listened to stories read by the teacher and the other, a music lesson where the children clapped, danced, and played musical instruments. The two groups of children did not differ in their attention and participation in the music lesson, but during storytelling, the diagnosed children were significantly less attentive. These results suggest that, when the setting allows for activity and responses from the children, children with attention deficits can manage as well as other children. The problems occur in settings that require sitting still.

In a series of important clinical studies, Campbell (1985) and her colleagues have followed groups of preschool children referred because of problems with attention and hyperactivity. In the first longitudinal study (Schleifer et al., 1975), children were recruited from pediatric private practices for observation in a research nursery. One subgroup of children was rated by both parents and teachers as extremely active. For the other subgroup of children, only the parents judged their activity level to be problematic. The investigators found that the children rated as hyperactive by both parents and teachers were more aggressive, more active during structured tasks, and more impulsive than either control children or the children rated as hyperactive by only the parents.

These two groups of children were followed into their early elementary school years (Campbell, Endman, & Bernfeld, 1977; Campbell, Schleifer, Weiss, & Perlman, 1977). At 6.5 years of age, the children rated as hyperactive by both parents and teachers tended to be more impulsive and to make more errors on a modified version of the Matching Familiar Figures Test, a test that requires attention to detail. The children also requested more feedback and made more comments on their performance while working on a task with their mothers, and their mothers tended to offer more guidance around impulse control. When the children were 7 to 9 years of age, classroom observations revealed that the children rated as hyperactive by both parents and teachers were more often out of their seats and not attending to the current task than either classroom controls or the children originally rated as hyperactive by only the parents. They were also judged by their teachers to be more inattentive. Thus, young children who show problems across situations may have more severe deficits, and hence, higher predictability for problems in the future than do children who show problems in only one setting.

In a later, more detailed, longitudinal study (Campbell et al., 1982; Campbell, Breaux, Ewing, & Szumowski, 1984; Campbell, Ewing, Breaux, & Szumowski, 1986), 46 children between the ages of 2 and 3 years were referred by their parents because of concerns about overactivity, impulsivity, lack of attention, and noncompliance. Twenty-two children whose parents were not concerned about them served as controls. At both 3 and 4 years of age, all children were observed during a free-play session, during interaction with their mothers, and during structured tasks. In analyzing the data from this study, Campbell and her colleagues first compared the referred children to control children at 3 years of age (Campbell et al., 1982). During free play, the referred children changed activities more often, displayed more frequent short episodes of a single activity, and had fewer episodes longer than 2 minutes; they were also more likely than control children to attend to other objects in the room. The two groups did not differ on absolute level of activity, but during the structured tasks, the referred children were more often out of their seats and off task.

On a delay task, in which the children were asked to wait before retrieving a small piece of cookie from its hiding place, referred children delayed less often, and thus, made more impulsive responses. They were lower in IQ on the Stanford-Binet test and were more likely to be rated by their mothers as hostile and aggressive. In the preschool setting, the referred children were observed to have more aggressive encounters with other children and were rated by their teachers as more aggressive and hyperactive (Campbell & Cluss, 1982). A year later at follow-up, the two groups of children still differed on the same measures. Thus, Campbell's observations of referred preschool children are in keeping with descriptions of older children diagnosed with attention deficits with hyperactivity, suggesting that parents may see the relevant constellation of problems as early as 2 years of age.

Another evaluation at 6 years revealed that referred children tended to be rated as more problematic than control children by both parents and teachers (Campbell et al., 1986). In fact, 30% of the referred group met the official criteria for attention deficit with hyperactivity (*DSM-III*, 1980), while none of the control children did so. There was little difference between the two groups on laboratory measures of attention and activity, however. The greater challenges posed by the requirements of school, such as sitting still and following instructions from the teacher, may make the school setting better than the laboratory setting for detecting problems in attention and behavior at this age.

Developmental Patterns

In Campbell's longitudinal study, differences between the parent-referred group and the control group diminished when the children were 6 years old. Noting, however, that group results may obscure individual patterns of development, Campbell (1987) divided the referred group into those who had improved over the years and those whose behavior problems had persisted. Children in the persistent group were either classified by official criteria (*DSM-III*, 1980) as showing Attention Deficit Disorder, were rated by their mothers on the Children's Behavior Checklist (see Achenbach, 1992) as outside the normal range, or were otherwise judged to be showing moderate to severe symptoms. Children in the improved group met none of these criteria and were generally judged by parents and teachers to have no problems or very mild ones. Campbell then asked how these groups differed in their earlier ratings at 3 years and in their ratings over time.

At 3 years, referred children in both the persistent and improved groups were rated as more restless, more disobedient, and showing less concentration than control children. The mothers also complained of more behavior problems in both subgroups. However, the children whose problems persisted were judged to be more destructive and less popular with peers, to lie more, and to share less than control children, while the ratings of children in the improved group were intermediate between those of the control children and persistent children. When ratings from 3, 4, and 6 years were combined, the persistent group was rated as significantly more destructive and more physically aggressive than either the improved group or the control group.

Figure 11.1 shows the profiles of the three groups on these three variables. Children with persistent problems and control children show relatively little change over time. In contrast, those in the improved group show a steady decrease in ratings on each of the variables. By 4 years, they have converged with the control group on ratings of disobedience; by 6 years, they have converged with the control group on ratings of concentration. Though improved, they still are rated as somewhat more restless than controls. In another analysis, Campbell plotted the children's activity ratings on the Werry-Weiss-Peters Activity Scale (Routh et al., 1974). Again, the improved children match the control group by 4 years, though they had been rated as considerably more active at 3 years. See figure 11.2. Thus, extreme restlessness and inattention may be transient characteristics for some children in the preschool years, giving way to increasing maturity and socialization. For other children, especially those who also show more aggressive and antisocial behavior, restlessness and inattention are more likely to continue.

In a follow-up study when the children were 9 years old, Campbell and Ewing (1990) found that children in the persistent group had three times as many symptoms of both attention deficit with hyperactivity and conduct disorders than the improved group or the control group. Children in the persistent group were also rated by their mothers as higher in aggression and delinquent behavior and lower in social compe-

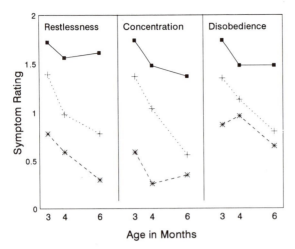

Figure 11.1. Profiles of scores on restlessness, low concentration, and disobedience over age for referred children whose behavior stayed problematic (■), referred children who improved (+), and control children (*). From ''Parent-referred problem three-year-olds: Developmental changes in symptoms'' by S. B. Campbell, 1987, *Journal of Child Psychology and Psychiatry, 28,* p. 841. Copyright 1987 by the Association for Child Psychology and Psychiatry. Adapted with permission.

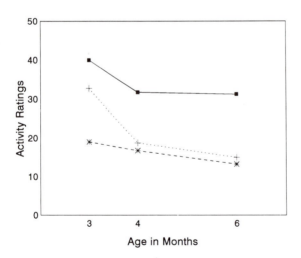

Figure 11.2. Profiles of the same three groups as depicted in Figure 11.1 on their activity ratings over time. From ''Parent-referred problem three-year-olds: Developmental changes in symptoms'' by S. B. Campbell, 1987 *Journal of Child Psychology and Psychiatry, 28,* p. 841. Copyright 1987 by the Association for Child Psychology and Psychiatry. Adapted with permission.

tence than the other groups. These results demonstrate the long-range predictive value of early measures and the value of knowing the developmental course of symptoms.

PRECURSORS TO ATTENTION DEFICITS WITHOUT HYPERACTIVITY

Attention deficits without hyperactivity have received much less attention and clinical investigation than deficits with hyperactivity. Therefore, less information about early precursors is available. Data that may be pertinent come from a longitudinal study of children from 1 to 3.5 years (Ruff & Lawson, 1988, 1991; Ruff, 1990). A small subgroup of children was identified on the basis of extreme and persistent inattention according to the global ratings discussed in chapter 10. These ratings were made by observers unfamiliar with the children on the basis of videotaped sessions involving several procedures. At both 1 and 2 years of age, 125 children were rated on a three-point scale: (1) very inattentive; (2) of average attentiveness; and (3) very attentive. These ratings were validated against quantitative measures of attention taken at the same age, with good agreement between the two types of measures (Ruff, Lawson et al., 1990).

Only 5 children were rated as very attentive at both ages and only 6 children were rated as very inattentive at both ages, the latter group being composed solely of boys. These two extreme subgroups were compared on measures of attention obtained when they were 3.5 years of age, measures that were independent of the criteria for group formation. The extreme low attenders showed less focused attention during free play with toys and they took their eyes off the toys more often. During a structured reaction-time task, they had slower reaction times and more errors of omission, further indices of inattention. In figures 11.3 and 11.4, the means for these two extreme groups are compared to each other, but also to a comparison group of children rated as average at both 1 and 2 years of age. These extreme groups of children remained very different for several years, and the low attenders differed more from the average children than the high attenders.

Consistent with our emphasis on the integration of attention with other aspects of functioning, these two subgroups differed from each other on a number of temperament dimensions. The mothers rated them on the Carey Toddler Temperament Scale (Fullard et al., 1984) at 1 year of age. As can be seen in figure 11.5, the extreme low attenders were judged to be less adaptable, less likely to approach new objects and situations, and more negative in mood. The low attenders also tended to be *higher* in threshold—that is, less sensitive or responsive to sounds and sights—and *lower* on distractibility, a measure of responsivity to sounds. Although these latter two results are only marginally significant, they raise the intriguing possibility that the low attenders, compared to the high attenders, had a higher threshold for arousal by environmental stimulation. Similar differences in mood and adaptability were seen at 2 years when mothers rated them on the Colorado Temperament Inventory (Rowe & Plomin, 1977; see figure 11.6). In contrast, the low attenders were never rated as more active by their mothers nor did they show more active inattention at any age.

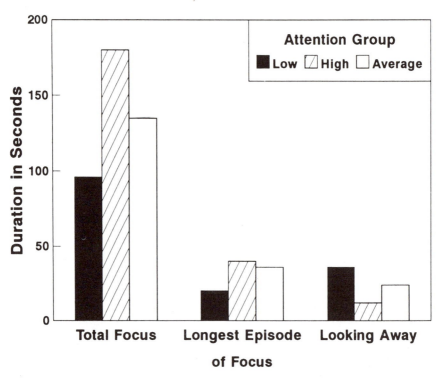

Figure 11.3. Comparison of extremely attentive and extremely inattentive subgroups on measures of attention during free play at 3.5 years. Taken from Ruff and Lawson (1988).

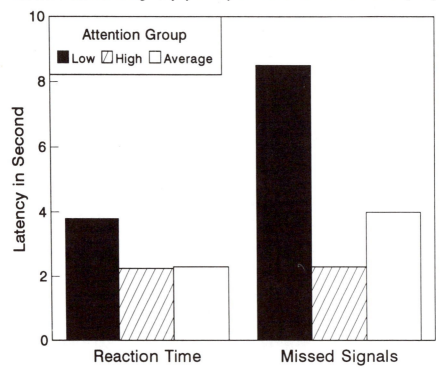

Figure 11.4. Comparison of the same two extreme attention groups depicted in Figure 11.3 on measures of attention during the reaction time task at 3.5 years. Taken from Ruff and Lawson (1988).

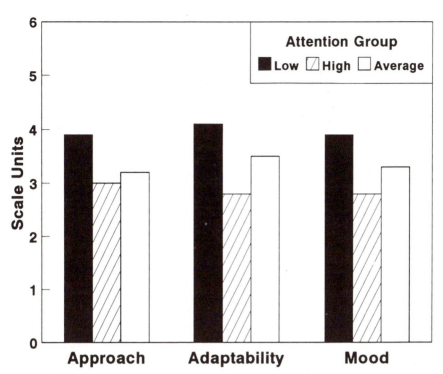

Figure 11.5. Comparison of the two extreme groups on several dimensions of the Carey Toddler Temperament Scale. Higher scores represent non-approach, unadaptability, and negative mood. Taken from Ruff and Lawson (1988).

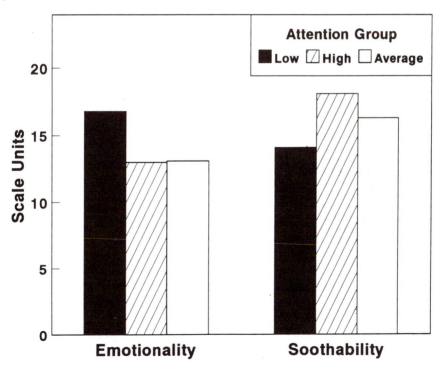

Figure 11.6. Comparison of the two extreme groups on two dimensions of the Colorado Temperament Survey. Taken from Ruff and Lawson (1988).

There was no evidence that they were more impulsive than average on our impulse control task at 2 years, nor did they make more errors of commission on the reaction time task at 3.5 years, another measure of impulsivity.

Based on the Conners parent questionnaire at 3.5 years, the mothers found the low attenders to be no more problematic than average. Thus, although this small group of children was consistently inattentive from 1 to 3.5 years of age, they did not fit the picture of hyperactivity, as Campbell's parent-referred sample did. They seemed to be relatively unreactive children, closer to the description of attention deficits without hyperactivity. Such an attention deficit might be expected to have serious consequences for cognitive development. Indeed, the low attenders, though not different from the high attenders in their performance on the Bayley Mental Development Scale (Bayley, 1969) at 1 and 2 years, were significantly lower in IQ at 3.5 years (see figure 11.7).

ATTENTION DEFICITS IN OTHER CONDITIONS

Although school-age children, and even some preschoolers, may be officially diagnosed as having attention deficits, problems with attention are also known to accom-

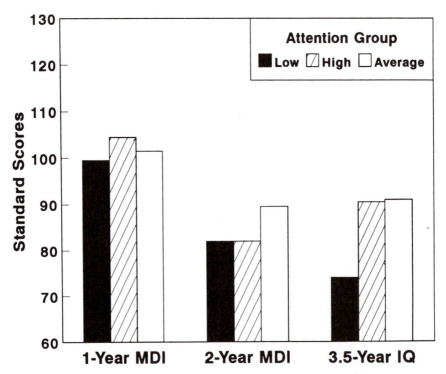

Figure 11.7. Comparison of the two extreme groups on their scores on standardized tests of cognitive functioning (Bayley Mental Development Index and Stanford-Binet IQ). Taken from Ruff and Lawson (1988).

pany other types of disorders. Distractibility and impaired ability to sustain attention, for example, are considered to be part of the general cognitive disorganization accompanying schizophrenia (Cornblatt & Erlenmeyer-Kimling, 1985). Here, we illustrate inattentiveness in the context of other disorders of infancy and early childhood with brief discussions of regulatory-disordered infants and young autistic children.

Infants with Regulatory Disorders

In earlier chapters, we have pointed to the intimate relation between attention and various aspects of self-regulation. Thus, the potential for attention deficits seems reasonably high for infants who exhibit serious problems with regulation. Although all very young infants have immature regulatory processes, regulatory-disordered infants are defined as those whose difficulties in self-regulation continue past 6 months of age (DeGangi et al., 1991). The classification of disordered infants is based on normal perinatal history, developmental test scores above 80, and at least two of the following symptoms: (1) disturbances in sleep (e.g., repeated awakening at night); (2) difficulties in consoling self (e.g., unable to use hand to mouth activity or visual distraction to calm down); (3) difficulties around feeding (e.g., refusing to eat); and (4) hyperarousal (e.g., disorganization and distractibility in face of new stimulation).

In a study designed to assess physiological and behavioral responses in 8- to 11-month-old infants, DeGangi et al. (1991) compared 24 normal infants with 11 infants showing problems with self-regulation. The investigators measured heart rate and respiratory sinus arrhythmia (RSA) before and during the administration of the Bayley Scales of Development (Bayley, 1969). As we discussed in earlier chapters, both heart rate and the degree of variability as measured by RSA are expected to decrease during attention-demanding and cognitively challenging tasks (Porges, 1992). In the study by DeGangi et al., this expectation was supported by a mean decrease in RSA from resting baseline levels to levels during the administration of the Bayley Mental Development Scale. It was also supported by individual differences in the degree of change exhibited and performance on the Bayley; the greater the extent to which RSA was suppressed from baseline to the administration of the test, the higher were the infants' Bayley scores.

The infants with regulatory problems tended to have higher baseline levels of vagal tone (derived from RSA). Yet a scatterplot of baseline levels with the degree of change during the Bayley reveals the expected negative relationship between the two only for the normal infants; the baseline and task levels for the disordered infants were unrelated (see figure 11.8). This difference between groups suggests that the disordered infants may have had more difficulty regulating the underlying state necessary for sustained and focused attention (see chapters 6 and 7). Porges (1992) concludes that ''these infants, although highly reactive to the environment, can not inhibit ongoing physiological activity to attend and may have difficulties behaviorally engaging with the environment'' (p. 220). In this way, early manifestations of poor self-regulation may be accompanied by concurrent low performance on attention-demanding tasks, such as the Bayley, and presage later deficits in attention.

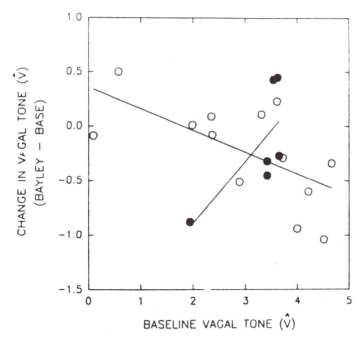

Figure 11.8. Scatterplots comparing the relationship between baseline vagal tone and the change in response to the task for regulatory-disordered infants (●) and normally developing infants. (○) From ''Psycholphysiological characteristics of the regulatory disordered infant,'' by G. A. DeGangi, J. A. DiPietro, S. I. Greenspan, and S. W. Porges, 1991, *Infant Behavior and Development, 14,* p. 44. Copyright 1991 by Ablex. Adapted with permission.

Impaired Attention in Autistic Children in Social Situations

In quite a different arena, young children with autism have been compared to both normal and mentally retarded children in terms of their patterns of attention, including joint attention with others. As Dawson and Lewy (1989) write:

> *It is well recognized that autistic children attend to their environments in unusual ways. Perhaps of most concern is their abnormal attention to people. In many instances, they appear oblivious to others and, despite bids for attention from those around them, fail to pay attention to them. In other instances, they may physically withdraw from people when approached. Along with these abnormal responses to people, unusual responses to objects are common. Autistic children often become fascinated with certain objects—a fascination that can lead to overly focused attention on the object, to the exclusion of the rest of the environment.* (p. 49)

How are these abnormal patterns manifested in the preschool child? In one study, Ferrara and Hill (1980) compared autistic children with a mean mental age of about 3.5 years to normal children whose chronological age was equivalent. All children were given a set of toys, with dolls chosen to represent the social domain, and blocks and slinkys, the object domain. Perceptually simple and complex versions of all these toys were presented, with the complex toys incorporating more detail and movement. The toys appeared on a stage at either predictable or unpredictable intervals. Several differences between the two groups were found. The autistic children looked at and manipulated the toys less than the normal children. Their attention was particularly low in the unpredictable condition, whereas the normal children seemed to be unaffected by the degree of predictability. The normal children, as would be expected, attended more to the complex than the simple toys, presumably because the complex toys were more interesting and challenging. The autistic children, on the other hand, manipulated the simple toys more. Interestingly, when complexity was low, the autistic children preferred the social to the nonsocial toys.

Other investigators have been concerned specifically with shared or joint attention in situations affording interaction between child and adult. Children diagnosed with autism seem to be less responsive to adults' points, shifts in gaze, and displays of objects than are matched controls who are either mentally retarded or who have developmental language delay (Mundy, Sigman, Ungerer, & Sherman, 1987; Loveland & Landry, 1986). They are also less likely to communicate with gesture themselves or to look back and forth from toy to adult (Mundy et al., 1987). In addition, when autistic children do use gestures that elicit another's attention to a toy, they are less likely to display positive emotion than other children; their facial expressions tend to remain neutral (Kasari, Sigman, Mundy, & Yirmiya, 1990).

Mundy and Sigman (1989) hypothesize that ''joint-attention deficits [seen in autistic children] involve a disturbance in the capacity to share common affective experiences with others'' (p. 178). Using Bakeman and Adamson's (1984; Adamson & Bakeman, 1991) account of the development of shared attention (see also chapter 8), Mundy and Sigman suggest that this deficit may first manifest itself in poor reciprocal attention and shared affect during early face to face play. They argue that, without this early experience, the motivation and ability to share attention to a common object may be impaired. This impairment in shared attention may, in turn, be an obstacle in the development of both comprehension and production of language; comprehension, which contributes to the development of productive language, depends in part on the child's response to adult speech and accompanying attention-directing gestures (Schmidt, 1991). Investigating this potential relationship, Mundy et al. (1987) found the extent of observed joint attention to be related to level of language development within a group of autistic children, even with general cognitive level and level of symbolic play controlled for. Thus, the relationship between joint attention and language skills may be specific to the impairment in attention and not a by-product of delays in symbolic development or in global cognitive functioning.

Dawson and Lewy (1989) conjecture that the complex and unpredictable nature of social interactions is what makes attention to and with people a problem for children with autism. That is, autistic children have low thresholds for the stimulation involved in complex and unpredictable events, and because they easily become overstimulated, they tend to avoid these events. It follows that if social interactions can be made simpler and more predictable, autistic children should be better able to attend. In a test of this prediction, Dawson and Galpert (reported in Dawson &

Lewy, 1989) implemented an intervention with 15 autistic children between 2 and 6 years and their mothers. In the first, pre-intervention session, the children were observed while they played with a set of toys; each mother was asked to play with her child as she wished. Then the mother was given an identical set of toys so that both mother and child had a set of toys; the mother was instructed to imitate her child's actions, body movements, and vocalizations. At the end of the session, the two sets of toys were given to the mother and she was asked to use this imitative procedure for 20 minutes every day for two weeks. After two weeks, the children and mothers returned to the lab setting, where a free play session with a *new* set of toys was followed by an imitative session with the same new set and finally by an imitative session with the old set of toys.

The intervention seemed to be quite effective. Figure 11.9 shows that the duration of time looking at the mother increased in the imitative conditions while the time

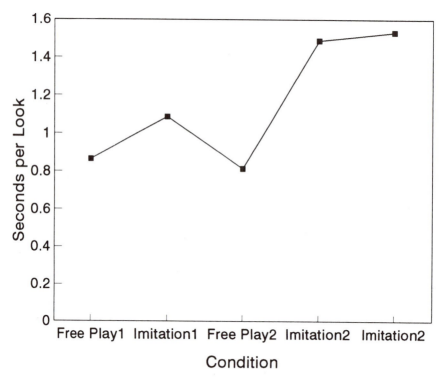

Figure 11.9. *Mean duration of gaze at mother's face (average number of seconds per gaze) for 15 autistic children during each of five conditions: (1) free play with mother, pre-2-week intervention—Free Play 1; (2) mother imitates child's play, pre-2-week-intervention— Imitation 1; (3) free play with mother, post-2-week intervention—Free Play 2; (4) mother imitate child's play with unfamiliar toys, post-2-week intervention—Imitation 2 [novel toys]; and (5) mother imitates child's play with familiar toys, post-2-week intervention—Imitation 2 [familiar toys].* Caption and figure in Dawson and Lewy (1989). From *Autism: Nature, diagnosis and treatment* (p. 65), G. Dawson (Ed.), 1989, New York: Guilford. Copyright 1989 by Guilford. Adapted with permission.

looking at her actions decreased; the effect is particularly striking after the two weeks of intervention, even though the second lab session involved novel toys. The children were more likely, after intervention, to change toys more frequently and to use a larger variety of play schemes (see figure 11.10). Although not definitive, the results suggest that the children exhibited longer attention and greater flexibility when the mother's behavior was not only more predictable, but also more contingent on the children's behavior.

In summary, this short review of research on the attention of children with regulatory disorders and autism is intended to illustrate the diversity that exists in deficits in attention. The types of deficiencies observed in children, including those discussed in previous sections, have implications for our understanding of attention and its underlying mechanisms. We turn now to a consideration of how processes of attention may deviate from normal.

UNDERLYING DEVIATIONS IN EARLY ATTENTION DEFICITS

Throughout this book, we have considered processes that may underlie attention and normal individual differences. Here, we explore several theoretical accounts of the processes underlying attention deficits. These include ideas about a neurodevelopmental lag, temperamental deviations, optimal level of arousal, and processes of activation and inhibition. Most accounts are limited to the attention deficits with and without hyperactivity, but some also address the deficits peculiar to autism.

Attention Deficit as Neurodevelopmental Lag

Eisenberg (1966) noted that hyperactivity often follows a course in which symptoms lessen considerably once the children reach adolescence, although recent studies suggest more continuity (Hinshaw, 1994). The symptoms also seem to be characteristic of normal children several years younger. Along similar lines, Kinsbourne (1973) suggested that much of the behavior seen in children diagnosed with minimal brain dysfunction is immature, appropriate at early ages but unacceptable at the child's current age. Thus, factors affecting behavior at younger ages may affect dysfunctional children at later ages. Defining an abnormality in terms of the child's age can be referred to as a neurodevelopmental lag (Kinsbourne, 1973).

Given the constellation of characteristics that lead to the diagnosis of attention deficit with hyperactivity, this is not an unreasonable hypothesis. As described in earlier chapters, activity level decreases markedly with age. Duration of sustained, focused attention increases over the first few years and is observed in a wider variety of situations as children develop. Impulse control and compliance increase dramatically. Thus, a school-age child displaying high activity, inattention, and impulsivity could be considered immature. In addition, as we described earlier, 4- to 5-year-old children have a hard time "waiting" in a monitoring task if the rewards for completing the task are visible to them throughout. Older hyperactive children could be like younger children in that they are less patient and more impulsive in the presence of

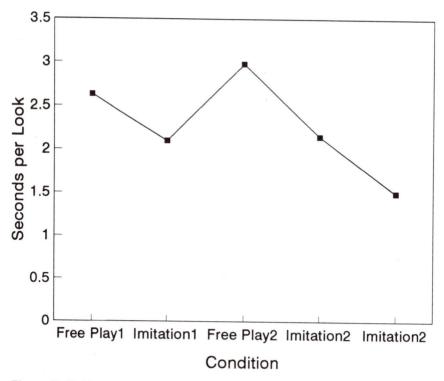

Figure 11.10 *Mean duration of gaze at mother's actions with toys (average number of seconds per gaze) for 15 autistic children during each of the five conditions described for* Figure 11.9. Caption and figure in Dawson and Lewy (1989). From *Autism: Nature, diagnosis and treatment* (p. 66), G. Dawson (Ed.), 1989, New York: Guilford. Copyright 1989 by Guilford. Adapted with permission.

rewards (Douglas & Peters, 1979). Another way of viewing the problem as a developmental lag is that one or more control processes do not develop fully for some children with attentional deficits. They will then look like younger children, but may also be unable to demonstrate appropriate attentional and behavioral controls even at a later date.

A Temperament Approach to Attention Deficits

Although general developmental trends are consistent with the hypothesis of neurodevelopmental lag, any evidence of long-term individual differences in the key dimensions of behavior would argue against immaturity, per se. The similarity between attention deficits with hyperactivity in children and extreme extraversion in adults is one example. Extraverted adults, compared to introverts, have been characterized as more impulsive, more sensation-seeking, more responsive to rewards, and less able to sustain attention in situations of low stimulation (Eysenck, 1976). This description is strikingly concordant with the one provided by Douglas (1983) for hyperactive children. Continuity between characteristics observed in the preschool years and the personality of adults indicates not so much a developmental lag as persistent individuality—individuality that may sometimes be extreme enough to be problematic. In this section, we consider how individual differences in extraversion might interact with weak control systems to produce attention deficits.

In the previous chapter on individual differences in children's temperament, we described three broad dimensions, including (1) extraversion as opposed to fear; (2) a general tendency to become distressed; and (3) effortful or attentional control. The dimensions of extraversion and effortful control show strong similarities to the two dimensions of attention deficits emerging from factor analyses of symptoms—motor overactivity and problems with attention (Lahey et al., 1988). These dimensions can also be connected to the two major control systems on behavior discussed in chapters 8 and 10 (Kochanska, 1993; Rothbart, 1989c; Rothbart & Ahadi, 1994). The first control system of behavioral inhibition is associated with wariness or fear. The second control system, effortful control, is involved in inhibiting behavior inappropriate for the situation and in flexibly shifting and focusing attention.

If we apply these temperament dimensions, including the control systems, to the two subtypes of attention deficit, a fairly clear picture would emerge for the child with attention deficits and hyperactivity. The child would be high in extraversion and low on behavioral inhibition. The child would also be relatively low in the higher level attentional processes that allow for effortful control. There would be more complexity in characterizing the child with attention deficits but no hyperactivity. This child would also have deficiencies in effortful control. The child might, however, also be either less reactive than average and low in extraversion; or the child could be of average reactivity and extraversion, but very high in the behavioral inhibition associated with fearfulness. The tendency of attention deficits without hyperactivity to be associated more with anxiety and depression than with impulsivity and aggression (Lahey et al., 1987) would be congruent with the latter possibility.

A temperament approach suggests that, rather than a neurodevelopmental lag, the two attention deficits may involve poor effortful control, control that usually evolves during the preschool period. Because the children look like younger children, a maturational lag may be postulated, and indeed some children may attain controls later than others. Some children, however, may never develop adequate levels of effortful control and attention.

Hypotheses About Optimal Arousal Level

A topic that could also be considered under the rubric of temperament is an arousal hypothesis explicated by Zentall and Zentall (1983). A number of theories address the role of individual differences in arousal level in the development of adult personality and temperament (Eysenck, 1972; Rothbart, 1989b). In agreement with these, Zentall and Zentall argue that human beings modulate incoming sensory stimulation to maintain an optimal level of arousal. Abnormally high or abnormally low levels of sensory input for normal individuals lead to ''disordered'' behavior—distress and sensory deprivation, respectively. For some individuals, sensory input is chronically and abnormally low (in Eysenck's view, the extreme extravert), and for others, sensory input is chronically and abnormally high (in Eysenck's view, the extreme introvert). These differences may lead to chronically disordered behavior as these individuals attempt to regulate input that is too high or too low. Specifically, Zentall and Zentall propose that hyperactive children fall on the chronically understimulated end of the spectrum. Their activity, impulsivity, and sensation-seeking are, in this view, an adaptation to this chronic condition; sensation-seeking may raise arousal levels through the excitement of novel and risky situations; high activity level may do so by increasing the level of auditory, visual, and tactual stimulation. As a consequence, tasks demanding attention to repetitive, familiar stimulus events, such as continuous performance tests, are likely to be problematic for chronically under-aroused children.

From this perspective, it also follows that the performance of children with attention deficits and hyperactivity may improve in an environment that provides a high level of background stimulation. Barlow (1977, cited in Zentall & Zentall, 1983) compared the effect of low and high environmental stimulation crossed with low and high levels of stimulant medication (placebo versus methylphenidate) on a continuous performance task. For hyperactive children, number of errors decreased in both high-stimulation conditions, so environmental manipulation and drugs seemed to have similar effects, at least in the short run. A point to consider is that the task was simple and required only sustained attention. Because it did not involve learning new material or new patterns of response, we do not know whether increasing overall arousal level would help or hinder learning.

One difficulty with the Zentall and Zentall model (1983) is that it does not distinguish between the major subtypes of attention deficit. Behaviorally, children with attention deficits but no hyperactivity appear to be less aroused, but they do *not* have problems with impulsivity. Thus, the children who seem to be most under-aroused may be no more sensation-seeking than are normal children. Chronic under-arousal and its compensating behavior may nevertheless explain some types of attention deficits.

In contrast, a tendency to become overaroused and its accompanying behavior may be manifest in other types of attention deficits, such as those accompanying autism. Zentall and Zentall suggest that repetitive behavior and withdrawal from social interaction could be ways of reducing uncomfortably high levels of arousal caused by average levels of stimulation. Consistent with this view is evidence for higher than average physiological responsiveness to novel events in autistic children, accompanied by slower than average rates of habituation (Zentall & Zentall, 1983).

A specific consequence of being abnormally aroused by average levels of stimulation may be overfocusing (Kinsbourne, 1991). As Kinsbourne notes, "Overfocusing involves a narrow focus of attention. . . . Constricted attention limits the amount of experienced stimulation. But a corollary drawback is that it reduces the individual's ability to detect and monitor unexpected change in the environment" (p. 18). Children who focus on particular objects or activities to an unusually narrow degree may prefer familiar routines and surroundings and be upset by change. They may prefer to limit the number of objects or events they attend to at one time and resist shifting attention when asked by someone else to do so. They may also maintain the same posture or the same facial expression for long periods of time. Kinsbourne hypothesizes that, for these children, such behaviors are adaptive in that they limit the amount of experienced stimulation and keep arousal levels within a more comfortable zone. In this sense, stability of internal state would be a more dominant motivator than adjusting to the demands of changing circumstances and of normal social interchange.

Imbalances of Activation and Inhibition

Another way of viewing the processes underlying attention is in terms of activation and inhibition. Attention that is appropriately modulated to meet the needs of external constraints and self-determined goals requires a balance between these two influences. Many aspects of attention discussed in this book are the product of these opponent processes operating at many levels. These levels include: (1) behavior, in that particular activities are promoted or suppressed; (2) the autonomic nervous system, in sympathetic or parasympathetic excitation and inhibition; (3) subcortical and cortical neural functions that depend on both inhibitory and excitatory processes. Adequate deployment of attention and organized activity occurs when these opponent processes are integrated and work in concert. Imbalances may lead to maladaptive distribution of attention and poorly organized responses.

Porges (1976, 1984, 1992) has developed this hypothesis in terms of both the autonomic and central nervous systems. Specifically, he hypothesizes that hyperactive individuals are deficient in inhibitory control of behavior with a parallel deficit in parasympathetic control. The lack of parasympathetic control is observed in their failure to slow heart rate and suppress heart rate variability (e.g., respiratory sinus arrhythmia) in response to demands for sustained attention. The parasympathetic system is controlled by the vagus nerve, which is, in turn, controlled by the brainstem and by other central systems via the brainstem. Thus, the inability to modulate heart rate and inhibit spontaneous behavior can be considered a deficit with origins in the central nervous system.

In support of Porges's hypothesis are the results of a study in which 16 school-age hyperactive children were tested with a reaction-time task involving a variable period between the warning and the signal to respond (Porges, Walter, Korb, & Sprague, 1975). The children were seen under two conditions—after administration of a placebo and after methylphenidate. The investigators counterbalanced conditions and measured reaction time, heart rate, and heart rate variability during the task. Heart rate and variability were significantly lower with methylphenidate than with the placebo; presumably the drug changed the balance of excitatory and inhibitory forces acting on the parasympathetic system, whereas the placebo had no effect.

In addition, Porges (1976) speculates that the attention deficits of autistic children are related to a dysfunctional sympathetic system, where unstable levels of excitation lead to inconsistent responses to environmental events. Yet other imbalances may cause some individuals to be "lethargic . . . (and lacking in) structured cognitive activity" (p. 42), suggestive of attention deficit without hyperactivity.

Along similar lines, Schaughency and Hynd (1989) suggest that attention deficits with hyperactivity represent a dysfunction in inhibitory processes (see also Quay, 1988), whereas attention deficits without hyperactivity are a dysfunction in excitatory processes. Following Posner and Peterson (1990) and Tucker and Williamson

(1984), they argue that two functional networks can be discriminated on the basis of both neurochemistry and neuroanatomy. The arousal network controls reactivity to external events; this network is located in the right posterior part of the brain, with norepinephrine and serotonin pathways providing the neurotransmitter substrate. The second network, more related to motor control, is located in the left frontal region of the brain with dopamine and acetylcholine as the relevant neurotransmitters. Note the parallels with our orienting/investigative system and system of higher level controls. Attention deficits with hyperactivity, in this framework, result from functional deficits in the network related to motor control. Such a possibility is supported by animal work showing that rats with depleted dopamine levels exhibit increased activity levels and respond favorably to administration of stimulants. In clinical studies with human patients with hyperactivity, investigators have observed poorer than normal blood supply in the prefrontal cortex and motor cortical areas (Lou, Henriksen, & Bruhn, 1984) and lower levels of glucose metabolism (Zametkin et al., 1990); stimulant medication results in increased blood supply to pathways leading from subcortical areas to the frontal cortex (Lou et al., 1984).

There are two ways in which this formulation may connect to Porges's hypotheses. One is that acetylcholine, the neurotransmitter important to the frontal system, is also important to parasympathetic control. The second is that a major subcortical to cortical route would be input from the limbic system—important in evaluating adaptive significance of events—to the frontal systems controlling motor activity (Tucker, 1991). The limbic system also can directly inhibit the vagus, thus reducing parasympathetic excitation and inhibiting heart rate and heart rate variability (Porges, 1992).

The arousal system, in contrast, may be an important factor in attention deficits without hyperactivity (Schaughency & Hynd, 1989). This would suggest a deficit manifested in low behavioral reactivity, low arousal in the spatial orienting system of the central posterior brain (Posner & Peterson, 1990), and deficiencies in the norepinephrine pathways. The locus coeruleus of the brain stem is a major source of norepinephrine, and its activity is closely tied to orienting reactions. Low levels of activity in the locus coeruleus, and therefore low norepinephrine levels, lead to low reactivity to environmental events (Aston-Jones, 1994).

A third theoretical formulation about attention deficits comes from Posner and colleagues (Posner & Raichle, 1994; Posner & Rothbart, 1991; see also Voeller, 1991), who speculate that at least some attention deficits may reflect a problem with the vigilance network of the right frontal cortex (see chapter 3). This is an interesting possibility given the extensive use of vigilance or reaction-time tasks in the study of attention deficits. Vigilance tasks involve relatively long waiting periods during which the subject must be prepared to respond to an infrequent auditory or visual signal, often embedded in a stream of irrelevant stimuli. Accurate and fast responses require the subject to maintain alertness and motor preparedness during the waiting periods. If the vigilance network in the frontal cortex is not operating efficiently, inhibitory control over cortical and autonomic activity will be weak. If metabolic and electrical activity in the cortex (outside the right frontal area) remains at normal levels, as they might with weak inhibitory controls, signals are not amplified; thus they may be responded to slowly or missed altogether. The vigilance task is an experimental technique that does not obviously reflect the normal circumstances of preschool or school-age children. One practical example, however, might be those occasions when parents or teachers tell the child to listen to what they are going to say or to watch how something is done. Children with immature or inefficient vigilance systems may have difficulty achieving the appropriate state of alertness and preparedness and thus, have difficulty picking up the information that they have been told is coming. This difficulty, in turn, would have negative implications for socialization, where attention to and compliance with instructions from others is essential.

This very brief overview cannot do justice to the complex topic of the integration and balance of excitatory and inhibitory processes occurring at all levels of the nervous system. Our review also has not included a number of current hypotheses about the neurotransmitter substrate of hyperactivity and the effect of stimulant medication (e.g., Hynd, Hern, Voeller, & Marshall, 1991; Zametkin & Rapoport, 1987). Some of the uncertainty in our approach to mechanisms exists because of the field's inadequate discrimination of subtly different deficits on the one hand and the possibility that similar behavioral deficits may arise from different underlying causes on the other. Research in the future will certainly lead to a more refined understanding of the specific neural sources of difficulties in attention as more articulated descriptions of behavioral and cognitive deficits become available.

SUMMARY

In this chapter, we have considered difficulties experienced by young children in the control of attention. Because attention is itself multifaceted, it is not surprising that multiple deficits of attention have been identified. Most research focuses on attention deficits found in school-age children. These are quite stable over time and have been linked to antisocial behavior and interpersonal difficulties.

The evidence points to at least two major forms of attention deficit at school age. The first, attention deficit disorder with hyperactivity, has been identified by Douglas (1983) as including disorganized and poorly maintained attention, impulsivity, and poor modulation of arousal level. A second variant, attention deficit without hyperactivity, shares with the first type problems of arousal and sustained attention; it is otherwise characterized by cognitive disorganization, low reactivity, and sluggish tempo.

We then reviewed studies of possible precursors to attention deficits with hyperactivity; these suggest that some children who will have future problems with attention can be identified as early as 2 to 3 years of age. From an early age, some children tend to be rated by their mothers as more restless, more disobedient, and showing less concentration. Preliminary findings were also reported on a set of characteristics in preschool children that may be associated with later development of attention deficits without hyperactivity. These include less focused attention and a propensity for negative emotionality and withdrawal from environmental stimulation.

Inattentiveness has been connected with other disorders of infancy and early childhood, including regulatory disorders and early childhood autism, and we provided a brief review of these. Finally, we considered processes that might underlie deficiencies in attention. One possibility is a neurodevelopmental lag; some children with attention deficits behave in many ways like younger children. Another possibility is that some deficits represent deviations in temperamental characteristics; hyperactive children might be portrayed as having high levels of extraversion not regulated by behavioral inhibition and also low levels of effortful control; children with attention deficits without hyperactivity may also have low levels of effortful control, but be unreactive or dominated by behavioral inhibition. A third account stresses individual differences in optimal levels of arousal; disordered behavior such as hyperactivity is seen as an adaptation to chronically and abnormally low arousal. In a fourth section, we discussed several hypotheses about imbalances in activation and inhibition; hyperactive children have relatively weak inhibitory processes, while other deficits may stem from weak activation relative to inhibition.

In chapter 12, we return to the topic of attention deficits by considering the biological and social contributions to the development of abnormal patterns of attention. Our discussion there is set within the framework of individuality as seen in profiles of attentional development.

12

Individuality and Development

In the last two chapters, our review and summary of research on individual differences strongly suggested that stable individual differences in components of attention exist in infancy and early childhood. In some cases, these differences may herald later deficits in attention. Although stability of individual differences across time and context implies some modicum of predictability in the attentiveness of individuals, the explanation of those differences involves the contribution of many interacting factors. In this chapter, we address issues of explanation by asking the following questions: How do differences in attention originate? What are some of the contributors to the development of these differences? How are these contributors related to one another in the development of individual children? How is attention related to variability in patterns of development? Although we cannot answer these questions in detail, we do wish to consider individual differences, including attention deficits, within the framework of development. As Cairns and Hood (1983) note, "much of the variance that is predictable across ontogeny is not 'in' the organism, but 'in' its developmental context, its physical ecology, its relationships, and its likely course of subsequent development" (pp. 344–345).

ORIGINS OF INDIVIDUAL DIFFERENCES

First we consider two large domains of variation important to early development: organismic variables, the characteristics a child brings to a situation; and environmental variables, characteristics of the child's surroundings that have an impact on development.

Early Biological Variation

Differences among children are apparent on the first day of life, even earlier to mothers in their second or later pregnancies. These differences observed early in life are determined by the complex interplay of the child's genetic makeup, influences in the intrauterine environment, and the current situation. The behavioral endpoint of prenatal development serves as a starting point for postnatal development where the same general forces are operating. At the end of this section, we discuss biologically based dispositions that emerge later in development.

Some behavioral dimensions showing noticeable variability in the newborn are reactivity, emotionality, and alertness (Rothbart, 1989c; Sroufe, 1979). These dimensions could be considered propensities for: (1) quick, strong reactions versus slow, weaker ones; (2) negative or positive emotional tone; and (3) low to high levels of alertness. Where an individual infant falls on these dimensions will vary from situation to situation, but, as we have seen, the dimensions are stable enough to qualify as individual dispositions. These early dispositions are, in Horowitz's (1990) words, "functional elements in the processes of development" (p. 16). They structure the child's environment in particular ways and help determine the nature of the child's earliest experiences.

Level of alertness in the newborn can serve as an example. Thoman and Whitney (1990; also Becker & Thoman, 1983) report that extended observations of neonates led to highly reliable estimates of the amount of time spent in alert waking states and nonalert waking states; coefficients of stability for these two states in the second through fifth weeks were .71 and .62, respectively. The duration of nonalert waking states, defined as those times when the baby's eyes are open but have a vacant look, was inversely correlated with the overall stability of state (Becker & Thoman, 1983). Thoman and Whitney (1990) argue that stability of state is a reflection of early integrity of the central nervous system. Infants with extremely unstable states are likely to be dysfunctional, with such instability potentially leading to later regulatory disorders. For our purposes here, with the exception of these extremes, the range of stability and the amount of time spent in alert and nonalert waking states are considered to represent normal individual differences in state control.

Given that individual neonates vary in their control and distribution of various states, how might these differences influence infants' early experiences? Thoman and Whitney (1990) note:

The behavioral states are a system of species-specific behaviors that express CNS integration and serve endogenous needs of the organism. This is accomplished by two major functions of state. State functions as a gating mechanism for the infant's perception of internal processes and external events and as a modulating mechanism for the infant's behaviors. These functions are intimately linked to the role of state as an interface with the environment, primarily as a mediator of interactions between the infant and the caregiver. Thus, state functions in complex, dynamic ways to express the infant's neurobehavioral status while, at the same time, influencing the developmental course of that status. (p. 131)

An infant who is frequently alert and whose states are stable and predictable may be easier for the mother or other caregiver to manage than a less alert infant; the alert infant may also be more responsive to the mother's interventions. In turn, the mother may feel generally more positive about her own competence as a caregiver, an experience that is likely to affect her later interactions with the infant (Rothbart, 1989c). In addition, the alert infant will have a larger window of time in the first few weeks to take in visual and auditory events, creating a different base for later cognitive development than a less alert infant will have. On the other hand, the infant's alertness may create situations in which overstimulation is possible or that create demands on the new mother who may be tired and in need of rest.

New biologically based propensities emerge later in development. These include fear, an emotion that appears in the latter half of the first year; its intensity and duration in strange situations is highly variable across infants (Bronson, 1972; Rothbart, 1981). As the infant becomes more mobile and more capable of acting on intentions, frustration is experienced when the infant's actions are blocked (Bertenthal & Campos, 1990). The degree of frustration felt and the tolerance for frustrating circumstances differs markedly across children (Rothbart, 1981). The inhibitory controls so important for development in the preschool years vary in strength (Kochanska et al., in press). These later-emerging dispositions are certainly based, in part, on biological and genetic differences. As with the neonatal dispositions, they have a significant impact on the rate and nature of individual children's development of attention.

Environment as a Contributor

The child's early dispositions put constraints on those aspects of the environment that are effective in the child's development. "Environment," however, is a term covering many different facets of the social milieu and the physical surroundings of the child. In chapter 8, we discussed the social context for the development of attention. This context included the adult's role in helping the child to: (1) regulate arousal levels through calming and stimulation; (2) learn strategies of attending through demonstration and instruction; and (3) move to increasing self-control of attention. All of these aspects of the social environment are relevant here, although different children may respond differentially to the same interventions and require different levels of intervention in order to function adaptively. We discuss this issue further when we take up the topic of interactions between child and environment.

One general aspect of the environment we have not yet addressed is the physical environment. In recent years, Wachs (1989, 1990, 1993) and others (Gottfried & Gottfried, 1984; Wohlwill, 1983) have argued that the physical environment exerts important influences on child development. Wachs (1989), expanding on Wohlwill's (1983) classification, uses three dimensions to define or classify features of the physical environment: (1) whether stimulation is in the background or foreground for the child; (2) whether the stimulation is animate or inanimate; and (3) whether the stimulation is responsive or nonresponsive to the child's activity. Much movement of people in and out of the room with no attention paid to the child is an example of background, animate, and nonresponsive stimulation, whereas noise from television, radio, and street traffic would be background, inanimate, and nonresponsive if the child had no control over the sources of noise. Crowded, noisy environments may interfere more with the development of attention than quiet environments, everything else, including number and nature of toys, being equal. If objects and events do not clearly stand out from background stimulation, we would expect a child to have difficulty selecting and maintaining a focus of attention.

There are, Wachs (1993) contends, also indirect effects of these physical features. Crowded, noisy conditions in homes with a high level of traffic in and out of them are associated with lower levels of responsivity and attention to the child by the parent. He suggests several routes by which crowding and noise may interfere with parents' responsivity. One is that parents may habituate to high noise levels and tune out the child as well as the background noise. A second possibility is that parents may feel helpless in the face of uncontrollable conditions and thus be less motivated to engage in interaction with the child. Third, the number of competing events may make it difficult for the parents to focus their attention on the child. Finally, noise and constant activity may tire the parents out, with fatigue lowering their tolerance for demands from the child. Given the importance of social structuring in the child's early development, the unavailability of parental support may lead some children to develop lower levels of attentiveness and weaker controls on attention and behavior than children who have more parental support.

In summary, both the social and physical contexts for development vary widely from child to child and thus contribute to individual variation in the different components of attention. Some physical conditions and some social interactions will predispose a child to extensive exploratory activity and high levels of attention to novel objects and events (Bornstein, 1989). Other conditions and interactions may interfere with sustained attention to novelty. Some environments will be conducive to rapid development of self-control while other environments may actually discourage control over impulsivity and activity. In addition, children encounter different models in their parents, with some who are highly focused, others who distribute their attention more broadly, some who sustain concentration for long periods of time, and others who move quickly from one activity to the next. All of these possibilities could contribute to the development of normal and expected differences among children.

An Interactionist Approach to Individual Differences

Although we initiated our discussion of how children develop differences in attention by introducing early biological variation and diverse environmental conditions, we have said little about how these organismic and environmental variables relate to one another in determining development. It is commonplace now in the literature on child development to consider development as the result of interacting biological and environmental influences. These interactions may take many forms. One interaction particularly relevant for our current discussion is simply that individuals will respond in different ways to the same input (Escalona, 1968; Schneirla, 1965). Wachs and his colleagues (e.g., Wachs & Gandour, 1983) refer to this interaction as "organismic specificity."

We have already discussed associations between attention and aspects of temperament, such as negative emotionality and activity level. A reasonable question is whether these temperamental characteristics interact with environmental factors to influence patterns of attention. For example, Wachs (1987) found that the number of people moving around in the home was positively related to the amount of time 12-month-olds spent "off-task" when playing with toys ($r = .22$). However, the relationship was much stronger in children who were rated as temperamentally difficult (negative mood and unadaptable; $r = .49$) than it was in those who were rated as easy ($r = .08$). It may be that infants prone to distress have a narrower range of manageable arousal, and that too much traffic in the home raises their arousal above a level optimal for sustained or concentrated play with toys.

Gandour (1989) found the same level of maternal intervention to have different effects on individual children according to their activity level. Her hypothesis was that relatively inactive children living with mothers who were highly stimulating would attend to and explore objects more than similar children living with low stimulating mothers (see also Escalona, 1968). On the other hand, she hypothesized that highly active children with highly stimulating mothers would actually show lower levels and quality of attention and exploration than highly active children with less stimulating mothers.

Mothers and children were observed in their homes six times when the children were 15 months of age. Activity level was determined by maternal ratings on the Carey Toddler Temperament Scale (Fullard et al., 1984). Maternal level and intensity of stimulation was determined by direct observation and coding of mothers' attention-focusing activity, both physical and verbal. Finally, the children's exploratory activities were coded in terms of the length of engagement with toys and level of play using the system of Belsky and Most (1981). As shown in figure 12.1, the expected interaction was found; children with low activity level and highly stimulating mothers and children with high activity level and low stimulating mothers played at a higher level and for longer periods than the other subgroups of children.

The findings by Wachs and Gandour suggest that some early-appearing temperamental characteristics of children may, in interaction with physical and social features of the environment, help determine the amount and nature of attention paid to objects. Another characteristic, however, may be the child's attention level itself. In the last two chapters, we reviewed evidence for early, relatively stable, differences in the amount of attention spontaneously focused on objects. We also suggested in chapter 8 that parents often attempt to direct and sustain children's attention when they play jointly with toys. How does parental activity interact with children's tendency to sustain and focus attention as seen in their independent play?

A study with 10-month-olds (Parrinello & Ruff, 1988) addressed this question. After a baseline period in which infants were given four objects, one at a time, to play with, the infants were assigned to one of three levels of intervention or a no-intervention control condition. The two major independent variables were level of intervention and children's baseline durations of focused attention. The interventions were scaled in intensity of stimulation provided by an adult who played with the child and several new objects. The level of intervention was defined by: (1) speed and frequency of demonstrating object properties; (2) frequency and volume of accompanying speech; (3) physical proximity; and (4) timing of efforts to refocus the child's attention when it lapsed. The measure of the intervention's effectiveness was the total amount of time spent in focused attention to the object. The intervention was partly contingent on the child's behavior and attention, and the conditions varied in the total amount of time the child had available to focus attention independently on the objects; therefore, the measure of focused attention was corrected for the time available.

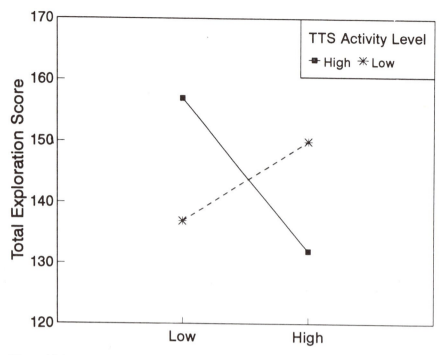

Figure 12.1. The differential outcomes for low and high active children in relation to level of maternal stimulation (low vs. high). From ''Activity level as a dimension of temperament in toddlers: Its relevance for the organismic specificity hypothesis,'' by M. J. Gandour, 1989, *Child Development, 60,* p. 1096. Copyright 1989 by the Society for Research in Child Development. Adapted with permission.

Level of intervention was an important factor for the low attenders—those below the median on attention during baseline—while it had relatively little effect on the high attenders. Figure 12.2 shows that the low attenders were more focused in the medium level of intervention than in the lowest level; specifically, they had more episodes of focused attention and a lengthening of the longest single episode. The highest level seemed to increase the number of episodes of focused attention without affecting their length. These results suggest that low attenders (like the low-active children in Gandour's study) benefited from the adult's stimulation and intervention, whereas high-attending children did not. Although there was room for improvement, the attention of high attenders remained at the same level during all types of interaction with the adult. Their emotional reactions to the experimenter and the situation, however, varied with level of intervention. They looked less at the examiner in the highest level of intervention than in the lower levels; they smiled less and showed more negative affect as the level of intervention increased, suggesting that high levels of intervention may have been overstimulating for them.

While these results are based on a single encounter with a strange adult, the results of other studies reveal similar effects of maternal intervention (e.g., Belsky, Goode, & Most, 1980; Riksen-Walraven, 1978). Lawson et al. (1992) found essen-

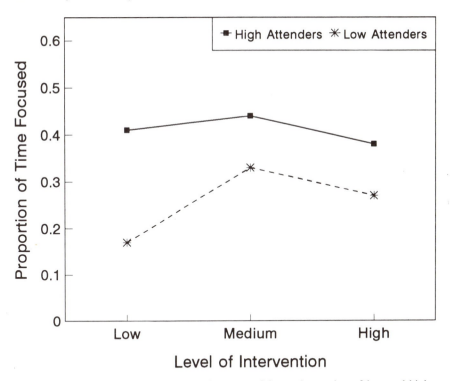

Figure 12.2. The differential responses in terms of focused attention of low and high attenders to different levels of intervention. From "The influence of adult intervention on infants' level of attention," by R. M. Parrinello and H. A. Ruff, 1988, *Child Development, 59*, p. 1129. Copyright 1988 by the Society for Research in Child Development. Adapted with permission.

tially the same interaction when mothers played with their 1-year-old infants. Mothers appeared to be most effective in increasing focused attention and decreasing active forms of inattention, such as dropping and throwing the toys, for low-attending infants. Low attenders, during play with their mothers, were as attentive as average attenders, though still less than high attenders. Although mothers of the three groups did not differ in the frequency or type of behavior displayed during this period of interaction, children in the three groups responded quite differently to their efforts. The mothers of high attenders were, however, rated as taking more pleasure in their children. This finding raises the possibility that mothers of infants who are well regulated in attention and behavior may derive particular satisfaction from interacting with their infants and may allow their infants to take more control of their own actions.

The results of these studies suggest that the attention of some infants is not strongly engaged by objects and toys when they play by themselves. Their attention will increase, however, when stimulated, aroused, instructed, and/or restricted by their mothers during joint play with objects. The attention of other infants seems to be well regulated during independent play; intervention does not enhance it, and at high levels, may interfere with it. That does not mean that spontaneously high attenders do not benefit from participating in interactive play with objects; such experiences are important for emerging skills of joint attention and for continuing intimacy with parents. Sensitive parents, however, will adjust their level of intervention to give low attenders a boost and avoid disrupting the high-attending child's patterns of concentration.

The results with the low attenders have important implications for development. If low-active or low-attending children are affected by efforts to stimulate and enhance their attention to and activities with toys, then their spontaneous levels of attention may increase with the repeated assistance of more experienced members of the family. In a recent study (Lawson & Ruff, 1995a), the following hypothesis, based on previous research, was tested: low-attending children who are positive in affect and easy to manage will increase their attention over time more than low-attending children who are more irritable and difficult to manage. A possible mediator is a greater amenability in the first group than the second to parental attempts to encourage attention. Preterm infants were seen at 7, 12, and 24 months, corrected age; they were rated by their mothers on the Bates Infant Characteristics Questionnaire (Bates, Freeland, & Lounsbury, 1979) and were observed during the administration of the Bayley Mental Development Scale (Bayley, 1969), free play with toys, and joint play with the mother.

The level of independent focused attention and the temperament rating at 7 months interacted to predict attentiveness at 15 and 24 months of age. That is, the correlation between focused attention at 7 months and focused attention averaged for 15 and 24 months was high for the relatively negative children and very low for relatively positive children. The more negative children were consistent in their focused attention, an indication that they were less influenced by external factors than more positive children. When the children were divided into subgroups on the basis of the combined 7-month attention and temperament scores, the negative, low attenders were the least attentive children at 24 months. The levels of attention displayed by the positive low attenders increased significantly and approached the levels of attention seen in the high attenders. These results suggest that child characteristics help determine the child's response to environmental forces and subsequent development. Children's attention changes with age, but it changes more in some cases than others.

Parents do not always facilitate their children's attentiveness. An example of a possible negative influence comes from Breznitz and Friedman (1988), who compared toddlers whose mothers were clinically depressed with those whose mothers were free of any psychiatric diagnosis. The investigators predicted that toddlers of depressed mothers would be less attentive during play than toddlers of normal mothers; however, they hypothesized that the mother's degree of availability and her own attention to toys when she was available would mediate the child's attention to toys. After familiarizing the children with the lab, furnished like a living room, the investigators recorded the children's behavior during a period of free play. Mothers were asked to give their children toys from a suitcase, but were not instructed further. Most mothers spent some time showing the toys to their children.

The results generally supported the investigators' expectations. Children of depressed mothers attended to significantly more objects and spent less time with each object. The depressed mothers and their toddlers spent as much time engaged in joint attention to objects as did normal mothers and their toddlers. The depressed mothers, however, terminated their children's attention to objects significantly more often than normal mothers.

Breznitz and Friedman speculate that the depressed mothers' own attention patterns are disturbed by their disorder; in turn, the mothers are more likely to disrupt their children's attention. Thus, they provide their children with poorer models of sustained attention as well as less practice in maintaining attention over time. Further work along these lines would not only elucidate a potential risk factor for children's poor development of attention but also add to our understanding of social influences on the development of attentional control.

THE DEVELOPMENT OF ATTENTION DEFICITS

In this section, we explore contributions made by both biological and social factors, interacting with one another, to the development of children who are considered to have attention deficits. Because more information is available for children diagnosed as having attention deficits with hyperactivity, we use the development of these children as an example.

Biological Bases

Most discussions of the development of hyperactivity are based on a strong presumption that it is biologically based. For example, Lou et al. (1984) found evidence of low metabolic activity in the white matter of the frontal lobes of child patients with hyperactivity. This evidence is consistent with an early lack of oxygen as a possible origin of the neurological deficit underlying the disorder. Although disordered behavior is related to biological or neurological variation on the one hand and personal social and behavioral histories on the other, biological deviations may be extreme enough to give them a greater weight in the equation than is the case for normal children. Szumowski, Ewing, and Campbell (1987) offer a case study that seems to illustrate a very strong influence of the child's early dispositions. In this case, David's parents had sought professional help when he was only 2 years of age because of problems present since early infancy. In the words of Szumowski et al.,

In David's history, there are indications of difficulties almost immediately after birth. Although his perinatal respiratory problems remitted quite rapidly with only minimal intervention, he is described as a temperamentally difficult infant who resisted cuddling and soothing. Feeding and sleeping problems persisted throughout the first year, and as he added walking to his repertoire at 8 1/2 months, it became another source of distress for his parents who were unable to contain his activity. . . .

At the home visit, our first contact with David, he was noted to have a high level of activity, described as frenetic, and an extremely limited attention span. He virtually ricocheted from one toy to another. . . .

During both visits to our laboratory playroom, David's short attention span and high

activity were again apparent, as were a moderate amount of irritability and non-compliance. For example, during free play, David flitted rapidly from one toy to another, but failed to become engaged in a constructive or sustained play activity. . . . David could be coaxed to complete structured tasks if he was provided with frequent redirection and praise. David's mother was observed to provide him with both clear limits and liberal praise throughout their interactions. She was frequently and appropriately firm, but also warm and supportive.

David was not observed at preschool since he had been expelled prior to . . . our study. But that incident and teacher accounts of his aggression toward his peers provided additional data which further validated the pervasiveness of his problems. . . .

David's parents . . . were helped to implement several different behavior management strategies and to target the most troublesome behavior for intervention. . . . At our first follow-up one year later, David (age 4 1/2) was managing relatively well in a specialized preschool program. . . .

When David was 5, his pediatrician suggested a trial of methylphenidate. . . . By age 6, David was in public kindergarten, but there was some question whether he would remain. . . . David met DSM-III criteria for Attention Deficit Disorder with Hyperactivity. . . . David's very severe behavior problems have persisted in spite of his parents' ability to provide consistency, structure, well-established limits, an intact, loving family environment, and low levels of additional family stress. (pp. 80–83)

This case describes the development of a child with persistent problems with activity, attention, and aggression. The authors of the case study make the important point, however, that the particular manifestations of his problems were not static throughout his early development.

Rather, they seem to have appeared first as difficulties with mood, consolability, and self-regulation in infancy; as overactivity and recklessness in early toddlerhood; as a short attention span, difficulty playing alone, tantrums and aggressive outbursts in the preschool years; and more recently, as age-inappropriate[,] excessive defiance and tantrum behavior in addition to continued overactivity, poor impulse control, limited attentional capacities, and suspected learning disabilities. (p. 83)

Underscoring biological contributions to the disorder, Alessandri and Schramm (1991) provide an experimental case study of a single child. A boy of 4 years was diagnosed as having an attention deficit with hyperactivity and was subsequently observed in a preschool setting. There were four 4-week periods of observation: a baseline, a trial of stimulant medication, another baseline, and a second trial of medication. Neither teachers nor observers were informed of the child's medication status at any point. As can be seen in figure 12.3, the boy's behavior changed in accordance with the medication. During the medication periods, compared to the baseline periods, he spent less time off-task—that is, unoccupied or in transition from one activity to another; he spent more time engaged in play and the quality of his play was more mature; he was rated as more attentive during structured activities. The medication was apparently influencing some of the neural processes described in chapter 11 and thereby affecting his behavior.

Social Contributions to Developmental Patterns

In some cases, even the most supportive care by parents may not eliminate the symptoms of a severe disorder. The child's social experiences are nonetheless important in the development of attention and self-regulation. These experiences may exacerbate or mitigate early biological vulnerabilities (Conners & Wells, 1986) and

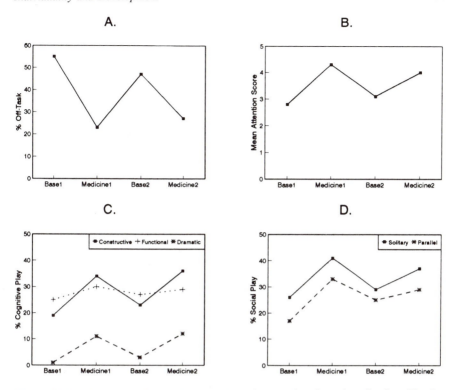

Figure 12.3. Changes in a boy's classroom behavior as a function of medication. The first and third points represent baseline periods with no medication, the second and fourth points, periods of medication. (A) The amount of "off-task" behavior during a 50-minute free-play period, including unoccupied behavior and aggression. (B) The degree of attentiveness during circle time, a structured period with the teacher and other children. (C) The percentage of play time spent in "simple repetitive play," in construction with materials, and in pretend play. (D) The percentage of time spent playing alone or beside another child. From "Effects of dextroamphetamine on the cognitive and social play of a preschooler with ADHD" by S. M. Alessandri and K. Schramm, 1991, *Journal of the American Academy of Child and Adolescent Psychiatry, 30,* p. 770. Copyright 1991 by the American Academy of Child and Adolescent Psychiatry. Adapted with permission.

thus are important to consider. Jacobvitz and Sroufe (1987), in a prospective study of children followed from birth, assessed the contribution of early measures of both child and parental behavior to hyperactivity as assessed in kindergarten when the children were 5 years old. They found that children judged to be hyperactive, compared to problem-free children, were more likely to have been motorically immature at birth and more distractible at 3.5 years; their mothers, however, were also more likely to have given them intrusive care at 6 months and overstimulating care at 42 months. Mothers' intrusive care at 6 months was significantly related to the child's distractibility at 42 months.

The investigators speculated that early individual differences in vulnerability, as seen in the motor maturity score, and maternal intrusive style interacted to produce consistent problem behavior in some children. Their speculation is plausible because at least some aspects of the mother's behavior were measured long before the outcome at 5 years. At the same time, intrusive mothers may themselves be highly impulsive and inattentive and thus contribute to the child's behavior "passively" through heredity, as well as "actively" through interaction with their children. These two possibilities are difficult to tease apart.

In their longitudinal study, Campbell and colleagues observed mothers' behavior during free play with their children at the children's 3- and 4-year visits (Campbell, Breaux, Ewing, Szumowski, & Pierce, 1986). Because the referred families were somewhat lower in socioeconomic status (SES) than the control families, and because SES is associated with different parental styles of interaction and discipline, group differences on observed measures of interaction were examined with SES partialled out. Even so, mothers of referred children at the 3-year visit were more likely to suggest activities to the child that were different from the child's current activity. When the data from the 3- and 4-year visits were combined, the mothers of referred children were significantly more likely to utter negative statements directed at controlling the child; this difference seemed to result from the fact that mothers of control children substantially reduced the number of negative control statements from 3 to 4 years, while the mothers of the referred children did not.

Although the differences between referred and control children were not extensive, they are consistent with differences found in studies of interaction between mothers and older hyperactive children. Cunningham and Barkley (1979), for example, found mothers of school-age hyperactive boys, during both free play and structured tasks, to be less likely to initiate interaction with their sons or to respond to their sons' initiatives; they tried to control their children's activity more than mothers of normal children. Using the same procedures and coding scheme, Mash and Johnston (1982) found similar results with younger children. Mothers of 5- and 8-year-old hyperactive children were more directive and more negative than mothers of control children. They were also more likely to ignore the child's questions and bids for interaction. This pattern was most apparent during structured activity and was stronger for 5-year-olds than for 8-year-olds. The interaction of mothers with the older hyperactive children was, in fact, more like the interaction of mothers with younger normal children.

We do not know from these studies whether the mothers were *reacting* to the children's behavior or whether their behavior was characteristic of their general style. One way to determine whether maternal behavior is reactive is to manipulate the child's behavior without the mother's being aware of the particular conditions. To our knowledge, this has not been done with preschool hyperactive children. A study by Barkley and Cunningham (1979) with school-age children, however, was designed for this purpose. Hyperactive children and their mothers were observed twice, once after the children had been given stimulant medication and once after they had been given a placebo. Mothers, experimenters, and children were blind to the order of drug and placebo. The results suggest that the children were less active and more compliant when on the medication than when on the placebo. The mothers also uttered fewer commands, were less negative, and were more responsive when their children were on medication. The conclusion is that "coercive, controlling, critical parent behaviors are, at least in part, elicited by the . . . child's deficits in attention, impulse, and activity control" (Conners & Wells, 1986, pp. 121–122).

Stylistic characteristics of parents, it should be noted, were not assessed in this study. Such an assessment would allow a test of the possibility that reactions to children's behavior vary systematically with parents' general approaches to interaction and discipline.

Even reactive parental behavior, if continued over a long enough period, may reinforce the child's undesirable behavior and have long-term emotional consequences for both parent and child. Patterson and Bank (1989) have identified patterns of family interaction where coercive behavior escalates as family members attempt to control each other. These behaviors, such as "yelling, hitting, whining, crying, [and] sarcasm" (p. 170) are associated with the development of children's aggressive and antisocial behavior. A parent's negative or controlling response to the child's behavior may begin as a reaction to early temperamental characteristics or deficiencies in a child. The interactive chain described by Patterson, however, then leads to an increasing likelihood that the children will engage in negative and coercive behavior in the future. Other disciplinary techniques—use of reprimands early in the interaction and reinforcement of positive behaviors—might lead to quite different results, as they seem to when used with hyperactive children in the school setting (Swanson, 1992).

INDIVIDUAL PROFILES OF DEVELOPMENT

Thelen (1990) argues that outcomes for any given individual cannot be explained or predicted from knowledge about the average effects of either organismic or environmental variables. Nor can they be predicted from statistical interactions based on groups of children. This relative lack of predictability stems in part from the fact that the parameters influencing development of one individual can never be exactly the same as those influencing another. Although differences in experience early in life may be very small, these small variations can lead to widely divergent outcomes. Unpredictability of outcome also stems from inevitable accidental events in the history of an individual. If these accidents, which are likely to be small events of the everyday variety rather than major traumas, occur at critical times in development, they may push an individual's developmental trajectory into quite a different direction.

Thus, as Thelen (1990) puts it: "Developing human organisms share universal internal and external boundary conditions that produce normal functioning adults. Within these boundaries are a nearly infinite and indeterminate number of permissible endstates" (p. 26). Tucker (1991), speaking in neurological terms, writes:

Each brain is so reflective of its local environment, and so much a product of its own self-organizing process, that it becomes unlike any other brain. For simpler organisms whose end structure is specified by the genetic plan, individuals in the species are highly similar. For organisms whose features are formed by epigenetic mechanisms, each individual is different. Because of the radical extension of ontogenetic plasticity, each human brain may become a highly unique experiment of nature. (p. 111)

Fentress (1989) argues that the "nature-nurture" issue cannot be resolved by a simple interactionist approach; we need to "grasp fully what it means to be both self-organizing and interactive within a dynamically ordered context" (p. 38). Fentress's emphasis is on the necessity for a developing organism to be sensitive to environmental influences and yet sufficiently protected to allow self-ordering processes to operate. What does it mean to be self-organizing? Again, to quote Fentress (1989):

Throughout development, the child . . . refines properties of its expression, combines previously isolated properties together into new packages, and opens up new windows of receptivity to its world while closing other windows on the way to establishing a unique individuality. (p. 35)

That is, the organism is active in seeking out situations that will propel it in certain directions rather than others.

This conceptual approach leads to the study of development at the level of the individual rather than of the group. In observations of children whose development has not proceeded normally, case studies are common; clinicians, of necessity, gather extensive data on individual children. The case study by Szumowski et al. (1987) described earlier is an example. In the study of normal development, a number of researchers have argued that an alternative approach to averaging data over groups of children seen infrequently is to describe the course of development in individuals who are followed intensively. A case in point is the study of infant state regulation by Thoman and Whitney (1990) cited earlier; infants were observed for 7-hour periods over several weeks in order to describe each child's individual range and consistency in state. In principle, any aspect of behavior can be observed and measured on frequent occasions. The resulting descriptions can then serve as the basis for aggregating over similar individual profiles to make generalizations about development in subgroups of children (Fogel, 1990; Cairns, 1986; Thorngate, 1986). Such an approach puts more emphasis on individuals as total systems than on variables (Magnusson, 1985), and it calls for descriptive rather than inferential statistics (Thorngate & Carroll, 1986).

There are no existing data on the development of attention from studies that would meet these specifications. However, we present here hypotheses about different possible developmental profiles along with speculation about why individual children might follow different routes. Changes with age in duration of focused attention will serve to illustrate this approach. The first profile is globally consistent with findings reviewed in chapter 7 on the development of focused attention, and it can be provisionally considered the modal profile. Figure 12.4 represents our hypothetical model in which duration of focused attention devoted to examining and inspecting objects during *independent free play* increases and then declines with age (asterisks), while at the same time, focused attention devoted to more complex activities increases (squares), causing an inflection in a combined curve around 12 to 14 months. In chapter 7, we speculated that these two curves reflect different underlying processes that could be linked, in the first case, to the orienting/investigative attention system and, in the second case, to the later-developing attention system related to planning and goal-oriented activity.

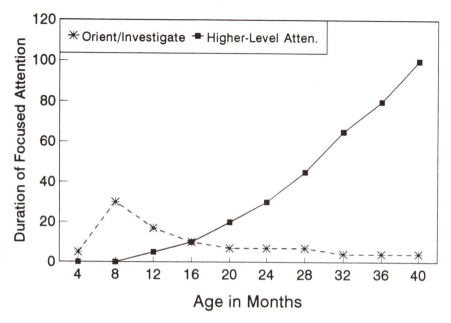

Figure 12.4. Schematic representation of the course of focused attention within the two underlying systems, as proposed in chapter 7. The scale on the y-axis is arbitrary and is intended to show only the relative levels of focused attention in the two overlapping systems. Notice the hypothesized dip in overall level of focused attention around 12 months.

What would cause *individuals* to develop along this particular pathway? One child—a baby girl, for example—of average reactivity and activity level might rarely encounter periods of over- or understimulation, and thus, be able early to engage in fairly long periods of face-to-face play. The development of the orienting/investigative system would lead to flexible engagement and disengagement of attention in her interactions with people and objects. As grasping and manipulation develop and her interest turns to objects, the child's attention would be strongly activated by novelty; in conjunction with her temperamental disposition for moderate approach, she is led to involvement in exploration of objects. Her environment serves to support this responsiveness by providing the physical props (a changing array of toys, space to play with them), social support (help when needed, freedom to control activity), and experience (some instruction on how things work). Her parents may encourage her interest in objects by joining her at times, but not interfering, thus allowing her responses to objects to organize themselves to some extent. From 6 to 10 months, the child habituates to novel objects at a moderate rate, and reasonably extended periods of focused attention alternate with other forms of play, such as joyful banging. During the periods of focused attention, she will experience internal states derived from her arousal level and her posture and facial expression. These are part of her exploratory activity and the accompanying attention to objects.

By 11 months, however, she habituates to the physical properties of objects very quickly and her focused attention occurs less frequently and in shorter spurts as extended exploration of objects is less necessary. This child is now in a transition period. New processes are becoming functional; she approaches new objects more slowly and begins to play with familiar toys in quite different ways as she discovers how to stack and combine objects. Her response to novelty may actually be diminishing; to the extent that her attention is still governed by the orienting/investigative system, her attention will not be as strongly engaged as before. Her cognitive skills, however, do not yet allow her to engage in very complex activities, to formulate goals, or to plan ahead to meet those goals. Only as these become possible with the later-maturing attention system will her focused attention begin to increase again.

In the preschool years, the young girl's observation of her parents and her own desire to master the environment lead her to seek out activities that challenge her developing cognitive and self-regulative skills. Her continued moderate level of reactivity means that she is not easily distressed and tends to approach new experiences. Her advancing cognitive skills give her many experiences of success. These experiences reward her efforts and encourage her to accept and seek other challenges. These challenges, even though self-imposed, involve an element of tension; this, in itself, tends to narrow her attentional focus and promote organized activity. As before, her parents and teachers support these manifestations of self-control, but do not cause them to occur. The child's attention and activity have become organized around the objects and important events in the environment, and she has developed, through a dynamic interplay with her environment, cognitive and regulatory skills that ensure her ability to carry through on what she plans. These plans are clearly structured in part by the materials at hand and by her observation of others' activities, but her own motivation activates the appropriate activity. Her growing inhibitory controls help her to be even more organized and efficient in her approach to tasks.

A highly reactive and active child with weaker self-regulation could develop along the same course but would require more regulative input from parents and others. Components in the organism-environment system may be balanced in different ways but result in the same profile. Other developmental profiles might look quite different from the modal profile. A child, for example, might show little systematic decline in inspection and little systematic increase in focused attention with development. The child may be lower than average in both earlier and later types of attention and may also be more variable than average across time and situation. This profile may stem from the child's difficulty in modulating and organizing early reactivity and response to objects; development of later attention based on more complex activities may be interfered with by a delay in cognitive development and a continued balance favoring excitatory over inhibitory processes.

In yet another child, the first attention system may develop along the modal route, while the later system does not. The child shows a systematic rise and decline in focused attention devoted to inspection, but shows little subsequent increase of overall duration of focused attention. Such a profile is most likely to happen where the child's reactivity to objects leads to interest in novel objects and where the orienting/investigative system efficiently supports both habituation and arousal. Focused attention supported by later-developing processes is limited, however, suggesting the possibility that the second attention system is maturing more slowly. This slower maturation could be due in part to biological factors. However, because the development of planning and self-regulation do not occur without a physical and social environment encouraging self-evaluation and control (see chapter 8), these must also be implicated. For example, a young boy's parents may actively discourage inhibitory skills by rewarding impulsive responses; he gets what he wants by throwing tantrums or grabbing, while his verbal requests are ignored. This slows the growth of verbal regulation of behavior; the delay in this regulation then contributes to social interactions that tend to maintain his immature behavior. The boy also contributes to the ordering of behavior along these principles; he does not focus attention long enough to reap potential cognitive and emotional benefits gained from mastering tasks in the course of play and other activities. The attention of this child, then, remains governed more by the earlier orienting/investigative system, and because he now habituates very quickly to new objects and situations, there is little external activation of prolonged attention. In the extreme, such a profile might reflect an early attention deficit.

A fourth profile is also possible in which the first type of focused attention is limited, but focused attention begins to increase as more complex activities emerge and the child begins to devote attention to them. This profile might suggest a lower than average level of reactivity to external events, but cognitive and motivational progress allows attention to be recruited and maintained for self-generated schemes. Conversely, the same general profile might stem from heightened reactivity that can be regulated only by withdrawing attention from and avoiding novel objects and situations. In the first year, this withdrawal might take the form of longer periods of sleep or time spent in quiet thumb-sucking. Later, long periods of focused attention during independent play, either in construction or pretend play, may serve the same function of keeping the child's arousal level within a manageable range.

Although these profiles are hypothetical, they are intended to illustrate the dynamic, individual nature of the development of attention. They also underscore the variation that can occur when the two systems of attention are affected differentially by both organismic and environmental factors.

SUMMARY

In this chapter, we have integrated developmental themes presented earlier in the book with issues concerning individual children. We first discussed general organismic, environmental, and interactional approaches to the development of attention and then considered specific cases of development.

In the first individual case study (Szumowski et al., 1987), we described what seemed to be a strong biological disposition to attentional problems that persisted throughout early development. This case description was followed by a discussion of studies investigating environmental influences on the development of attention deficits. In the final section of the chapter, we considered hypothetical cases of normal children differing in characteristics related to the orienting/investigative system and the system of higher level control. We noted ways in which both organismic and environmental factors can influence the development of each system, leading to quite different trajectories in the development of attention.

Whether considering individual variability within the normal range or deviations leading to major difficulties for the child and others, development can only be treated as the interplay of both dispositional and environmental conditions and events. The study of development can and should proceed through the use of different approaches—those that emphasize the commonalities across groups of children and those that stress the unique development of individuals. Both approaches, and the methods they entail, will contribute to our knowledge of the various components of attention and the way in which the underlying processes operate to produce individuals who differ markedly from one another in patterns of attention.

13

Recapitulation

We have come to the end of our account of themes and variations in the early development of attention. In this final summary, we wish to emphasize the major points of our discussion. We also try to place our book in a larger context.

We have argued that attention has many facets, including the processes by which we select a target for perusal or concentration, the alterations in physiological and psychological state that accompany attention, and the mechanisms of control that make our attention voluntary and deliberate. Attention is intimately related to motivational and emotional systems. These systems provide information about the adaptive significance of events and thus influence the control processes that compose attention.

DEVELOPMENT

We have described the development of attention as involving two systems. The orienting/investigative system is functional in the first year of life and underlies the attention infants give to exploring the novel aspects of the environment. It appears to depend on the maturation of neural pathways in the posterior cortex and pathways from subcortical regions to the posterior cortex. These pathways begin to strongly influence infants' behavior after 2 or 3 months of age.

The second system of higher level controls emerges at the end of the first year and continues to develop throughout the preschool years. This system underlies the attention involved in planning ahead, carrying plans to completion, and organizing complex sequences of action. Inhibition in many forms is essential to the operation of this system. It appears to depend on maturation of the frontal cortex and connections from other brain regions to the frontal cortex. Developmental transitions at 18 months and 4 years mark steps forward in the control of attention.

Higher level controls would not develop fully without the child's interaction with older, more experienced members of society. The young child depends on parents and siblings for help in regulating state, for information about what is important to attend to, and for guidance in how to meet social and cognitive demands. Parents and siblings, in turn, transmit values of the larger culture; their behavior directs the child to objects and events worthy of attention and demonstrates appropriate techniques of attending to everyday events and tasks.

Many types of learning would not procced without attention. For the infant, learning may be promoted when attention is captured by novel and significant events. Infants also concentrate on practicing newly developed skills—so much so that they may be unable to attend to other important features of the context until the skills become second nature to them. Other learning requires more deliberate deployment of attention. This is likely when children learn to recognize and anticipate complex sequences of events, when they themselves engage in sequential actions, and when tasks are structured by adults and the materials are not intrinsically compelling.

INDIVIDUAL DIFFERENCES

Many individual differences are observed in the context of normal development of attention. Infants and children vary in the speed and strength of their reactions to events around them. These reactions determine, in part, how intense and sustained their attention to those events will be. Infants and children vary in the duration of time they spend looking at displays and events, and these variations may have implications for what is learned during attention. Variations in the extent and duration of focused attention can be observed at any age. For older children, the propensity for sustained focused attention is related to cognitive skills and to the higher level controls developing from 1 to 5 years.

Stable variations in attention are related to individual differences in other domains. We noted three of these. Attention is related to activity level. High levels of motor activity are antithetical to sustained attention if the child has difficulty modulating the level of activity in situations that demand lower levels. Sustained, focused attention is also related to children's inhibitory control over their own actions. Children with strong inhibitory skills can prevent extraneous actions from interfering with an organized response to environmental demands. Children with weak inhibitory skills are likely to be impulsive and have difficulty attending to tasks structured by others or themselves. Finally, control of attention is related to negative emotionality. Infants and children who can redirect and focus their attention on external events and activities away from unpleasant events or thoughts seem to be less susceptible to anger and distress. That is, children vary in their ability to make use of attentional states to control incompatible states of distress.

Some children fall at the extremes of variability and are considered to be deficient in attention. These deficiencies may reflect reactivity that is too high or too low to be adaptive. They may stem from a relative inability to mobilize and sustain effort over time when the situation demands it. The deficits may reflect weak inhibitory controls relative to activation of behavior, leading to inattention and impulsive responses.

Individual children take many routes to mature control of attention. The variation in developmental profiles derives from the complex and continuing interplay of biological and social forces. Attention deficits arise in the same dynamic way, though biological differences may have a stronger influence than in development of normal patterns of attention. Children help to determine their own paths of development and, within the normal range, there are many variations in the rate of development and the relative strength of the two attention systems.

THE LARGER CONTEXT

At the outset, we stated that our emphasis was on visual attention. This emphasis reflected our own research interests but also the focus of many other investigations. Attention to auditory events, or auditory attention, is certainly just as important. Some of the operations involved in orienting to and exploring auditory sources of information may be quite different from those involved in the orienting/investigative system we discussed. On the other hand, auditory and visual aspects of events are integrated and thus mutually influence each other and the child's reactions and actions. We think many of the state variables considered in this book will apply just as well to auditory as to visual events, although auditory events seem to have more power to alert the organism than visual events. Higher level controls are influenced by auditory input and also govern attention and behavior toward auditory events. The socialization of attention certainly depends on spoken language, as we have had many occasions to note. Thus, many of our generalizations about visual attention are relevant for attention to sound and language.

A point we have made in several ways is that the study of attention requires an array of behavioral and physiological measures. Different methods are also necessary to provide converging information about attention. These methods range from observational, descriptive approaches to highly controlled experiments to marker tasks that help to specify brain-behavior relationships. The value of multiple measures and methods applies no matter what specific form of attention is being investigated.

Our understanding of attention as a construct and of the processes that underlie its deployment has advanced so far in recent years that it is becoming difficult to keep abreast of developments. Every journal that arrives contains relevant articles. We hope this book, although destined to soon be out of date in some respects, will provide a structure for organizing and integrating new data as they are generated. Attention is a difficult construct that will evolve in the future but will, we think, continue to be essential to any complete account of development and adaptive behavior.

References

Achenbach, T. N. (1992). *Manual for the Child Behavior Checklist*. Burlington, VT: Department of Psychiatry, University of Vermont.

Adamson, L. B., & Bakeman, R. (1991). The development of shared attention during infancy. In R. Vasta (Ed.), *Annals of child development* (Vol. 8, pp. 1–41). London: Kingsley.

Adamson, L.B., & Bakeman, R. (1992). [Average levels of engagement with toys during independent play from 6 to 18 months of age.] Unpublished raw data.

Adler, S. A., & Rovee-Collier, C. (1994). The effect of enhanced attention on infant memory [Abstract]. *Infant Behavior and Development, 17*, 484.

Ahadi, S. A., Rothbart, M. K., & Ye, R. (1993). Children's temperament in the US and China: Similarities and differences. *European Journal of Personality, 7*, 359–378.

Alessandri, S. M. (1992). Attention, play, and social behavior in ADHD preschoolers. *Journal of Abnormal Child Psychology, 20*, 289–302.

Alessandri, S. M., & Schramm, K. (1991). Effects of dextroamphetamine on the cognitive and social play of a preschooler with ADHD. *Journal of the American Academy of Child & Adolescent Psychiatry, 30*, 768–772.

Ambrose, J. A. (1961). The development of the smiling response in early infancy. In B. M. Foss (Ed.), *Determinants of infant behaviour* (Vol. 1, pp. 179–210). New York: Wiley.

American Psychiatric Association. (1980). *Diagnostic and statistical manual of mental disorders* (3rd ed.). Washington, DC: Author.

American Psychiatric Association. (1994). *Diagnostic and statistical manual of mental disorders* (4th ed.). Washington, DC: Author.

Anderson, D. R., Choi, H. P., & Lorch, E. P. (1987). Attentional inertia reduces distractibility during young children's TV viewing. *Child Development, 58*, 798–806.

Anderson, D. R., & Levin, S. R. (1976). Young children's attention to "Sesame Street." *Child Development, 47*, 806–811.

Anderson, D. R., & Lorch, E. P. (1983). Looking at television: Action or reaction? In J. Bryant & D. R. Anderson (Eds.), *Children's understanding of television: Research on attention and comprehension* (pp. 1–33). New York: Academic Press.

Anderson, D. R., Lorch, E. P., Field, D. E., Collins, P. A., & Nathan, J. G. (1986). Television viewing at home: Age trends in visual attention and time with TV. *Child Development, 57*, 1024–1033.

245

Anderson, D. R., Lorch, E. P., Field, D. E., & Sanders, J. (1981). The effects of TV program comprehensibility on preschool children's visual attention to television. *Child Development, 52,* 151–157.

Anderson, D. R., Lorch, E. P., Smith, R., Bradford, R., & Levin, S. R. (1981). Effects of peer presence on preschool children's television-viewing behavior. *Developmental Psychology, 17,* 446–453.

Anisfeld, M. (1984). *Language development from birth to three.* Hillsdale, NJ: Erlbaum.

Anthony, B. J., & Graham, F. K. (1983). Evidence for sensory-selective set in young infants. *Science, 220,* 742–744.

Aslin, R. N. (1981). Development of smooth pursuit in human infants. In D. F. Fisher, R. A. Monty, & J. W. Senders (Eds.), *Eye movements: Cognition and visual perception* (pp. 31–51). Hillsdale, NJ: Erlbaum.

Aslin, R. N. (1987). Visual and auditory development in infancy. In J. D. Osofsky (Ed.), *Handbook of infant development* (2nd ed., pp. 5–97). New York: Wiley.

Aslin, R. N., & Ciuffreda, K. J. (1983). Eye movements of preschool children. *Science, 222,* 74–75.

Aston-Jones, G. (1994, March). The role of the locus coeruleus in vigilance. Lecture given at the Albert Einstein College of Medicine, Rose F. Kennedy Center for Research in Mental Retardation and Human Development, Bronx, NY.

Azmitia, M. (1988). Peer interaction and problem solving: When are two heads better than one? *Child Development, 59,* 87–96.

Bahrick, L. E., Walker, A. S., & Neisser, U. (1981). Selective looking by infants. *Cognitive Psychology, 13,* 377–390.

Baillargeon, R. (1987). Object permanence in 3$^{1}/_{2}$- and 4$^{1}/_{2}$-month-old infants. *Developmental Psychology, 23,* 655–664.

Bakeman, R., & Adamson, L. B. (1984). Coordinating attention to people and objects in mother-infant and peer-infant interaction. *Child Development, 55,* 1278–1289.

Bakeman, R., & Brown, J. V. (1980). Early interaction: Consequences for social and mental development at three years. *Child Development, 51,* 437–447.

Bakeman, R., Adamson, L. B., Konner, M., & Barr, R. G. (1990). !Kung infancy: The social context of object exploration. *Child Development, 61,* 794–809.

Baker-Ward, L., Ornstein, P. A., & Holden, D. J. (1984). The expression of memorization in early childhood. *Journal of Experimental Child Psychology, 37,* 555–575.

Baldwin, D. A. (1991). Infants' contribution to the achievement of joint reference. *Child Development, 62,* 875–890.

Baldwin, D. A., & Markman, E. M. (1989). Establishing word-object relations: A first step. *Child Development, 60,* 381–398.

Baldwin, D. A., & Moses, L. J. (1994). The ontogeny of social information-gathering. Unpublished manuscript.

Bandura, A. (1965). Vicarious processes: A case of no-trial learning. In L. Berkowitz (Ed.), *Advances in Experimental Social Psychology, 2,* 1–55. New York: Academic Press.

Bandura, A. (1986). *Social foundations of thought and action.* Englewood Cliffs, NJ: Prentice-Hall.

Bandura, A., & Walters, R. H. (1963). *Social learning and personality development.* New York: Holt, Rinehart and Winston.

Banks, M. S., & Ginsburg, A. P. (1985). Infant visual preferences: A review and new theoretical treatment. *Advances in Child Development and Behavior, 19,* 207–246.

Barkley, R. A., & Cunningham, C. E. (1979). The effects of methylphenidate on the mother-child interactions of hyperactive children. *Archives of General Psychiatry, 36,* 201–208.

Barrera, M. E., & Maurer, D. (1981). The perception of facial expressions by the three-month-old. *Child Development, 52,* 203–206.

Barten, S., & Ronch, J. (1971). Continuity in the development of visual behavior in young infants. *Child Development, 42,* 1566–1571.

Bates, J. E., Freeland, C. A. B., & Lounsbury, M. L. (1979). Measurement of infant difficultness. *Child Development, 50,* 794–803.

Bayley, N. (1969). *Bayley Scales of Infant Development.* New York: Psychological Corporation.

Beatty, J. (1982). Task-evoked pupillary responses, processing load, and the structure of processing resources. *Psychological Bulletin, 91,* 276–292.

Becker, P. T., & Thoman, E. B. (1983). Organization of sleeping and waking states in infants: Consistency across contexts. *Physiology and Behavior, 31,* 405–410.

Bell, M. A., & Fox, N. A. (1994). Brain development over the first year of life. In G. Dawson & K. W. Fischer (Eds.), *Human behavior and the developing brain* (pp. 314–345). New York: Guilford.

Belsky, J., Goode, M. K., & Most, R. K. (1980). Maternal stimulation and infant exploratory competence: Cross-sectional, correlational, and experimental analyses. *Child Development, 51,* 1168–1178.

Belsky, J., & Most, R. K. (1981). From exploration to play: A cross-sectional study of infant free play behavior. *Developmental Psychology, 17,* 630–639.

Bentall, R. P., Lowe, C. F., & Beasty, A. (1985). The role of verbal behavior in human learning: II. Developmental differences. *Journal of the Experimental Analysis of Behavior, 43,* 165–181.

Berg, C. A., & Sternberg, R. J. (1985). Response to novelty: Continuity versus discontinuity in the developmental course of intelligence. *Advances in Child Development and Behavior, 19,* 1–47.

Berg, W. K., & Berg, K. M. (1987). Psychophysiological development in infancy: State, startle, and attention. In J. D. Osofsky (Ed.), *Handbook of infant development* (2nd ed., pp. 238–317). New York: Wiley.

Berk, L. E. (1986). Relationship of elementary school children's private speech to behavioral accompaniment to task, attention, and task performance. *Developmental Psychology, 22,* 671–680.

Berk, L. E., & Garvin, R. A. (1984). Development of private speech among low-income Appalachian children. *Developmental Psychology, 20,* 271–286.

Berlyne, D. E. (1970). Attention as a problem in behavior theory. In D. I. Mostofsky (Ed.), *Attention: Contemporary theory and analysis* (pp. 25–49). New York: Appleton-Century-Crofts.

Berlyne, D. E., Borsa, D. M., Craw, M. A., Gelman, R. S., & Mandell, E. E. (1965). Effects of stimulus complexity and induced arousal on paired-associate learning. *Journal of Verbal Learning and Verbal Behavior, 4,* 291–299.

Berlyne, D. E., & Lewis, J. L. (1963). Effects of heightened arousal on human exploratory behaviour. *Canadian Journal of Psychology, 17,* 398–410.

Berntson, G. G., Cacioppo, J. T., & Quigley, K. S. (1993). Respiratory sinus arrhythmia: Autonomic origins, physiological mechanisms, and psychophysiological implications. *Psychophysiology, 30,* 183–196.

Bertenthal, B. I., & Campos, J. J. (1990). A systems approach to the organizing effect of self-produced locomotion during infancy. *Advances in Infancy Research, 6,* 1–60.

Bertenthal, B. I., Campos, J. J., & Barrett, K. C. (1984). Self-produced locomotion: An organizer of emotional, cognitive, and social development in infancy. In R. N. Emde & R. J. Harmon (Eds.), *Continuities and discontinuities in development* (pp. 175–210). New York: Plenum Press.

Birns, B. B., Barten, S., & Bridger, W. H. (1969). Individual differences in temperamental characteristics of infants. *Transactions of the New York Academy of Sciences, 31,* 1071–1082.

Bivens, J. A., & Berk, L. E. (1990). A longitudinal study of the development of elementary school children's private speech. *Merrill-Palmer Quarterly, 36,* 443–463.

Bjorklund, D. F., & Harnishfeger, K. K. (1990). The resources construct in cognitive development: Diverse sources of evidence and a theory of inefficient inhibition. *Developmental Review, 10,* 48–71.

Blake, J., McConnell, S., Horton, G., & Benson, N. (1992). The gestural repertoire and its evolution over the second year. *Early Development and Parenting, 1,* 127–136.

Blass, E. M. (1992, Spring). Linking developmental and psychobiological research. Society for Research in Child Development Newsletter. Chicago: University of Chicago Press.

Block, J. H., & Block, J. (1980). The role of ego-control and ego-resiliency on the organization of behavior. In A. Collins (Ed.), *Minnesota Symposium on Child Psychology: Vol. 13. Development of cognition, affect, and social relations* (pp. 39–101). Hillsdale, NJ: Erlbaum.

Bloom, L., & Beckwith, R. (1989). Talking with feeling: Integrating affective and linguistic expression in early language development. *Cognition and Emotion, 3,* 313–342.

Boring, E. G. (1970). Attention: Research and beliefs concerning the conception in scientific psychology before 1930. In D. I. Mostofsky (Ed.), *Attention: Contemporary theory and analysis* (pp. 5–8). New York: Appleton-Century-Crofts.

Bornstein, M. H. (1985a). Habituation of attention as a measure of visual information processing in human infants: Summary, systematization, and synthesis. In G. Gottlieb & N. A. Krasnegor (Eds.), *Development of audition and vision during the first year of postnatal life: A methodological overview* (pp. 253–300). Norwood, NJ: Ablex.

Bornstein, M. H. (1985b). How infant and mother jointly contribute to developing cognitive competence in the child. *Proceedings of the National Academy of Science, 82,* 7470–7473.

Bornstein, M. H. (1989). Between caretakers and their young: Two modes of interaction and their consequences for cognitive growth. In M. H. Bornstein & J. S. Bruner (Eds.), *Interaction in human development* (pp. 197–214). Hillsdale, NJ: Erlbaum.

Bornstein, M. H., Azuma, H., Tamis-LeMonda, C., & Ogino, M. (1990). Mother and infant activity and interaction in Japan and in the United States: I. A comparative macroanalysis of naturalistic exchanges. *International Journal of Behavioral Development, 13,* 267–287.

Bornstein, M. H., & Benasich, A. A. (1986). Infant habituation: Assessments of individual differences and short-term reliability at five months. *Child Development, 57,* 87–99.

Bornstein, M. H., Maital, S. L., Tal, J., & Baras, R. (1995). Mother and infant activity and interaction in Israel and in the United States: A comparative study. *International Journal of Behavioral Development, 18,* 63–82.

Bornstein, M. H., & Sigman, M. S. (1986). Continuity in mental development from infancy. *Child Development, 57,* 251–274.

Bornstein, M. H., Tamis-LeMonda, C. S., Pêcheux, M. G., & Rahn, C. W. (1991). Mother and infant activity and interaction in France and the United States: A comparative study. *International Journal of Behavioral Development, 14,* 21–43.

Bosco, J. J., & Robin, S. S. (1980). Hyperkinesis: Prevalence and treatment. In C. K.

Whalen & B. Henker (Eds.), *Hyperactive children: The social ecology of identification and treatment* (pp. 173–187). New York: Academic Press.

Brazelton, T. B. (1984). *Neonatal Behavioral Assessment Scale* (2nd ed.). London: Spastics International Medical Publications.

Brazelton, T. B., Nugent, J. K., & Lester, B. M. (1987). Neonatal Behavioral Assessment Scale. In J. D. Osofsky (Ed.), *Handbook of infant development* (2nd ed., pp. 780–817). New York: Wiley.

Breznitz, Z., & Friedman, S. L. (1988). Toddlers' concentration: Does maternal depression make a difference? *Journal of Child Psychology and Psychiatry, 29,* 267–279.

Bridger, W. H., Birns, B. M., & Blank, M. (1965). A comparison of behavioral and heart rate measurements in human neonates. *Psychosomatic Medicine, 27,* 123–134.

Brock, S. E., Rothbart, M. K., & Derryberry, D. (1986). Heart-rate deceleration and smiling in 3-month-old infants. *Infant Behavior and Development, 9,* 403–414.

Bronson, G. W. (1972). Infants' reactions to unfamiliar persons and novel objects. *Monographs of the Society for Research in Child Development, 37* (3, Serial No. 148).

Bronson, G. (1974). The postnatal growth of visual capacity. *Child Development, 45,* 873–890.

Bronson, G. W. (1991). Infant differences in rate of visual encoding. *Child Development, 62,* 44–54.

Brown, M. W. (1930). Continuous reaction as a measure of attention. *Child Development, 1,* 255–291.

Brownell, C. A. (1988). Combinatorial skills: Converging developments over the second year. *Child Development, 59,* 675–685.

Bullock, M., & Lütkenhaus, P. (1988). The development of volitional behavior in the toddler years. *Child Development, 59,* 664–674.

Burns, J. J., & Anderson, D. R. (1993). Attentional inertia and recognition memory in adult television viewing. *Communication Research, 20,* 777–799.

Bursill, A. E. (1958). The restriction of peripheral vision during exposure to hot and humid conditions. *Quarterly Journal of Experimental Psychology, 10,* 113–129.

Bushnell, E. W. (1985). The decline of visually guided reaching during infancy. *Infant Behavior and Development, 8,* 139–155.

Bushnell, E. W., Shaw, L., & Strauss, D. (1985). Relationship between visual and tactual exploration by 6-month-olds. *Developmental Psychology, 21,* 591–600.

Bushnell, I. W. R. (1979). Modification of the externality effect in young infants. *Journal of Experimental Child Psychology, 28,* 211–229.

Buss, A. (1989). Temperaments as personality traits. In G. A. Kohnstamm, J. E. Bates, & M. K. Rothbart (Eds.), *Temperament in childhood* (pp. 49–58). Chichester, England: Wiley.

Buss, D. M., Block, J. H., & Block, J. (1980). Preschool activity level: Personality correlates and developmental implications. *Child Development, 51,* 401–408.

Butterworth, G. (1991). The ontogeny and phylogeny of joint visual attention. In A. Whiten (Ed.), *Natural theories of mind* (pp. 223–232). Oxford: Oxford University Press.

Butterworth, G., & Cochran, E. (1980). Towards a mechanism of joint visual attention in human infancy. *International Journal of Behavioral Development, 3,* 253–272.

Butterworth, G., & Jarrett, N. (1991). What minds have in common is space: Spatial mechanisms serving joint visual attention in infancy. *British Journal of Developmental Psychology, 9,* 55–72.

Cairns, R. B. (1986). Phenomena lost: Issues in the study of development. In J. Valsiner (Ed.), *The individual subject and scientific psychology* (pp. 97–111). New York: Plenum Press.

Cairns, R. B., & Hood, K. E. (1983). Continuity in social development: A comparative perspective on individual difference prediction. In P. B. Baltes & J. O. G. Brim (Eds.), *Life-span development and behavior* (Vol. 5, pp. 301–358). New York: Academic Press.

Campbell, S. B. (1985). Hyperactivity in preschoolers: Correlates and prognostic implications. *Clinical Psychology Review, 5,* 405–428.

Campbell, S. B. (1987). Parent-referred problem three-year-olds: Developmental changes in symptoms. *Journal of Child Psychology and Psychiatry, 28,* 835–845.

Campbell, S. B., Breaux, A. M., Ewing, L. J., & Szumowski, E. K. (1984). A one-year follow-up study of parent-referred hyperactive preschool children. *Journal of the American Academy of Child Psychiatry, 23,* 243–249.

Campbell, S. B., Breaux, A. M., Ewing, L. J., Szumowski, E. K., & Pierce, E. W. (1986). Parent-identified problem preschoolers: Mother-child interaction during play at intake and 1-year follow-up. *Journal of Abnormal Child Psychology, 14,* 425–440.

Campbell, S. B., & Cluss, P. (1982). Peer relations of young children with behavior problems. In K. H. Rubin & H. S. Ross (Eds.), *Peer relationships and social skills in childhood* (pp. 323–351). New York: Springer.

Campbell, S. B., Endman, M. W., & Bernfeld, G. (1977). A three-year follow-up of hyperactive preschoolers into elementary school. *Journal of Child Psychology and Psychiatry, 18,* 239–249.

Campbell, S. B., & Ewing, L. J. (1990). Follow-up of hard-to-manage preschoolers: Adjustment at age 9 and predictors of continuing symptoms. *Journal of Child Psychology and Psychiatry, 31,* 871–889.

Campbell, S. B., Ewing, L. J., Breaux, A. M., & Szumowski, E. K. (1986). Parent-referred problem three-year-olds: Followup at school entry. *Journal of Child Psychology and Psychiatry, 27,* 473–488.

Campbell, S. B., Schleifer, M., Weiss, G., & Perlman, T. (1977). A two-year follow-up of hyperactive preschoolers. *American Journal of Orthopsychiatry, 47,* 149–162.

Campbell, S. B., Szumonski, E. K., Ewing, L. J., Gluck, D. S., & Breaux, A. M. (1982). A multidimensional assessment of parent-identified behavior problem toddlers. *Journal of Abnormal Child Psychology, 10,* 569–591.

Campos, J. J., Emde, R. N., Gaensbauer, T., & Henderson, C. (1975). Cardiac and behavioral interrelationships in the reactions of infants to strangers. *Developmental Psychology, 11,* 589–601.

Canfield, R. L., & Haith, M. M. (1991). Young infants' visual expectations for symmetric and asymmetric stimulus sequences. *Developmental Psychology, 27,* 198–208.

Capaldi, D. M., & Rothbart, M. K. (1992). Development and validation of an early adolescent temperament measure. *Journal of Early Adolescence, 12,* 153–173.

Carpenter, G. C., Tecce, J. J., Stechler, G., & Friedman, S. (1970). Differential visual behavior to human and humanoid faces in early infancy. *Merrill-Palmer Quarterly, 16,* 91–108.

Case, R. (1992). The role of the frontal lobes in the regulation of cognitive development. *Brain and Cognition, 20,* 51–73.

Case, R., & Khanna, F. (1981). The missing links: Stages in children's progression from sensorimotor to logical thought. *New Directions for Child Development: Vol. 12. Cognitive development* (pp. 21–32). San Francisco: Jossey-Bass.

Casey, B. J., & Richards, J. E. (1988). Sustained visual attention in young infants measured with an adapted version of the visual preference paradigm. *Child Development, 59,* 1514–1521.

Casey, B. J., & Richards, J. E. (1991). A refractory period for the heart rate response in infant visual attention. *Developmental Psychobiology, 24,* 327–340.

Casey, M. B. (1979). Color versus form discrimination learning in 1-year-old infants. *Developmental Psychology, 15,* 341–343.

Choi, H. P., & Anderson, D. R. (1991). A temporal analysis of free toy play and distractibility in young children. *Journal of Experimental Child Psychology, 52,* 41–69.

Chugani, H. T. (1994). Development of regional brain glucose metabolism in relation to behavior and plasticity. In G. Dawson & K. W. Fischer (Eds.), *Human behavior and the developing brain* (pp. 153–175). New York: Guilford.

Clohessy, A. B. (1994). Visual anticipation and sequence learning in 4- and 10-month-old infants and adults. Unpublished doctoral dissertation, University of Oregon.

Clohessy, A. B., Posner, M. I., Rothbart, M. K., & Vecera, S. P. (1991). The development of inhibition of return in early infancy. *Journal of Cognitive Neuroscience, 3,* 345–350.

Cohen, A., Ivry, R. I., & Keele, S. W. (1990). Attention and structure in sequence learning. *Journal of Experimental Psychology: Learning, Memory, and Cognition, 16,* 17–30.

Cohen, L. B. (1972). Attention-getting and attention-holding processes of infant-visual preferences. *Child Development, 43,* 869–879.

Cohen, L. B. (1973). A two process model of infant visual attention. *Merrill-Palmer Quarterly, 19,* 157–180.

Cohen, L. B., DeLoache, J. S., & Strauss, M. S. (1979). Infant visual perception. In J. D. Osofsky (Ed.), *Handbook of infant development* (pp. 393–438). New York: Wiley.

Coldren, J. T. (1987). *Infant visual attention during social interaction and information-processing tasks.* Unpublished master of arts thesis, University of Kansas.

Coldren, J. T., & Colombo, J. (1994). The nature and processes of preverbal learning: Implications from nine-month-old infants' discrimination problem solving. *Monographs of the Society for Research in Child Development, 59* (4, Serial No. 241).

Coles, M. G. H. (1984). Heart rate and attention: The intake-rejection hypothesis and beyond. In M. G. H. Coles, J. R. Jennings, & J. A. Stern (Eds.), *Psychophysiological perspectives: Festschrift for Beatrice and John Lacey* (pp. 276–294). New York: Van Nostrand Reinhold.

Coles, M. G. H., & Gratton, G. (1986). Cognitive psychophysiology and the study of states and processes. In G. R. J. Hockey, A. W. K. Gaillard, & M. G. H. Coles (Eds.), *Energetics and human information processing* (pp. 409–424). Dordrecht: Martinus Nijhoff Publishers.

Colombo, J. (1993). *Infant cognition: Predicting later intellectual functioning.* Newbury Park, CA: Sage.

Colombo, J. (1995). On the neural mechanisms underlying developmental and individual differences in visual fixation in infancy: Two hypotheses. *Developmental Review, 15,* 97–135.

Colombo, J., & Bundy, R. S. (1981). A method for the measurement of infant auditory selectivity. *Infant Behavior and Development, 4,* 219–223.

Colombo, J., & Bundy, R. S. (1983). Infant response to auditory familiarity and novelty. *Infant Behavior and Development, 6,* 305–311.

Colombo, J., Freeseman, L. J., Coldren, J. T., & Frick, J. E. (1995). Individual differences in infant visual fixation: Dominance of global versus local stimulus properties. *Cognitive Development, 10,* 271–285.

Colombo, J., & Mitchell, D. W. (1990). Individual differences in early visual attention: Fixation time and information processing. In J. Colombo & J. Fagen (Eds.), *Indi-*

vidual differences in infancy: Reliability, stability, prediction (pp. 193–227). Hillsdale, NJ: Erlbaum.

Colombo, J., Mitchell, D. W., Coldren, J. T., & Atwater, J. D. (1990). Discrimination learning during the first year: Stimulus and positional cues. *Journal of Experimental Psychology: Learning, Memory, and Cognition 16*, 98–109.

Colombo, J., Mitchell, D. W., Coldren, J. T., & Freeseman, L. J. (1991). Individual differences in infant visual attention: Are short lookers faster processors or feature processors? *Child Development, 62*, 1247–1257.

Colombo, J., Mitchell, D. W., & Horowitz, F. D. (1988). Infant visual attention in the paired-comparison paradigm: Test-retest and attention-performance relations. *Child Development, 59*, 1198–1210.

Colombo, J., Mitchell, D. W., O'Brien, M., & Horowitz, F. D. (1987). The stability of visual habituation during the first year of life. *Child Development, 58*, 474–487.

Conners, C. K., & Wells, K. C. (1986). *Hyperkinetic children: A neuropsychosocial approach.* Beverly Hills, CA: Sage.

Corbetta, M., Miezin, F. M., Dobmeyer, S., Shulman, G. L., & Petersen, S. E. (1990). Attentional modulation of neural processing of shape, color, and velocity in humans. *Science, 248*, 1556–1559.

Cornblatt, B. A., & Erlenmeyer-Kimling, L. (1985). Global attentional deviance as a marker of risk for schizophrenia: Specificity and predictive validity. *Journal of Abnormal Psychology, 94*, 470–486.

Courchesne, E. (1990). Chronology of postnatal human brain development: Event-related potential, positron emission tomography, myelinogenesis, and synaptogenesis studies. In J. W. Rohrbaugh, R. Parasuraman, & R. Johnson (Eds.), *Event-related brain potentials: Basic issues and applications* (pp. 210–241). New York: Oxford University Press.

Cowan, N. (1988). Evolving conceptions of memory storage, selective attention, and their mutual constraints within the human information-processing system. *Psychological Bulletin, 104*, 163–191.

Cunningham, C. E., & Barkley, R. A. (1979). The interactions of normal and hyperactive children with their mothers in free play and structured tasks. *Child Development, 50*, 217–224.

Curran, T., & Keele, S. W. (1993). Attentional and nonattentional forms of sequence learning. *Journal of Experimental Psychology: Learning, Memory, and Cognition, 19*, 189–202.

Dannemiller, J. L., & Banks, M. S. (1983). Can selective adaptation account for early infant habituation? *Merrill-Palmer Quarterly, 29*, 151–158.

Davies, D. R., & Jones, D. M. (1975). The effects of noise and incentives upon attention in short-term memory. *British Journal of Psychology, 66*, 61–68.

Dawson, G., & Lewy, A. (1989). Arousal, attention, and the socioemotional impairments of individuals with autism. In G. Dawson (Ed.), *Autism: Nature, diagnosis and treatment* (pp. 49–74). New York: Guilford.

DeGangi, G. A., DiPietro, J. A., Greenspan, S. I., & Porges, S. W. (1991). Psychophysiological characteristics of the regulatory disordered infant. *Infant Behavior and Development, 14*, 37–50.

DeLoache, J. S., Rissman, M. W., & Cohen, L. B. (1978). An investigation of the attention-getting process in infants. *Infant Behavior and Development, 1*, 11–25.

DeMarie-Dreblow, D., & Miller, P. H. (1988). The development of children's strategies for selective attention: Evidence for a transitional period. *Child Development, 59*, 1504–1513.

Dember, W. N. (1989). Historical overview. In W. N. Dember & C. L. Richman (Eds.), *Spontaneous alternation behavior* (pp. 1–17). New York: Springer-Verlag.

Derryberry, D., & Rothbart, M. K. (1988). Arousal, affect, and attention as components of temperament. *Journal of Personality and Social Psychology, 55,* 958–966.

Derryberry, D., & Tucker, D. M. (1990). The adaptive base of the neural hierarchy: Elementary motivational controls on network function. In R. Dienstbier (Ed.), *Nebraska Symposium on Motivation: Vol. 38. Perspectives on motivation* (pp. 289–342). Lincoln, NE: University of Nebraska Press.

de Schonen, S., McKenzie, B., Maury, L., & Bresson, F. (1978). Central and peripheral object distances as determinants of the effective visual field in early infancy. *Perception, 7,* 499–506.

Diamond, A. (1985). Development of the ability to use recall to guide action, as indicated by infants' performance on A$\overline{B}$. *Child Development, 56,* 868–883.

Diamond, A. (1991). Neuropsychological insights into the meaning of object concept development. In S. Carey & R. Gelman (Eds.), *The epigenesis of mind: Essays on biology and cognition.* Hillsdale, NJ: Erlbaum.

Diamond, A., & Gilbert, J. (1989). Development as progressive inhibitory control of action: Retrieval of a contiguous object. *Cognitive Development, 4,* 223–249.

Diamond, A., & Goldman-Rakic, P. (1989). Comparison of human infants and rhesus monkeys on Piaget's A$\overline{B}$ task: Evidence for dependence on dorsolateral prefrontal cortex. *Experimental Brain Research, 74,* 24–40.

Diamond, A., Towle, C., & Boyer, K. (1994). Young children's performance on a task sensitive to the memory functions of the medial temporal lobe in adults—the delayed nonmatching-to-sample task—reveals problems that are due to non-memory-related task demands. *Behavioral Neuroscience, 108,* 659–680.

Diamond, A., Werker, J. F., & Lalonde, C. (1994). Toward understanding commonalities in the development of object search, detour navigation, categorization, and speech perception. In G. Dawson & K. W. Fischer (Eds.), *Human behavior and the developing brain* (pp. 380–426). New York: Guilford.

Diamond, A., Zola-Morgan, S., & Squire, L. R. (1989). Successful performance by monkeys with lesions of the hippocampal formation on A$\overline{B}$ and object retrieval, two tasks that mark developmental changes in human infants. *Behavioral Neuroscience, 103,* 526–537.

DiLalla, L. F., Thompson, L. A., Plomin, R., Phillips, K., Fagan, J. F., Haith, M. M., Cyphers, L. H., & Fulker, D. W. (1990). Infant predictors of preschool and adult IQ: A study of infant twins and their parents. *Developmental Psychology, 26,* 759–769.

Di Leo, J. H. (1970). *Young children and their drawings.* New York: Brunner/Mazel.

DiPietro, J. A., Larson, S. K., & Porges, S. W. (1987). Behavioral and heart rate pattern differences between breast-fed and bottle-fed neonates. *Developmental Psychology, 23,* 467–474.

DiPietro, J. A., Porges, S. W., & Uhly, B. (1992). Reactivity and developmental competence in preterm and full-term infants. *Developmental Psychology, 28,* 831–841.

Dittrichova, J., & Lapackova, V. (1964). Development of the waking state in young infants. *Child Development, 35,* 365–370.

Dixon, R. A., & Hertzog, C. (1988). A functional approach to memory and metamemory in adulthood. In F. W. Weinert & M. Perlmutter (Eds.), *Memory development: Universal changes and individual differences* (pp. 3–30). Hillsdale, NJ: Erlbaum.

Douglas, V. I. (1983). Attentional and cognitive problems. In M. Rutter (Ed.), *Developmental neuropsychiatry* (pp. 280–329). New York: Guilford.

Douglas, V. I., & Peters, K. G. (1979). Toward a clearer definition of the attentional deficit of hyperactive children. In G. A. Hale & M. Lewis (Eds.), *Attention and cognitive development* (pp. 173–247). New York: Plenum Press.

Draeger, S., Prior, M., & Sanson, A. (1986). Visual and auditory attention performance in hyperactive children: Competence or compliance. *Journal of Abnormal Child Psychology, 14,* 411-424.

Duffy, F. H. (1994). The role of quantified electroencephalography in psychological research. In G. Dawson & K. W. Fischer (Eds.), *Human behavior and the developing brain* (pp. 93–133). New York: Guilford.

Easterbrook, J. A. (1959). The effect of emotion on cue utilization and the organization of behavior. *Psychological Review, 66,* 183–201.

Eisenberg, L. (1966). The management of the hyperkinetic child. *Developmental Medicine and Child Neurology, 8,* 593–598.

Eisenberg, N., Fabes, R. A., Bernzweig, J., Karbon, M., Poulin, R., & Hanish, L. (1993). The relations of emotionality and regulation to preschoolers' social skills and sociometric status. *Child Development, 64,* 1418–1438.

Ekman, P., & Friesen, W. V. (1975). *Unmasking the face: A guide to recognizing emotions from facial clues.* Englewood Cliffs, NJ: Prentice-Hall.

Emde, R. N., Gaensbauer, T. J., & Harmon, R. J. (1976). Emotional expression in infancy: A biobehavioral study. *Psychological Issues Monograph Series* (1, No. 37).

Epstein, S. (1980). The stability of behavior: II. Implications for psychological research. *American Psychologist, 35,* 790–806.

Eriksen, C. W., & St. James, J. D. (1986). Visual attention within and around the field of focal attention: A zoom lens model. *Perception and Psychophysics, 40,* 225–240.

Eriksen, C. W., & Schultz, D. W. (1979). Information processing in visual search: A continuous flow conception and experimental results. *Perception and Psychophysics, 25,* 249–263.

Eriksen, C. W., & Yeh, Y. (1985). Allocation of attention in the visual field. *Journal of Experimental Psychology, 11,* 583–597.

Escalona, S. K. (1968). *The roots of individuality: Normal patterns of development in infancy.* Chicago: Aldine.

Eysenck, H. (1972). Human typology, higher nervous activity, and factor analysis. In V. D. Nebylitsyn & J. A. Gray (Eds.), *Biological bases of individual behavior* (pp. 165–181). New York & London: Academic Press.

Eysenck, H. J. (1976). *The measurement of personality.* Baltimore: University Park Press.

Fähndrich, D., & Schneider, K. (1987). Emotional reactions of preschool children while exploring and playing with a novel object. *Journal of Genetic Psychology, 148,* 209–217.

Fagan, J. F. (1974). Infant recognition memory: The effects of length of familiarization and type of discrimination task. *Child Development, 45,* 351–356.

Fagan, J. F. (1984). The relationship of novelty preferences during infancy to later intelligence and recognition memory. *Intelligence, 8,* 339–346.

Fantz, R. L. (1961). The origin of form perception. *Scientific American, 204,* 66–72.

Fantz, R. L. (1963). Pattern vision in newborn infants. *Science, 140,* 296–297.

Fantz, R. L. (1964). Visual experience in infants: Decreased attention to familiar patterns relative to novel ones. *Science, 146,* 668–670.

Fantz, R. L., & Fagan, J. F. (1975). Visual attention to size and number of pattern details by term and preterm infants during the first six months. *Child Development, 46,* 3–18.

Fantz, R. L., & Miranda, S. B. (1975). Newborn infant attention to form of contour. *Child Development, 46,* 224–228.

Fantz, R. L., & Nevis, S. (1967). Pattern preferences and perceptual-cognitive development in early infancy. *Merrill-Palmer Quarterly, 13,* 77–108.

Fenson, L., Sapper, V., & Minner, D. G. (1974). Attention and manipulative play in the one-year-old child. *Child Development, 45,* 757–764.

Fentress, J. C. (1989). Developmental roots of behavioral order: Systematic approaches to the examination of core developmental issues. In M. R. Gunnar & E. Thelen (Eds.), *Minnesota Symposium on Child Psychology: Vol. 22. Systems and development* (pp. 35–76). Hillsdale, NJ: Erlbaum.

Ferrara, C., & Hill, S. D. (1980). The responsiveness of autistic children to the predictability of social and nonsocial toys. *Journal of Autism and Developmental Disorders, 10,* 51–57.

Field, T. M. (1979). Interaction patterns of pre-term infants. In T. M. Field, A. M. Sostek, S. Goldberg, & H. H. Shuman (Eds.), *Infants born at risk: Behavior and development.* New York: SP Medical and Scientific Books.

Field, T. M. (1981). Infant arousal and affect during early interactions. *Advances in Infancy Research, 1,* 57–100.

Field, T. M., Vega-Lahr, N., Goldstein, S., & Scafidi, F. (1987). Face-to-face interaction behavior across early infancy. *Infant Behavior and Development, 10,* 111–116.

Finlay, D., & Ivinskis, A. (1982). Cardiac and visual responses to stimuli presented both foveally and peripherally as a function of speed of moving stimuli. *Developmental Psychology, 18,* 692–698.

Finlay, D., & Ivinskis, A. (1984). Cardiac and visual responses to moving stimuli presented either successively or simultaneously to the central and peripheral visual fields in 4-month-old infants. *Developmental Psychology, 20,* 29–36.

Fogel, A. (1977). Temporal organization in mother-infant face-to-face interaction. In H. R. Schaffer (Ed.), *Studies in mother-infant interaction* (pp. 119–151). New York: Academic Press.

Fogel, A. (1990). The process of developmental change in infant communicative action: Using dynamic systems theory to study individual ontogenies. In J. Colombo & J. Fagen (Eds.), *Individual differences in infancy: Reliability, stability, prediction* (pp. 341–358). Hillsdale, NJ: Erlbaum.

Fogel, A., & Thelen, E. (1987). Development of early expressive and communicative action: Reinterpreting the evidence from a dynamic systems perspective. *Developmental Psychology, 23,* 747–761.

Foreman, N., & Stevens, R. (1987). Relationships between the superior colliculus and hippocampus: Neural and behavioral considerations. *Behavioral and Brain Sciences, 10,* 101–151.

Fox, N. A. (1989). Psychophysiological correlates of emotional reactivity during the first year of life. *Developmental Psychology, 25,* 364–372.

Fox, N. A., & Field, T. M. (1989). Individual differences in preschool entry behavior. *Journal of Applied Developmental Psychology, 10,* 527–540.

Fox, N., Kagan, J., & Weiskopf, S. (1979). The growth of memory during infancy. *Genetic Psychology Monographs, 99,* 91–130.

Fox, N. A., & Stifter, C. A. (1989). Biological and behavioral differences in infant reactivity and regulation. In G. A. Kohnstamm, J. E. Bates, & M. K. Rothbart (Eds.), *Temperament in childhood* (pp. 169–183). Chichester, England: Wiley.

Fraiberg, S. (1977). *Every child's birth right: In defense of mothering.* New York: Basic Books.

Frankel, D. G., Shapira, R., Arbel, T., Shapira, Y., & Ayal, F. (1982). The visual attention at 4-months of full-term small-for-gestational-age and full-term appropriate-weight-for-gestational-age infants. In L. P. Lipsitt & T. M. Field (Eds.), *Infant behavior and development: Perinatal risk and newborn behavior* (pp. 121–129). Norwood, NJ: Ablex.

Frederickson, W. T., & Brown, J. V. (1975). Posture as a determinant of visual behavior in newborns. *Child Development, 46,* 579–582.

Freeseman, L. J., Colombo, J., & Coldren, J. T. (1993). Individual differences in infant visual attention: Four-month-olds' discrimination and generalization of global and local stimulus properties. *Child Development, 64,* 1191–1203.

Friedman, S. (1972). Habituation and recovery of visual response in the alert human newborn. *Journal of Experimental Child Psychology, 13,* 339–349.

Fullard, W., McDevitt, S. C., & Carey, W. B. (1984). Assessing temperament in one- to three-year-old children. *Journal of Pediatric Psychology, 9,* 205–217.

Gallup, G. G. (1979). Self-awareness in primates. *American Scientist, 67,* 417–421.

Gandour, M. J. (1989). Activity level as a dimension of temperament in toddlers: Its relevance for the organismic specificity hypothesis. *Child Development, 60,* 1092–1098.

Gardner, J. M., & Karmel, B. Z. (1983). Attention and arousal in preterm and full-term neonates. In T. Field & A. Sostek (Eds.), *Infants born at risk: Physiological, perceptual, and cognitive processes* (pp. 69–98). New York: Grune & Stratton.

Gibson, E. J. (1969). *Principles of perceptual learning and development.* New York: Appleton-Century-Crofts.

Gibson, E. J. (1988). Exploratory behavior in the development of perceiving, acting, and the acquiring of knowledge. *Annual Review of Psychology, 39,* 1–41.

Gibson, E. J., & Rader, N. (1979). Attention: The perceiver as performer. In G. A. Hale & M. Lewis (Eds.), *Attention and cognitive development* (pp. 1–21). New York: Plenum Press.

Gibson, J. J. (1979). *The ecological approach to visual perception.* Boston: Houghton-Mifflin.

Gibson, J. J., & Gibson, E. J. (1955). Perceptual learning: Differentiation or enrichment? *Psychological Review, 62,* 32–41.

Gibson, J. J., & Pick, A. D. (1963). Perception of another person's looking behavior. *American Journal of Psychology, 76,* 386–394.

Girton, M. R. (1979). Infants' attention to intra-stimulus motion. *Journal of Experimental Child Psychology, 28,* 416–423.

Goodman, S. H. (1981). The integration of verbal and motor behavior in preschool children. *Child Development, 52,* 280–289.

Goodyear, P., & Hynd, G. W. (1992). Attention-deficit disorder with (ADD/H) and without (ADD/WO) hyperactivity: Behavioral and neuropsychological differentiation. *Journal of Clinical Child Psychology, 21,* 273–305.

Goren, C. C., Sarty, M., & Wu, P. Y. K. (1975). Visual following and pattern discrimination of face-like stimuli by newborn infants. *Pediatrics, 56,* 544–549.

Gorenstein, E. E., & Newman, J. P. (1980). Disinhibitory psychopathology: A new perspective and a model for research. *Psychological Review, 87,* 301–315.

Gottfried, A. W., & Gottfried, A. E. (1984). Home environment and cognitive development in young children of middle-socioeconomic-status families. In A. W. Gottfried (Ed.), *Home environment and early cognitive development* (pp. 57–115). Orlando, FL: Academic Press.

Gottfried, A. W., Rose, S. A., & Bridger, W. H. (1977). Cross-modal transfer in human infants. *Child Development, 48,* 118–123.

Goyette, C. H., Conners, C. K., & Ulrich, R. F. (1978). Normative data on revised Conners

Parent and Teacher Rating Scales. *Journal of Abnormal Child Psychology, 6,* 221–236.

Graham, F. K., Anthony, B. J., & Ziegler, B. L. (1983). The orienting response and developmental processes. In D. Siddle (Ed.), *Orienting and habituation: Perspectives in human research* (pp. 371–430). New York: Wiley.

Graham, F. K., & Clifton, R. K. (1966). Heart-rate change as a component of the orienting response. *Psychological Bulletin, 65,* 305–320.

Graham, F. K., Strock, B. D., & Ziegler, B. L. (1981). Excitatory and inhibitory influences on reflex responsiveness. In W. A. Collins (Ed.), *Minnesota Symposium on Child Development: Vol 14. Aspects of the development of competence* (pp. 1–38). Hillsdale, NJ: Erlbaum.

Gray, J. A. (1982). *The neuropsychology of anxiety: An enquiry into the functions of the septo-hippocampal system.* Oxford: Clarendon Press.

Greenberg, D., Uzgiris, I. C., & Hunt, J. McV. (1970). Attentional preference and experience: III. Visual familiarity and looking time. *Journal of Genetic Psychology, 117,* 123–135.

Gregg, C. L., Haffner, M. E., & Korner, A. F. (1976). The relative efficacy of vestibular-proprioceptive stimulation and the upright position in enhancing visual pursuit in neonates. *Child Development, 47,* 309–314.

Groves, P. M., & Thompson, R. F. (1970). Habituation: A dual process theory. *Psychological Review, 77,* 419–450.

Guitton, D., Buchtel, H. A., & Douglas, R. M. (1985). Frontal lobe lesions in man cause difficulties in suppressing reflexive glances and in generating goal-directed saccades. *Experimental Brain Research, 58,* 455–472.

Gunnar, M. R. (1990). The psychobiology of infant temperament. In J. Colombo & J. Fagen (Eds.), *Individual differences in infancy: Reliability, stability, prediction* (pp. 387–409). Hillsdale, NJ: Erlbaum.

Gusella, J. L., Muir, D., & Tronick, E. Z. (1988). The effect of manipulating maternal behavior during an interaction on three-and six-month-olds' affect and attention. *Child Development, 59,* 1111–1124.

Hageküll, B., & Bohlin, G. (1981). Individual stability in dimensions of infant behavior. *Infant Behavior and Development, 4,* 97–108.

Haider, M. (1970). Neuropsychology of attention, expectation, and vigilance. In D. I. Mostofsky (Ed.), *Attention: Contemporary theory and analysis* (pp. 419–432). New York: Appleton-Century-Crofts.

Hainline, L. (1981). Eye movements and form perception in human infants. In D. F. Fisher, R. A. Monty, & J. W. Senders (Eds.), *Eye movements: Cognition and visual perception* (pp. 3–19). Hillsdale, NJ: Erlbaum.

Hainline, L., & Abramov, I. (1992). Assessing visual development: Is infant vision good enough. *Advances in Infancy Research, 7,* 39–102.

Haith, M. M. (1980). *Rules that babies look by: The organization of newborn visual activity.* Hillsdale, NJ: Erlbaum.

Haith, M. M., Hazan, C., & Goodman, G. S. (1988). Expectation and anticipation of dynamic visual events by 3.5-month-old babies. *Child Development, 59,* 467–479.

Haith, M. M., & McCarty, M. E. (1990). Stability of visual expectations at 3.0 months of age. *Developmental Psychology, 26,* 68–74.

Halverson, C. F., & Waldrop, M. F. (1973). The relations of mechanically recorded activity levels to varieties of preschool play behavior. *Child Development, 44,* 678–681.

Harman, C., Posner, M. I., Rothbart, M. K., & Thomas-Thrapp, L. (1994). Development of orienting to objects and locations in human infants. *Canadian Journal of Experimental Psychology, 48,* 301–318.

Harman, C., Rothbart, M. K., & Posner, M. I. (1995). The interaction of distress and attention in early infancy. Manuscript in preparation.

Harris, C. M. (1989). The etiology of saccades: A non-cognitive model. *Biological Cybernetics, 60,* 401–410.

Harris, C. M., Hainline, L., Abramov, I., Lemerise, E., & Camenzuli, C. (1988). The distribution of fixation durations in infants and naive adults. *Vision Research, 28,* 419–432.

Harris, P. L. (1973). Eye movements between adjacent stimuli: An age change in infancy. *British Journal of Psychology, 64,* 215–218.

Harris, P., & MacFarlane, A. (1974). The growth of the effective visual field from birth to seven weeks. *Journal of Experimental Child Psychology, 18,* 340–348.

Hayes, L. A., Ewy, R. D., & Watson, J. S. (1982). Attention as a predictor of learning in infants. *Journal of Experimental Child Psychology, 34,* 38–45.

Higgins, A. T., & Turnure, J. E. (1984). Distractibility and concentration of attention in children's development. *Child Development, 55,* 1799–1810.

Hillyard, S. A., Munte, T. F., & Neville, H. J. (1985). Visual-spatial attention, orienting, and brain physiology. In M. I. Posner & O. S. M. Marin (Eds.), *Attention and performance XI* (pp. 63–84). Hillsdale, NJ: Erlbaum.

Hinshaw, S. P. (1994). *Attention deficits and hyperactivity in children.* Thousand Oaks, CA: Sage.

Hockey, G. R. J. (1970). Effect of loud noise on attention selectivity. *Quarterly Journal of Experimental Psychology, 22,* 28–36.

Hockey, G. R. J., Coles, M. G. H., & Gaillard, A. W. K. (1986). Energetical issues in research on human information processing. In G. R. J. Hockey, A. W. K. Gaillard, & M. G. H. Coles (Eds.), *Energetics and human information processing* (pp. 3–21). Dordrecht: Martinus Nijhoff Publishers.

Hofer, M. (1981). *The roots of human behavior.* San Francisco: W.H. Freeman.

Hood, B. M. (1993). Inhibition of return produced by covert shifts of visual attention in 6-month-old infants. *Infant Behavior and Development, 16,* 245–254.

Hood, B. M., & Atkinson, J. (1993). Disengaging visual attention in the infant and adult. *Infant Behavior and Development, 16,* 405–422.

Hornik, R., Risenhoover, N., & Gunnar, M. (1987). The effects of maternal positive, neutral, and negative affective communications on infant responses to new toys. *Child Development, 58,* 937–944.

Horobin, K., & Acredolo, L. (1986). The role of attentiveness, mobility history, and separation of hiding sites on Stage IV search behavior. *Journal of Experimental Child Psychology, 41,* 114–127.

Horowitz, F. D. (Ed.). (1975). Visual attention, auditory stimulation, and language discrimination in young infants. *Monographs of the Society for Research in Child Development, 39* (5–6, Serial No. 158).

Horowitz, F. D. (1990). Developmental models of individual differences. In J. Colombo & J. Fagen (Eds.), *Individual differences in infancy: Reliability, stability, prediction* (pp. 3–18). Hillsdale, NJ: Erlbaum.

Houghton, G., & Tipper, S. P. (1994). A model of inhibitory mechanisms in selective attention. In D. Dagenbach & T. Carr (Eds.), *Inhibitory processes in attention, memory, and language* (pp. 53–112). Orlando, FL: Academic Press.

Hubley, P., & Trevarthen, C. (1979). Sharing a task in infancy. In I. Uzgiris (Ed.), *New*

Directions for Child Development: Vol. 4. Social interaction and communication during infancy (pp. 57–80). San Francisco: Jossey-Bass.

Hughes, M. (1978). Sequential analysis of exploration and play. *International Journal of Behavioral Development, 1,* 83–97.

Hughes, M. (1979). Exploration and play re-visited: A hierarchical analysis. *International Journal of Behavioral Development, 2,* 215–224.

Hughes, M., & Hutt, C. (1979). Heart-rate correlates of childhood activities, play, exploration, problem-solving and daydreaming. *Biological Psychology, 8,* 253–263.

Humphrey, M. M. (1982). Children's avoidance of environmental, simple task internal, and complex task internal distractors. *Child Development, 53,* 736–745.

Huttenlocher, P. R. (1979). Synaptic density in human frontal cortex—developmental changes and effects of aging. *Brain Research, 163,* 195–205.

Huttunen, M. O., & Nyman, G. (1982). On the continuity, change and clinical value of infant temperament in a prospective epidemiological study. In R. Porter & G. M. Collins (Eds.), *Temperamental differences in infants and young children* (pp. 240–251). London: Pitman.

Hynd, G. W., Hern, K. L., Voeller, K. K., & Marshall, R. M. (1991). Neurobiological basis of attention-deficit hyperactivity disorder (ADHD). *School Psychology Review, 20,* 174–186.

Izard, C. E. (1977). *Human emotions.* New York: Plenum Press.

Izard, C. E. (1979). *The maximally discriminative facial coding system (Max).* Newark, DE: University of Delaware Office of Instructional Technology.

Izard, C. E., Dougherty, L. M., & Hembree, E. A. (1989). *A system for identifying affect expressions by holistic judgements (Affex).* Newark, DE: Instructional Resources Center, University of Delaware.

Izard, C. E., Porges, S. W., Simons, R. F., Haynes, O. M., Hyde, C., Parisi, M., & Cohen, B. (1991). Infant cardiac activity: Developmental changes and relations with attachment. *Developmental Psychology, 27,* 432–439.

Jacob, R. G., O'Leary, K. D., & Rosenblad, C. (1978). Formal and informal classroom settings: Effects of hyperactivity. *Journal of Abnormal Child Psychology, 6,* 47–59.

Jacobson, S. W., Jacobson, J. L., O'Neill, J. M., Padgett, R. J., Frankowski, J. J., & Bihun, J. T. (1992). Visual expectation and dimensions of infant information processing. *Child Development, 63,* 711–724.

Jacobvitz, D., & Sroufe, L. A. (1987). The early caregiver-child relationship and attention-deficit disorder with hyperactivity in kindergarten: A prospective study. *Child Development, 58,* 1496–1504.

James, W. (1890/1950). *The principles of psychology* (Vol. 1). New York: Dover.

Jeannerod, M. (1994). The representing brain: Neural correlates of motor intention and imagery. *Behavioral and Brain Sciences, 17,* 187–245.

Jeffrey, W. E. (1968). The orienting reflex and attention in cognitive development. *Psychological Review, 75,* 323–334.

Jennings, J. R. (1986). Bodily changes during attending. In M. G. H. Coles, E. Donchin, & S. W. Porges (Eds.), *Psychophysiology: Systems, processes, and applications* (pp. 268–289). New York: Guilford.

Jennings, K. D. (1991). Early development of mastery motivation and its relation to the self-concept. In M. Bullock (Ed.), *The development of intentional action: Cognitive, motivational, and interactive processes* (pp. 1–13). Basel, Switzerland: Karger.

Johnson, M. H. (1990). Cortical maturation and the development of visual attention in early infancy. *Journal of Cognitive Neuroscience, 2,* 81–95.

Johnson, M. H., & Morton, J. (1991). *Biology and cognitive development*. Cambridge, MA: Basil Blackwell.

Johnson, M. H., Posner, M. I., & Rothbart, M. K. (1991). Components of visual orienting in early infancy: Contingency learning, anticipatory looking, and disengaging. *Journal of Cognitive Neuroscience, 3*, 335–344.

Jones, M. R., & Boltz, M. (1989). Dynamic attending and responses to time. *Psychological Review, 96*, 459–491.

Jonides, J. (1983). Further toward a model of the mind's eye's movement. *Bulletin of the Psychonomic Society, 21*, 247–250.

Kagan, J. (1970). Attention and psychological change in the young child. *Science, 170*, 826–832.

Kagan, J., Reznick, J. S., & Gibbons, J. (1989). Inhibited and uninhibited types of children. *Child Development, 60*, 838–845.

Kagan, J., Reznick, J. S., & Snidman, N. (1987). The physiology and psychology of behavioral inhibition in children. *Child Development, 58*, 1459–1473.

Kagan, J., McCall, R. B., Reppucci, N. D., Jordan, J., Levine, J., & Minton, C. (1971). *Change and continuity in infancy*. New York: Wiley.

Kahneman, D. (1973). *Attention and effort*. Englewood Cliffs, NJ: Prentice-Hall.

Kaler, S. R., & Kopp, C. B. (1990). Compliance and comprehension in very young toddlers. *Child Development, 61*, 1997–2003.

Karmel, B. Z., & Maisel, E. B. (1975). A neuronal activity model for infant visual attention. In L. B. Cohen & P. Salapatek (Eds.), *Infant perception: From sensation to cognition* (Vol. 1, pp. 77–131). New York: Academic Press.

Kasari, C., Sigman, M., Mundy, P., & Yirmiya, N. (1990). Affective sharing in the context of joint attention interactions of normal, autistic, and mentally retarded children. *Journal of Autism and Developmental Disorders, 20*, 87–100.

Kaye, K. (1978). Discriminating among normal infants by multivariate analysis of Brazelton scores: Lumping and smoothing. In A. J. Sameroff (Ed.). *Organization and stability of newborn behavior: A commentary on the Brazelton Neonatal Behavior Assessment Scale. Monographs of the Society for Research in Child Development, 43* (5-6, Serial No. 177), 60–80.

Kaye, K., & Fogel, A. (1980). The temporal structure of face-to-face communication between mothers and infants. *Developmental Psychology, 16*, 454–464.

Keller, H., & Gauda, G. (1987). Eye contact in the first months of life and its developmental consequences. In H. Rauh & H.-Ch. Steinhausen (Eds.), *Psychobiology and early development* (pp. 129–143). North-Holland: Elsevier.

Keller, H., Schölmerich, A., Miranda, D., & Gauda, G. (1987). Exploratory behavior development in the first four years. In D. Gorlitz & J. F. Wohlwill (Eds.), *Curiosity, imagination, and play* (pp. 127–150). Hillsdale, NJ: Erlbaum.

Kinsbourne, M. (1973). Minimal brain dysfunction as a neurodevelopmental lag. *Annals of the New York Academy of Sciences, 205*, 268–273.

Kinsbourne, M. (1991). Overfocusing: An apparent subtype of attention deficit-hyperactivity disorder. *Pediatric and Adolescent Medicine, 1*, 18–35.

Kochanska, G. (1993). Toward a synthesis of parental socialization and child temperament in early development of conscience. *Child Development, 64*, 325–347.

Kochanska, G., Murray, K., Jacques, T. Y., Koenig, A. L., & Vandegeest, K. A. (in press). Inhibitory control in young children and its role in emerging internalization. *Child Development*.

Kohlberg, L. (1971). The cognitive-developmental approach to socialization. In D. A. Goslin

(Ed.), *Handbook of socialization theory and research* (pp. 347–480). Chicago: Rand-McNally.

Kopp, C. B. (1982). Antecedents of self-regulation: A developmental perspective. *Developmental Psychology, 18,* 199–214.

Kopp, C. B. (1991). Young children's progression to self-regulation. In M. Bullock (Ed.), *The development of intentional action: Cognitive, motivational, and interactive processes* (pp. 38–54). Basel, Switzerland: Karger.

Korner, A. F., & Grobstein, R. (1966). Visual alertness as related to soothing in neonates. *Child Development, 37,* 867–876.

Koslowski, B., & Bruner, J. S. (1972). Learning to use a lever. *Child Development, 43,* 790–799.

Kowler, E., & Martins, A. J. (1982). Eye movements of preschool children. *Science, 215,* 997–999.

Krakow, J. B., Kopp, C. B., & Vaughn, B. E. (1982). Sustained attention during the second year: Age trends, individual differences, and implications for development. Unpublished manuscript.

Krupski, A., & Boyle, P. R. (1978). An observational analysis of children's behavior during a simple-reaction-time task: The role of attention. *Child Development, 49,* 340–347.

Kuczynski, L., Kochanska, G., Radke-Yarrow, M., & Girnius-Brown, O. (1987). A developmental interpretation of young children's noncompliance. *Developmental Psychology, 23,* 799–806.

Kunst-Wilson, W. R., & Zajonc, R. B. (1980). Affective discrimination of stimuli that cannot be recognized. *Science, 207,* 557–558.

Kurtzberg, D., & Vaughan, H. G. (1979). Maturation and task specificity of cortical potentials associated with visual scanning. In D. Lehmann & E. Callaway (Eds.), *Human evoked potentials* (pp. 185–199). New York: Plenum Press.

LaBerge, D. (1990). Thalamic and cortical mechanisms of attention suggested by recent positron emission tomographic experiments. *Journal of Cognitive Neuroscience, 2,* 358–372.

Labrell, F., & Simeoni, F. (1992). ZPD revisited: Parental presence may be enough [Abstract]. *Infant Behavior and Development, 15,* 507.

Lacey, J. I., & Lacey, B. C. (1962). The law of initial values in the longitudinal study of autonomic constitution: Reproducibility of autonomic response patterns over a four year interval. *Annals of the New York Academy of Sciences, 98,* 1257–1290.

Lacey, J. I., & Lacey, B. C. (1970). Some autonomic-central nervous system interrelationships. In P. Black (Ed.), *Physiological correlates of emotion* (pp. 205–227). New York: Academic Press.

Lahey, B. B., Pelham, W. E., Schaughency, E. A., Atkins, M. S., Murphy, H. A., Hynd, G. W., Russo, M., Hartdagen, S., & Lorys-Vernon, A. (1988). Dimensions and types of attention deficit disorder. *Journal of the American Academy of Child & Adolescent Psychiatry, 27,* 330–335.

Lahey, B. B., Schaughency, E. A., Hynd, G. W., Carlson, C. L., & Nieves, N. (1987). Attention deficit disorder with and without hyperactivity: Comparison of behavioral characteristics of clinic-referred children. *Journal of the American Academy of Child & Adolescent Psychiatry, 26,* 718–723.

Lamb, M. E., Morrison, D. C., & Malkin, C. M. (1987). The development of infant social expectations in face-to-face interaction: A longitudinal study. *Merrill-Palmer Quarterly, 33,* 241–254.

Landau, B., Smith, L. B., & Jones, S. S. (1988). The importance of shape in early lexical learning. *Cognitive Development, 3,* 299–321.

Landau, S., & Milich, R. (1988). Social communication patterns of attention deficit-disordered boys. *Journal of Abnormal Child Psychology, 16,* 69–81.

Landers, D. M. (1980). The arousal-performance relationship revisited. *Research Quarterly for Exercise and Sport, 51,* 77–90.

Lane, D. M., & Pearson, D. A. (1982). The development of selective attention. *Merrill-Palmer Quarterly, 28,* 317–337.

Langsdorf, P., Izard, C. E., Rayias, M., & Hembree, E. A. (1983). Interest expression, visual fixation, and heart rate changes in 2- to 8-month-old infants. *Developmental Psychology, 19,* 375–386.

Lawson, K. R., Parrinello, R., & Ruff, H. A. (1992). Maternal behavior and infant attention. *Infant Behavior and Development, 15,* 209–229.

Lawson, K. R., & Ruff, H. A. (1984). Infants' visual following: The effects of size and sound. *Developmental Psychology, 20,* 427–434.

Lawson, K. R., & Ruff, H. A. (1995a, March). Temperament and attention in infancy interact to predict later attention and cognition. Poster presented at the biennial meeting of the Society for Research in Child Development, Indianapolis, IN.

Lawson, K. R., & Ruff, H. A. (1995b). The relationship of attention and temperament in early development. Manuscript submitted for publication.

Lawson, K. R., & Turkewitz, G. (1980). Intersensory function in newborns: Effect of sound on visual preferences. *Child Development, 51,* 1295–1298.

LeDoux, J. E. (1989). Cognitive-emotional interactions in the brain. *Cognition and Emotion, 3,* 267–289.

Lepper, M. R., & Greene, D. (1978). Overjustification research and beyond: Toward a means-ends analysis of intrinsic and extrinsic motivation. In M. R. Lepper & D. Greene (Eds.), *New perspectives on the psychology of human motivation* (pp. 109–148). Hillsdale, NJ: Erlbaum.

Leung, E. H. L., & Rheingold, H. L. (1981). Development of pointing as a social gesture. *Developmental Psychology, 17,* 215–220.

Levy, F. (1980). The development of sustained attention (vigilance) and inhibition in children: Some normative data. *Journal of Child Psychology and Psychiatry, 21,* 77–84.

Lewis, M., & Brooks-Gunn, J. (1979). *Social cognition and the acquisition of self.* New York: Plenum Press.

Lewis, M., & Goldberg, S. (1969). The acquisition and violation of expectancy: An experimental paradigm. *Journal of Experimental Child Psychology, 7,* 70–80.

Lewis, M., Goldberg, S., & Campbell, H. (1969). A developmental study of information processing within the first three years of life: Response decrement to a redundant signal. *Monographs of the Society for Research in Child Development, 34* (9, Serial No. 133).

Lewis, M., Kagan, J., Campbell, H., & Kalafat, J. (1966). The cardiac response as a correlate of attention in infants. *Child Development, 37,* 63–71.

Lewis, T. L., Maurer, D., & Brent, H. P. (1989). Optokinetic nystagmus in normal and visually deprived children: Implications for cortical development. *Canadian Journal of Psychology, 43,* 121–140.

Linnemeyer, S. A., & Porges, S. W. (1986). Recognition memory and cardiac vagal tone in 6-month-old infants. *Infant Behavior and Development, 9,* 43–56.

Lipton, E. L., Steinschneider, A., & Richmond, J. B. (1961). Autonomic function in the neonate: IV. Individual differences in cardiac reactivity. *Psychosomatic Medicine, 23,* 472–484.

Lipton, E. L., Steinschneider, A., & Richmond, J. B. (1966). Autonomic function in the neonate: VII. Maturational changes in cardiac control. *Child Development, 37,* 1–16.

23   ECHOES IN THE LABYRINTH

☐ Brian Ferneyhough: *Collected Writings* (London, 1996)
Paul Hillier: *Arvo Pärt* (Oxford, 1997)

◯ Ferneyhough: *Unity Capsule*, etc. – Elision (Etcetera)
Grisey: *Les espaces acoustiques* – Pierre-André Valade and
Sylvain Cambreling (Accord)
Lachenmann: *Schwankungen am Rand*, etc. – Eötvös (ECM)
Kurtág: *Kafka-Fragmente* – Adrienne Csengery (Hungaroton)
Messiaen: *Saint François d'Assise* – Kent Nagano (DG)
Pärt: *Tabula rasa*, etc. – Saulius Sondeckis (ECM)

24   INTERLUDE

◯ Adès: *Asyla*, etc. – Simon Rattle (EMI)
Birtwistle: *Pulse Shadows* – Reinbert de Leeuw (Teldec)
Carter: *Symphonia*, etc. – Oliver Knussen (DG)
Kyburz: *The Voynich Cipher Manuscript*, etc. – Rupert Huber
(Kairos)
Ligeti: *With Pipes, Drums, Fiddles*, etc. – Amadinda (Teldec)
Sciarrino: *Infinito nero*, etc. – Ensemble Recherche (Kairos)

Index

Llamas, C., & Diamond, A. (1991, April). Development of frontal cortex abilities in children between 3–8 years of age. Paper presented at the biennial meeting of the Society for Research in Child Development, Seattle, WA.

Lockman, J. J., & McHale, J. P. (1989). Object manipulation in infancy: Developmental and contextual determinants. In J. J. Lockman & N. L. Hazen (Eds.), *Action in a social context: Perspectives on early development* (pp. 129–167). New York: Plenum Press.

Logan, G. D. (1988). Toward an instance theory of automatization. *Psychological Review, 95,* 492–527.

Lorch, E. P., & Horn, D. G. (1986). Habituation of attention to irrelevant stimuli in elementary school children. *Journal of Experimental Child Psychology, 41,* 184–197.

Lou, H. C., Henriksen, L., & Bruhn, P. (1984). Focal cerebral hypoperfusion in children with dysphasia and/or attention deficit disorder. *Archives of Neurology, 41,* 825–829.

Loveland, K. A., & Landry, S. H. (1986). Joint attention and language in autism and developmental language delay. *Journal of Autism and Developmental Disorders, 16,* 335–349.

Lütkenhaus, P., & Bullock, M. (1991). The development of volitional skills. In M. Bullock (Ed.), *The development of intentional actions: Cognitive, motivational, and interactive processes* (pp. 14–23). Basel, Switzerland: Karger.

Luria, A. R. (1973). *The working brain: An introduction to neuropsychology.* New York: Basic Books.

Luria, A. R., & Homskaya, E. D. (1970). Frontal lobes and the regulation of arousal processes. In D. I. Mostofsky (Ed.), *Attention: Contemporary theory and analysis* (pp. 303–330). New York: Appleton-Century-Crofts.

MacFarlane, A., Harris, P., & Barnes, I. (1976). Central and peripheral vision in early infancy. *Journal of Experimental Child Psychology, 21,* 532–538.

Mackie, R. R. (1977). *Vigilance: Theory, operational performance and physiological correlates.* New York: Plenum Press.

Mackworth, N. H. (1965). Visual noise causes tunnel vision. *Psychonomic Science, 3,* 67–68.

Mackworth, N. H., & Bruner, J. S. (1970). How adults and children search and recognize pictures. *Human Development, 13,* 149–177.

Mackworth, N. H., & Morandi, A. J. (1967). The gaze selects informative details within pictures. *Perception and Psychophysics, 2,* 547–552.

Magnusson, D. (1985). Implications of an interactional paradigm for research on human development. *International Journal of Behavioral Development, 8,* 115–137.

Martin, R. P. (1989). Activity level, distractibility, and persistence: Critical characteristics in early schooling. In G. A. Kohnstamm, J. E. Bates, & M. K. Rothbart (Eds.), *Temperament in childhood* (pp. 451–461). Chichester, England: Wiley.

Martini, M., & Kirkpatrick, J. (1992). Marquesan caregiver-infant interactions [Abstract]. *Infant Behavior and Development, 15,* 555.

Marx, M. H., & Hillix, W. A. (1963). *Systems and theories in psychology.* New York: McGraw-Hill.

Mash, E. J., & Johnston, C. (1982). A comparison of the mother-child interactions of younger and older hyperactive and normal children. *Child Development, 53,* 1371–1381.

Masters, J. C., & Binger, C. G. (1978). Interrupting the flow of behavior: The stability and development children's initiation and maintenance of compliant response inhibition. *Merrill-Palmer Quarterly, 24,* 229–242.

Maurer, D. (1975). Infant visual perception: Methods of study. In L. B. Cohen & P. Salapatek

(Eds.), *Infant perception: From sensation to cognition* (Vol. 1, pp. 1–76). New York: Academic Press.

Maurer, D., & Lewis, T. L. (1981). The influence of peripheral stimuli on infants' eye movements. In D. F. Fisher, R. A. Monty, & J. W. Senders (Eds.), *Eye movements: Cognition and visual perception* (pp. 21–29). Hillsdale, NJ: Erlbaum.

Maurer, D., & Lewis, T. L. (1991). The development of peripheral vision and its physiological underpinnings. In M. J. Weiss & P. R. Zelazo (Eds.), *Newborn attention: Biological constraints and the influence of experience* (pp. 218–255). Norwood, NJ: Ablex.

Maurer, D., & Maurer, C. (1988). *The world of the newborn.* New York: Basic Books.

Maurer, D., & Salapatek, P. (1976). Developmental changes in the scanning of faces by young infants. *Child Development, 47,* 523–527.

Mayer, D. L., & Fulton, A. B. (1993). Development of the human visual field. In K. Simons (Ed.), *Early visual development: Normal and abnormal.* New York: Oxford University Press.

McCall, R. B., & Carriger, M. S. (1993). A meta-analysis of infant habituation and recognition memory performance as predictors of later IQ. *Child Development, 64,* 57–79.

McCall, R. B., & Mash, C. W. (1995). Infant cognition and its relation to mature intelligence. In R. Vasta (Ed.), *Annals of child development* (Vol.10, pp. 27–56). London: Kingsley.

McDevitt, S. C., & Carey, W. F. (1981). Stability of ratings vs. perceptions of temperament from early infancy to 1–3 years. *American Journal of Orthopsychiatry, 51,* 342–345.

McKenzie, B. E., & Day, R. H. (1976). Infants' attention to stationary and moving objects at different distances. *Australian Journal of Psychology, 28,* 45–51.

Meltzoff, A. N. (1988a). Infant imitation after a 1-week delay: Long-term memory for novel acts and multiple stimuli. *Developmental Psychology, 24,* 470–476.

Meltzoff, A. N. (1988b). Infant imitation and memory: Nine-month-olds in immediate and deferred tests. *Child Development, 59,* 217–225.

Meltzoff, A. N. (1990). Towards a developmental cognitive science. In A. Diamond (Ed.), *The development and neural bases of higher cognitve functions* (pp. 1–37). New York: New York Academy of Sciences.

Mendelson, M. J. (1983). Attentional inertia at four and seven months? *Child Development, 54,* 677–685.

Merigan, W. H., & Maunsell, J. H. R. (1993). How parallel are the primate visual pathways? *Annual Review of Neuroscience, 16,* 369–402.

Mesulam, M. M. (1981). A cortical network for directed attention and unilateral neglect. *Annals of Neurology, 10,* 309–325.

Mesulam, M. M. (1983). The functional anatomy and hemispheric specialization for directed attention: The role of the parietal lobe and its connectivity. *Trends in NeuroScience, 6,* 384–387.

Michel, G. F., Camras, L. A., & Sullivan, J. (1992). Infant interest expressions as coordinative motor structures. *Infant Behavior and Development, 15,* 347–358.

Milewski, A. E. (1976). Infants' discrimination of internal and external pattern elements. *Journal of Experimental Child Psychology, 22,* 229–246.

Milich, R., & Landau, S. (1989). The role of social status variables in differentiating subgroups of hyperactive children. In L. Bloomingdale & J. M. Swanson (Eds.), *Attention deficit disorder* (pp. 1–16). Oxford: Pergamon.

Miller, D. J. (1972). Visual habituation in the human infant. *Child Development, 43,* 481–493.

Miller, D. J., Ryan, E. B., Aberger, E., Jr., McGuire, M. D., Short, E. J., & Kenny, D. A. (1979). Relationships between assessments of habituation and cognitive performance in the early years of life. *International Journal of Behavioral Development, 2,* 159–170.

Miller, D. J., Ryan, E. B., Sinnott, J. P., & Wilson, M. A. (1976). Serial habituation in two-, three-, and four-month-old infants. *Child Development, 47,* 341–349.

Miller, P. H. (1990). The development of strategies of selective attention. In D. F. Bjorklund (Ed.), *Children's strategies: Contemporary views of cognitive development* (pp. 157–184). Hillsdale, NJ: Erlbaum.

Miller, P. H., & Harris, Y. R. (1988). Preschoolers' strategies of attention on a same-different task. *Developmental Psychology, 24,* 628–633.

Miller, P. H., Seier, W. L., Probert, J. S., & Aloise, P. A. (1991). Age differences in the capacity demands of a strategy among spontaneously strategic children. *Journal of Experimental Child Psychology, 52,* 149–165.

Miller, P. H., Woody-Ramsey, J., & Aloise, P. A. (1991). The role of strategy effortfulness in strategy effectiveness. *Developmental Psychology, 27,* 738–745.

Miller, P. H., & Zalenski, R. (1982). Preschoolers' knowledge about attention. *Developmental Psychology, 18,* 871–875.

Milner, A. D., Carey, D. P., & Harvey, M. (1994). Visually guided action and the "need to know." *Behavioral and Brain Sciences, 17,* 213–214.

Mischel, W. (1983). Delay of gratification as process and as person variable in development. In D. Magnusson & V. L. Allen (Eds.), *Human development: An interactional perspective* (pp. 149–165). New York: Academic Press.

Mischel, W., & Ebbeson, E. B. (1970). Attention in delay of gratification. *Journal of Personality and Social Psychology, 16,* 329–337.

Mischel, W., Ebbeson, E. B., & Zeiss, A. R. (1972). Cognitive and attentional mechanisms in delay of gratification. *Journal of Personality and Social Psychology, 21,* 204–218.

Morgan, J. J. B. (1916). The overcoming of distraction and other resistances. *Archives of Psychology, 35,* 1–84.

Morissette, P., Ricard, M., & Gouin-Décarie, T. (1992). Comprehension of pointing and joint visual attention: A longitudinal study [Abstract]. *Infant Behavior and Development, 15,* 591.

Morrison, F. J. (1982). The development of alertness. *Journal of Experimental Child Psychology, 34,* 187–199.

Moss, M., Colombo, J., Mitchell, D. W., & Horowitz, F. D. (1988). Neonatal behavioral organization and visual processing at three months. *Child Development, 59,* 1211–1220.

Mountcastle, V. B. (1978a). Brain mechanisms for directed attention. *Journal of the Royal Society of Medicine, 71,* 14–28.

Mountcastle, V. B. (1978b). An organizing principle for cerebral function: The unit module and the distributed system. In G. M. Edelman & V. B. Mountcastle (Eds.), *The mindful brain* (pp. 7–50). Cambridge, MA: MIT Press.

Moyer, K. E., & Gilmer, B. H. (1955). Attention spans of children for experimentally designed toys. *Journal of Genetic Psychology, 87,* 187–201.

Mundy, P., & Sigman, M. (1989). The theoretical implications of joint-attention deficits in autism. *Development and Psychopathology, 1,* 173–183.

Mundy, P., Sigman, M., Ungerer, J., & Sherman, T. (1987). Nonverbal communication and play correlates of language development in autistic children. *Journal of Autism and Developmental Disorders, 17,* 349–364.

Murphy, C. M., & Messer, D. J. (1978). Mothers, infants, and pointing: A study of a gesture. In H. R. Schaffer (Ed.), *Studies in mother-infant interaction* (pp. 325–354). London: Academic Press.

Näätänen, R., & Michie, P. T. (1979). Early selective-attention effects on the evoked potential: A critical review and reinterpretation. *Biological Psychology, 8,* 81–136.

Nachman, P. A., Stern, D. N., & Best, C. (1986). Affective reactions to stimuli and infants' preferences for novelty and familiarity. *Journal of the American Academy of Child Psychiatry, 25,* 801–804.

Nadel, L., & Zola-Morgan, S. (1984). Infantile amnesia: A neurobiological perspective. In M. Moscovitch (Ed.), *Infant memory: Its relation to normal and pathological memory in humans and other animals* (pp. 145–172). New York: Plenum Press.

Navon, D. (1977). Forest before trees: The precedence of global features in visual perception. *Cognitive Psychology, 9,* 353–383.

Navon, D. (1984). Resources—A theoretical soup stone? *Psychological Review, 91,* 216–234.

Navon, D., & Gopher, D. (1979). On the economy of the human processing system. *Psychological Review, 86,* 214–255.

Neisser, U. (1967). *Cognitive psychology.* Englewood Cliffs, N.J.: Prentice-Hall.

Neisser, U. (1979). The control of information pickup in selective looking. In A.D. Pick (Ed.), *Perception and its development: A tribute to Eleanor J. Gibson* (pp. 201–219). Hillsdale, NJ: Erlbaum.

Nelson, C. A., & deRegnier, R. A. (1992). Neural correlates of attention and memory in the first year of life. *Developmental Neuropsychology, 8,* 119–134.

Nicolich, L. M. (1977). Beyond sensorimotor intelligence: Assessment of symbolic maturity through analysis of pretend play. *Merrill-Palmer Quarterly, 23,* 89–99.

Nissen, M. J., & Bullemer, P. (1987). Attentional requirements of learning: Evidence from performance measures. *Cognitive Psychology, 19,* 1–32.

Norman, D. A., & Shallice, T. (1986). Attention to action. In R. J. Davidson, G. E. Schwartz, & D. Shapiro (Eds.), *Consciousness and self-regulation: Advances in research and theory* (pp. 1–18). New York: Plenum Press.

Oakes, L. M., & Tellinghuisen, D. J. (1994). Examining in infancy: Does it reflect active processing? *Developmental Psychology, 30,* 748–756.

Obrist, P. A., Howard, J. L., Sutterer, J. R., Hennis, R. S., & Murrell, D. J. (1973). Cardiac-somatic changes during a simple reaction-time task: A developmental study. *Journal of Experimental Child Psychology, 16,* 346–362.

Obrist, P. A., Webb, R. A., & Sutterer, J. R. (1969). Heart rate and somatic changes during aversive conditioning and a simple reaction time task. *Psychophysiology, 5,* 696–723.

Obrist, P. A., Webb, R. A., Sutterer, J. R., & Howard, J. L. (1970). Cardiac deceleration and reaction time: An evaluation of two hypotheses. *Psychophysiology, 6,* 695–706.

Osofsky, J. D., & Danzger, B. (1974). Relationships between neonatal characteristics and mother-infant interaction. *Developmental Psychology, 10,* 124–130.

O'Sullivan, J. T. (1993). Preschoolers' beliefs about effort, incentives, and recall. *Journal of Experimental Child Psychology, 55,* 396–414.

Overman, W. H. (1990). Performance on traditional matching to sample, non-matching to sample, and object discrimination tasks by 12- to 32-month-old children. In A. Diamond (Ed.), *The development and neural bases of higher cognitive functions* (pp. 365–393). New York: New York Academy of Sciences.

Parasuraman, R. (1984). Sustained attention in detection and discrimination. In R. Parasuraman & D. R. Davies (Eds.), *Varieties of attention* (pp. 243–271). Orlando, FL: Academic Press.

Parrinello, R. M., & Ruff, H. A. (1988). The influence of adult intervention on infants' level of attention. *Child Development, 59,* 1125–1135.

Parrinello-Ruttner, R. (1986). The influence of adult intervention on infants' level of attention. Unpublished doctoral dissertation, Ferkauf Graduate School of Psychology, Yeshiva University.

Passingham, R. E. (1993). *The frontal lobes and voluntary action.* Oxford: Oxford University Press.

Patterson, C. J. (1982). Self-control and self-regulation in childhood. In T. M. Field, A. Huston, H. C. Quay, L. Troll, & G. E. Finley (Eds.), *Review of human development* (pp. 290–303). New York: Wiley.

Patterson, C. J., & Mischel, W. (1975). Plans to resist distraction. *Developmental Psychology, 11,* 369–378.

Patterson, G. R., & Bank, L. (1989). Some amplifying mechanisms for pathologic processes in families. In M. R. Gunnar & E. Thelen (Eds.), *Minnesota Symposium on Child Psychology: Vol. 22. Systems and development* (pp. 167–209). Hillsdale, NJ: Erlbaum.

Pêcheaux, M.-G., & Lécuyer, R. (1983). Habituation rate and free exploration tempo in 4-month-old infants. *International Journal of Behavioral Development, 6,* 37–50.

Piaget, J. (1952). *The origin of intelligence in children.* New York: International Universities Press.

Piaget, J. (1955). *The language and thought of the child.* Cleveland, OH: World Publishing Company.

Piaget, J. (1962). *Play, dreams and imitation in childhood.* New York: W.W. Norton.

Pick, H. L., & Pick, A. D. (1970). Sensory and perceptual development. In P. H. Mussen (Ed.), *Carmichael's manual of child psychology* (3rd ed., Vol. 1, pp. 773–847). New York: Wiley.

Pillow, B. H. (1988). Young children's understanding of attentional limits. *Child Development, 59,* 38–46.

Porges, S. W. (1972). Heart rate variability and deceleration as indexes of reaction time. *Journal of Experimental Psychology, 92,* 103–110.

Porges, S. W. (1974). Heart rate indices of newborn attentional responsivity. *Merrill-Palmer Quarterly, 20,* 231–254.

Porges, S. W. (1976). Peripheral and neurochemical parallels of psychopathology: A psychopathological model relating autonomic imbalance to hyperactivity, psychopathy, and autism. *Advances in Child Development and Behavior, 2,* 35–65.

Porges, S. W. (1984). Physiologic correlates of attention: A core process underlying learning disorders. *Pediatric Clinics of North America, 31,* 371–385.

Porges, S. W. (1986). Respiratory sinus arrhythmia: Physiological basis, quantitative methods, and clinical implications. In P. Grossman, K. Janssen, & D. Vaitl (Eds.), *Cardiorespiratory and cardiosomatic psychophysiology* (pp. 101–115). New York: Plenum Press.

Porges, S. W. (1991). Vagal tone: An autonomic mediator of affect. In J. Garber & K. A. Dodge (Eds.), *The development of emotion regulation and dysregulation* (pp. 111–128). Cambridge, England: Cambridge University Press.

Porges, S. W. (1992). Autonomic regulation and attention. In B. A. Campbell, H. Hayne, & R. Richardson (Eds.), *Attention and information processing in infants and adults* (pp. 201–223). Hillsdale, NJ: Erlbaum.

Porges, S. W., Doussard-Roosevelt, J. A., & Maiti, A. K. (1994). Vagal tone and the physiological regulation of emotion. In N. A. Fox (Ed.), The development of emotion regulation: Biological and behavioral considerations. *Monographs of the Society for Research in Child Development, 59* (2–3, Serial No. 240).

Porges, S. W., & Raskin, D. C. (1969). Respiratory and heart rate components of attention. *Journal of Experimental Psychology, 81*, 497–503.

Porges, S. W., & Smith, K. M. (1980). Defining hyperactivity: Psychophysiological behavioral strategies. In C. K. Whalen & B. Henker (Eds.), *Hyperactive children: The social ecology of identification and treatment* (pp. 75–104). New York: Academic Press.

Porges, S. W., Stamps, L. E., & Walter, G. F. (1974). Heart rate variability and newborn heart rate responses to illumination changes. *Developmental Psychology, 10*, 507–513.

Porges, S. W., Walter, G. F., Korb, R. J., & Sprague, R. L. (1975). The influences of methylphenidate on heart rate and behavioral measures of attention in hyperactive children. *Child Development, 46*, 727–733.

Posner, M. I. (1978). *Chronometric explorations of mind.* Hillsdale, NJ: Erlbaum.

Posner, M. I. (1982). Cumulative development of attentional theory. *American Psychologist, 37*, 168–179.

Posner, M. I., & Boies, S. J. (1971). Components of attention. *Psychological Review, 78*, 391–408.

Posner, M. I., & Cohen, Y. (1984). Components of visual orienting. In H. Bouma & D. G. Bouwhuis (Eds.), *Attention and performance X: Control of language processes* (pp. 531–556). Hillsdale, NJ: Erlbaum.

Posner, M. I., Cohen, Y., Choate, L. S., Hockey, R., & Maylor, E. (1984). Sustained concentration: Passive filtering or active orienting? In S. Kornblum & J. Requin (Eds.), *Preparatory states and processes* (pp. 49–65). Hillsdale, NJ: Erlbaum.

Posner, M. I., & Dehaene, S. (1994). Attentional networks. *Trends in NeuroScience, 17*, 75–79.

Posner, M. I., & Peterson, S. E. (1990). The attention system of the human brain. *Annual Review of Neuroscience, 13*, 25–42.

Posner, M. I., & Presti, D. E. (1987). Selective attention and cognitive control. *Trends in NeuroScience, 10*, 13–17.

Posner, M. I., & Raichle, M. E. (1994). *Images of mind.* New York: W. H. Freeman.

Posner, M. I., & Rothbart, M. K. (1981). The development of attentional mechanisms. In J. H. Flowers (Ed.), *Nebraska Symposium on Motivation* (Vol. 28, pp. 1–52). Lincoln, NE: University of Nebraska Press.

Posner, M. I., & Rothbart, M. K. (1991). Attentional mechanisms and conscious experience. In A. D. Milner & M. D. Rugg (Eds.), *Neuropsychology of consciousness* (pp. 91–111). San Diego: Academic Press.

Posner, M. I., Rothbart, M. K., Gerardi, G., & Thomas-Thrapp, L. (in press). Functions of orienting in early infancy. In P. Lange, M. Balaban, & R. F. Simmons (Eds.), *The study of attention: Cognitive perspectives from psychophysiology, reflexology, and neuroscience: Festschrift for Frances Graham.* Hillsdale, NJ: Erlbaum.

Posner, M. I., Rothbart, M. K., Thomas-Thrapp, L., & Gerardi, G.(in press). Development of orienting to locations and objects. In R. Wright (Ed.), *Visual attention: The Simon Fraser Conference.* New York: Oxford University Press.

Posner, M. I., & Snyder, C. R. R. (1975). Attention and cognitive control. In R. L. Solso (Ed.), *Information processing and cognition: The Loyola Symposium* (pp. 55–85). Hillsdale, NJ: Erlbaum.

Pribram, K. H., & McGuinness, D. (1975). Arousal, activation, and effort in the control of attention. *Psychological Review, 82*, 116–149.

Prior, M., Leonard, A., & Wood, G. (1983). A comparison study of preschool children diagnosed as hyperactive. *Journal of Pediatric Psychology, 8,* 191–207.

Prior, M., & Sanson, A. (1986). Attention deficit disorder with hyperactivity: A critique. *Journal of Child Psychology and Psychiatry, 27,* 307–319.

Quay, H. C. (1988). The behavioral reward and inhibition system in childhood behavior disorder. In L. M. Bloomingdale (Ed.), *Attention deficit disorder* (pp. 176–186). New York: Pergamon.

Rafal, R. D., Calabresi, P. A., Brennan, C. W., & Sciolto, T. K. (1989). Saccade preparation inhibits reorienting to recently attended locations. *Journal of Experimental Psychology: Human Perception and Performance, 15,* 673–685.

Raine, A., & Jones, F. (1987). Attention, autonomic arousal, and personality in behaviorally disordered children. *Journal of Abnormal Child Psychology, 15,* 583–599.

Reason, J. (1984). Lapses of attention in everyday life. In R. Parasuraman & D.R. Davies (Eds.), *Varieties of attention* (pp. 515–549). Orlando, FL: Academic Press.

Reed, E. S. (1982). An outline of a theory of action systems. *Journal of Motor Behavior, 14,* 93–134.

Reed, M. A., Pien, D. L., & Rothbart, M. K. (1984). Inhibitory self-control in preschool children. *Merrill-Palmer Quarterly, 30,* 131–147.

Renninger, K. A., & Leckrone, T. G. (1991). Continuity in young children's actions: A consideration of interest and temperament. In L. Oppenheimer & J. Valsiner (Eds.), *The origins of actions: Interdisciplinary and international perspectives* (pp. 205–238). New York: Springer-Verlag.

Renninger, K. A., & Wozniak, R. H. (1985). Effect of interest on attentional shift, recognition, and recall in young children. *Developmental Psychology, 21,* 624–632.

Reznick, J. S., & Kagan, J. (1981). Dishabituation and category detection in infancy. *Advances in Infancy Research, 2,* 79–111.

Ribot, T. H. (1911). *The psychology of attention.* Chicago: Open Court Publishing.

Richards, J. E. (1985). The development of sustained visual attention in infants from 14 to 26 weeks of age. *Psychophysiology, 22,* 409–416.

Richards, J. E. (1987). Infant visual sustained attention and respiratory sinus arrhythmia. *Child Development, 58,* 488–496.

Richards, J. E. (1988). Heart rate responses and heart rate rhythms, and infant visual sustained attention. *Advances in Psychophysiology, 3,* 189–221.

Richards, J. E. (1989). Development and stability in visual sustained attention in 14, 20, and 26 week old infants. *Psychophysiology, 26,* 422–430.

Richards, J. E. (1991). Neurophysiological basis of eye movements, and the effect of attention on eye movements in the development of infant saccades, smooth pursuit, and visual tracking. Unpublished manuscript, University of South Carolina.

Richards, J. E. (1994). Infants' recognition of briefly presented visual stimuli as a function of attention status [Abstract]. *Infant Behavior and Development, 17,* 895.

Richards, J. E., & Cameron, D. (1989). Infant heart-rate variability and behavioral developmental status. *Infant Behavior and Development, 12,* 45–58.

Richards, J. E., & Casey, B. J. (1991). Heart rate variability during attention phases in young infants. *Psychophysiology, 28,* 43–53.

Richards, J. E., & Casey, B. J. (1992). Development of sustained visual attention in the human infant. In B. Campbell, H. Hayne, & R. Richardson (Eds.), *Attention and information processing in infants and adults* (pp. 30–60). Hillsdale, NJ: Erlbaum.

Riksen-Walraven, J. M. (1978). Effects of caregiver behavior on habituation rate and self-efficacy in infants. *International Journal of Behavioral Development, 1,* 105–130.

Robertson, S. S., & Bacher, L. F. (1992). Coupling of spontaneous movement and visual attention in infants [Abstract]. *Infant Behavior and Development, 15,* 657.

Robson, K. S., & Moss, H. A. (1970). Patterns and determinants of maternal attachment. *Journal of Pediatrics, 77,* 976–985.

Rocissano, L., & Yatchmink, Y. (1983). Language skill and interaction patterns in prematurely born toddlers. *Child Development, 54,* 1229–1241.

Rogoff, B. (1990). *Apprenticeship in thinking: Cognitive development in social context.* New York: Oxford University Press.

Rogoff, B., Mistry, J., Göncü, A., & Mosier, C. (1993). Guided participation in cultural activity by toddlers and caregivers. *Monographs of the Society for Research in Child Development, 58*(8, Serial 236).

Rose, S. A., & Feldman, J. F. (1987). Infant visual attention: Stability of individual differences from 6 to 8 months. *Developmental Psychology, 23,* 490–498.

Rose, S. A., Gottfried, A. W., Melloy-Carminar, P., & Bridger, W. H. (1982). Familiarity and novelty preferences in infant recognition memory: Implications for information processing. *Developmental Psychology, 18,* 704–713.

Rose, S. A., & Wallace, I. F. (1985). Visual recognition memory: A predictor of later cognitive functioning in preterms. *Child Development, 56,* 843–852.

Ross-Kossak, P., & Turkewitz, G. (1986). A micro and macro developmental view of the nature of changes in complex information processing: A consideration of changes in hemispheric advantage during familiarization. In R. Bruyer (Ed.), *The neuropsychology of face perception and facial expression* (pp. 125–145). Hillsdale, NJ: Erlbaum.

Rosvold, H. E., Mirsky, A. F., Sarason, I., Bransome, E. D., & Beck, L. H. (1956). A continuous performance test of brain damage. *Journal of Consulting Psychology, 20,* 343–350.

Rothbart, M. K. (1981). Measurement of temperament in infancy. *Child Development, 52,* 569–578.

Rothbart, M. K. (1986). Longitudinal observation of infant temperament. *Developmental Psychology, 22,* 356–365.

Rothbart, M. K. (1988a). Attention and emotion in the development of temperament. In M. I. Posner (Ed.), *The role of attention in normal development and psychopathology, Technical Report No. 88-3* (pp. 2–6). Eugene, OR: University of Oregon, Center for the Study of Emotion.

Rothbart, M. K. (1988b). Temperament and the development of inhibited approach. *Child Development, 59,* 1241–1250.

Rothbart, M. K. (1989a). Behavioral approach and inhibition. In J. S. Resnick (Ed.), *Perspectives on behavioral inhibition* (pp. 139–157). Chicago: University of Chicago Press.

Rothbart, M. K. (1989b). Biological processes in temperament. In G. A. Kohnstamm, J. E. Bates, & M. K. Robthbart (Eds.), *Temperament in childhood* (pp. 77–110). Chichester, England: Wiley.

Rothbart, M. K. (1989c). Temperament and development. In G. A. Kohnstamm, J. E. Bates, & M. K. Rothbart (Eds.), *Temperament in childhood* (pp. 187–247). Chichester, England: Wiley.

Rothbart, M. K. (1989d). Temperament in childhood: A framework. In G. A. Kohnstamm, J. E. Bates, & M. K. Rothbart (Eds.), *Temperament in childhood* (pp. 59–73). Chichester, England: Wiley.

Rothbart, M. K., & Ahadi, S. A. (1994). Temperament and the development of personality. *Journal of Abnormal Psychology, 103,* 55–66.

Rothbart, M. K., Ahadi, S. A., & Hershey, K. L. (1994). Temperament and social behavior in childhood. *Merrill-Palmer Quarterly, 40,* 21–39.

Rothbart, M. K., Ahadi, S. A., Hershey, K. L., & Fisher, P. (1994). Temperament in children 4–7 years as assessed in the Children's Behavior Questionnaire. Manuscript in preparation.

Rothbart, M. K., & Derryberry, D. (1981). Development of individual differences in temperament. In M. E. Lamb & L. Brown (Eds.), *Advances in developmental psychology* (pp. 37–86). Hillsdale, NJ: Erlbaum.

Rothbart, M. K., Derryberry, D., & Posner, M. I. (1994). A psychobiological approach to the development of temperament. In J. E. Bates & T. D. Wachs (Eds.), *Temperament: Individual differences at the interface of biology and behavior* (pp. 83–116). Washington, DC: American Psychological Association.

Rothbart, M. K., & Goldsmith, H. H. (1985). Three approaches to the study of infant temperament. *Developmental Review, 5,* 237–260.

Rothbart, M. K., & Mauro, J. A. (1990). Questionnaire approaches to the study of infant temperament. In J. Colombo & J. Fagen (Eds.), *Individual differences in infancy: Reliability, stability, prediction* (pp. 411–429). Hillsdale, NJ: Erlbaum.

Rothbart, M. K., Posner, M. I., & Boylan, A. (1990). Regulatory mechanisms in infant development. In J. T. Enns (Ed.), *The development of attention: Research and theory* (pp. 47–66). North-Holland: Elsevier.

Rothbart, M. K., Rundman, D., Gerardi, D., & Posner, M. I. (1995). Learning of unique and context-sensitive associations by 18-month-old infants. Manuscript in preparation.

Rothbart, M. K., Ziaie, H., & O'Boyle, C. G. (1992). Self-regulation and emotion in infancy. In N. Eisenberg & R. A. Fabes (Eds.), *New Directions for Child Development: Vol. 55. Emotion and its regulation in early development* (pp. 7–23). San Francisco: Jossey-Bass.

Routh, D. K., Schroeder, C. S., & O'Tuama, L. A. (1974). Development of activity level in children. *Developmental Psychology, 10,* 163–168.

Routh, D. K., Walton, M. D., & Padan-Belkin, E. (1978). Development of activity level in children revisited: Effects of mother presence. *Developmental Psychology, 14,* 571–581.

Rovee-Collier, C., Earley, L., & Stafford, S. (1989). Ontogeny of early event memory: III. Attentional determinants of retrieval at 2 and 3 months. *Infant Behavior and Development, 12,* 147–161.

Rowe, D. C., & Plomin, R. (1977). Temperament in early childhood. *Journal of Personality Assessment, 41,* 150–156.

Rudel, R. G., & Teuber, H. L. (1963). Discrimination of direction of line in children. *Journal of Comparative and Physiological Psychology, 56,* 892–898.

Ruff, H. A. (1975). The function of shifting fixations in the visual perception of infants. *Child Development, 46,* 857–865.

Ruff, H. A. (1978). Infant recognition of the invariant form of objects. *Child Development, 49,* 293–306.

Ruff, H. A. (1982). The role of manipulation in infants' responses to invariant properties of objects. *Developmental Psychology, 18,* 682–691.

Ruff, H. A. (1986). Components of attention during infants' manipulative exploration. *Child Development, 57,* 105–114.

Ruff, H. A. (1988). The measurement of attention in high risk infants. In P. M. Vietze & H. G. Vaughan (Eds.), *Early identification of infants with developmental disabilities* (pp. 282–296). Philadelphia, PA: Grune & Stratton.

Ruff, H. A. (1989). [Average levels of looking at a television screen during puppet skits and in anticipation of puppet skits at 2.5, 3.5, and 4.5 years.] Unpublished raw data.

Ruff, H. A. (1990). Individual differences in sustained attention during infancy. In J. Colombo & J. Fagen (Eds.), *Individual differences in infancy: Reliability, stability, prediction* (pp. 247–269). Hillsdale, NJ: Erlbaum.

Ruff, H. A. (1991, January). The relationship between development of attention and the development of self-regulation. Paper presented at a roundtable of the ABC Initiative, Bethesda, MD.

Ruff, H. A. (1992). [The effect of periodic distractors on the focused attention of 3.5-year-olds during free play.] Unpublished raw data.

Ruff, H. A., & Birch, H. G. (1974). Infant visual fixation: The effect of concentricity, curvilinearity, and number of directions. *Journal of Experimental Child Psychology, 17,* 460–473.

Ruff, H. A., & Capozzoli, M. (1991). [The relationship of looking away from screen and visual reaction time.] Unpublished raw data.

Ruff, H. A., Capozzoli, M., Dubiner, K., & Parrinello, R. (1990). A measure of vigilance in infancy. *Infant Behavior and Development, 13,* 1–20.

Ruff, H. A., Capozzoli, M., & Saltarelli, L. M. (in press). Focused attention and distractibility in 10-month-old infants. *Infant Behavior and Development.*

Ruff, H. A., & Dubiner, K. (1987). Stability of individual differences in infants' manipulation and exploration of objects. *Perceptual and Motor Skills, 64,* 1095–1101.

Ruff, H. A., & Lawson, K. R. (1988). Development and individual differences in sustained attention [Abstract]. *Infant Behavior and Development, 11,* 383.

Ruff, H. A., & Lawson, K. R. (1990). Development of sustained, focused attention in young children during free play. *Developmental Psychology, 26,* 85–93.

Ruff, H. A., & Lawson, K. R. (1991). Assessment of infants' attention during play with objects. In C. E. Schaefer, K. Gitlin, & A. Sandgrund (Eds.), *Play diagnosis and assessment* (pp. 115–129). New York: Wiley.

Ruff, H. A., Lawson, K. R., Kurtzberg, D., McCarton, C., & Vaughan, H. G., Jr. (1982). Visual following of moving objects by fullterm and preterm infants. *Journal of Pediatric Psychology, 7,* 375–386.

Ruff, H. A., Lawson, K. R., Parrinello, R., & Weissberg, R. (1990). Long-term stability of individual differences in sustained attention in the early years. *Child Development, 61,* 60–75.

Ruff, H. A., & Saltarelli, L. M. (1993). Exploratory play with objects: Basic cognitive processes and individual differences. In M. H. Bornstein & A. W. O'Reilly (Eds.), *New Directions for Child Development: Vol. 59. The role of play in the development of thought* (pp. 5–15). San Francisco, CA: Jossey-Bass.

Ruff, H. A., Saltarelli, L. M., Capozzoli, M., & Dubiner, K. (1992). The differentiation of activity in infants' exploration of objects. *Developmental Psychology, 28,* 851–861.

Ruff, H. A., & Turkewitz, G. (1975). Developmental changes in the effectiveness of stimulus intensity on infant visual attention. *Developmental Psychology, 11,* 705–710.

Ruff, H. A., & Turkewitz, G. (1979). The changing role of stimulus intensity in infants' visual attention. *Perceptual and Motor Skills, 48,* 815–826.

Ruff, H. A., Weissberg, R., Lawson, K., & Capozzoli, M. (1995). Development and individuality in sustained attention in the preschool years. Unpublished manuscript.

Rutter, M. (1989). Attention deficit disorder/hyperkinetic syndrome: Conceptual and research issues regarding diagnosis and classification. In T. Sagvolden & T. Archer (Eds.), *Attention deficit disorder: Clinical and basic research* (pp. 1–24). Hillsdale, NJ: Erlbaum.

Ryther, J. S., Colombo, J., Frick, J. E., & Coleman, S. (1994). Minding your O's and Q's: Visual pop-out and fixation duration in three-month-olds [Abstract]. *Infant Behavior and Development, 17,* 920.

Salapatek, P. (1975). Pattern perception in early infancy. In L. B. Cohen & P. Salapatek (Eds.), *Infant perception: From sensation to cognition* (Vol. I, pp. 133–248). New York: Academic Press.

Saltarelli, L., Ruff, H. A., & Capozzoli, M. (1990, April). Distractibility during focused attention in infants. *Infant Behavior and Development, 13,* 606.

Sameroff, A. J. (1983). Developmental systems: Contexts and evolution. In P. H. Mussen (Series Ed.) & W. Kessen (Volume Ed.), *Handbook of child psychology: Vol. 1. History, theory, and methods* (4th ed., pp. 237–294). New York: Wiley.

Schaefer, E. S., & Bayley, N. (1963). Maternal behavior, child behavior, and their intercorrelations from infancy through adolescence. *Monographs of the Society for Research in Child Development, 28*(3, Serial No. 87).

Schaffer, H. R. (1974). Cognitive components of infant's response to strangeness. In M. Lewis & L.A. Rosenblum (Eds.), *The origins of fear* (pp. 11–24). New York: Wiley.

Schaffer, H. R. (1984). *The child's entry into a social world.* London: Academic Press.

Schaffer, H. R., & Crook, C. K. (1980). Child compliance and maternal control techniques. *Developmental Psychology, 16,* 54–61.

Schaughency, E. A., & Hynd, G. W. (1989). Attentional control systems and the attention deficit disorders (ADD). *Learning and Individual Differences, 1,* 423–449.

Schleifer, M., Weiss, G., Cohen, N., Elman, M., Cvejic, H., & Kruger, E. (1975). Hyperactivity in preschoolers and the effect of methylphenidate. *American Journal of Orthopsychiatry, 45,* 38–50.

Schmidt, C. L. (1991). *The scrutability of reference.* Unpublished doctoral dissertation, University of Chicago.

Schneirla, T. C. (1965). Aspects of stimulation and organization in approach/withdrawal processes underlying vertebrate behavioral development. *Advances in the Study of Behavior, 1,* 1–74.

Schroeder, S. R., & Holland, J. G. (1968). Operant control of eye movements during human vigilance. *Science, 161,* 292–293.

Sergeant, J. A., & Scholten, C. A. (1983). A stages-of-information approach to hyperactivity. *Journal of Child Psychology and Psychiatry, 24,* 49–60.

Shiffrin, R. M., & Schneider, W. (1977). Controlled and automatic human information processing: II. Perceptual learning, automatic attending, and a general theory. *Psychological Review, 84,* 127–190.

Shoda, Y., Mischel, W., & Peake, P. K. (1990). Predicting adolescent cognitive and self-regulatory competencies from preschool delay of gratification: Identifying diagnostic conditions. *Developmental Psychology, 26,* 978–986.

Shulman, G. L., & Wilson, J. (1987). Spatial frequency and selective attention to local and global information. *Perception, 16,* 89–101.

Sigman, M., Cohen, S. E., Beckwith, L., & Parmelee, A. H. (1986). Infant attention in relation to intellectual abilities in childhood. *Developmental Psychology, 22,* 788–792.

Sinha, C. (1994). Canonical representation and constructive praxis: Some developmental and linguistic considerations. *Behavioral and Brain Sciences, 17,* 223–224.

Slater, A., & Morison, V. (1985). Selective adaptation cannot account for early infant habituation: A response to Dannemiller and Banks. *Merrill-Palmer Quarterly, 31,* 99–103.

Slater, A., Morison, V., & Rose, D. (1984). Habituation in the newborn. *Infant Behavior and Development, 7*, 183–200.

Smith, P. H. (1984). Five-month-old infant recall and utilization of temporal organization. *Journal of Experimental Child Psychology, 38*, 400–414.

Smith, P. H., Jankowski, J. J., Brewster, M., & Loboschefski, T. (1990). Preverbal infant response to spatiotemporal events: Evidence of differential chunking abilities. *Infant Behavior and Development, 13*, 129–146.

Smothergill, D. W., & Kraut, A. G. (1989). Developmental studies of alertness and encoding effects of stimulus repetition. *Advances in Child Development and Behavior, 22*, 249–270.

Sokolov, E. N. (1963). *Perception and the conditioned reflex.* Oxford: Pergamon.

Sorce, J. F., Emde, R. N., Campos, J., & Klinnert, M. D. (1985). Maternal emotional signaling: Its effect on the visual cliff behavior of 1-year-olds. *Developmental Psychology, 21*, 195–200.

Sorsby, A. J., & Martlew, M. (1991). Representational demands in mothers' talk to preschool children in two contexts: Picture book reading and a modelling task. *Journal of Child Language, 18*, 373–395.

Spelke, E. (1976). Infants' intermodal perception of events. *Cognitive Psychology, 8*, 553–560.

Spelke, E. S., Breinlinger, K., Macomber, J., & Jacobson, K. (1992). Origins of knowledge. *Psychological Review, 99*, 605–632.

Spelke, E. S., Hirst, W. C., & Neisser, U. (1976). Skills of divided attention. *Cognition, 4*, 215–230.

Spitzer, H., Desimone, R., & Moran, J. (1988). Increased attention enhances both behavioral and neuronal performance. *Science, 240*, 338–340.

Sroufe, A. L. (1979). Socioemotional development. In J. D. Osofsky (Ed.), *Handbook of infant development* (pp. 462–516). New York: Wiley.

Stack, D. M., & Muir, D. W. (1992). Adult tactile stimulation during face-to-face interactions modulates five-month-olds' affect and attention. *Child Development, 63*, 1509–1525.

Stechler, G., & Latz, E. (1966). Some observations on attention and arousal in the human infant. *Journal of the American Academy of Child Psychiatry, 5*, 517–525.

Steele, D., & Pederson, D. R. (1977). Stimulus variables which affect the concordance of visual and manipulative exploration in six-month-old infants. *Child Development, 48*, 104–111.

Steinschneider, M., Kurtzberg, D., & Vaughan, H. G. (1992). Event-related potentials in developmental neuropsychology. In I. Rapin & S. J. Segalowitz (Eds.), *Handbook of neuropsychology* (Vol. 6, pp. 239–299). North-Holland: Elsevier Science Publishers.

Stern, D. N. (1974). Mother and infant at play: The dyadic interaction involving facial, vocal and gaze behaviors. In M. Lewis & L. Rosenblum (Eds.), *The effect of the infant on its caregiver.* New York: Wiley.

Stevenson, H. W. (1970). Learning in children. In P. H. Mussen (Ed.), *Carmichael's manual of child psychology* (3rd ed., Vol. 1, pp. 849–938). New York: Wiley.

Stifter, C. A., & Fox, N. A. (1990). Infant reactivity: Physiological correlates of newborn and 5-month temperament. *Developmental Psychology, 26*, 582–588.

Stifter, C. A., Fox, N. A., & Porges, S. W. (1989). Facial expressivity and vagal tone in 5- and 10-month-old infants. *Infant Behavior and Development, 12*, 127–137.

Stipek, D., Recchia, S., & McClintic, S. (1992). Self-evaluation in young children. *Monographs of the Society for Research in Child Development, 57*(1, Serial No. 226).

Strauss, M. E., & Rourke, D. L. (1978). A multivariate analysis of the Neonatal Behavioral

Assessment Scale in several samples. In A. J. Sameroff (Ed.), *Organization and stability of newborn behavior: A commentary on the Brazelton Neonatal Behavior Assessment Scale* (pp 81–91). *Monographs of the Society for Research in Child Development, 43*(5–6, Serial No. 177).

Strommen, E. A. (1973). Verbal self-regulation in a children's game: Impulsive errors on "Simon Says." *Child Development, 44,* 849–853.

Stuss, D. T., & Benson, D. F. (1984). Neuropsychological studies of the frontal lobes. *Psychological Bulletin, 95,* 3–28.

Sugarman, S. (1982). Transitions in early representational intelligence: Changes over time in children's production of simple block structures. In G. E. Forman (Ed.), *Action and thought: From sensorimotor schemes to symbolic operations* (pp. 65–93). New York: Academic Press.

Sullivan, M. W., & Lewis, M. (1988). Facial expression during learning in 1-year-old infants. *Infant Behavior and Development, 11,* 369–373.

Swanson, J. M. (1992). *School-based assessments and interventions for ADD students.* Irvine, CA: K.C. Publishing.

Symons, D. K., & Moran, G. (1987). The behavioral dynamics of mutual responsiveness in early face-to-face mother-infant interactions. *Child Development, 58,* 1488–1495.

Szumowski, E. K., Ewing, L. J., & Campbell, S. B. (1987). What happens to "hyperactive" preschoolers? In J. Loney (Ed.), *The young hyperactive child.* New York: Haworth Press.

Tamis-LeMonda, C. S., & Bornstein, M. H. (1993). Antecedents of exploratory competence at one year. *Infant Behavior and Development, 16,* 423–439.

Taylor, R. (1990). PET illuminates how the brain pays attention. *Journal of NIH Research, 2,* 56–59.

Tennes, K., Emde, R., Kisley, A., & Metcalf, D. (1972). The stimulus barrier in early infancy: An exploration of some formulations of John Benjamin. In R. R. Holt & E. Peterfreund (Eds.), *Psychoanalysis and contemporary science: An annual of integrative and interdisciplinary studies* (Vol. 1, pp. 206–234). New York: Macmillan.

Thatcher, R. W. (1994). Cyclic cortical reorganization: Origins of human cognitive development. In G. Dawson & K.W. Fischer (Eds.), *Human behavior and the developing brain* (pp. 232–266). New York: Guilford.

Thelen, E. (1990). Dynamical systems and the generation of individual differences. In J. Colombo & J. Fagen (Eds.), *Individual differences in infancy: Reliability, stability, prediction* (pp. 19–44). Hillsdale, NJ: Erlbaum.

Thoman, E. B., & Whitney, M. P. (1990). Behavioral states in infants: Individual differences and individual analyses. In J. Colombo & J. Fagen (Eds.), *Individual differences in infancy: Reliability, stability, prediction* (pp. 113–135). Hillsdale, NJ: Erlbaum.

Thorley, G. (1984). Review of follow-up and follow-back studies of childhood hyperactivity. *Psychological Bulletin, 96,* 116–132.

Thorngate, W. (1986). The production, detection, and explanation of behavioral patterns. In J. Valsiner (Ed.), *The individual subject and scientific psychology* (pp. 71–93). New York: Plenum Press.

Thorngate, W., & Carroll, B. (1986). Ordinal pattern analysis: A strategy for assessing hypotheses about individuals. In J. Valsiner (Ed.), *The individual subject and scientific psychology* (pp. 201–232). New York: Plenum Press.

Tinsley, V. S., & Waters, H. S. (1982). The development of verbal control over motor behavior: A replication and extension of Luria's findings. *Child Development, 53,* 746–753.

Tipper, S. P. (1992). Selection for action: The role of inhibitory mechanisms. *Current Directions in Psychological Science, 1,* 105–109.

Tipper, S. P., Bourque, T. A., Anderson, S. H., & Brehaut, J. C. (1989). Mechanisms of attention: A developmental study. *Journal of Experimental Child Psychology, 48,* 353–378.

Tipper, S. P., & Driver, J. (1988). Negative priming between pictures and words in a selective attention task: Evidence for semantic processing of ignored stimuli. *Memory and Cognition, 16,* 64–70.

Tipper, S. P., Lortie, C., & Baylis, G. C. (1992). Selective reaching: Evidence for action-centered attention. *Journal of Experimental Psychology: Human Perception and Performance, 18,* 891–905.

Tipper, S. P., MacQueen, G. M., & Brehaut, J. C. (1988). Negative priming between response modalities: Evidence for the central locus of inhibition in selective attention. *Perception and Psychophysics, 43,* 45–52.

Tipper, S. P., & McLaren, J. (1990). Evidence for efficient visual selectivity in children. In J. T. Enns (Ed.), *The development of attention: Research and theory* (pp. 197–210). North-Holland: Elsevier.

Tomasello, M., & Farrar, M. J. (1986). Joint attention and early language. *Child Development, 57,* 1454–1463.

Tucker, D. M. (1991). Developing emotions and cortical networks. In M. Gunnar & C. Nelson (Eds.), *Minnesota Symposium on Child Psychology: Vol. 24. Developmental behavioral neuroscience* (pp. 75–128). Hillsdale, NJ: Erlbaum.

Tucker, D. M., & Derryberry, D. (1992). Motivated attention: Anxiety and the frontal executive functions. *Neuropsychiatry, Neuropsychology & Behavioral Neurology, 5,* 233–252.

Tucker, D. M., & Williamson, P. A. (1984). Asymmetric neural control systems in human self-regulation. *Psychological Review, 91,* 185–215.

Turkewitz, G., Gardner, J. M., & Lewkowicz, D. J. (1984). Sensory/perceptual functioning during early infancy: The implications of a quantitative basis for responding. In G. Greenberg & E. Tobach (Eds.), *Behavioral evolution and integrative levels* (pp. 167–195). Hillsdale, NJ: Erlbaum.

Turnure, C. (1971). Response to voice of mother and stranger by babies in the first year. *Developmental Psychology, 4,* 182–190.

Turnure, J. E. (1970). Children's reactions to distractors in a learning situation. *Developmental Psychology, 2,* 115–122.

Turnure, J. E. (1971). Control of orienting behavior in children under five years of age. *Developmental Psychology, 4,* 16–24.

Ungerleider, L. G., & Mishkin, M. (1982). Two cortical visual systems. In D. J. Ingle, M. A. Goodale, & R. J. W. Mansfield (Eds.), *Analysis of visual behavior* (pp. 549–550 and 578–579). Cambridge, MA: MIT Press.

Uzgiris, I. C., Benson, J. B., Kruper, J. C., & Vasek, M. E. (1989). Contextual influences on imitative interactions between mothers and infants. In J. J. Lockman & N. L. Hazen (Eds.), *Action in social context: Perspectives on early development* (pp. 103–127). New York: Plenum Press.

Valenza, E., Simion, F., & Umiltá, C. (1994). Inhibition of return in newborn infants. *Infant Behavior and Development, 17,* 293–302.

Vanderwolf, C. H., & Robinson, T. E. (1981). Reticulo-cortical activity and behavior: A critique of the arousal theory and a new synthesis. *Behavioral and Brain Sciences, 4,* 459–514.

van Hover, K. I. (1974). A developmental study of three components of attention. *Developmental Psychology, 10,* 330–339.

Vaughn, B. E., Kopp, C. B., & Krakow, J. B. (1984). The emergence and consolidation of self-control from eighteen to thirty months of age: Normative trends and individual differences. *Child Development, 55,* 990–1004.

Vecera, S. P., Rothbart, M. K., & Posner, M. I. (1991). Development of spontaneous alternation in infancy. *Journal of Cognitive Neuroscience, 3,* 351–354.

Voeller, K. K. S. (1991). What can neurological models of attention, intention, and arousal tell us about attention-deficit hyperactivity disorder? *Journal of Neuropsychiatry, 3,* 209–216.

Volkmann, F. C., & Dobson, M. V. (1976). Infant responses of ocular fixation to moving visual stimuli. *Journal of Experimental Child Psychology, 22,* 86–99.

von Bargen, D. M. (1983). Infant heart rate: A review of research and methodology. *Merrill-Palmer Quarterly, 29,* 115–149.

von Hofsten, C., & Lindhagen, K. (1979). Observations on the development of reaching for moving objects. *Journal of Experimental Child Psychology, 28,* 158–173.

Vurpillot, E. (1976). *The visual world of the child.* New York: International Universities Press.

Vygotsky, L. S. (1962). *Thought and language.* Cambridge, MA: MIT Press.

Vygotsky, L. S. (1978). *Mind in society: The development of higher psychological processes* (Translated by: Cole, M. John-Steiner, V., Scribner, S. & Souberman, E.). Cambridge, MA.: Harvard University Press.

Wachs, T. D. (1987). Specificity of environmental action as manifest in environmental correlates of infant's mastery motivation. *Developmental Psychology, 23,* 782–790.

Wachs, T. D. (1989). The nature of the physical microenvironment: An expanded classification system. *Merrill-Palmer Quarterly, 35,* 399–419.

Wachs, T. D. (1990). Must the physical environment be mediated by the social environment in order to influence development?: A further test. *Journal of Applied Developmental Psychology, 11,* 163–178.

Wachs, T. D. (1993). Nature of relations between the physical and social microenvironment of the two-year-old child. *Early Development and Parenting, 2,* 81–87.

Wachs, T. D., & Gandour, M. J. (1983). Temperament, environment, and six-month cognitive-intellectual development: A test of the organismic specificity hypothesis. *International Journal of Behavioral Development, 6,* 135–152.

Wagner, S. H., & Sakovitz, L. J. (1986). A process analysis of infant visual and cross-modal recognition memory: Implications for an amodal code. *Advances in Infancy Research, 4,* 195–217.

Walden, T. A., & Ogan, T. A. (1988). The development of social referencing. *Child Development, 59,* 1230–1240.

Waldrop, M. F., Bell, R. Q., McLaughlin, B., & Halverson, C. F. (1978). Newborn minor physical anomalies predict short attention span, peer aggression, and impulsivity at age 3. *Science, 199,* 563–565.

Ward, T. B. (1990). The role of labels in directing children's attention. In J. T. Enns (Ed.), *The development of attention: Research and theory* (pp. 321–342). North-Holland: Elsevier.

Waters, W. F., & Wright, D. C. (1979). Maintenance and habituation of the phasic orienting response to competing stimuli in selective attention. In H. D. Kimmel, E. H. van Holst, & J. F. Orlebeke (Eds.), *The orienting reflex in humans* (pp. 101–121). Hillsdale, NJ: Erlbaum.

Weinberg, M. K., & Tronick, E. Z. (1994). Beyond the face: An empirical study of infant affective configurations of facial, vocal, gestural, and regulatory behaviors. *Child Development, 65,* 1503–1515.

Weiss, G., & Hechtman, L. T. (1986). *Hyperactive children grown up.* New York: Guilford Press.

Weissberg, R., Ruff, H. A., & Lawson, K. R. (1990). The usefulness of reaction time tasks in studying attention and organization of behavior in young children. *Journal of Developmental and Behavioral Pediatrics, 11,* 59–64.

Weizmann, F., Cohen, L. B., & Pratt, R. J. (1971). Novelty, familiarity, and the development of infant attention. *Developmental Psychology, 4,* 149–154.

Wellman, H. M. (1988). The early development of memory strategies. In F. E. Weinert & M. Perlmutter (Eds.), *Memory development: Universal changes and individual differences* (pp. 3–29). Hillsdale, NJ: Erlbaum.

Welsh, M. C., & Pennington, B. F. (1988). Assessing frontal lobe functioning in children: Views from developmental psychology. *Developmental Neuropsychology, 4,* 199–230.

Wenckstern, S., Weizmann, F., & Leenaars, A. A. (1984). Temperament and tempo of play in eight-month-old infants. *Child Development, 55,* 1195–1199.

Wentworth, N., & Haith, M. M. (1992). Event-specific expectations of 2- and 3-month-old infants. *Developmental Psychology, 28,* 842–850.

Werner, H. (1948). *The comparative psychology of mental development.* New York: International Universities Press.

Wertsch, J. V. (1985). *Vygotsky and the social formation of mind.* Cambridge, MA: Harvard University Press.

Wertsch, J. V., McNamee, G. D., McLane, J. B., & Budwig, N. A. (1980). The adult-child dyad as a problem-solving system. *Child Development, 51,* 1215–1221.

Wetherford, M. J., & Cohen, L. B. (1973). Developmental changes in infant visual preferences for novelty and familiarity. *Child Development, 44,* 416–424.

Whalen, C. K., & Henker, B. (1985). The social worlds of hyperactive (ADDH) children. *Clinical Psychology Review, 5,* 447–478.

White, S. H., & Plum, G. E. (1964). Eye movement photography during children's discrimination learning. *Journal of Experimental Child Psychology, 1,* 327–338.

Wickens, C. D. (1984). Processing resources in attention. In R. Parasuraman & D. R. Davies (Eds.), *Varieties of attention* (pp. 63–102). Orlando, FL: Academic Press.

Wiener-Margulies, M., Rey-Barboza, R. Cabrera, E., & Anisfeld, M. (in press). During play children speak less when they exert more effort. *Journal of Genetic Psychology.*

Willats, P., & Rosie, K. (1989, April). Planning by 12-month-old infants. Paper presented at the biennial meeting of the Society for Research in Child Development, Kansas City, KS.

Wilson, F. A. W., Ó Scalaidhe, S. P., & Goldman-Rakic, P. S. (1993). Dissociation of object and spatial processing domains in primate prefrontal cortex. *Science, 260,* 1955–1958.

Wohlwill, J. F. (1983). Physical and social environment as factors in development. In D. Magnusson & V. L. Allen (Eds.), *Human development: An interactional perspective* (pp. 111–129). New York: Academic Press.

Wolff, P. H. (1987). *The development of behavioral states and the expression of emotions in early infancy.* Chicago: Chicago University Press.

Woodworth, R. S., & Schlosberg, H. (1965). *Experimental psychology* (3rd ed.). New York: Holt, Rinehart & Winston.

Wozniak, R. H. (1986). Notes toward a co-constructive theory of the emotion-cognition relationship. In D. J. Bearison & H. Zimiles (Eds.), *Thought and emotion: Developmental perspectives* (pp. 39–64). Hillsdale, NJ: Erlbaum.

Wright, J. C., & Vlietstra, A. G. (1975). The development of selective attention: From perceptual exploration to logical search. *Advances in Child Development and Behavior, 10,* 195–239.

Yarbus, A. L. (1967). *Eye movements and vision.* New York: Plenum Press.

Yates, J. F., & Revelle, G. L. (1979). Processes operative during delay of gratification. *Motivation and Emotion, 3,* 103–115.

Yendovitskaya, T. V. (1971). Development of attention. In A.V. Zaporozhets & D.B. Elkonin (Eds.), *The psychology of preschool children* (pp. 65–88). Cambridge, MA: MIT Press.

Younger, B. A. (1985). The segregation of items into categories by ten-month-old infants. *Child Development, 56,* 1574–1583.

Zametkin, A. J., & Rapoport, J. L. (1987). Neurobiology of attention deficit disorder with hyperactivity: Where have we come in 50 years? *Journal of the American Academy of Child & Adolescent Psychiatry, 26,* 676–686.

Zametkin, A. J., Nordahl, T. E., Gross, M., King, A. C., Semple, W. E., Rumsey, J., Hamburger, S., & Cohen, R. M. (1990). Cerebral glucose metabolism in adults with hyperactivity of childhood onset. *New England Journal of Medicine, 323,* 1361–1366.

Zeaman, D., & House, B. J. (1963). The role of attention in retardate discrimination learning. In N. R. Ellis (Ed.), *Handbook of mental deficiency: Psychological theory and research* (pp. 159–223). New York: McGraw-Hill.

Zentall, S. S., & Zentall, T. R. (1983). Optimal stimulation: A model of disordered activity and performance in normal and deviant children. *Psychological Bulletin, 94,* 446–471.

Zinchenko, V. P., Chzhi-tsin, V., & Tarakanov, V. V. (1964). The formation and development of perceptual activity. *Soviet Psychology and Psychiatry, 2,* 3–12.

Author Index

Subject Index